Bach, Handel, Scarlatti

Tercentenary Essays

Bach, Handel, Scarlatti
Tercentenary Essays

EDITED BY PETER WILLIAMS

The right of the
University of Cambridge
to print and sell
all manner of books
was granted by
Henry VIII in 1534.
The University has printed
and published continuously
since 1584.

CAMBRIDGE UNIVERSITY PRESS

CAMBRIDGE
LONDON NEW YORK NEW ROCHELLE
MELBOURNE SYDNEY

Published by the Press Syndicate of the University of Cambridge
The Pitt Building, Trumpington Street, Cambridge CB2 1RP
32 East 57th Street, New York, NY 10022, USA
10 Stamford Road, Oakleigh, Melbourne 3166, Australia

First published 1985

Printed in Great Britain at the University Press, Cambridge

Library of Congress catalogue card number: 84-11394

British Library Cataloguing in Publication Data

Bach, Handel, Scarlatti
1. Bach, Johann Sebastian   2. Handel, George Frideric
3. Scarlatti, Domenico
I. Williams, Peter, 1937 May 14
780'.92'2   ML410.B13
ISBN 0 521 25217 2

ME

Contents

Contents

Illustrations

Illustrations

Preface

There will be few major certainties established by the essays in this commemorative volume. But what they are commemorating in their different ways is the work of three of the most gifted composers ever to show on paper their views on what music is and what it can do. In attempting to understand such men and such work, knowledge and experience seem to join to give us not a greater certainty but only a wider and more sophisticated awareness of the uncertainties. There is nothing new in this observation, of course. But the physicist of our period knows that the art and skill of research are geared towards asking the right question, and that many 'answers' or 'solutions' are no more than one verbal formula substituting for another. Musical studies too know the 'substitute' statement – the kind of statement that expresses or explains a phenomenon only by giving it a label ('apples fall to the ground because of *gravity*' is an example from physics). A problem is that musicians and music students seem not to realize how often they are making such statements.

To put precisely into words what one's question is requires knowledge and imagination. But it must also be an experience familiar to many musicians that the act of framing the question as carefully as possible brings knowledge and prompts imagination in a way unknown to those eager to rush to judgement. This is the reason for writing about an aural and non-literate art. Because it brings with it a simple, direct pleasure, music allows many to rush to judgement – especially players setting out to win audiences – but in many areas neither players nor audiences have even begun to ask the right question. All of the composers concerned here, like so many major figures in 'early music', composed works which have become part of the common musical background and which took a major part in creating the language. One cannot say that they 'transcend their period' because all later periods have built on them and taken them as part of a heritage which, without them as individuals, would have been very different. This means that although the music of those three composers can and usually does 'speak to us' through quite inappropriate means (just as a film of *Hamlet* will speak to us however inappropriate the medium), we are still not understanding it in any real sense if we do not seek to find out what *is* appropriate.

'Appropriate' is a technical term involving those details that were part of the composer's original intentions or expectations – for the production of their stage works, the singing of their vocal works, the playing of their instrumental. Because great music is supposed to 'transcend its period' and its context, these three composers have been followed by at least two centuries of greater or lesser misinterpretation, not total of course but such as still to leave open very basic questions. Every contributor here knows that there are still very large gaps in our knowledge about these men and their development, just as there are about their music and its performance, gaps sometimes so wide (e.g. on the chronology of the keyboard music of each of them) as to complicate beyond solution so far the pressing practical problems (e.g. what kind of everyday keyboard did they each play?). No contributor or reader needs reminding of what we do not know. Yet perhaps the time will come, even in connection with one or other of our three composers on whom so much time is already spent,[1] when a volume of this kind will frankly set out to frame the unknown questions, listing them with an exactness made possible by the easy convenience of historical research today.

In thinking about music, it must be right to avoid false ideals – the musical equivalent of *faux-pastoralisme* – such as assuming that the composer himself always cared much about details that are important to us. Our reaching towards framing a question and then finding its answer ought not to delude us into thinking it was one that the composer himself could have answered or would even have seen in that way. Composers have a natural wish to see their music performed – at any time, under almost any conditions whatsoever – and it cannot be expected that a few years after Handel served at Cannons or Bach at Cöthen either of them cared about – or perhaps could even have remembered – the exact conditions under which they composed or performed their music at those places. But of course we will never know what those conditions were without at least learning to define or refine questions about them. Nor does our trying to understand those conditions mean that the end-result of research and knowledge would be to insist on them as the only 'correct' conditions of performance (as to type of acoustic, types of instruments and singers, 'correct' tempo or articulation or pitch, etc.) without which a performance would be a travesty. For one thing, neither the aim nor the end-result of research – the winning of knowledge – is necessarily practical, and generally an oversimplification results from believing it is. For another, the re-creating of those conditions – and no player once converted to this viewpoint can help but wish to re-create them to at least some extent – is only a starting-point and does not guarantee

1 Bach scholarship in particular is probably the most developed and in many ways the most like a model for all branches of historical music study today, just as it was in the nineteenth century.

success. Any modern performance is no more than a revival, and it is difficult to see how a circumspect scholar – as distinct from the teacher simplifying truths for students or the performer satisfying the ears of listeners – could entertain such a notion as 'authentic performance'.

Rather, the end-result of knowledge seems to be to understand how it was that the composer came to compose what he did compose, and accordingly how it was that he saw it. Not only is this a fair starting-point for any performer now as then, but it becomes itself a discipline for the thinker – to whittle away the rushed judgement and to expose the likeliest answer to a given problem. In the process he may question whether the highest aim of music, in general or in particular, is to play it. This is not to raise hares of speculation on how or whether the *Art of Fugue* was written for performance, or to ignore the phenomenal care taken by Handel to get his stage works exactly right, or to question the intimate awareness of harpsichord touch demonstrated time and again by Scarlatti; it is to ask whether even the most pressing requirements for music at Cannons or Cöthen or Madrid actually resulted in music whose sole *raison d'être* was that it be performed. There are other things to do with music besides playing it, and while it must be true that these three composers were practical men with an astonishing gift for touching the ears and minds of their listeners, it is also true that they had a fidelity to music itself, music as a mode of thought, with a logic and grammar and rhetoric in the mastering of which even the most gifted and creative composers are taxed. The very practicability of their music could come only from very sharp and disciplined intellects. When D. F. Tovey, with characteristic cleverness, remarked of the *Art of Fugue* that 'no rule of counterpoint is kept more meticulously by Bach than the confinement of the part-writing to the stretch of two hands' he was still not quite saying that the *Art of Fugue* was keyboard music: its playability was itself a factor in the makeup of the piece and one that had had to be meticulously calculated.

While it is an occasion for countless performances and publications, the tercentenary year is therefore also a time to take stock and to see present understanding as having achieved no particular peak of truth but at least as having laid bare many questions that some had already thought satisfactorily answered. Some of the essays in this volume ask questions in such a way as almost to inaugurate fields of research in the future; others attempt to establish a background knowledge for reference purposes in a next stage of research; yet others trace the learning or teaching activities of men whose extraordinary grasp of the language of music (its vocabulary, grammar and rhetoric) will always serve as some kind of model for thinkers, performers and composers. Running below the surface of all of them is an unspoken admiration that, though first prompted by instinct or sheer pleasure, becomes the more intense the better one understands the technique of the composer concerned. Up to a point, any centenary volume however planned will be an accidental collection of essays, since no two writers on music ever seem to have quite the same way of thinking and writing about it. But all of them here are stimulated by that combination of admiration and wish-to-understand that seems a particular characteristic of studies about the greatest composers. It is a combination that, at its best, seems to question rather than to answer – or (when it does) to give answers which themselves only open up new areas to explore.

PETER WILLIAMS
Edinburgh, October 1983

Abbreviations

AfMw	*Archiv für Musikwissenschaft*
AM	*Acta musicologica*
AMZ	*Allgemeine musikalische Zeitung*
BG	*Gesamtausgabe der Bach-Gesellschaft* (Leipzig, 1851–99)
BJ	*Bach-Jahrbuch*
BL	British Library (formerly British Museum Library), London
Bodleian	Bodleian Library, Oxford
BR	H. T. David & A. Mendel, *The Bach Reader* (New York, 1945; rev. edn 1966)
BWV	W. Schmeider, *Thematisch-systematisches Verzeichnis der musikalischen Werke von Johann Sebastian Bach* (Leipzig, 1950)
Cfm	Fitzwilliam Museum, Cambridge
DDT	*Denkmäler deutscher Tonkunst*
Deutsch *Doc*	O. E. Deutsch, *Handel: A Documentary Biography* (London, 1955)
Dok I, II, III	*Bach-Dokumente, herausgegeben vom Bach-Archiv Leipzig*, I, ed. W. Neumann & H.-J. Schulze (Leipzig, 1963); II, ed. W. Neumann & H.-J. Schulze (Leipzig, 1969); III, ed. H.-J. Schulze (Leipzig, 1972)
DSB	Deutsche Staatsbibliothek, formerly Preussische Staatsbibliothek (previously Königliche Bibliothek), East Berlin
DTB	*Denkmäler der Tonkunst in Bayern*
DTÖ	*Denkmäler der Tonkunst in Österreich*
EM	*Early Music*
Forkel	J. N. Forkel, *Ueber Johann Sebastian Bachs Leben, Kunst und Kunstwerke* (Leipzig, 1802)
Hamburg	Staats- und Universitätsbibliothek, Hamburg
Hannover NH	Niedersächsische Landesbibliothek, Hanover
HG	*G. F. Händels Werke: Ausgabe der Deutschen Händelgesellschaft*, ed. F. W. Chrysander (Leipzig/Bergedorff, 1858ff)

Abbreviations

HHA	*Hallische Händel-Ausgabe im Auftrage der Georg Friedrich Händelgesellschaft* (Leipzig/Kassel, 1955ff)
Hicks (nos.)	A. Hicks, 'Handel Worklist' in W. Dean, 'Handel, G. F.', *New Grove*; reprint in W. Dean, *Handel* (London, 1983)
HJ	*Händel-Jahrbuch*
Huntington	Huntington Library, San Marino, California
HWV	B. Baselt, 'Verzeichnis der Werke Georg Friedrich Händels (HWV)', *HJ* 25 (1979), pp. 1–139
JAMS	*Journal of the American Musicological Society*
JbP	*Jahrbuch der Musikbibliothek Peters*
Kk	R. Kirkpatrick, *Domenico Scarlatti* (Princeton NJ, 1953), pp. 442–456
KmJb	*Kirchenmusicalisches Jahrbuch*
Mainwaring	[J. Mainwaring], *Memoirs of the Life of the late George Frederic Handel* (London, 1760)
Mf	*Die Musikforschung*
MGG	*Die Musik in Geschichte und Gegenwart*, ed. F. Blume (Kassel, 1949ff)
ML	*Music and Letters*
MQ	*Musical Quarterly*
MT	*Musical Times*
NBA (*NBA KB*)	*Neue Bach-Ausgabe: Johann Sebastian Bach. Neue Ausgabe sämtlicher Werke* (Leipzig/Kassel, 1954ff) (*Kritischer Bericht*)
New Grove	*The New Grove Dictionary of Music and Musicians*, 20 vols., ed. S. Sadie (London, 1980)
New York PL	New York Public Library
NH	see Hannover
Paris BN	Bibliothèque Nationale, Paris
Parma Bib. Pal.	Biblioteca Palatina, Sezione musicale, Parma
PRMA	*Proceedings of the Royal Musical Association*
PRO	Public Record Office, London
Spitta, I, II	P. Spitta, *Johann Sebastian Bach*, 2 vols. (Leipzig 1873, 1880)
SPK	Staatsbibliothek Preussischer Kulturbesitz, West Berlin
Venice Bib. Marc.	Biblioteca Nazionale Marciana (B. N. di San Marco), Venice
Versuch	C. P. E. Bach, *Versuch über die wahre Art das Clavier zu spielen* (Berlin, 1753)
Vienna NB	Österreichische Nationalbibliothek, Musiksammlung, Vienna
Wo	A. Wotquenne, *Catalogue thematique des oeuvres de Ph. E. Bach* (Leipzig, 1905)
WTC	*Das wohltemperirte Clavier*, Bk 1 (BWV 846–869), Bk 2 (BWV 870–893)
ZfMw	*Zeitschrift für Musikwissenschaft*

Handel and Music for the Earl of Carnarvon

GRAYDON BEEKS

(Claremont, California)

'Two years he spent at CANNONS, a place which was then in all its glory. . .' (Mainwaring 1760 p. 95). So wrote John Mainwaring in his pioneering biography of Handel, describing the composer's patronage by James Brydges, from October 1714 Earl of Carnarvon and from April 1719 first Duke of Chandos. Since then scholars have sought the answers to a number of questions. When, exactly, did Handel work for Brydges, what were his duties, and what was his remuneration? Did Handel actually live at Cannons (Brydges's newly built Palladian home near Edgware, northwest of London)? What music did he compose for the 'Cannons Concert' of musicians, and when and where was it performed?

The most perceptive and accurate early account of the Cannons period in Handel's life was by R. A. Streatfeild (Streatfeild 1916), and it remains a model of its kind. However, Streatfeild did not have access to the surviving letters and documents from Cannons, which were then at Stowe in the possession of the Duke of Buckingham. These papers, together with the rest of the Stowe manuscripts, were acquired by Henry E. Huntington in 1925 and are now housed at the Huntington Library in San Marino, California. After detailed study of these documents, Charles Henry Collins Baker of the library staff published his definitive biography of James Brydges (Baker 1949).

Baker, however, was not a music historian, and his presentation of the documents bearing on music and musicians at Cannons left something to be desired. Since 1949 several students have examined the documents again (Rogers 1977 and Beeks 1981a), several studies have been made of Handel's music written for Cannons (Dean 1959 pp. 153–224, Beeks 1981a, Burrows 1981 and Serwer 1981), and a detailed study has been made of Handel's autograph scores (Burrows 1982). It is the purpose of this article to review the current state of knowledge concerning Handel's patronage by James Brydges as we approach the tercentenary of the composer's birth. A number of questions will still remain unanswered, but it seems desirable to marshal all available evidence in one place and draw what conclusions one can.

1

In his classic study of the oratorios, Winton Dean wrote:

From his complete disappearance between the Water Concert of 17 July 1717 and February 1719, during which period the newspapers contain not a single reference to his activities, it is safe to conclude that he was out of London; and the only private reference to him at this time . . . implies that he was in residence at Cannons. (Dean 1959 p. 159)

No evidence gathered since that time has served to contradict these dates for Handel's service to Carnarvon.

Both Hatton (Hatton 1978 p. 265) and Burrows (Burrows 1981, I p. 195) have suggested that Handel's decision to accept Carnarvon's patronage coincides with the departure for the Continent in August 1717 of his previous patron, the Earl of Burlington. The underlying motive may well have been a desire to escape the developing quarrel between King George I and his son, George Ludwig, Prince of Wales. The details are dealt with elsewhere (Hatton 1978 pp. 201–10 and Beattie 1967 pp. 262–78), but in brief the dispute stemmed from the actions of the prince while serving as Regent during the king's absence on his visit to Hanover from 7 July 1716 to 18 January 1717. Matters continued to deteriorate during the spring of 1717, when the prince's supporters began openly to vote with the opposition in Parliament. When the royal family moved to Hampton Court in July 1717, the king maintained a high degree of visibility, in contrast to his habitual and preferred seclusion, and the Prince and Princess of Wales, in contrast to their behavior the previous summer, were kept in the background (Beattie 1967. p. 264). The king, for example, attended the famous Water Concert of 17 July 1717, sponsored by the Baron de Kielmansegg, but Bonet, the Prussian *Resident*, noted that 'neither the Prince nor the Princess took any part in this festivity' (Deutsch *Doc* p. 77).

The Italian Opera had closed with a performance of *Tito Manlio* on 29 June 1717, and it must have been clear to Handel that another season would be impossible unless the conflicts were resolved among the primary financial supporters of opera in London, the nobility and the royal family. Relations continued to deteriorate, however, and the break came in early November at the christening of George William, Duke of Gloucester, when the prince insulted the Duke of Newcastle and (or so the latter thought) challenged him to a duel. The prince was arrested, confined under guard and, on 2 December, expelled from the palace. In early 1718 he and the Princess of Wales purchased Leicester House, which quickly became a center of the opposition, and the king let it be known that anyone paying court at Leicester House would be unwelcome at St James's.

Handel must have been aware of the desirability of maintaining good, or at least passable, relations with both factions, just as he must have seen that the Italian Opera was finished for a time in London. He seems likely to have seized the opportunity to look for a wealthy and neutral patron to provide work and income to go with his court pension. The Earl of Carnarvon must have seemed a good choice, for although he spent a good deal of time in town and at court in pursuit of his dukedom, even dining with the king at Hampton Court on 22 August 1717 (Burrows 1981, I p. 196), he was not a member of the government or the opposition. He

2

was, in fact, steadily withdrawing himself from political life altogether, and by 29 November 1719 he could say:

My inclinations lead me not in the least to desire Prefermt at Court; to Serve the King & Parl: in Winter, & to enjoy quiet in ye Country in Summer, is the utmost of my Ambition, & the Way in wch I covet to Spend the rest of my Life. (Huntington MS ST 57, xvi p. 393)[1]

The first mention of Handel at Cannons comes in the oft-quoted postscript to Carnarvon's letter of 25 September 1717 to Dr Arbuthnot at Bath:

Mr Hendle has made me two new Anthems very noble ones & Most think they far exceed the two first. He is at work for 2 more & some Overtures to be plaied before the first lesson. You had as good take Cannons in on your way to London. (Huntington MS ST 57, xv pp. 231–2)

This letter seems clearly to have been written at Cannons and to imply Handel's presence there. The anthems would have been written for and performed by the small but flourishing Cannons Concert.

The hiring of musicians for Cannons seems to have begun in late 1715. On 5 November the Duchess Cassandra wrote as follows to Eliza, Dowager Duchess of Bedford:

Madam, My Ld puts me upon giving yr Grace the trouble of desiring to know upon wt terms Mr Hyems yt plays upon the Base Viol served the Duke of Bedford, whether he had a sallery, & whether he Eat at the Stewards Table, my Ld is inform'd yt he would be willing to live with him, & therefore he would bee glad to know upon what foot he served his Grace (Huntington MS STB Box 2(3), p. 9 – letter no. 12)

This was a reference to Nicola Francesco Haym (1678–1727), cellist, composer and librettist, who had served the Duke of Bedford as chamber musician from 1710 until 1711 at an annual salary of 100 guineas (Dean 1980 p. 415). He was subsequently employed by Carnarvon until Michaelmas 1718 at a salary of £50 per year (Huntington MS ST 87, 5, 12, 30).

Haym wrote six anthems for Cannons, and his presentation volume of them was dedicated to Brydges on 29 September 1716 (for the MS, see Christie 1981 p. 38). The dedication makes it clear that these anthems were written specifically to employ all the members of the Cannons Concert and were performed in the church of St Lawrence, Little Stanmore, also known as Whitchurch. This edifice, which lay just beyond the gate of Cannons proper and is still standing, was rebuilt by Brydges between 1713 and 1715 in an Italianate style, and served as his chapel until the opening of the chapel at Cannons on 29 August 1720 (Deutsch *Doc* p. 112). Haym's anthems require from one to three voices, at least two violins, bass strings (cello and/or double bass), oboe and flute ('traversa').

A year later Handel wrote his first six Chandos Anthems for a slightly expanded Cannons Concert still engaged in services at Whitchurch. For these performances the musicians were apparently located on the paved floor area at the east end of the building, together with the organ (Burrows 1981, II p. 125). The Earl of Carnarvon,

---

1 Quotations from manuscripts in the Huntington Library, San Marino, California are given here by permission of the library.

his family and guests sat in a gallery at the west end facing east, perhaps flanked by his Serjeants-at-Arms. There is a reference in the duke's letterbooks to a gallery (presumably not the west gallery) being removed to St John the Evangelist, Great Stanmore, in 1735 (Huntington MS ST 57, xlvi p. 282), but whether this could have been used for placement of musicians or the organ is not known.

I have discussed elsewhere the question of the chronology of Handel's Chandos Anthems (Beeks 1981b, and Beeks 1981a pp. 301–34). The first six anthems were clearly written in pairs, on the evidence of Carnarvon's letter to Arbuthnot, and I concluded for other reasons that the next two were likewise written as a set. I suggested that they were probably written in the following order:

Anthem 2	*In the Lord put I my Trust*	(*HG* 34 pp. 37–78)
Anthem 5A	*I will magnifie thee*	(*HG* 34 pp. 133–68)
Anthem 1	*O be joyfull in the Lord*	(*HG* 34 pp. 1–36)
Anthem 3	*Have mercy upon me, O God*	(*HG* 34 pp. 79–108
Anthem 4	*O sing unto the Lord*	(*HG* 34 pp. 109–32)
Anthem 6A	*As pants the Hart*	(*HG* 34 pp. 207–38)
Anthem 11A	*Let God arise*	(*HG* 35 pp. 211–62)
Anthem 7	*My song shall be allway*	(*HG* 35 pp. 1–40)

I was unable to suggest whether Anthem 4 was written before or after Anthem 6A.

Donald Burrows, on the basis of an extensive examination of the paper characteristics of Handel's autographs, confirmed the pairings but suggested a different chronology (Burrows 1981, I pp. 199–220):

Anthem 6A	*As pants the Hart*
Anthem 4	*O sing unto the Lord*
Anthem 7	*My song shall be allway*
Anthem 11A	*Let God arise*
Anthem 3	*Have mercy upon me, O God*
Anthem 1	*O be joyfull in the Lord*
Anthem 2	*In the Lord put I my trust*
Anthem 5A	*I will magnifie thee*

As noted, this is the order found in a manuscript formerly owned by William H. Cummings, with the order of the first two anthems reversed. Cummings thought that the volume came from the library of the Duke of Chandos and preserved the anthems 'in the order of composition' (Cummings 1915 pp. 11–12), although he gave no reasons for his belief. The manuscript was acquired at the sale of his library on 17 May 1917 (Sotheby 1917 item 816) by Bernard Quaritch, Ltd, who subsequently advertised it for sale in their catalogue of October 1919 (Quaritch 1919 item 168). Its present whereabouts are unknown.

It is now clear, from an examination of Burrows's 'Handlist of Paper Characteristics of Handel's English Autographs' (Burrows 1982 passim), that the watermarks and rastra of the Chandos Anthem autographs argue strongly for a paper flow as suggested in the Burrows–Cummings ordering rather than as suggested by me. Furthermore, from my own additional work with the Stowe Manuscripts at the

Huntington Library, I am now convinced that the Cannons Concert did not grow steadily in every detail from its inception to its dispersal in 1721, although that was the overall effect. This had been one of the assumptions underlying my suggested chronology.

Finally, two volumes of Handel's Chandos Anthems have surfaced which seem definitely to have come from the Duke of Chandos's music library (Christie 1981 p. 36). These volumes had been in the possession of the Lords Leigh of Stoneleigh Abbey, Warwickshire, from the eighteenth century, apparently having passed to them on the marriage of James Brydges's granddaughter, Caroline, to her cousin, James Leigh of Adlestrop, Gloucestershire, in 1755. They were acquired by the British Library in 1981 and catalogued as Add. MSS 62099 and 62100. There can be little doubt that the two volumes derive from Cannons, and they seem clearly to contain items 7-12 in the 1720 'A Catalogue of Anthems Cantatas and Other Musick Belonging to His Grace James Duke of Chandos &c' (Huntington MS ST 66). This would seem to eliminate the possibility that the lost Cummings manuscript derived from Cannons, unless the duke possessed duplicate copies not reflected in the catalogue. The anthems in these two volumes, however, are numbered from I to VI in the exact order found in the Cummings manuscript.

It is not possible to settle the question of chronology in these pages, but something along the lines of the Burrows–Cummings ordering must be held to be the most likely. Orderings within pairs should, perhaps, be reversed in some cases, but the overall flow seems to make the most sense based upon the evidence currently at hand.

Regardless of the exact chronology, it is clear that the first four anthems were in existence by the time of the earl's letter of 25 September 1717, with another two in preparation. Both Burrows and I feel fairly certain that the first eight anthems were written before the end of the year. From the vocal and instrumental requirements of these works we may deduce the minimum number of musicians with whom Handel worked at Cannons – or at least for whom he wrote the first eight anthems – in the last four months or so of 1717.

For the first eight Chandos Anthems Handel's instrumental forces are specified in some detail in the autographs. He required at least three violins (with solo, first and second appearing in Anthem 6A), no viola, and one each of violoncello, bassoon, 'Contrabasso', oboe and organ. On the vocal side, he required a treble, a tenor with extensive solo skills, and a bass. When the anthem pair of 11A and 7 was written, he also had an alto of some sort available. Thus, the Cannons Concert in late 1717 contained a minimum of eleven musicians.

From Lady Day Quarter 1718 through to Michaelmas Quarter 1720 Cannons maintained a 'Receipt Book for Wages' (Huntington MS ST 87), which each employee signed upon receipt of his quarterly wages. Although none is identified by title or position, it is possible to identify some musicians from other sources including lists of the duke's 'Family' at New Year 1721 and New Year 1722 (in Huntington MS ST 44 – see Plates A and B), and to suggest other likely musicians

A List of His Grace the Duke of Chandos: Family
At New Years Day 1720/1

	Persons Names	Sallaries £ s d	Totall £ s d
His Graces Table			
1 His Grace			
2 Her Grace			
3 Mrs Cornwallis			
4 Coll: Watkins			
5 The Chaplain who reads for his Week			
The Chaplains Table			
1 The Chaplain who does not read			
2 Secretary	Nic.o Philpott	070	
3 Master of the Musick	Dr. Xtr Papusch	100	
4 House Steward	Lionell Herman	050	
5 Head Gardiner	Sitsman Robert	100	
6	Jo.n Lowthorp		320
Gentlemen of the Horses Table			
1 Gentleman of the Horse	George Wright	30	
2 Gentleman to His Grace	Leyson Sayer	30	
3 Gentleman Usher	Pardini	50	
4 Waiting Page	Monrow	30	
5 2d Waiting Page	Amos Rogers / Martin	15	
6 Gentlewoman to Her Grace	Wm Oakly	10	
8 Chamber Maid to Her Grace	Mrs Bolteux	6	171
Officers Table			
1 Second Gentleman to His Grace	Vanderolyn	15	
2 Clerk of the Cheque	Francis Hopwood	20	
3 Clerk of the Kitchin (in lieu of a Head Cook)	Phillip Baree	32	
4 Head Butler	Edward Hill	12	
5 Under Butler and Baker	Jos Barlow	20	
6 Confectioner	Solom Sifans	25	
7 Groom of the Chambers	Jn Gisbert	20	
8 Under Gentleman Usher	Wm Rogers	10	
9 House Keeper	Harris	10	
19	Richardson		
10 Black Boy	David Ockra		199
	Carryed Over	£	

Plates A and B. List of the Duke of Chandos's 'Family' at New Year 1721 (Huntington MS ST 44 pp. 27–8)

6

	Persons Names	Sallaries £ s d	Totall £ s d
The Musick Table	Brought Over		
1 Violino 1.°	Biti	40	
2 D.°	Scarpitini	30	
3 D.°		30	
4 Violino 2.°	Girardo	30	
5 D.°	Rawlins	30	
6 D.°	Burges	20	
7 Violino Tenor	Ostamain	20	
8 Violoncello	Angell	30	
9 Basson	Weston	30	
10 Trumpet	Lemon	30	
11 Hautbois	Kitch	50	
12 Treble Voice	Person		
13 D.°	Rigs		
14 D.°	Sallaway		
15 Contraalto	Morphew	30	
16 Counter Tenor	Gerling	40	
D.°	Bell		
17 Tenor	Rogers Sen.°		
18 Bass	Perry	30	
19 D.°	Vanbrugh	30	470
20			
Servants Hall Table 1			
1 Usher of the Hall	Martin Parsly	15	
2 Head Laundry Maid	Alice Cole	6	
3 Under Laundry Maid	Elizabeth Kirkman	5	
4 Dairy Maid	Eliz. Squelch	5 10	
5 First House Maid	Ellin Hurst	5	
6 Second Ditto	Mary Hill	5	
7 Third Ditto	Mary Mitchell	5	
Second Table in s.d Hall			
8 Under Usher of the Hall	James Cole	10	
9 Porter and Poulterer	Thomas Symson	10	
10 Brewer	Charles Gunter	12	
11 His Graces Coachman	John Wright	10	
12 Her Graces Coachman	Matth. Copham	10	
13 another Coachman	Rich.d Kits	8	106 10
	Carry.d Over	£	

7

on the basis of wages drawn. The musicians available to Handel at Cannons in 1718 are listed in Table 1.

Table 1. *Musicians at Cannons in 1718*
(Information from Huntington MSS ST 87 and ST 44 unless noted)
LD = Lady Day Quarter, MS = Midsummer Quarter, MM = Michaelmas Quarter,
CM = Christmas Quarter, NY = New Year's Day

Instrumentalists name	instrument(s)	quarterly wage	employment
Georg Angel	cello, bass	£7 10s	MS 1718[a] – NY 1722
Sigr Biancardi	oboe[b]	£7 10s	LD 1718 – CM 1720
Alexander Bitti	violin	£10	LD 1718 – NY 1721
Sigr Pietro Chabond (Chaboud)	bassoon, bass viol,[b] flute, composer	£10	LD 1718[c]
?Johan Christian dürCop (Mr. Duurcopt)	?trumpet/?bassoon	£10	MM 1718 – MS 1719
Nicola Francesco Haym	cello, violone, composer	£12 10s	LD 1718 – MM 1718
Luis Mercy (Merci)	recorder, ?flute	£10	LD 1718 – LD 1719
Charles Pardini (Perdini)	cello, ?bass	£10	LD 1718 – LD 1724[d]
John Ruggiero (Rogiero)	violin[b]	£7 10s	MS 1718 – MM 1720
Sigr Scarpettini	violin	£7 10s	LD 1718 – NY 1721

Singers name	voice part	quarterly wage	employment
James Blackley	tenor	£10	LD 1718 – CM 1719[e]
'A Singing Boy'[f]	treble		?MM 1718 – ?
?Josh: Harrison	?bass	£7 10s	LD 1718 – MM 1718
?George Monro[g] (Munro, Monroe)	?treble		c1714 – LD 1724[h]
William Perry	bass	£7 10s	CM 1718 – Nov. 1725[i]
?Amos Rogers[j]	treble		? – Jan. 1724[k]
?William Rogers[l]	?tenor		? – Nov. 1723[m]
Francis Rowe (Mr. Row)	tenor		1718[n]

[a] Paid £1 3s at Midsummer 1718 for a fortnight's wages (i.e. from c10 June).
[b] See Milhous 1983 pp. 158–61.
[c] His name is listed in the Receipt book at Lady Day 1718, but no receipt or signature appears with it.
[d] Huntington MS ST 82, p. 54.
[e] Paid a year in advance at Michaelmas 1719, but paid half salary 'by the Duke's leave' at Christmas 1719.
[f] Mentioned in letters of 12 June 1718 (Huntington MS ST 57, pp. 250–2) as being sent up from Hereford around Midsummer 1718.
[g] Although primarily known as a keyboard-player, Monro came to Cannons around 1714 as a page (Huntington MS ST 57, p. 21) and probably also sang treble.
[h] Huntington MS ST 82 p. 12
[i] Huntington MS ST 82 p. 185
[j] On 22 December 1719 the duke said that he doubted that Amos Rogers's voice was about to break (Huntington MS ST 57, xvi p. 412). If he was at Cannons in 1718 he undoubtedly sang treble. He may well have been the 'Singing Boy' from Hereford, since we know he came from that town (Huntington MS ST 57, xviii p. 241).
[k] He was last employed in January 1724 (Huntington MS ST 24, i. p. 268).
[l] William Rogers ('the older Rogers') was listed as a tenor on the list of the duke's 'Family' at New Year's 1721. Whether he was at Cannons or sang tenor in 1718 is not known.

Except for the addition of a second and third tenor and a third cellist, and the departure of a bassoon (Chaboud), the Cannons Concert in 1718 was not appreciably different from what it would seem to have been in autumn 1717. There is evidence in the later Chandos Anthems (Anthem 8 in particular) that Handel could count on four rather than three violins.

Curiously, Handel's name does not appear in the Receipt Book for Wages, nor in any of the other surviving Cannons accounts. As mentioned above, Rowe's name never appears in the Receipt Book either, nor does Pepusch's until Michaelmas 1719, although the duke refers to him as his musical director as early as 21 May 1719 (Huntington MS ST 57, xvi p. 163). Presumably they, and perhaps others, were paid in other ways.

When Brydges hired Haym in 1715 he had his wife inquire 'whether he had a sallery, & whether he Eat at the Stewards Table' (see above). He made similar inquiries concerning other prospective employees, including Francesco Scarlatti (Huntington MS ST 57, xvi p. 445) and Baron de Kielmansegg's oboe-player (Huntington MS ST 57, xv pp. 168-9). Presumably he did the same concerning Handel, and we should no doubt expect to find that the composer served the Earl of Carnarvon on terms similar to those under which he served his former patron, the Earl of Burlington. Unfortunately, we do not now know the details of Handel's patronage by Burlington, but we do know a good deal about his service to Cardinal Ruspoli in 1707-8. As Ursula Kirkendale has summarized it,

although Handel was treated as a favorite guest – and no official salary was paid to him – his activity had the character of a clearly regulated employment. A definite number of compositions was expected from him; by (probably informal) agreement he was obliged to remain and do his duties. (Kirkendale 1967 p. 251)

Handel's position with Brydges may well have been similar. If so, the expected output of new compositions was certainly smaller, but we have no way of knowing how much performing and teaching Handel was expected to do for his supper. It is, of course, possible that Handel's compositions for Cannons were straight commissions, payments for which do not appear in the incompletely surviving Chandos documents.

Whether and to what extent Handel actually resided at Cannons has always been a matter of dispute. The only references to Handel in this period clearly connect him with Cannons, and the complete lack of newspaper references seems curious if he was in London. In 1724 the Duke of Chandos wrote that George Munro

hath been so successful in his improvement under Mr. Handell and Dr. Pepusch that he is become, though young, a perfect master both for composition & performance on the organ & Harpsichord. (Huntington MS ST 57, xxiv p. 21)

However, by 1720 Munro was assigned to wait 'wherever his Grace is', whether in

---

[m] The last reference to him is in November 1723 (Huntington MS ST 24, p. 268).

[n] Rowe's name never appears in the receipt book for wages, but it does appear on Handel's autographs of *Acis and Galatea* (BL RM 20.a.2), Chandos Anthem 8 (BL RM 20.d.8) and the Chandos Te Deum (BL RM 20.d.7).

London or at Cannons (Huntington MS ST 44, pt I p. 35). If this was also true earlier, he could have studied with Handel in London.

It is clear that the members of the Cannons Concert were not always in attendance nor at full strength at Cannons, at least in a later period, from the 'Regulations for the allowance of Strong Beer and Ale' of January 1720:

The Musick Table when the consort is at Cannons, strong Beer 2 bottles, Ale 6 Bottles, when any of them are about a proportionable abatemt. to be made. (Huntington MS ST 44, pt I p. 22)

In addition Mercy, Keitch and some members of the Royal Academy of Music orchestra are known to have participated in London concerts while employed by Brydges (see *The London Stage*, and Milhous 1983 pp. 158–61). One can imagine that Handel, too, divided his time between town and country. It is suggestive, though, that Pepusch also disappears from the London scene during most of his term as Director of the Cannons Concert (see Table 2 below, notes 7 and 8), although he seems to have kept his house in Boswell Court (Huntington MS ST 66). On 8 October 1719 Chandos specifically states that he leaves 'the Choice as well as ye Direction of the Concert entirely to Dr Pepusch who lives with Me, & hath the care of it' (MS ST 57, xvi p. 322). I think we may assume, unless evidence is found to the contrary, that Handel spent a good portion of his time during late 1717 and 1718, but probably not all of it, at Cannons.

The next mention of Handel in connection with Cannons comes in a letter of 27 May 1718 from Sir David Dalrymple to Hugh Campbell, third Earl of Loudoun:

My Dear Lord
    Since my last [i.e. 24 May 1718] I have been at Canons with E. of Carnarvan who lives *en Prince* & to boot is a worthy beneficent man. I heard [a] sermon at his paroch church which for painting and ornament exceeds every thing in this Country he has a Choorus of his own, the Musick is made for himself and sung by his own servants, besides which there is a litle opera now a makeing for his diversion whereof the Musick will not be made publick. The words are to be furnished by Mrs Pope & Gay, the musick to be composed by Hendell, It is as good as finished, and I am promised some of the Songs by Dr Arbuthnot who is one of the club of composers which your Ld shall have as soon as I get it . . . (Huntington MS LO 8340, printed in Dickinson 1973 and Rogers 1973)

This seems clearly to be a reference to *Acis and Galatea*, for the performance of which the Earl of Carnarvon must have acquired a second oboe-player not reflected in surviving documents. It also gives a date for the composition and probable first performance of the work of early summer 1718. In fact, since Georg Angel seems to have been primarily a string-bass-player rather than a cellist, and since *Acis and Galatea* calls for two cellists and no double bass (Dean 1959 p. 169), it is quite likely that *Acis and Galatea* was performed before Angel's arrival around 10 June 1718.

Handel wrote three large-scale anthems for Cannons:

Anthem 8	*O come let us sing unto the Lord*	(*HG* 35 pp. 41–97)
Anthem 9	*O praise the Lord with one consent*	(*HG* 35 pp. 98–150)
Anthem 10	*The Lord is my light*	(*HG* 35 pp. 151–210)

and a setting of the Te Deum in B flat (*HG* 37 pp. 25–108). It has been apparent for some time that these were written after his first eight anthems, and that at least one of them – Anthem 8 – is closely related to *Acis and Galatea*. Some support for these conclusions may be derived from a close examination of the outgoing letterbooks of early 1718.

During this period the Earl of Carnarvon was endeavoring to disentangle himself from court and city affairs in order to spend most of his time at Cannons, the building of which he anticipated would soon be completed. This desire was not at odds with his largely monetary efforts to acquire a dukedom. He had put a great deal of his fortune into real estate and stocks, thus lessening the business demands on his time, and a good deal of his energy was spent in attempting to persuade the auditors to approve and seal his Paymaster General's Accounts from the period of the War of Spanish Succession. His desire, as he expressed it in a letter of 15 May 1718, was 'that I shall for the future be the greatest part of my time in the Country' (Huntington MS ST 57, xiii pp. 97–8).

His desire was not fulfilled during the first part of 1718. He was still an active member of the House of Lords, and Parliament kept him in Lodnon most of the time during its sitting, which in 1717 began on 21 November. Duchess Cassandra's journal ('An Account of ye Journeys I have taken. . . ', Leigh Papers, Shakespeare Birthplace Trust) shows that his customary winter routine was to leave London on Friday afternoon or Saturday and return the following Monday or Tuesday. He was certainly at Cannons over Christmas 1717, but hoped to be in Town on Wednesday 1 January 1718 (Huntington MS ST 57, xiii and xv, *passim*). We know for certain that Carnarvon was at Cannons every weekend in January, as likewise for the third weekend in February and the first in March. This would almost certainly have been his regular pattern until the coming of spring and the dismissal of Parliament, certainly by early June. However, in early March his second son, Henry, Lord Wilton (1708–71), came down with smallpox. He was soon considered out of danger, and by 6 March his father could write that 'he is in a fair way of doing well' (Huntington MS ST 57, xv p. 132), but he was confined to the house in London and with him his parents.

Lord Henry's illness upset Carnarvon's regular pattern of weekends at Cannons. On Saturday 15 March he promised Captain Herring that 'as soon as I get down to Canons where I have not been able to have been for some time past (& where I have left your other Accts) I will tend you a Bill for the Remainder' (Huntington MS ST 57, xv p. 142). Carnarvon originally hoped that Lord Henry would be well enough to travel to Cannons for the beginning of Holy Week (i.e. 7–13 April), but by 10 April his son was 'not yet able to put his Feet to ye Ground & will not be in a condition to go down to Cannons I fear this fortnight yet' (Huntington MS ST 57, xv p. 183). He may, in fact, have been unable to travel to Cannons until some time in May 1718.

Regardless of Lord Henry's condition, Carnarvon and his wife travelled to Cannons (again according to Duchess Cassandra's journal) on the weekends of

22–3 March, 29 March – 3 April, and 4–7 April. Their return to Cannons for 10–14 April, the weekend of Easter, seems to have marked the return to normal. April also marked a renewal of interest in the Cannons Concert. On Friday 4 April he wrote to Haym:

Not having seen you of some weeks at Cannons, & having recd no Excuse from you for your absence, I take it for granted, you are not willing to continue longer with me, upon which I have order'd Mr. Gray to pay you the Quarter due at last Lady Day – & shall think of agreeing with another Bass in your stead . . . (Huntington MS ST 57, xv p. 168)

Of course, the Earl of Carnarvon had not been at Cannons himself for some weeks, and it seems clear that little in the way of musical activity had been going on there in March and late February. Haym may well have been in London performing in one or more of the benefit concerts staged during this period. In any event, he returned to Carnarvon's service and collected his wages through to Michaelmas 1718.

The next day, Saturday 5 April, Carnarvon wrote to his friend Sir Matthew Decker:

I forgot wn I saw you last to beg the favour of you, wn you see Madam de Kielmansegge next to enquire of her if she be willing to part with the Hautbois Monsieur de Kielmansegge kept & in the case she is, that she'l let you know what wages he gave him; because as I want one in my Concert I shou'd be glad to take him. (Huntington MS ST 57, xv pp. 168–9)

The identity of this oboe-player is not known, nor whether he subsequently joined the Cannons Concert. It should be remembered, however, that while most pieces written for Cannons in this period require a single oboe, *Acis and Galatea* of May or June 1718 calls for paired oboes.

The renewed interest in the Cannons Concert also signals an apparent increase in the amount of entertaining at Cannons. Carnarvon had guests the weekend of 9–11 May (Huntington MS ST 57, xv p. 215), entertained Dr Arbuthnot at some point prior to 24 May (Huntington MS ST 57, xv p. 230), and hosted Sir David Dalrymple sometime between Saturday 24 May and Tuesday 27 May but certainly including a Sunday morning service at Whitchurch (see the letter quoted above). At this point plans for *Acis and Galatea* were well under way.

Handel's later works for Cannons (Anthems 8–10, *Acis and Galatea* and *The Oratorium*, i.e. the original version of *Esther*), are all similar in requiring at least two and sometimes three ensemble tenors, in calling for two separate tenor soloists, and in never mentioning a bassoon. The autographs of all, except *The Oratorium*, were prepared in whole or in part with each stave ruled separately (@1 8.5 or @1 9), something not found at all in the first eight anthems.[2] Even paper types found in both groups of anthems are ruled differently. For example, the *Dl* paper in the autograph of Anthem 10 is ruled @4 73, @2 31–31.5 or @4 85.5, while in the earlier works it is always ruled @5 86–86.5. Likewise, the *Oratorium* autograph is on *Cb* paper ruled @2 29.5–30 or @2 31, while the only appearances of *Cb* paper in

---

2 This information and the following derived from Burrows 1982a. For a description of rastra and types of paper, see Burrows's essay in the present volume, especially notes 44–6.

the first eight anthems were ruled either @5 86 or @2 30–30.5 (a single folio in Anthem 3).

I propose that the winter of 1717–18 and the confusion and dislocation surrounding Lord Henry's smallpox infection completely disrupted the normal functioning of the musical establishment at Cannons, and that Handel was not called upon to provide additional new music until sometime in April 1718, coinciding with Carnarvon's renewed interest in the Cannons Concert. Handel's later works for Cannons, described above, probably date from after April.

The two later works which seem most closely related are Anthem 8 and *Acis and Galatea*. The former is written on paper type *Be* ruled @1 8.5–9. Except for a gathering near the end of the Chandos Te Deum autograph, this paper occurs in the Cannons works only in *Acis and Galatea*, where it accounts for most of the first two gatherings ruled @1 9, then giving way to paper type *Cb* ruled @1 8.5–9 for the remainder of the piece. Both works require two tenor soloists, although *Acis and Galatea* requires an additional ensemble tenor and a solo bass, and both call for paired recorders; only *Acis and Galatea* asks for paired oboes as well. Anthem 8 would appear to have preceded *Acis and Galatea*, which we know to have been in the final stages of preparation by 24 May 1718. It is probably the anthem referred to in Carnarvon's letter of 6 May 1718 to Dr John Cockburn (1652–1729), Vicar of Northholt, Middlesex, which concludes:

I think it long till I see you, & if you'l come over and give us a sermon on Sunday [i.e. 11 May], & hear a new Anthem your Company will be very acceptable to your Humble Servant. (Huntington MS ST 57, xiii p. 95)

From May 1718 through to the opening of Parliament on 11 November 1718, Carnarvon seems to have spent as much of his time at Cannons as he could, sometimes even riding down to London in the morning and returning the same evening (cf. Tuesday 10 June 1718, Huntington MS ST 57, xv p. 246). He was detained in London during early July by the Commissioners' meeting to consider his Paymaster General's Accounts, but they soon adjourned. Handel's remaining works for Cannons could have been performed at almost any time during this period.

If paper flow alone is considered, Anthem 9, written entirely on *Cb* paper ruled @1 8.5, might have been composed immediately after *Acis and Galatea*. It does contain the only bass aria in the Chandos Anthems, reminding one immediately of the character of Polyphemus. However, it requires only two ensemble tenors, a single oboe and no recorders. The Chandos Te Deum looks more like *Acis and Galatea*, requiring two solo tenors and three ensemble tenors. Since it begins with several gatherings of *Cb* paper ruled @1 9, it could conceivably have been written after either *Acis and Galatea* or Anthem 9. It does, however, require only a single oboe and recorder, while calling for an additional solo trumpet. This latter is difficult to explain, since no other Cannons work by Handel except *The Oratorium* asks for a trumpet, and a trumpeter is not documented at Cannons until June 1719 when A. G. Lemon was hired (Huntington MS ST 87). Perhaps the mysterious Mr Duurcopt, who joined the Cannons staff at Midsummer 1718, was a trumpeter.

The Chandos Te Deum autograph ends with 9+ gatherings of *Bd* paper ruled almost entirely @1 8.5, and Anthem 10 begins with 2+ gatherings of the same paper. Anthem 10, like *Acis and Galatea* and the Chandos Te Deum, required two solo tenors and three ensemble tenors (at least in the opening chorus), while like *Acis and Galatea* it calls for paired recorders. Like the Chandos Te Deum, Anthem 10 requires only a single oboe, but it does not call for a trumpet.

Perhaps the best that can be said with the available evidence is that the later Chandos works almost certainly date from after April 1718; that Anthem 8 and *Acis and Galatea* seem to be closely related, and the former is likely to have been the 'new anthem' performed on 11 May 1718; that the Chandos Te Deum and Anthem 10 may well form a pair; and that Anthem 9, in many ways, seems the odd man out.

Before discussing *The Oratorium* I would like to digress a bit and comment on several smaller works which Handel may have written for Cannons. In his letter to Dr Arbuthnot of 25 September 1717, Carnarvon mentions that Handel 'is at work on . . . some Overtures to be plaied before the first lesson'. Just what these might have been is not clear, nor whether Handel ever completed them. They might, of course, have been the introductory instrumental sonatas which precede all but one of the Chandos Anthems, but it seems extremely unlikely that those should ever have been detached from the anthems for which they were composed or, in at least one case, appended. The Catalogue of the Chandos Music Library (Huntington MS ST 66) lists as item 117 a 'Sonata for 2 Violins 1 Hautboi and a Bass composed by Mr. Handel'. This might fit the bill as an 'Overture', and it certainly would seem to have been written for Cannons. Although neither the autograph nor the Duke of Chandos's copy seems to survive, this piece is almost certainly the Sonata in G minor HWV 404, for the same forces. (This has been edited by Terence Best from a manuscript in the Malmesbury collection and published in *HHA* IV/15 (Kassel, 1979).)

The first movement of the sonata generally associated with Anthem 11A seems only to have been coupled with that anthem from the time of the compilation of the Op. V trio sonatas published by Walsh in 1739 (see Beeks 1981c, and Burrows 1983 pp. 97–102). Based on the paper type (*Bd*) of the autograph, this movement also seems to date from the Cannons period and could be a detached movement from one of the 'Overtures'.

The Chandos Music Library Catalogue also lists a single cantata by Handel, *Sento là che ristretto* for canto solo, as item 36. This is bound in a collection of twenty-four cantatas by various Italian composers and J. C. Pepusch now in the British Library (BL Add. MS 62102). The cantata exists in several versions, and the autograph of version B (BL RM 20.d.12, ff. 28–30) is on *Cb* paper, one of the longest-lived of Handel's watermarks (1717/18–1728) but not inconsistent with composition during the Cannons period. We know, in fact, that the Chandos version, at least, was composed before the completion of the Music Library Catalogue, which was subscribed by Pepusch on 23 August 1720. The location of item

36 in the catalogue is more consistent with a date of 1718, and another copy of this cantata is found in a volume from Elizabeth Legh's collection dated '1718' (Bodleian MS Mus d 61).

Other Italian cantatas whose autographs are written on *Ba*, *Cb* and *Dl* papers could well have been written during the Cannons period of 1717–18 (see Burrows 1982 pp. 94–5, 104), but there is presently no evidence to connect them with Cannons or the Cannons Concert. On the other hand, the Chandos Music Library Catalogue may represent only a portion of the musical repertoire of the Cannons Concert; it may, in fact, largely reflect the existence of presentation rather than performance copies.

The surviving Chandos documents make no reference to keyboard works by Handel, nor to any solo or trio sonatas, but this should not necessarily be taken to exclude the possibility that some of them were written or revised during the Cannons period. The lack of autograph sources and datable early copies for most of these works makes it extremely difficult to establish their dates of composition and/or revision.

Finally, the Op. III concerti grossi are often said to have been 'largely composed at Cannons'. This is true but misleading. In the words of Donald Burrows,

Only Nos 1, 2 and 4 of Op. 3 seem to have had an existence as separate integral works before Walsh's publication [in early 1734]: the rest were put together from other sources, mainly the Chandos Anthems. (Burrows 1983, p. 86)

Concerto no. 4, or most of it at any rate, dates from at least as early as 1716, when it was added to a revival of *Amadigi* as the 'Orchestra Concerto' or 'Second Overture' (Sadie 1972 p. 16). Concertos no. 1 and 2 may be even earlier works, but they were surely not written for Cannons. The two oboes, two violas and two bassoons required for Concerto no. 1 could not have been mustered by the Cannons Concert as we know it at any time, while the paired oboes and viola of Concerto no. 2 look unlike any work known to have been written for Cannons, except the orchestra for Pepusch's Magnificat of late 1720 or 1721 (BL Add. MS 34072). Concerto no. 6 consists of only two movements, the first composed for *Ottone*, probably in 1726 but containing curious echoes of the *Acis and Galatea* overture, and the second probably written shortly before the publication of Op. III but based on a thematic idea first heard in the 1712 *Il pastor fido* (Sadie 1972 pp. 19–20).

Concertos nos. 3 and 5 may only in the strictest sense be said to have been composed for Cannons, at least in part. The first two movements of Concerto no. 3 consist of the introductory instrumental sonata to Chandos Anthem 7, while the third movement is taken from the ritornello to the setting of 'We believe that Thou art come to be our judge' in the Chandos Te Deum. The final movement began life as a keyboard fugue (or, perhaps, a keyboard sketch for an instrumental fugue): no. 2 of the set of *Six Fugues or Voluntarys for the Organ or Harpsicord* published by Walsh in 1735. The autograph (BL RM 20.g.14, ff. 30–32a) is written on type *Bb2* paper and must also date from before or during the Cannons period (see Burrows

1982 pp. 103, 118 and *passim*). These disparate movements were later collected to form a concerto, evidently shortly before the publication of Op. III.

The original Concerto no. 5 consisted of the two-movement introductory sonata to Chandos Anthem 2. Three movements were subsequently added, the second of which is the fugal second movement of the introductory sonata to Anthem 6A transposed from E minor to D minor. The origin of the remaining two movements is not known, but the lack of an independent viola part certainly points to a trio-sonata origin and perhaps a Cannons one as well. As with Concerto no. 3 above, these movements were cobbled together to form a concerto, but this was clearly not Handel's original intention. (For additional details see Sadie 1972 and Burrows 1983).

The final work to be discussed in this article has always been associated with Cannons and James Brydges; that is, of course, *The Oratorium* (i.e. the original version of *Esther*). This identification with Chandos and the year 1720 dates from Bernard Gates's revival of the work in 1732. The Mathias copy of *Esther* in Gerald Coke's collection and the New York Public Library copy taken from it (New York PL MNZ) state on their title-pages:

ESTHER./ an ORATORIO; or, *Sacred Drama.*/ the MUSICK *as it was Composed for the MOST NOBLE*/ JAMES DUKE of CHANDOS./ by George Frederick Handel, in the Year 1720./ ——— / *And Perform'd by the CHILDREN of His MAJESTY's Chapel*, on/Wednesday 23: February 1731./ ——— / LONDON 1732. (see Serwer 1981, p. 36)

Furthermore, a published libretto in the Schoelcher Collection (Paris BN), printed for the Philharmonic Society performances of 23 February and 1 March 1732, provides the same information (Dean 1959 p. 191). What gives this information an added likelihood of truth is that the Duke of Chandos had in the winter of 1731–2 been accepted as a member of the Gentlemen Performers of Musick (Huntington MS ST 57, p. 311) who provided the instrumentalists for Gates's first two performances (Dean 1959 pp. 83 and 204).

Although a certain amount of evidence points to the year 1720 for the genesis of *The Oratorium*, a complete copy of it has been discovered which bears the title 'Composed by George Frederick Handel, Esq., London 1718', and the endorsement 'Eliz. Legh 171[8/9]' (Serwer 1981 p. 38). There would thus seem to be no doubt that 1718 is the correct date of composition. What, then, is the explanation for the 1720 date?

The vocal and instrumental requirements of *The Oratorium* far exceed the forces available at Cannons on a regular basis in 1718 (see Table 1 above). It calls for two solo sopranos, one alto, four tenors, two basses, and an orchestra including paired horns and bassoons, viola and harp, none of which would have been possible with the 1718 forces. However, these requirements almost exactly match the expanded membership of the Cannons Concert in Midsummer 1720, as shown in Table 2, a time when Handel could have been available to direct a performance (Dean 1959 p. 191).

Table 2. *Musicians at Cannons in 1720*

(Information from Huntington MSS ST 87 and ST 44 unless noted)
LD = Lady Day Quarter, MS = Midsummer Quarter, MM = Michaelmas Quarter,
CM = Christmas Quarter, NY = New Year's Day

Instrumentalists name	instrument(s)	quarterly wage	employment
Georg Angel	cello, bass	£7 10s	MS 1718[a] – NY 1722
Sigr Biancardi	oboe[b]	£7 10s	LD 1718 – CM 1720
Alexander Bitti	violin	£10	LD 1718 – NY 1721
Thomas Burges	violin	£5	LD 1719 – NY 1721
Richard de la Main (Delamain)	viola	£5	MS 1720[c] – NY 1721
Girardo (Giraldo, Ghirardo)	violin	£7 10s	MS 1720 – NY 1722
Jean Christian Kytch (Keutch, Keitch)	oboe, bassoon, recorder	£12 10s	CM 1719 – NY 1721
A. G. Lemon	trumpet	£8 15s	MM 1719[d] – NY 1721
George Monro (Munro, Monroe)	keyboard	£7 10s	MM 1719[e] – LD 1724[f]
Charles Pardini (Perdini)	cello, ?bass	£10	LD 1718 – LD 1724[g]
John Christopher Pepusch	composer, keyboard, violin	£25	MM 1719[h] – CM 1725[i]
Thomas Rawlins (Rawling, Rawlin)	violin	£7 10s	CM 1719 – NY 1721
John Ruggiero (Rogiero)	violin[b]	£7 10s	MS 1718 – MM 1720
Sigr Scarpettini	violin	£7 10s	LD 1718 – NY 1721
Olaus Westenson Linnert (Mr Weston)	bassoon	£7 10s	MS 1720 – NY 1721

Singers name	voice part(s)	quarterly wage	employment
Thomas Bell	countertenor	£10[j]	MM 1720[k] – NY 1721
Thomas Gethin	countertenor, tenor	£10[j]	MS 1720[l] – NY 1721

[a] Paid £1 3s at Midsummer 1718 for a fortnight's wages. A Mr Angel 'who never perform'd on the stage before' gave an entertainment on the German harp at Lincoln's Inn Fields Theatre on 27 March 1720 (*The London Stage*). Georg Angel had a brother who visited him at Cannons on 17 September 1721 (Huntington MS ST 59).

[b] See Milhous 1983 pp. 158–61.

[c] Paid £11 13s for the period from 28 November 1719 to Midsummer 1720 on 1 July 1720.

[d] Paid £10 for 4 months' wages at Michaelmas 1719; corrected from New Year's list 1721 (see Plate B): Huntington MS ST 44, ii p. 34.

[e] Came to Cannons around 1714 as a page (Huntington MS ST 57, xiv p. 21) but began drawing wages in 1719.

[f] Last payment recorded 26 August 1724 for LD 1724 (Huntington MS ST 82 p. 12), but he was still allotted a room on the 19 June 1725 Inventory (Huntington MS ST 83 f. 176').

[g] Huntington MS ST 82 p. 54; but £50 per annum in New Year's list 1721 (see Plate A)

[h] Referred to as 'Director of the Concert' in a letter of 21 May 1719 (Huntington MS ST 57, xvi p. 163), so must have been employed prior to Midsummer 1719 on a different basis. Pepusch was heavily involved in the 1718/19 season at Lincoln's Inn Fields Theatre until 1 June 1719 (*The London Stage*). Presumably he was drawing a salary from the theatre until Midsummer 1719.

[i] Huntington MS ST 82 p. 173. Pepusch had returned to Lincoln's Inn Fields Theatre for the 1724/25 season with a new version of *Dioclesian* on 28 November 1724 (*The London Stage*), and seems to have been providing music for Cannons on Sundays only during 1725.

[j] Bell apparently shared his salary and room with Gethin at NY 1721, but they were both paid for the earlier period.

[k] Paid £11 10s for 1 June 1720 to Michaelmas 1720 as initial payment.

[l] Paid £6 13s for 29 April 1720 to 24 June 1720 on 1 July 1720.

17

Table 2 (cont.)

Singers name	voice part(s)	quarterly wage	employment
Morphow	'Contra alto'	£7 10s	NY 1721
Peirson	treble		NY 1721
William Perry	bass	£7 10s	CM 1718 – MM 1725[m]
Rigs	treble		NY 1721
Amos Rogers	?treble		?[n] – Jan. 1724[o]
William Rogers	tenor	£2 10s	NY 1721[p] – Nov. 1723[q]
Thomas Salloway (Salway)	treble		NY 1721 – Oct. 1724[r]
George Vanbrugh (Vanbrughe, Ghentbrughe)	bass	£7 10s	CM 1719[s] – NY 1721

[m] Paid £8 8s on 6 November 1725 'for his performance (in singing) at Cannons to this day' (Huntington MS ST 82 p. 185).

[n] On 22 December 1719 the Duke thought that Amos Rogers's voice was not about to break (Huntington MS ST 57, xviii p. 207). He must have been in Chandos's service before this date.

[o] He was last employed in January 1724 (Huntington MS ST 24, i p. 286).

[p] William Rogers may well have been in Chandos's service for some time before this date but not drawing a salary. See Table 1, note l.

[q] The last reference to him is in November 1723 (Huntington MS ST 24, i p. 268).

[r] Huntington MS ST 82 p. 110, but he was still allotted a room on the 19 June 1725 Inventory (Huntington MS ST 83 f. 177').

[s] Paid £8 4s for 15 September 1719 to Christmas 1719 at Christmas 1719.

Even more interesting is the presence of two compositional layers in the *Oratorium* autograph (BL RM 20.e.7), first pointed out by Winton Dean (Dean 1959 pp. 222–3). The earliest layer, which Handel composed as far as the middle of Sc. 5, is scored for single oboe, two violins and undesignated bass instruments; a chorus of canto, alto, tenors I and II, and bass; and canto, alto, bass and four tenor soloists. With the exception of the alto voice, this matches almost exactly the known resources of the Cannons Concert in 1718, assuming some doubling of tenor roles.

In the middle of Sc. 5 Handel apparently decided to rework his earlier material employing a somewhat revised libretto and an expanded instrumental and vocal scoring. The reasons for these changes are not known, but as the revised version is found complete in the score dated '1718', the alterations must have been made before the end of that year, or before 25 March 1719 if the old calendar was employed. Handel, apparently, wrote the expanded version of *The Oratorium* either for a performance by the 1718 Cannons Concert augmented by a relatively large number of extra players and singers from London, or for a projected performance by the Cannons Concert at a time when it had expanded its own resources sufficiently. The first suggestion, though certainly possible, seems to me unlikely in view of the apparent tailoring of works by Haym, Handel and Pepusch to the peculiarities of the Cannons Concert at the time of their composition, and the references of Sir David Dalrymple and others to the fact that Carnarvon/Chandos had his music 'made for himself and sung by his own servants'.

The possibility of a projected future performance, although according ill with our perception of Handel's usual working procedures, does seem to fit the facts at hand, and all indications point to 1720 as the date for that performance. Even the placement of *The Oratorium* as item 123 in the Chandos Music Library Catalogue (Huntington MS ST 66) indicates a date of acquisition of 1720, certainly before 23 August when the catalogue was subscribed by Pepusch, and perhaps after late May when item 107, Pepusch's *Six English Cantatas* dedicated to the Duke of Chandos, was first published (Smith 1948 p. 164). That the catalogue entry fails to mention the harp or the two bassoons may simply reflect the presence of an inattentive scribe or the fact that these instruments were included in partbooks labelled for other instruments.

In conclusion, it might be well to speculate concerning Handel's departure from Carnarvon's employ. Mainwaring reports that

During the last year of his residence at Cannons, a project was formed by the Nobility for erecting an academy at the Haymarket. The intention of this musical Society, was to secure to themselves a constant supply of Operas to be composed by Handel, and performed under his direction. For this end a subscription was set on foot . . . The sum subscribed being very large, it was intended to continue for fourteen years certain. But as yet it was in its embrio-state, being not fully formed till a year or two after. (Mainwaring 1760 p. 96)

In a letter to his brother-in-law, M. D. Michaelsen, dated London, 20 February 1719, Handel himself writes:

Ne jugez pas, je Vous supplie, de mon envie de Vous voir par le retardement de mon depart, c'est à mon grand regret que je me vois arreté icy par des affaires indispensables et d'ou, j'ose dire, mà fortune depend, et les quelles ont trainé plus longtems que je n'avois crû . . . mais a la fin j'espere d'en venir à bout dans un mois d'icy . . . (Deutsch *Doc* p. 84)

I beg that you will not judge of my eagerness to see you by the lateness of my departure; it is greatly to my regret that I find myself kept here by affairs of the greatest moment, on which (I venture to say) all my fortunes depend; but they have continued much longer than I had anticipated . . . but I am hoping to conclude it all in a month from now . . . (translation Deutsch *Doc* p. 85)

He was clearly referring to plans for the Royal Academy of Musick, and preparations for it would seem to have been afoot from late 1718. That Carnarvon (soon to be Chandos) was involved seems indicated by his subscription of £1,000 to the Academy in May 1719, and by the presence of his associates Sir Hungerford Hoskins, Sir Matthew Decker and Dr John Arbuthnot on the same list of subscribers (Deutsch *Doc* p. 91). Another figure to be directly involved with the Royal Academy was Haym, who was to prepare the libretto for Handel's first Academy opera, *Radamisto* of 1720. He left the Cannons Concert at Michaelmas 1718 (Huntington MS ST 83 p. 30). Could his departure have been in some way connected with preparations for the Royal Academy? Could Handel have ceased providing music for Cannons at around the same time, having become enmeshed in the preliminary planning for the new Academy which both his patrons, Carnarvon and Burlington, supported? Should we shorten Mainwaring's 'Two years he spent at CANNONS' (Mainwaring 1760 p. 95) to just over one year? How ironic it would be if all of Handel's works for Cannons were written before James Brydges finally received the long-sought title by which he and they are remembered.

References

Baker, C. H. C. & M. I., *The Life and Circumstances of James Brydges, First Duke of Chandos, Patron of the Liberal Arts* (Oxford, 1949)

Beattie, J. M., *The English Court in the Reign of George I* (Cambridge, 1967)

Beeks, G. F., 'The Chandos Anthems and Te Deum of George Frideric Handel (1685–1759)', Ph.D. diss., University of California, Berkeley, 1981 [Beeks 1981a]

Beeks, G. F., 'Zur Chronologie von Händels Chandos Anthems und Te Deum B-dur', *HJ* 27 (1981), pp. 89–105 [Beeks 1981b]

Beeks, G. F., 'Handel's Chandos Anthems: More "Extra" Movements', *ML* 62 (1981), pp. 155–61 [Beeks 1981c]

Burrows, D. J., 'Handel and the English Chapel Royal during the Reigns of Queen Anne and King George I', 2 vols., Ph. D. diss., The Open University, 1981

Burrows, D. J., 'A Handlist of the Paper Characteristics of Handel's English Autographs', typescript, The Open University, 1982

Burrows D. J., 'Walsh's Editions of Handel's Opera 1–5: The Texts and their Sources', in C. Hogwood & R. Luckett (eds.), *Music in Eighteenth-Century England: Essays in Memory of Charles Cudworth* (Cambridge, 1983), pp. 79–102

Christie, Manson & Woods Ltd, *Printed Books . . . which will be Sold at Christie's Great Rooms Wednesday 18 November 1981* (London, 1981)

Cummings, W. H., *Handel, the Duke of Chandos and the Harmonious Blacksmith* (London, 1915)

Dean, W., *Handel's Dramatic Oratorios and Masques* (London, 1959)

Dean, W., 'Haym, Nicola Francesco', *New Grove* (London, 1980)

Dickinson, H. T., *The Scriblerian* 5/2 (1973), p. 118

Hatton, R., *George I. Elector and King* (London, 1978)

Kirkendale, U., 'The Ruspoli Documents on Handel', *JAMS* 20 (1967), pp. 222–73

The London Stage 1660–1800, ed. E. L. Avery *et al.* (Carbondale, Ill., 1960–8)

[Mainwaring, J.], *Memoirs of the Life of the late George Frederic Handel* (London, 1760)

Milhous, J. & Hume, R. D., 'New Light on Handel and the Royal Academy of Music in 1720', *Theatre Journal* 35/2 (May 1983), pp. 149–67

Quaritch Ltd, *A Catalogue of Manuscripts and Books Relating to Music* (London, 1919)

Rogers, P. J., 'Dating "Acis & Galatea": A Newly Discovered Letter', *MT* 114 (1973), p. 792

Rogers, P. J., 'Music and Musicians at Cannons: The Huntington Library Documents', M.A. thesis, University of California, Santa Barbara, 1977

Sadie, S., *Handel Concertos* (London, 1972)

Serwer, H., 'Die Anfänge des Händelschen Oratoriums ("Esther" 1718)', in W. Siegmund-Schultze (ed.), *Anthem, Ode, Oratorium – ihre Ausprägung bei G. F. Händel*, Martin-Luther-Universität Halle-Wittenberg Wissenschaftliche Beiträge 14 (Halle, 1981), pp. 34–45

Smith, W. C., *A Bibliography of the Musical Works published by John Walsh during the Years 1695–1720* (London, 1948)

Sotheby, Wilkinson & Hodge, *Catalogue of the Famous Music Library . . . of the late W. H. Cummings* (London, 1917)

Streatfeild, R. A., *Handel, Canons and the Duke of Chandos* (London, 1916)

Aria and Ritornello: New Aspects of the Comparison Handel/Bach

PAUL BRAINARD

(Princeton, New Jersey)

It is a premise of this study that the particular questions to be addressed here cut directly across the demarcation lines of genre, language and, to a large extent, movement form as well, so that we can safely follow the example of the late Sir Anthony Lewis[1] in treating 'aria' as a single phenomenon for Handel, as it is for Bach. That is not to imply anything like uniformity in either composer's work; rather, it asserts that in respect to the matters at issue here, the wide range of variations found in both men's *oeuvre* is independent of the cantata/oratorio/opera distinction, and that Handel's German settings are as different from Bach's and in many of the same fundamental ways, as are his Italian or English ones.

A part of the involved history of the aria 'O placido il mare' from *Siroe* can serve as a useful beginning. In Handel's autograph[2] we find a discarded early version of the ritornello that originally read as in Ex. 1. Of its ten bars, Handel cancelled the fifth

Ex. 1.

---

1 See References below, under Lewis 1958–9.
2 BL RM 20.c.9 ff. 16′ ff, supplemented by Cfm 262 p. 21, which is discarded continuation of f. 16′ of the main MS, subsequently replaced by the present f. 17; cf. note 4 below.

and sixth at an early stage, before he had completed the orchestration. The remaining eight bars are made up of four two-bar segments, which I have labelled *a* to *d*. They correspond fairly closely to the final version of both the ritornello and the postlude[3] of the aria, except that in both of these their order has been changed to *a-c-b-d*. Handel achieved this peculiar rearrangement by directing his copyist to substitute the postlude – which shows the new order – for the original ritornello: 'l'ultimo Rittornello invece di questo'. Even this change entailed more than just a straightforward transferral, however, for the postlude itself shows both original and revised readings in its last three bars – Ex. 2 – the effect of the revision being to restore the *original* reading of phrase *d* of the now discarded ritornello.

Ex. 2.

The composer's ultimate choice of the altered, 'postlude' order of events (*a-c-b-d*) over the initial one is especially remarkable if we consider the vocal opening, in which Handel had originally used the 'new' succession *a-c* (Ex. 3), but from which

Ex. 3.

he subsequently deleted phrase *c*, substituting in its place the independent continuation printed by Chrysander.[4] We thus find him rejecting, in the vocal opening, the very succession of ideas which he later (?) went to some trouble to establish in the ritornello. In the event, phrase *c* figures only in the interior and towards the end of the aria's *A* section, associated now not with line 2 ('o porti con l'onda terrore e

---

3 For clarity's sake I suggest the use of the unqualified term 'ritornello' only in referring to the first appearance of the music in question, 'postlude' to designate the instrumental conclusion of the *A* section in *da capo* form, '*da capo* ritornello' to refer to an altered recurrence following the *B* section, and 'coda' in the event the aria concludes with other than a literal restatement of the postlude. The reasons for this will emerge presently.

4 *HG* 75 pp. 21–4. The vertical broken line in Ex. 3 represents the end of f. 16' of the autograph. What follows it is taken from the Fitzwilliam fragment (cf. note 2), showing that the completion of phrase *c* would have been still different had Handel retained this early version. The variant bar given in Ex. 3 is immediately followed in Cfm 262 by bars 13–27 of the final version, extending to the end of the recto side; thereupon the fragment breaks off.

spavento'), as in Handel's first attempt, but with the *last* line of the *A* text ('è colpa del vento, sua colpa non è'). In its most prominent appearance in the voice (bars 41–2) it is preceded by phrase *b* and followed by an expanded variant of *d*. Still another vocal statement of *c* (bars 47–8) ushers in the cadential Adagio and the postlude.

Of the several alterations cited here (the autograph shows others as well) only the first demonstrably preceded any performance of the piece; about the others one cannot be certain. We may in fact never know how many separate changes of mind on how many different occasions were involved, or to what extent the transferrals of material reflect piecemeal tinkering rather than calculated overall reshaping. But the mere occurrence of such reordering points up an important, instinctively 'known' but insufficiently realized fact about Handel's musical language: its high degree of segmentation, the discrete nature of its individual phrases being so pronounced as to permit, on occasion, a reshuffling of the very order in which they are presented.

The *Siroe* example is, in this last respect, admittedly an extreme case to which I know of no exact counterpart; but in most other ways it presents a picture that is altogether typical of Handel's composing scores – and exceptional in Bach's. Testimony to the 'block'-like manipulation of local contexts abounds in the Handel autographs. One repeatedly encounters not only the substitution of one phrase for a substantially different one of equal length, or the expansion of a given passage through the later insertion of anything from a half-bar (resulting in wholesale metrical shifts) to a succession of phrases not forming part of the original conception, but also – most tellingly – the outright excision of anything from a sub-phrase to an entire succession of phrases, no music being inserted in their place. Of this last type of revision there are, so far as I am aware from a fairly close acquaintance, no more than a handful of instances in all of the composing scores of Bach.

This contrast seems highly suggestive. Admittedly we know cutting and pruning to have been an everyday necessity of Handel's profession, whereas Bach was largely free of the constraints imposed by audiences' impatience and star singers' whims. Nonetheless it can be said that by no means all, and perhaps no more than a small majority, of Handel's cuts are demonstrably assignable to 'late' (post-composition) stages in the evolution of a given work, such as the revisions associated with a revival or a change of cast. That his music could, on such occasions, sustain the drastic amputations he frequently felt obliged to inflict upon it is itself a revealing fact. But more than this, 'surgery' was for him part and parcel of the composition process itself, a necessary concomitant perhaps of the rapid and seemingly inexhaustible flow of his melodic invention. Cuts, substitutions and transplantations at the phrase level occur in all phases of his work with a frequency that fundamentally distinguishes Handel's scores, and by implication his way of thinking, from those of Bach. More on this point follows below.

Revisions of the kind described can be peculiarly informative when, as in the *Siroe* example, they affect the voice–ritornello relationship of a given aria. In the Can-

23

nons autograph of *Acis and Galatea* (BL RM 20.a.2) two bars of the air 'Consider, fond shepherd' have been excised between the present bars 28 and 29. Handel's original entry reads as in Ex. 4. Clearly his curtailment of the phrase from six bars

Ex. 4.

that　flatters　our　　　　　　hope　in pursuit　　of　the　fair＿＿

to four is a correction in progress, occasioned by his discovery that the text could not be satisfactorily underlaid to the tune he had destined for it. Significantly, however, that melody is taken directly from bars 10–15 of the ritornello (the six-bar phrase there having been left intact). As an apparently intended, if not wholly successful, setting of line 2 of the poetry it forms part of a pattern in which each of three principal elements of the ritornello occupies a similar role: the first (bars 2–5) as a setting of line 1 and the third (bars 20–3) as the vehicle for successive repetitions of line 3 (in bars 48–51, 64–7 and 68–71, thus including the entire vocal segment immediately preceding the postlude). The introduction of 'Consider, fond shepherd' thus falls into one of the largest and most characteristic classes of Handelian ritornellos, in that it constitutes a kind of synopsis of prominent musical/textual events from (especially) the opening and closing portions of the *A* vocal section. Here each of the ideas in question anticipates one or more phrases from the voice line itself; an obvious alternative is for the ritornello to present figural material (like that of phrase *b* of Ex. 1) against which a separate voice line can subsequently be projected in the technique now known as *Einbau*.

Let me emphasize that I am confining myself here to instances of the *integral* restatement of ritornello passages in the body of the aria, as distinct from what one might call the 'non-structural' use of motivic material derived from, but contextually independent of, the ritornello. In my view such quotations-in-context can reveal particularly interesting aspects of the composer's craft, not the least of which are clues to the extent and nature of his forethought about a given setting, and (at least on occasion) the degree to which that forethought included specific consideration of the text to be set.

To turn for the moment to Bach, it is I think no exaggeration to say that for him the composition of the ritornello represented the largest single expenditure of creative effort in setting an aria text to music. What Marshall[5] has aptly termed 'formative' corrections are heavily concentrated in the opening portions of a large majority of Bach's arias and choruses (a fact that perhaps does not receive sufficient emphasis in Marshall's admirable survey). The advance notation of ritornello themes makes up a large and significant proportion of his 'sketching' activity (clearly distinct from his habit of jotting down 'continuation sketches' at the end of

5 Marshall 1972, I pp. 159ff.

a recto side in the interior of a piece). And repeatedly we gain the impression, in looking at his composing scores, that once the ritornello 'sits' and the vocal opening is under way, the main compositional hurdles have already been crossed. That this should be so is, it seems to me, entirely consistent with the prominent *structural* role played by the ritornello in the subsequent course of events in the great majority of Bach's concerted arias written after 1714. With a frequency and to an extent unmatched (so far as we know) by any composer of his time, Bach treats the ritornello as a determinant of context throughout long stretches of his vocal settings. From it emanate either extensive melodic quotations by the voice, or instrumental restatements against which the voice supplies counterpoint (so-called *Einbau* technique), or – most frequently – a combination of both. The practice, first pointed out by Werner Neumann some decades ago, constitutes the main argument in Neumann's more recent call for a wholesale revaluation of Bach's vocal music, on the grounds that it is for the most part 'instrumentally' conceived and dominated.[6] Of greater relevance here are the deep-seated differences we can observe in both the invention and the internal re-use of ritornellos in Handel's case.

Taking another fairly extreme instance for illustration's sake, one can usefully confront two compositions that might at first seem to constitute an unlikely pairing, but which in fact have a surprising amount in common: a second *Acis* aria, 'Where shall I seek the charming fair', and the Petrus aria 'Ach, mein Sinn' from Bach's *St John Passion*.[7] In each, the composer has evidently seized upon the imagery of 'seeking': the quest for an unattainable haven in the one case ('Wo willt du endlich hin, / wo soll ich mich erquicken?'), for the elusive Beloved in the other. The overall similarity of musical response – minor keys, triple time, similar tempos, restless dotted rhythms – invites comparison of the respective ritornellos and their relationship to the whole. For Bach it can almost be said that the sixteen-bar ritornello *is* the composition, for no fewer than 62 of the remaining 75 bars of the aria are made up of sustained quotations from it (none of them shorter than eight bars' duration, two of them comprising the entire sixteen), with *Einbau* prevailing except for the first eight bars of the vocal opening.

That Handel's ritornello is only half as long, and is confined moreover to the opening vocal theme alone, warns us that the analogy is only partial and should not be pursued too far; but this manner of simply 'setting the piece in motion' is on the other hand so typical of Handel (and generally uncharacteristic of Bach) as to justify the comparison. Here, after pre-stating the melody of the first two text lines as an 'antecedent', Handel appends a 'consequent' repetition of the same phrase-pair before turning matters over to the singer. But unlike Bach's succession of linked ritornello phrases, this particular arrangement of periods remains without thematic effect on the further course of the piece, once the voice has completed its

---

6 Especially Neumann 1981; see also Dürr 1971, I pp. 32–3; and Dürr 1977, especially pp. 132–7. I have suggested elsewhere (Brainard 1983) that there is considerable room for disagreement with Neumann's main contention.

7 I am indebted to Louis Bagger for having drawn my attention some years ago to the remarkable musical parallels between the two arias, which are a living demonstration of the *Affektenlehre* in action.

initial quotation (modified for purposes of modulation). Subsequent quotations of *intact* ritornello material (apart from the varied postlude) are limited to one embedded (*eingebaut*) statement of the antecedent phrase in each of the two vocal sections (on the threefold 'where' and on 'groves', respectively) and one three-bar instrumental interlude in the relative major. Thus, while it supplies a main thematic component of the aria, Handel's ritornello constitutes nothing like the tectonic nucleus we see in Bach's, a nucleus both subsuming and as it were generating the aria's context.

The sheer quantity of ritornello quotation is not precisely what is at issue here. One might cite a Handelian example like 'O godlike youth' from *Saul*, whose ritornello is simply an advance statement of the entire *A*-section vocal line (minus the latter's phrase-repetitions). The same technique can be found as far back as *Almira* ('Chi sa mia spema'), *Teseo* ('Deh! v'aprite'), and *Agrippina* ('Bella pur nel mio diletto'); it occurs in Bach as well (e.g. in BWV 197.iii, 'Schläfert aller Sorgen Kummer'), albeit more rarely, owing not least to Bach's strong penchant for alternating vocal quotation with long stretches of *Einbau* (these are in turn a rarity in Handel, whose preference is for a more rudimentary version of the device used over comparatively brief stretches). The more fundamental distinction between the two composers' ritornellos is harder to define, but might be likened to the difference between a distillation and a collection of samples. Bach's ritornello more commonly tends to remain integral and to shape the subsequent course of events from within; Handel's 'sampling' appears to work in the opposite direction, rather in the manner of a *résumé* before the event. Where energies do in fact 'flow outward' from the Handelian ritornello, they tend to be motivic rather than thematic or contextual – an observation not unrelated to what Winton Dean has called 'Handel's habit of improvising with a *datum*'.[8]

In the aria 'Da' tuoi begi'occhi' from *Giustino* (RM 20.b.4; *HG* 88) Handel initially set down a ritornello of seven bars' length; the first six bars of the final reading were originally to be rounded off by a cadential bar analogous to the present bar 9. Before proceeding further Handel deleted that seventh bar and substituted the present bars 7–9; only then did the writing of the vocal portions begin. Given this sequence of events it is of particular interest to note that the two added bars are devoted to an important 'circling' phrase that is later associated with the interior *A*-text lines 'Labbro vezzoso, volto amoroso'. That Handel might already have had this particular coupling of text and music in mind is an entirely plausible, if unprovable, interpretation of the correction. At all events, in the act of setting down his ritornello he was already mustering ideas whose future application extended well beyond the confines of the ritornello itself.

Similar forethought is sometimes revealed even by those ritornellos in whose final versions Handel has covered the traces of his original train of ideas. An example is 'La nobiltà del regno' from *Scipione* (printed in *HG* 71 with the text 'Del

---

8 Dean 1959 p. 57. The remark stems from a discussion of Handel's techniques of borrowing and of a point first made in Abraham 1954 pp. 266ff.

debellar la gloria'), which shows direct voice–ritornello correspondence only for the first $2\frac{1}{2}$ bars of the vocal opening. An in-progress correction in Handel's autograph (RM 20.c.6) reveals, however, that following the half-cadence in bar 4 he had initially had a different continuation in mind, containing music with which (in the event) the A section of the aria concludes: compare the bracketed music in Ex. 5

Ex. 5.

with the phrases of the published version beginning in bars 18 (voice) and 21 (instruments) respectively, as well as with the postlude. In this case the musical invention was apparently quite independent of any specific textual associations; nonetheless we again find Handel anticipating a prominent thematic event from the latter portions of the aria's main section. That he had barely begun to notate this theme before deleting it from the ritornello, only to resurrect it later on, admits of several explanations but demonstrates at all events that the 'synopsis' ritornello is in no sense a generative scheme or a consciously followed model, but rather the almost incidental (but not therefore insignificant!) product of a particular way of 'thinking ahead'.

That Handel attached no special importance to the 'synopsis' *per se* is further shown by his readiness on occasion to *eliminate* thematic anticipations from the ritornello when revising an already completed aria. 'Non ti fidar' from the third act of *Muzio Scevola* (RM 20.b.7; *HG* 64) is one of many such instances. Handel has made extensive cuts in both vocal sections as well as in the opening ritornello, which was originally identical with the postlude but has been shortened from fourteen to six bars. The material excised from the ritornello makes its only other sustained appearance in the aria just before the close of the A section. The reverse of this situation occurs in 'Fly, malicious spirit' from *Saul* (see *HHA* I/13, *Anhang*, no. 10, and *Kritischer Bericht*, pp. 90–1), whose autograph (RM 20.g.3) shows the deletion, following bar 52, of a near-literal quotation of the entire final stretch of the ritornello (bars 12–21), to the text 'Gracious Lord, his pain assuage'. The ritornello itself has been left intact, with the result that half of its music no longer figures in the body of the air.

The indifference seemingly implied by such cuts stands in sharp contrast to the considerable trouble Handel frequently took to bring ritornello and vocal sections into line with one another. In 'Mirth,admit me of thy crew' from *L'Allegro* (RM 20.d.5; *HG* 6) bars 5–8 of the ritornello are a late insertion replacing a single bar which Handel deleted in the process. The same new material is inserted by means of cues at its subsequent appearances in bars 29–30 and 58–9; but in the B section, at bars 75–8, it is an original entry. Clearly this is the 'lark' referred to in the B text,

27

and when Handel hit upon the idea in bars 75–8 he backtracked to include it in the ritornello and the *A* section as well.

Both the ritornello and the melodically identical vocal opening of the soprano aria 'Speranza mi dice' from *Giulio Cesare* (RM 20.b.3; the piece is not included in *HG* 68) show the same extensive corrections from identical original readings; internal quotations from the ritornello have been modified accordingly, but the postlude shows the revised tune as the original entry, suggesting that the changes were decided on at this point. In 'The god of battle' from *Hercules* (RM 20.e.8; *HG* 4) three ritornello bars have been cut between bars 8 and 9 of the final version. At the transposed recurrence of bars 9ff in bars 49–51, a three-bar segment analogous to the one excised from the ritornello has also been cut: surely more than a coincidence.

The aria 'Nube, che il sole ad ombra' from *Riccardo Primo* (RM 20.c.2; *HG* 74) contains a passage borrowed from the fourth movement of the well-known D major Violin Sonata. Each time these phrases appear in context in the aria, a two-bar segment has been cut (between the present bars 8 and 9, 27 and 28, and (in the postlude) 85 and 86): Ex. 6. As attested by the sonata's autograph (RM 20.g.13,

Ex. 6.

almost certainly Handel's composing score), the two bars are integral to the original conception. The composer's reasons for cutting them in the aria are obscure, but the consistency with which he has eliminated them from ritornello, *A* vocal section and postlude alike is striking. Ex. 7 illustrates a still more remarkable set of

Ex. 7.

excisions in 'Se non mi vuol amar' from *Tamerlano* (RM 20.c.11; *HG* 69), the fifth bar of whose ritornello originally comprised *two* full 6/8 bars, from which alternate beats have been cut in each appearance of the phrase except the *da capo* ritornello, where the single-bar version appears without correction. A conceivable reason for the changes might have been a decision on Handel's part that in the context

> Se non mi vuol amar,
> Almeno il traditor,
> Perfido ingannator,
> Il cor mi renda

the word-repetitions of his original *Einbau* setting of the phrase (Ex. 8) created a sense-distorting emphasis on the wrong word; these repetitions have in any case

Ex. 8.

almen   almen   almen il traditor

been eliminated in the final reading. 'Padre amato' from the same opera provides another instance of the 'retroactive' effect of the aria upon its ritornello. The present bar 4 was not part of the opening as originally written. Handel almost certainly incorporated it by working backwards from his composition of the vocal *A* section. He had introduced the idea for the first time in bar 48 as a phrase-bridging lead-in to the short *Einbau* segment beginning in bar 49. Later, in the postlude, he first started to reproduce the opening ritornello (still lacking bar 4), then changed its fourth bar to echo the line of bar 48. It was surely only now that he altered the opening correspondingly, inserting the new bar 4 and deleting the original seventh bar, leaving the total length of the ritornello unchanged.

Rather more puzzling, in view of the lengths Handel was obviously willing to go to to achieve consistency between the texted and untexted versions of a given tune, is a smaller but not inconsiderable group of instances in which his revisions have the opposite effect. These seem largely, and perhaps significantly, confined to vocal openings and their ritornello counterparts. The autograph of 'Joys that are pure' from *Samson* (RM 20.f.6; *HG* 10) shows initial agreement, and post-revision disagreement, between the respective beginnings: see Ex. 9. Corresponding changes

Ex. 9.

Joys that are   pure,

have been made in the later appearances of the ritornello opening (bars 31 and 106). It is just conceivable that they are connected with the circumstance that the *B* section of this air ('Where truth and peace') opens with the same ascending tetrachord found in the post-correction reading of bar 1.[9] In *Atalanta* (RM 20.a.9; *HG* 87) the vocal opening of 'Lascia ch'io parta' has been revised without concurrent alteration of the ritornello: see Ex. 10. Interestingly, Handel then proceeded to set down still another version of the tune in his *A*-section postlude (Ex. 11): a synthesis of the instrumental melody and the vocal rhythm from the aria's opening.

9 If true, that would make this an unusual case, for the thematic anticipations of Handel's ritornellos are normally confined to events that occur first in the *A* section. (Note the difference between this alteration and the one cited above from *L'Allegro*, where an idea actually emanating from the *B* section is inserted not only into the ritornello but into the *A* vocal section as well.) A series of extensive revisions in 'Powerful guardians' from *Alexander Balus* (RM 20.d.3), too space-consuming to be included in the present essay, had the effect if not the purpose of *eliminating* from the *A* section all original references to the phrase with which the *B* section ('Keep from insult') begins.

Ex. 10.

Lascia ch'io parta solo

Lascia ch'io

Ex. 11.

For some of these kinds of revision one can fairly readily adduce approximate counterparts in Bach. He too, particularly in the early stages of work on an aria, occasionally hit upon new ideas or modifications of the vocal setting which he subsequently incorporated into his ritornello as well. The late insertion of the second ritornello bar in BWV 42.vi (see Marshall 1972, I pp. 194–5), for example, surely results more directly from Bach's working-out of the vocal opening than from the more abstract considerations of pacing and register diagnosed by Marshall. Similarly, it was presumably the repetition of the first full bar of the voice entry in BWV 43. iii that triggered the late interpolation of the ritornello bars 2–3 (reproduced in Marshall 1972, I p. 195). Of the many instances one could cite of Bach's 'thinking ahead' while devising his ritornello, none is more remarkable than the evolution – no actual corrections are involved – from continuation-sketch (Marshall 1972, II Sketch 120) to final version of the chromatic concluding phrase of the ritornello of BWV 197. iii, a change clearly motivated (as Marshall perceptively observes: I p. 69) by the word 'Sorgenkummer'. Conversely, Bach was quite prepared on (rare) occasions to introduce departures from an already established ritornello context, especially when prompted by the discovery of new possibilities for enhancing the responsiveness of his music to its text. The correction in BWV 81.iii cited by Marshall (I pp. 123–4) was surely occasioned not only by Bach's choice of a vocally 'less demanding formulation' but also by his having hit upon the idea of lowered-chromatic inflection as the appropriate imagery for 'Belials Bächen'.

Several of the preceding cases notwithstanding, there is on the whole remarkably little trace in Bach of the 'surgical' procedures that are so common with Handel; nor, I venture to say, would the bulk of Bach's vocal music lend itself at all well to such treatment, even at the hands of so skilled and elegant a craftsman as Handel, schooled in the demands and potentialities of the musical theatre. In Bach there appear to be fewer of the necessary preconditions, e.g. successive phrases and phrase-groups having the same tonal goal; cadences tend more frequently to be bridged or overridden by longer-range linear 'vectors' including those set in motion by Bach's penchant for extensive (and often imitative) contrapuntal elaboration. His style might perhaps be likened to that of prose discourse, in which one thought is the premise of its successor. Handel's by contrast might be seen as analogous to a technique of versification in which the poetic line itself has a more nearly autonomous existence and import. The ritornello–aria relationship is but one of the ways in which this antithesis manifests itself.

Still a different aspect of the comparison concerns postludes, *da capo* ritornellos and codas – that is, those purely instrumental passages following the close of each of the two principal sections of the standard two- or three-part aria form. I have suggested the use of this multiplicity of terms in order to underscore the fact that in Handel's case they are often *not* musically synonymous with '*the* ritornello' stated at the outset. Winton Dean[10] has commented trenchantly on this phenomenon, of which several of the arias cited above provide examples. Quite apart from the reasons of plot and delineation of character plausibly adduced by Dean for the instances he cites, there seems to be a general readiness on Handel's part to let the later restatements of his ritornello be (as it were) filtered through the musical events of the intervening vocal section(s), producing subtle modifications for which there is often no obvious dramatic or other external motivation. The postludes of 'When sunk in anguish' from *Theodora* and 'The god of battle' from *Hercules* are but two of many examples one might name; see also Ex. 11 above. I know of no comparable instances in Bach, for whom the 'nuclear' function of the ritornello seems also to have implied its invariability (save for occasional curtailment) in postludes and at the *da capo*.

Handel's 'improvisatory' approach to such matters may also be seen, as Gerald Abraham and others have pointed out,[11] in his much-discussed expropriation of material from his own and others' compositions. Of obvious relevance to our topic is the well-known fact that in an aria Handel's *direct* borrowing is often limited to the ritornello (whether the ritornello corresponds to the vocal opening or not), following which the remainder of the source-composition is either ignored or so extensively rewritten as to constitute a new work. Where traces of this process turn up in Handel's working materials they can be particularly fascinating. I shall limit myself here to one example, the borrowing from Bononcini of ideas for the aria 'Meglio in voi' in Handel's version of *Serse*, to which Harold S. Powers has devoted an extensive discussion.[12] An added perspective on 'Meglio in voi' emerges from Handel's autograph (RM 20.c.7), where we learn that the piece was in fact originally even more *trasformato* (Power's term) than appears from the published final readings,[13] and that at least one of its more concrete resemblances to Bononcini emerged only gradually in the course of Handel's work on the aria – through what mental processes we can only guess. Handel's ritornello, for example, originally was to have begun as in Ex. 12. By the time he reached the vocal opening, he had already decided on the 'Bononcinian' descending triad in place of the repeated

10 Dean 1969, especially pp. 46–7 and 159–64.
11 Abraham 1954 pp. 266ff; see also Dean 1959, especially pp. 53ff, and Siegmund-Schultze 1962, 1965, 1966, and 1976.
12 Powers 1961 and 1962.
13 See the confrontation of Handel's final version and Bononcini's setting in Powers 1962 pp. 78–9.

Ex. 12.

notes at the start, and on the imitative gesture in the continuo, but his first phrase (before correction) still cadenced with tonic harmony: Ex. 13. It is possible that this was the point at which he revised both the vocal and ritornello openings to their

Ex. 13.

Meglio in voi col mio par - tire

final readings.[14] Even likelier, however, is that that decision was made still later, for in the postlude he once again initially (before correction) reverted to the first version of the tune and its original bass line. Finally, in the abbreviated *da capo* ritornello (later eliminated as part of a twenty-four-bar cut in the *B* section) we find all the features of the opening phrase established save for one small detail: the third beat of the melody in bar 4 has again had to be corrected from g′ to a′. The bearing of all this on the foregoing discussion will be evident. Equally clear, from all that we know about Bach's quite divergent approach to the practice of 'parody',[15] is that had he known and had occasion to use the Bononcinian model the results would have been entirely different.

14 The remainder of the ritornello shows several further substantial corrections including two two-bar cuts, at least one of which (between the present bars 6 and 7) was made concurrently with a twenty-four-bar excision from the *A* vocal section.
15 Notably the integral rather than 'improvisatory' nature of the vast majority of Bach's borrowings; see especially Neumann 1965, Finscher 1969, and Brainard 1969.

References

Abraham, G., 'Some Points of Style', in G. Abraham (ed.), *Concerning Handel* (Oxford, 1954), pp. 262–74

Brainard, P., 'Bach's Parody Procedure and the St. Matthew Passion', *JAMS* 22 (1969), pp. 241–60

——, 'The Aria and Its Ritornello: The Question of "Dominance" in Bach', in *Bachiana et alia musicologica: Festschrift Alfred Dürr zum 65. Geburtstag* (Kassel, 1983), pp. 39–51

Dean, W., *Handel's Dramatic Oratorios and Masques* (Oxford, 1959)

——, *Handel and the Opera Seria* (Berkeley/Los Angeles, 1969)

Dürr, A., *Die Kantaten von Johann Sebastian Bach*, 2 vols. (Kassel, 1971)

——, *Studien über die frühen Kantaten Johann Sebastian Bachs* (Leipzig, 1951), enlarged edn (Wiesbaden, 1977)

Finscher, L., 'Zum Parodieproblem bei Bach', in M. Geck (ed.), *Bach-Interpretationen* (Göttingen, 1969), pp. 94–105

Lewis, A., 'Handel and the Aria', *PRMA* 85 (1958–9), pp. 95–107

Marshall, R. L., *The Compositional Process of J. S. Bach*, 2 vols. (Princeton, 1972)

Neumann, W., 'Über Ausmass und Wesen des Bachschen Parodieverfahrens', *BJ* 51 (1965), pp. 63–85

——, 'Das Problem "vokal–instrumental" in seiner Bedeutung für ein neues Bach-Verständnis', in R. Brinkmann (ed.), *Bachforschung und Bachinterpretation heute*: *Bericht über das Bachfest-Symposium 1978* (Leipzig, 1981), pp. 72–85

Powers, H. S., '*Il Serse trasformato*', *MQ* 47 (1961) pp. 481–92, and 48 (1962), pp. 73–92

Siegmund-Schultze, W., 'Zu Händels Schaffensmethode', *HJ* 8 (1961–2), pp. 69–136

——, *Georg Friedrich Händel: Thema mit 20 Variationen* (Halle, 1965)

——, 'Bach und Händel', *HJ* 12 (1966), pp. 141–69

——, 'Zur "Wort-Ton"- Problematik bei Händel, dargestellt am Parodieverfahren', *HJ* 21/22 (1975–6), pp. 11–18

Handel and Hanover

DONALD BURROWS

(Milton Keynes, Buckinghamshire)

On 16 June 1710 Handel entered the service of the Elector of Hanover,[1] and for the following two and a half years he retained the post of Kapellmeister to the elector, notwithstanding his protracted absences from the court during that period. There are several references to Handel in the court and family papers of the electorate,[2] none of which was known to O. E. Deutsch when he compiled his documentary biography of the composer.[3] The Hanover papers help to fill in the background to Handel's service at the electoral court, but only to a limited extent; they do, however, provide some enlightenment about Handel's activities in London during the period 1710–14, immediately before his employer became King George I of Great Britain. In this article I shall review, first, Handel's relations with the Hanover court during these years, drawing on the court documents where these are relevant, and, secondly, the musical repertoire which may be associated with Handel's Hanoverian service.

The circumstances surrounding Handel's appointment at Hanover remain obscure. Handel probably received some approach while he was in Italy, but this would have been neither specific nor official. Chrysander stated that Steffani and Baron Kielmansegg were in Venice early in 1710,[4] but he reveals no source for this,

---

1 More correctly, the Elector of Brunswick and Lüneburg (*Kurfürst zu Braunschweig und Lüneburg*).

2 See Georg Schnath, *Geschichte Hannovers im Zeitalter der Neunten Kur und der englischen Sukzession 1674–1714*, III (Hildesheim, 1978), pp. 509–12. Papers now at the Niedersächsisches Hauptstaatsarchiv, Hanover, are designated NH in subsequent references. I thank His Royal Highness Prince Ernst August of Hanover, Duke of Brunswick and Lüneburg, for permission to consult and reproduce material from his family papers deposited there; the British Academy for a research grant which enabled me to study the sources at first hand in 1979; and Professor Ragnhild Hatton, of the University of London, for her advice on Hanoverian sources.

3 Deutsch *Doc* (published 1955).

4 Friedrich Chrysander, *G. F. Händel*, I (Leipzig, 1858), p. 311. According to Erich Graf von Kielmansegg, *Familien-Chronik* (Vienna, 1910), p. 447, Kielmansegg offered the kapellmeistership to Handel in Venice in 1710, but this source does not say that Steffani was also present. There is no comparable reference in the earlier edition of the *Familien-Chronik* (Leipzig/Vienna, 1872).

and the presence of Steffani in Venice at this time has been questioned.[5] In all probability Chrysander relied on the source which remains the only substantial one for information on this period of Handel's life, the *Memoirs of the Life of the late George Frederic Handel*, published anonymously in 1760 but probably the work of John Mainwaring.[6] The relevant section of the *Memoirs* runs thus:

HANDEL having now been long enough in Italy effectually to answer the purpose of his going thither, began to think of returning to his native country . . . HANOVER was the first [musical court] he stopped at. STEFFANI was there, and had met with favour and encouragement equal, if possible, to his singular desert. This person (whose character is elegantly sketched by a lover of his Art and friend to his memory) he had seen at Venice, the place of his nativity. Such an acquaintance he was glad to renew: for STEFFANI's compositions were excellent; his temper was exceedingly amiable; and his behaviour polite and genteel . . . We shall soon have occasion to mention him again, and therefore shall only add at present, that he was Master of the Chapel to his late MAJESTY, when he was only Elector of Hanover . . .

At Hanover there was also a Nobleman who had taken great notice of HANDEL in Italy, and who did him great service . . . when he came to ENGLAND for the second time. This person was Baron KILMANSECK. He introduced him at court, and so well recommended him to his Electoral Highness, that he immediately offered him a pension of 1500 Crowns per annum as an inducement to stay. Tho' such an offer from a Prince of his character was not to be neglected, HANDEL loved liberty too well to accept it hastily, and without reserve. He told the Baron how much he owed to his kind and effectual recommendation, as well as to his Highness's goodness and generosity. But he also expressed his apprehensions that the favour intended him would hardly be consistent either with the promise he had actually made to visit the court of the Elector Palatine, or with the resolution he had long taken to pass over into England, for the sake of seeing that of LONDON. . . Upon this objection, the Baron consulted his Highness's pleasure, and HANDEL was then acquainted, that neither his promise nor his resolution should be superseded by his acceptance of the pension proposed. He had leave to be absent for a twelve-month or more, if he chose it; and to go whithersoever he pleased. On these easy conditions he thankfully accepted it.

To this handsome pension the place of Chapel-master was soon after added, on the voluntary resignation of STEFFANI.[7]

From this it will be seen that the *Memoirs* do not say that Steffani and Kielmansegg were in Venice together in 1710, merely that Handel had previously met Steffani in Venice and that Kielmansegg had 'taken notice' of Handel in Italy. No doubt Handel received an invitation from Kielmansegg to visit Hanover, but there is no mention of an offer of an appointment and it is unlikely that Kielmansegg would have been empowered to make such an offer. In all probability Chrysander joined up the various threads from the *Memoirs* rather too tightly. I have found no record in the Hanover papers of a pension payment to Handel in addition to his sal-

5 Colin Timms, 'Handel and Steffani', *MT* 114 (1973), p. 374.

6 Evidence for Mainwaring's authorship comes from King George III's annotation to the title-page in his copy of the *Memoirs*, referred to in W. C. Smith, 'George III, Handel and Mainwaring', *MT* 65 (1924), p. 790. See also Benjamin Stillingfleet's comments, quoted below, on the authorship of the *Memoirs*.

7 I have extracted passages from pp. 69–73 of the *Memoirs*, retaining the paragraph sequence of the original.

ary as Kapellmeister: presumably the original offer was superseded by the subsequent appointment. In saying this I make the assumption that the *Memoirs*, fifty year later, relayed the facts correctly and that Handel did receive some offer in the first place. Where this section of the *Memoirs* can be tested against contemporary documents the narrative proves to be surprisingly accurate. A letter dated 4 June 1710 from the Electress Sophia to her granddaughter, to which I shall return presently, confirms the story from the *Memoirs* in two particulars. First, when Handel arrived in Hanover he had not previously received any formal offer of an appointment there. Far from this being the case, the electress remarked that the 'Saxon' would make a good Kapellmeister for the King of Prussia. Secondly, Handel was planning to investigate his prospects with the 'Electress Palatine' as well as those at Hanover, presumably in response to similar contacts made in Italy. The electress said that Handel was about to go to Düsseldorf to compose an opera. We may infer, perhaps, that Handel eventually rejected the Elector Palatine's offer when he discovered that operatic opportunities in Düsseldorf were less favourable than he had expected.

The accuracy of these details lends support to the hypothesis that one of the main sources for the *Memoirs* was Handel himself. Benjamin Stillingfleet, a friend of J. C. Smith the younger, claimed that the *Memoirs* were 'written by the Rev. Mr. Mainwaring, from material principally communicated by Mr. Smith'.[8] It is not completely clear whether the 'Mr. Smith' referred to by Stillingfleet is John Christopher Smith Senior or Junior, but neither of them can have had first-hand knowledge of Handel's career in Italy and Germany sufficient to provide the detailed narrative found in the *Memoirs*. More than half of the biographical section of the *Memoirs* is concerned with the years up to 1714, before Handel's association with Smith Senior commenced.[9] In the 1750s, when the material for the *Memoirs* was presumably collected, the only person in London who could have known as much about Handel's early life was Handel himself. Probably this section of the *Memoirs* was collected by some primitive interview technique: through the journalistic embroidery and 'writing-up' a tone of reminiscence can sometimes be detected in the style.[10] It is not unusual for old men to remember the days of their youth better than their middle years, and the proportions of the *Memoirs* may also have been affected by asking Handel to tell the story from the beginning, the narrative being curtailed by his death. Interviews were possibly, but not necessarily, conducted by one of the Smiths.[11]

8 Quoted in Percy Young's introduction to William Coxe, *Anecdotes of George Frederick Handel and John Christopher Smith [1799]*, facsimile edn (New York, 1979), pp. xi–xiv.

9 The earliest possible date for the commencement of Smith Senior's close association with Handel in London is 1717. The younger Smith was born in 1712.

10 See also Anthony Hicks, 'Handel's Early Musical development', *PRMA* 103 (1976–7), p. 81.

11 If Coxe (*Anecdotes*, pp. 48–9) is correct, Handel and the elder Smith were not close or concordant friends during Handel's last years, although still collaborating professionally. If either of the Smiths had questioned Handel about his earlier years, this is more likely to have been done by Smith Junior. For the years after 1720 both father and son could have supplied authoritative information to Mainwaring without involving Handel himself.

The proposition that Handel himself contributed some of the material which was eventually published in the *Memoirs* is not, of course, a reason for accepting sections of the *Memoirs* uncritically. Handel's recollections of his earlier years are unlikely to have been completely accurate. Furthermore, the *Memoirs* mix information which may have been derived from the composer with information from other sources. The writer of the *Memoirs* acknowledged his debt to one specific previous publication in this section of his narrative: the *Memoirs of the Life of Agostino Steffani* published anonymously in 1750, an early work of John Hawkins.[12] The last sentence in the extract quoted above is almost certainly derived from information in the Steffani memoirs,[13] and its inaccuracy is beyond question. Steffani's service as Kapellmeister to the court of Hanover had been directly related to the fortunes of the Court Opera. Appointed in 1688, he was succeeded by Pietro Torri in 1696; Torri's tenure was short, for the Opera was suspended after the death of the Elector Ernst August in 1698. Thereafter, any employment which Steffani received from Hanover was for diplomatic missions.[14] On present evidence, it appears that the kapellmeistership was revived for Handel in 1710, and that Steffani had not held this post for more than a decade. This does not rule out the possibility that Steffani's influence was critical in obtaining the post for Handel in 1710, however. As Bishop of Spiga and Apostolic Vicar of Northern Germany, Steffani's life from 1709 still centred on the region around Hanover, and his diplomatic activities kept him in close contact with the court; furthermore, he is known to have been in Hanover in June 1710, trying to arrange for the building of a Catholic church.[15]

Reference has already been made to the letters from the Electress Sophia to her granddaughter Sophia Dorothea, Princess Royal of Prussia. Handel is mentioned

12 For the likely date of this publication, see Colin Timms, 'Gregorio Piva and Steffani's Principal Copyist', in I. Bent (ed.), *Source Materials and the Interpretation of Music: A Memorial Volume to Thurston Dart* (London, 1981), p. 187 note 14.

13 See p. [v]: 'In the year 1708, he [Steffani] resigned his employment of Chapel-Master in favour of Mr. Handel.' On the same page, Hawkins claimed that he had received information for the *Memoirs* from Handel and Pepusch, yet even his date of 1708 must be wrong since Handel was still then in Italy. Some of Hawkins's material needs to be treated with even more caution than the independent sections of Mainwaring's *Memoirs*, and he seems particularly unreliable on dates. Colin Timms ('Handel and Steffani') interprets Hawkins's treatment of Handel and Steffani in his *History* as implying that the two composers met at Hanover in 1703. This is possible, but the passage quoted by Timms could equally refer to Handel's arrival in Hanover in 1710 if Hawkins was wrong in reporting Handel's age as being 'under twenty'.

14 For Steffani's career, see Timms, 'Gregorio Piva', and Philip Keppler, 'Agostino Steffani's Hannover Operas and a Rediscovered Catalogue', in H. Powers (ed.), *Studies in Music History: Essays for Oliver Strunk* (Princeton, N. J., 1698), p. 341.

15 Steffani's presence in Hanover is referred to in letters from Frederick William I of Prussia to the Electress Sophia, and from the Electress Sophia to the Raugräfin Louise, dated 10 and 15 June 1710. See E. Berner, *Aus den Briefwechsel König Friedrichs I von Preussen und seiner Familie*, Quellen und Untersuchungen zur Geschichte des Hauses Hohenzollern, Reihe 1, Bd 1, (Berlin, 1901), p. 224; and E. Bodemann, *Briefe der Kurfürstin Sophie von Hannover an die Raugräfinnen und Raugrafen zu Pfalz*, Publikationen aus dem Königlichen Preussischen Staatsarchiv 37 (Leipzig, 1888), pp. 318–19. A letter from Steffani himself, now in the Fondo Spiga, Rome, reveals that he was still in Hanover on 22 July 1710. I thank Colin Timms for these references and for his helpful criticism of this article.

three times in this correspondence, in letters from the period of his appointment in June 1710. The relevant passages run as follows:[16]

A Herenhausen, le 4 de Juin 1710

ie va [ca..] tous les iours voir nostre Princesse Electorale qui ce porte a present for bien et ne garde plus le lit   elle et diverti de la Musique d'un Saxson qui surpasse touse qu'on a iamais entandu sur le Clavesin et dans la Composition   on L'a fort admire en Italye   il est for propre a estre Maitre de chapelle si le Roy L'avoit sa Musique serat bien mieux en Ordre qu'elle est a present   il va a Dusseldorf pour y Composer un opera

A Herenhausen le 14 de juin 1710

car d'icy il n'y a pas grand chose a dire si non que L'Electeur a pris un maitre de chapelle qui sapelle Hendel qui ioue a mervelle du Clavesin dont le Prince et la Princesse Electorale ont beaucoup de ioye, il est assez bel home et la medisance dit qu'il a este amant de la Victoria, La P^es E^le ce porte si bien qu'elle ce promene tous les soirs avec moy au iardin, ce qui est un grand plesir pour moy

A Herenhausen le 15 de Juin 1710

Vous ne me [raendes] pas ma chere Princesse si le Roy a garde dans son service la bonne chanteuse dont V A R parle, L'Electeur a pris dans son service Henling qui ioue si bien du Clavesin et qui est (: a ce qu'on dit:) si savant en musique   le P^r et la P^es Electorale en sont charme et ravy que L'Electeur La retenu, pour moy ie ne m'y entants pas, depuis que i'ay perdu la feu Reyne ma fille la musique me rant melancolique

Herrenhausen, 4 June 1710

I go [almost] every day to see our electoral princess, who is very well at the moment and no longer confined to bed. She is entertained by the music of a Saxon who surpasses everyone who has ever been heard in harpsichord-playing and composition. He was much admired in Italy. He is very suitable to be [appointed] Master of the Chapel. If the king took him, his music would be in much better shape than it is at present. He is going to Düsseldorf to compose an opera there.

Herrenhausen, 14 June 1710

But there is not much to say from here except that the elector has taken on a Master of the Chapel named Handel, who plays marvellously on the harpsichord, in which the electoral prince and princess take a great deal of pleasure. He is quite a handsome man, and gossip says that he has been in love with Victoria. The electoral princess is so well that she walks every evening with me in the garden, which is a great pleasure for me.

Herrenhausen, 15 June 1710

You have not [informed] me, my dear princess, whether the king has retained in his service the fine singer of whom Your Royal Highness spoke. The elector has taken into his service Henling [sic], who plays the harpsichord so well and who is (so they say) so learned in music. The electoral prince and princess are charmed with him and delighted that the elector has kept him. For myself, I do not know much about it: since I lost the late queen, my daughter, music makes me melancholy.

16 Transcribed from Merseburg, Zentrales Staatsarchiv, HA Rep 46 T18, Vol. 1.2, ff. 152, 156–7, 158. I thank the staff of the Staatsarchiv for supplying me with copies of the originals. The electress's wayward orthography and (lack of) punctuation are reproduced here: doubtful words and editorial interpretations are shown in square brackets. Hanover dates were in New Style. Extracts from the letters of 4 June and 14 June were published in German translations in G. Schnath, *Briefwechsel der Kurfürstin Sophie von Hannover mit dem Preussischen Königshause* (Berlin/Leipzig, 1927), pp. 187–9: Anthony Hicks translated a section of Schnath's second letter in 'Handel's Early Musical Development' (see note 10 above), p. 83. I acknowledge the generous assistance of Sheila Hills with the translations from French originals in the present article, though the final form is my own.

'Victoria' may possibly have been the singer Vittoria Tarquini.[17] The 'king' referred to in these letters is Frederick I of Prussia, husband of the 'late queen', Sophia's daughter. 'The elector' is Georg Ludwig, Sophia's son and Sophia Dorothea's father, later King George I of Great Britain; 'the electoral prince and princess' are his son and daughter-in-law, subsequently King George II and Queen Caroline of Great Britain. From the letters it is clear that Handel's appointment received strong support from the prince and princess, who were of Handel's generation[18] – a fact that may have assumed some significance later in London when divisions appeared within the royal family. It is interesting to have this direct testimony to their admiration of Handel's musical accomplishments. The first letter also confirms that Handel's Italian reputation had run ahead of him to Hanover.

The following payments to 'Georg Friedrich Hendell' as Kapellmeister appear in the Hanover Chamber Accounts:[19]

Midsummer ('Johannis') 1710 – Midsummer 1711	1,000 Thaler
Midsummer 1711 – Midsummer 1712	1,000 Thaler, less deduction of 83 Thaler, 12 Groschen
Midsummer 1712	500 Thaler, for six months' salary, paid in arrears in 1715

Handel's first visit to London fell within his first year's salary, from which no deductions were made. At present not enough is known of Handel's activities during the second year to explain the reason for the deduction shown in the accounts. After Midsummer 1712 Handel was not in Hanover to collect his salary, even if it had been allowed to him. During the period of his service the Hanover Opera was still in abeyance for financial reasons, so the loan of the Kapellmeister to London may have been an arrangement completely favourable to the court, since it enabled Hanover to retain a right to his services while allowing Handel to fulfil his operatic ambitions.[20] The Hanover court moved to the hunting palace at Göhrde in October each year,[21] and my guess is that this provided a convenient occasion for Handel to be released from his duties to travel to London in 1710 and 1712. This worked in nicely with the London 'season' around which the performances at the

---

17 She is mentioned in the *Memoirs* as one of the singers in Handel's *Agrippina*, in a passage which tantalizingly concludes: 'HANDEL seemed almost as great and majestic as APOLLO, and it was far from the lady's intention to be so cruel and obstinate as DAPHNE' (p. 54). It is difficult to know whether to take this as a veiled reference to Handel's personal relationships or to the composition of his cantata *Apollo e Dafne*.

18 The prince and princess were both born in 1683, and were thus two years older than Handel.

19 NH Hannover Des. 76C (= Kammer-Rechnungen) Nr 235, pp. 393–4; Nr 236, p. 416; Nr 236a, p. 393. The original German entries are quoted in full by R. Doebner, 'Händel in Hannover', *Zeitschrift des Historischen Vereins für Niedersachsen*, ed. E. Bodemann (Hanover, 1885), pp. 297–8.

20 Ragnhild Hatton, *George I, Elector and King* (London, 1978), pp. 264–5 and p. 364 note 53.

21 NH Reisebuch, Hannover Dep. 103 IV Nr 318. Musical 'performances' at Göhrde seem to have been limited to those incidental to hunting: there is no evidence for the type of activity which would have required Handel's presence. See Jürgen Prüser, *Die Göhrde. Ein Beitrag zur Geschichte des Jagd- und Forstwesens in Niedersachsen* (Hildesheim, 1969).

Queen's Theatre, Haymarket, were planned. Precise dates for Handel's travels are not known, but a casual mention in a letter to Hanover reveals that in 1712 he was back in London by 21 October.[22]

The elector and his court were naturally looking towards their forthcoming British inheritance during the last years of Queen Anne's reign. A Hanoverian *Resident*, Kreienberg, was stationed in London from September 1710, and a succession of important Hanoverian diplomats – Grote, Schütz and Bothmer – served as envoys extraordinary. The representatives of Hanover no doubt used their influence to assist Handel when he arrived in England, and in this may lie the explanation of Handel's speedy and ready acceptance at Queen Anne's court. The extent of this acceptance is rather startling. One contemporary periodical reported a performance at court even before the successful production of *Rinaldo*, his first London opera:[23]

Tuesday, the 6th of February [1711], being the Queen's Birth-day, the same was observed with great Solemnity: the Court was extream numerous and magnificent; the Officers of state, Foreign Ministers, Nobility, and Gentry, and particularly the Ladies, vying with each other, who should most grace the Festival. Between One and Two in the Afternoon, was perform'd a fine Consort, being a Dialogue in *Italian*, in Her Majesty's Praise, set to excellent Musick by the famous Mr. *Hendel*, a Retainer to the Court of *Hanover*, in the Quality of Director of his Electoral Highness's Chapple, and sung by *Cavaliero Nicolini Grimaldi*, and the other Celebrated Voices of the *Italian* Opera: with which Her Majesty was extreamly well pleas'd.

This performance appears to have replaced the court birthday ode which was the traditional task of English musicians. The Poet Laureate and the Master of the Queen's Musick were ousted from the royal birthday odes for the rest of the reign: there is a hiatus in the payments to John Eccles, Master of the Queen's Musick, for composition of the odes after 1711, and they do not resume again until 1715.[24]

Although Handel's visits to London were, in the first instance, in furtherance of his musical career, the second 'visit' (which turned into permanent residence) must be seen against the background of English and European political developments.[25] His first visit had coincided with changes in the British government which had important consequences for direction of foreign policy: while Handel was back in Hanover momentous changes took place in England. The first Peace Articles were agreed between Britain and France in September 1711, and early in 1712 Marl-

---

22 Hanover, Niedersächsische Landesbibliothek, L.Br.97 (= letter from J. D. Brandshagen to Leibniz, London 21 October 1712 (presumably Old Style)).
23 Abel Boyer, *The History of the Reign of Queen Anne digested into Annals*, 11 vols. (London, 1703–13), IX, p. 315. Also printed in vol. I of the same author's *The Political State of Great Britain*, 2nd edn (London, 1718).
24 PRO LC5/155–6. The schedule of court odes for 1711–14 given in Rosamund McGuinness, *English Court Odes* (Oxford, 1971), p. 27, needs revision. See Donald Burrows, 'Handel and the English Chapel Royal during the Reigns of Queen Anne and King George I', Ph.D. diss., The Open University, 1981, pp. 60, 140–4.
25 For the political background to this period see Hatton, *George I* (note 20 above), ch. 4, and Edward Gregg, *Queen Anne* (London, 1980), Chs. 13, 14.

borough was dismissed from his post as Captain-General of the armed forces. After nearly a decade of concerted action by British, Imperial and Dutch forces, the alliance was broken by the 'restraining orders' given to the British army in May 1712, which effectively left the rest of the allied armies at the mercy of the French during the campaigns of that year. Such developments could only be regarded with horror in Hanover, and the elector made known his attitude to Queen Anne's unilateral peacemaking in strong terms. Perhaps it is not surprising that the Duke of Marlborough was among those reported as pressing for Handel's return to London in June 1712.[26] The elector himself may have been only too pleased to release Handel again: any Hanoverian influence, however indirect, must have been welcome in London at this time.

Yet only three months after returning to England Handel composed a Te Deum which was undoubtedly intended for the celebration of the forthcoming Peace of Utrecht;[27] it was eventually performed, with its accompanying Jubilate, at the official thanksgiving service at St Paul's Cathedral on 7 July 1713. Information on the music, though not mentioning Handel as the composer, had reached the London newspapers as early as the end of February, and Handel is first named in reports of rehearsals on 5 and 7 March.[28] News of the Te Deum's composition had been forwarded to the elector much earlier, however, in a letter from Thomas Grote to the elector dated 13 January:

Auch hat mir der Mylord Bolingbroke nahmens der Königin gesaget, es hatte Ihre Majestät Ew. Kurf. Durchlaucht Capellmeister Handel eine Musik für dieselbe zu componiren aufgegeben. Weil sie ihn nun zu solchem Ende gerne hier behalte, aber erfahren hatte, dass dessen von Ew. Kurf. Durchlaucht erhaltene Erlaubniss zu Ende sey, so mochte ich Ew. Kurf. Durchl. in truste referiren, dass Dieselbe Ihr zu gefallen besagten Haendel noch eine Weile hier zu belassen belieben mochte. Ich habe solches gerne versprochen und anbey bezeuget, wie ich nicht zweifelte, es würde Ew. Kurf. Durchl. froh seyn, dass jemand von Dero Bedienten Ihrer Majestät in einigen Sachen nach Gefallen zu dienen die Ehre hätte. Diese Musik ist, wie ich vernehme, ein Tedeum so in der St. Paulskirche bei Publicirung des Friedens soll gesungen werden und werden dazu über hundert Musicanten employiret werden. Die Zeit anlangend, so scheinet man damit ziemlich zu eilen und sollte man etwa auf vier Wochen a dato muthmassen.[29]

My lord Bolingbroke told me in the name of the queen that Her Majesty had commissioned Your Highness's Kapellmeister, Handel, to compose a piece of music for her. Because she would like him to remain here until this is done but has found out that Your Highness's permission for him to remain here has come to an end, I would like to inform Your Highness in confidence that Her Majesty wishes Handel to remain here for a while. I have promised that with pleasure and herewith report, as I didn't doubt that Your Highness would be pleased that one of your servants would have the honour of serving Her Majesty in some way. This music is, as I understand, a Te Deum, which shall be sung in St Paul's Cathedral when peace is proclaimed, and more than a hundred musicians are going to be employed for this.

26 Cal. Br. 24 Nr 1694, ff. 234–5 (= letter from Kreienberg to the elector, 23 May/3 June 1712).
27 Te Deum autograph, BL MS RM 20.g.5, dated 14 January 1712 (Old Style).
28 *Dawk's News-Letter* 19 February and 7 March 1713.
29 NH Hanover 91 Grote III Nr 2, f. 98. A German transcription of the relevant passage from the near-impenetrable handwriting of the original is printed in R. Pauli, 'Ueber einige Bestandtheile des Königlichen Staatsarchivs in Hannover', *Nachrichten von der Königlichen Gesellschaft der Wissenschaften und der Georg-August-Universität zu Göttingen* no. 9 (Göttingen, 1881), pp. 254–5 note 1.

Regarding the time, they seem to be rather in a hurry and one should assume it would take about four weeks from now.

It is likely that Handel's ode *Eternal source of light divine*, whose text refers directly to the Peace, was composed at the same period as the Utrecht Te Deum and was intended for performance on the queen's birthday, 6 February. The precarious state of the queen's health probably prevented any performance of the ode, but the fact of its composition demonstrates that Handel did not feel inhibited by Hanoverian political considerations. He is still described as 'Maestro di Capella di S.A.E. d'Hannover' on the word-book for *Silla*, dated 2 June 1713.

This word-book was no doubt prepared some time before the performance. Handel was, in fact, finally dismissed from his Hanover post at the beginning of June 1713. We can hardly doubt from the timing of the dismissal that it was Handel's part in the Utrecht celebrations which lost him his post as Kapellmeister, though his continued absence from Hanover may have been used as an excuse to justify the dismissal. Once Handel had committed himself to the composition of the Te Deum, it was only to be expected that he would see it through to performance at the thanksgiving service. We need not pay too much attention to Grote's estimate of four weeks, unrealistic though it proved in the event: the central point at issue was whether the elector would accept the generous view of Handel's activities which Grote suggested.

The circumstances of Handel's dismissal are revealed in a copy of a letter from Kreienberg, Hanoverian *Resident* in London, and I quote the complete section referring to Handel.[30]

Londres le 5/16 Juin 1713

Je vous ay ecrit il y a quelques jours sur le sujet de Mr. Hendel, que comme S.A.E. etoit resolüe de le casser, il s'y soumettoit et qu'il ne souhaittoit rien sinon que l'affaire se fit de bonne grace, et qu'on luy donnat un peu de tems pour entrer ici au service de la Reyne, aussi me semble-t-il par vos lettres que c'etoit l'intention genereuse de S.A.E. mais du depuis Mr. de Hattorf a fait scavoir à Mr. Hendel par Mr. de Kielmansegge que S.A.E. l'avoit cassé de son service, et qu'il n'eut qu'à aller ou il luy plairoit, de sorte qu'il a eu son congé d'une maniere qui le motifie beaucoup. Je vous avouë franchement, que Mr. Hendel n'est rien à moi, mais il faut que je dise en même tems, que si on m'avoit laissé faire pendant quelques semaines, j'aurois pû mener toute l'affaire à la satisfaction de S.A.E. et de Hendel et même à l'avancement du service du maitre, puisque le Medecin confident de la Reyne, homme d'importance, étant son grand patron et amy, et l'ayant jour et nuit chez lui, il auroit pu etre d'une fort grande utilité, méme il l'a été déja plusieurs fois, en m'informant des circonstances qui m'ont souvent eclairci sur l'etat de la santé de la Reyne. Ce n'est pas que ce Medecin luy dise justement comment cela va, mais e.g. lorsque j'ai scû par quelque assez bon canal, que la Reyne etoit mal, il a sceu me dire, par exemple qu'une belle nuit le medecin avait couché dans la maison de la Reyne et ces sortes de circonstances, qui jointes avec d'autres, dont on

---

30 NH Dep. 103 Nr 148 (*olim* Dep. 103 Gmunden I D 2c). Copy in French by Jean de Robethon, Secretary of the Embassies, to whom the letter was presumably addressed. This is probably Robethon's file copy, made after those sections written in cipher-code had been decoded. Schnath (*Geschichte Hannovers* (see note 2 above), III, p. 511) believed the document lost in the Second World War and had to rely on extracts made by a previous scholar. The original was successfully located by the staff of the NH at my instigation, and I thank them for their willingness to undertake the search.

est informé d'ailleurs, ne laissent pas de donner quelque eclaircissement; car il faut que vous sachiez que nos Whigs ne scavent presque jamais rien de la sante de la Reyne. Comme Elle n'est de rien si avide que d'entendre des histoires de Hannover, il peut la satisfaire à cette heure, puisqu'il scait beaucoup de choses; vous m'entendez bien quelles histoires je veux dire. On les raconte aprés à quelques Ecclesiastiques graves, ce qui fait un merveilleux effet. Peut-être que vous vous moquerez de tout cela, mais je le regarde autrement. J'ai fait en sorte que Hendel ait ecrit une lettre à Mr. de Kielmansegge pour en sortir de bonne grace, et j'ai laissé tomber quelques paroles pour Luy faire connoitre, que S.A.E. venant un jour ici, il pourra rentrer dans son service.

London 5/16 June 1713

A few days ago I wrote to you on the subject of Mr Handel, that since His Highness was determined to dismiss him, Mr Handel submitted to that wish, and desired nothing save that the affair be conducted with a good grace and [that] he be given a little time here so that he could enter the queen's service. Moreover, it seems to me from your letters that this was precisely the generous intention of His Highness. But since then M. Hattorf has informed Mr Handel via M. Kielmansegg that His Highness had dismissed him from his service, telling him that he could go wherever he pleased. In other words, he was given notice in a way which he found particularly mortifying. I will admit to you frankly that Mr Handel is nothing to me, but at the same time I must say that if I had been given a free hand for a week or two I could have resolved the whole affair to the satisfaction of both His Highness and Mr Handel, and even to the benefit of the elector's service. The queen's physician, who is an important man and enjoys the queen's confidence, is his great patron and friend, and has the composer constantly at his house. Mr Handel could have been extremely useful, and has been on several occasions, by giving me information of circumstances which have often enlightened me as to the condition of the queen's health. Not that the doctor tells him exactly how she is but, for example, when I have been informed by other reliable channels that the queen was ill, he has been able to tell me that on one particular night the physician slept at the queen's residence, and other circumstances of this kind which provide illumination when taken in conjunction with other information. You must know that our Whigs rarely know anything about the queen's health. [In return,] since the queen is more avid for stories about Hanover than anything else, the doctor can satisfy her curiosity when he is with her from his own information: you understand the stories to which I am referring. Afterwards they are passed on to some serious ecclesiastical gentlemen, and this has a marvellous effect. Perhaps you will not take this seriously, but I do. I arranged things so that Mr Handel could write to M. Kielmansegg to extricate himself gracefully, and I let slip a few words to inform him that, when some day His Highness comes here, he might re-enter his service.

Although the queen herself remained firmly and constantly behind the Hanoverian Succession (though opposed to any of the electoral family residing in England during her lifetime), the attitude of her chief ministers was more ambivalent. Harley and Bolingbroke did not drop their negotiations with the Pretender until March 1714, following his rejection of their appeals to declare himself a member of the Church of England. The sudden death of the queen, who was not in good health, might have precipitated a succession crisis at any time during the preceding two years. Information on the queen's medical condition was therefore of the first importance to the Hanoverian agents in London, who used a number cipher when referring to the topic in their newsletters to Hanover.[31] Handel was obviously regarded by them as a valuable source. The royal physician who was his

31 NH Calenburg Brief Archiv, Des. 24, England, Nr 1698 (1712–13).

'friend and patron' was presumably Dr John Arbuthnot, whose high opinion of Handel's music is related in an anecdote in Mainwaring's *Memoirs*.[32] This letter provides us with the earliest, and most specific, evidence of a connection between the doctor and the composer. No less interesting is the letter's revelation that the elector took a direct interest in the matter of Handel's dismissal.

It is not possible that Handel, any more than others in London in 1713, could have forgotten the imminence of the Elector of Hanover's succession to the British crown. Presumably, in the end, the Hanoverian court was content enough to have Handel in London as an advance cultural representative, and accepted his commitment to the British government of the time. Unfortunately the Hanoverian end of the correspondence does not seem to have survived, but from a second letter of Kreienberg it is apparent that his solicitations on Handel's part were effective:[33]

Londres le 3/14 juillet 1713

Monsieur,
je receus hier vôs deux Lettres du 30 de juin et du 4 de juillet, par lesquelles je voy que vous avés receu enfin toutes Mes Lettres . . .
Je suis bien aise de ce que Vous m'ecrivés sur le sujet de Mr. Hendel, je n'ay pas pretendù, qu'il restât au service de S.A.E., ni Luy n'y songe plus, c'est seulement la maniere de Le congedier; j'ay fait en sorte qu'il est fort content, en Luy faisant entendre, qu'il n'est nullement en disgrace auprés de S.A.E. et en laissant tomber quelque parole, qu'il ne pourra pas manquer d'estre fort bien 14 658 927 310 1160 483 1145 310 71 951 1158 773 106 565 483 scaura [=*fort bien quand Mgr l'Electeur sera icy. Il continuera a me dire tout ce qu'il* scaura].

London 3/14 July 1713

Sir,
I received your two letters of 30 June and 4 July yesterday, from which I see that you have finally received all of my letters . . .
I am pleased that you have written to me about Mr Handel. I had not expected that he would remain in His Highness's service, nor was I considering that but merely the manner of his dismissal; I have done it in such a way that he is quite content, giving him to understand that he is by no means in disgrace with His Highness, and dropping a few words to the effect that he will be quite all right when the elector comes here. He will continue to tell me all he knows.

Things turned out more or less as Kreienberg had hoped. On 28 December 1713 Handel 'entered the queen's service' to the extent that he was granted an annual pension of £200 in return for undefined services.[34] When George I arrived in London in September 1714 he heard Handel's music at his first Sunday service at the

---

32 *Memoirs* p. 93. Although Arbuthnot is not named by Kreienberg, he is the only one of Queen Anne's physicians known to have had any connection with Handel; furthermore, there is good evidence of Arbuthnot's personal attendance on the queen at this period from payments in PRO LC5/155. Of the other physicians, the queen paid most attention to Sir David Hamilton, but music does not seem to have been part of his life; see *The Diary of Sir David Hamilton 1709–1714*, ed. Philip Roberts, with notes by D. W A. Speck (London, 1976).

33 Huntington MS HM 44710, ff. 57–8. Kreienberg to Robethon, letter in French, with passages in cipher-code (here italicized). This letter was discovered by Ragnhild Hatton; see R. Hatton, 'The Anglo-Hanoverian Connection', Creighton Trust Lecture, University of London, 1982. I thank the Huntington Library for permission to quote from the letter.

34 Copy of warrant, PRO T52/25 p. 380.

Chapel Royal, and he subsequently continued the pension granted by Queen Anne.[35] There is no evidence here of any difficulties arising from the circumstances of Handel's dismissal from his Hanoverian post the previous year. On 10/21 October 1715 the king even ordered (from London) that Handel should be paid six months' arrears in respect of his Hanoverian service. It is possible that the king was entertained by Handel's music during one of the royal water parties on the River Thames in July and August 1715,[36] and that Kielmansegg used the opportunity to suggest the payment of some arrears: this may be the truth behind the famous anecdote in Mainwaring's *Memoirs* about a supposed reconciliation between Handel and the king at the first performance of the *Water Music*.[37]

I have found no important references to Handel in the Hanover papers after 1715.[38] The complete absence of any mention of him in the official records of the king's journeys must call into question the possibility that Handel travelled as a member of the royal entourage to Germany in 1716 or 1719.[39]

As to Handel's period of service in Hanover itself, some mystery still attaches to the nature of his duties there. The court employed an orchestra of sixteen or seventeen musicians,[40] but these were apparently under the direction of the Konzertmeister, J. B. Farinelli. We might gain some idea of Handel's activities if it proved possible to identify music composed by him in Hanover. It was frequently Handel's practice to date his composition autographs on completion, naming the place of composition; examples from his London works are quite well known, and there are five similarly endorsed autographs of works composed in Italy during 1707-8.[41] Unfortunately there are no known autographs from the Hanover period that give either date or place of origin. In the absence of documentary identifications or a definable 'Hanover' musical style, how are we to look for Handel's Hanover compositions? Given the survival of such a large proportion of Handel's autographs,

35 Pension payments can be followed through W. A. Shaw (ed.), *Calendar of Treasury Books*, 32 vols. (London, 1904–57), vols. XIX-XXXII. For the Chapel Royal service, see Deutsch *Doc* p. 63.

36 The king attended water parties on 13 July and 13 August. Newspapers reported that music was performed, but without naming any composers.

37 *Memoirs* pp. 90–2.

38 The royal water party of July 1717 at which Handel's music was performed is mentioned in a newsletter from London (= NH Cal.Br.24, England 1720, f. 49'), but the information seems to have been taken solely from London newspaper reports. Receipts for the king's private expenditure in NH K.G.Anhang No. 3 include some referring to benefit nights at the London opera house signed by Diana Vico, Anastasia Robinson, Grimaldi and others; a receipt for the orchestra's benefit performance in June 1717 is signed by 'Dahuron'.

39 NH K.G. Hann.Br.92 Domestica Nr 34b (= Reisebuch). Nor is there mention of Handel in the English Public Records listing expenses connected with the king's journeys. See also Burrows, 'Handel and the English Chapel Royal' (see note 24 above), pp. 241–2.

40 I assume that all of them were instrumentalists; the account books show three of them as 'French musicians' (presumably string soloists, but possibly woodwind instrumentalists), but they give no further information on the matter.

41 *Dixit Dominus, Laudate pueri* (D major), *Lungi dal mio bel nume, Aci Galatea e Polifemo* and *Se tu non lasci amore* (trio). The completion date of *Nisi Dominus* is also known to fall within this period, though the relevant section of the autograph bearing Handel's date is lost.

paper characteristics may suggest some lines of approach although, as will become apparent, evidence of this type does not lead to simple definitive conclusions. We may resort to some guesswork about compositions for which no autograph material survives, but this is a rather arbitrary procedure which is likely to foist on the Hanover period works from Handel's Italian and English years (or, worse still, works of dubious authorship). However the problem is attacked, the approach must initially be a negative one: we are looking for works which cannot be identified with other periods in Handel's life. There are a couple of concertos, published much later in London, for which no autograph material survives,[42] and similarly some trio sonatas from the set published as Op. II but lacking autograph sources, which might have originated in Hanover. But there is nothing positive to make the connections, not even a basis for guesswork. There are no works of German church music by Handel which can be attributed to the Hanover period. The Electress Sophia's letters refer to Handel's keyboard-playing, yet here again no 'Hanover' keyboard music by Handel can be identified, all of the surviving autographs being on paper of 'English' type.[43] As already noted, there was no scope for operatic activity in Hanover, though an 'English singer' is reported to have visited Handel there in December 1711 on the pretext of having lessons from him.[44]

One important area of Handel's music remains for consideration: cantata-type works in the Italian language. Many of these can be attributed with confidence to Handel's Italian years: the autographs are on 'Italian' paper, many of the titles are listed in the Ruspoli documents for 1707-9,[45] and many even survive in copies from the Ruspoli library.[46] Handel also composed works of this type in England: there are composition autographs of Italian solo cantatas on 'English' paper, and he was still writing Italian duets as late as 1745. Although composition of the bulk of Handel's cantatas can be attributed to Italy or England, there is one orchestrally accompanied cantata for soprano and bass voices which does, at last, give us a lead towards music composed in Hanover. *Apollo e Dafne* ('La terra è liberata') was first ascribed to Handel's Hanover years by Keiichiro Watanabe in the course of an exposition of the results of his study of the 'Italian' papers used by Handel and his copyists.[47] Watanabe also usefully drew attention to the work of a music copyist who can be associated with Hanover sources. I shall briefly review and amplify

---

42 Concerto grosso Op. III No. 1 and Concerto in B flat for Oboe and strings (*HG* 21, p. 85). Anthony Hicks has suggested that the overtures to *Il pastor fido* and *Silla* may also have originated from earlier works possibly composed for Hanover (private communication to the author, June 1982).

43 Full details will be available in the catalogue of Handel's autographs at present being prepared by Martha Ronish and Donald Burrows. The autographs of keyboard music from the collections at the British Library and the Fitzwilliam Museum are included in Donald Burrows, 'A Handlist of the Paper Characteristics of Handel's English Autographs', typescript, The Open University, 1982.

44 See Schnath, *Geschichte Hannovers*, III, p. 510 note 50.

45 U. Kirkendale, 'The Ruspoli Documents on Handel', *JAMS* 20 (1967), pp. 222–73, 517–18.

46 Rudolf Ewerhart, 'Die Händel-Handschriften der Santini-Bibliothek in Münster', *HJ* 6 (1960), pp. 111–50. The Santini collection includes some copies of later provenance in addition to autographs and manuscript copies from Ruspoli sources.

47 'The paper used by Handel and His Copyists during the Time of 1706-1710', *Journal of the Japanese Musicological Society* 27/2 (1981), p. 129.

Watanabe's findings before applying the results to a group of works which have been associated from time to time with Handel's sojourn in Hanover – his Italian duets with basso continuo accompaniment.

No fewer than five types of paper are represented in the 39 folios which make up the composer's autograph of *Apollo e Dafne*, BL MS RM 20.e.1:

folios	watermark type[48]	stave-ruling[49]
1–6, 13–16, 21–24	(1) Three Crescents, type 'N'	10 @10 184
7–10, 12	(2) Fleur-de-lys, within Crowned Coat-of-Arms, over initials CV	8 @1 11 (ff. 7–10) 8 @1 10 (f. 12)
11, 17–19	(3) without watermark – i.e. chain lines only – Type 'B'	10 @5 82.5
20, 25–31, 36–37'	(4) Unicorn	10 @1 11
32–35	(5) Fleur-de-lys/countermark DS	8 @1 10

Further examples of the 'Unicorn' paper, which does not occur anywhere else in Handel's autographs, are found in manuscripts of some Italian works by Handel (including *Apollo e Dafne*) copied by the 'Hanover' scribe; these are now BL MSS RM 19.a.6 and RM 19.a.7 ff. 9–23. Colin Timms has identified the scribe as one of two principal copyists associated with a collection of opera scores originating from the library of the Hanover court.[50] Using Timms's designation, I shall refer to this scribe as 'Hanover B'. Although Watanabe does not make the connection explicit, the Hanover opera scores are the clinching link in the chain of associations between *Apollo e Dafne* and Handel's service at Hanover. The scores are by way of a 'collected edition' of the dramatic works performed by the Hanover Opera in its heyday: their bindings carry Hanoverian emblems, with the Hanover horse on the front covers and the 'wild man' on the rear. Hanover B was responsible for the following copies:

BL reference	title	composer	date of Hanover performance[51]
RM 23.k.23	*Paride in Ida*	Steffani	–
RM 23.h.11	*Henrico Leone*	Steffani	1689
RM 23.h.15	*La lotta d'Hercole con Archeloo*	?Steffani	1689
RM 23.h.13	*La superbia d'Alessandro*	Steffani	1690
RM 23.h.16	*La libertà contenta*	Steffani	1693
RM 23.f.16	*Baccanali*	?Steffani	1695
RM 23.i.1	*I trionfi del fato*	Steffani	1695
RM 23.g.21	*Briseide*	?Torri	1696
RM 23.h.1	*La costanza nelle selve*	Mancia	1697
RM 23.i.17	*I rivali concordi*	Steffani	1697

48 Watanabe's classifications are used here.

49 Descriptions of rastra follow the system I evolved for my 'Handlist' (see note 44 above). Entries give *first* number of staves per page, *secondly* structure of rastra (i.e. number of staves ruled simultaneously), *thirdly* the span of rastra (i.e. distance between the outermost stave-lines) given in mm and here measured to the nearest 0.5 mm. Thus '10 @5 82.5' indicates ten-stave pages ruled with five-stave rastra whose span is 82.5 mm.

50 Timms, 'Gregorio Piva' (see note 13 above).

51 These are the dates given on the title-pages of the volumes, all in the hand of the same scribe as the music.

The 'Unicorn' paper makes a brief appearance in one of these volumes, occurring in Act III only of *La superbia d'Alessandro*, RM 23.h.3. Otherwise, this collection was copied on paper of three types, none of them having watermarks identical to any of the papers in the *Apollo e Dafne* autograph. Nevertheless the pattern of connections is explicit enough: the bindings of these volumes establish the copyist's association with Hanover, the combination of the copyist with the 'Unicorn' paper in RM 19.a.6, RM 19.a.7 and RM 23.h.3 ties this paper to Hanover, and the occurrence of the 'Unicorn' paper in the autograph of *Apollo e Dafne* establishes that cantata's connection with Hanover. Although the Hanover opera collection is of works performed during the 1690s, I interpret the volumes as library reference copies prepared at about the same time as Handel's appointment as Kapellmeister. This interpretation is supported by the single volume of the collection which was the work of another copyist (Timms's scribe A), RM 23.h.2: this is a copy of Steffani's *Amor vien dal destino* bearing the date 1709 on its title-page.[52]

Of the three main paper types in the Hanover Opera collection, one requires further investigation. This has a watermark which I shall designate type (6) for the present purpose:

> (6) Fleur-de-lys within Crowned Coat-of-Arms,
> over initials GVH/countermark IV

Four volumes are copied on this paper, RM 23.h.16, RM 23.i.1, RM 23.g.21 and RM 23.h.1. The same paper also occurs in RM 18.b.11, a copy of Italian duets and trios by Handel in the hand of Hanover B. The watermark is not listed by Watanabe but it does in fact occur in Handel's autographs at RM 20.d.2 f. 11, a single sheet carrying his composition copy of the aria 'Pur ch'io ti stringa' from *Agrippina*. It is necessary to divert the main course of the argument here to establish the origin of this aria, pursuing briefly the history of the composition of its parent opera. *Agrippina* was the second opera performed at the Teatro S. Giovanni Grisostomo, Venice, during the Carnival season 1709–10: the main autograph (RM 20.a.3) is undated, but we can assume that it was written by Handel towards the end of 1709.[53] The paper of this autograph has a watermark identical with *Apollo e Dafne*, type (1). As composed, Act III Sc. 10 included an aria/duet for the characters Ottone and Poppea, 'No, ch'io non apprezzo',[54] but this was replaced by Ottone's aria 'Pur ch'io ti stringa' before the first performance: conclusive evidence for this is provided by the printed libretto,[55] which has the text of 'Pur ch'io ti stringa' in place of the duet text. Therefore, although RM 20.d.2 f.11 was not part of the original composition autograph of *Agrippina* it was written before the first performance and there can be no doubt of its Italian origin.

52 This opera was performed at Düsseldorf in 1709 but had been composed some years earlier in Hanover.
53 The opera was probably first performed in January 1710.
54 BL RM 20.a.3 ff. 98′–99. This was not published by Chrysander in *HG* 57.
55 *Agrippina Drama per Musica. Da Rappresentarsi nel Famosissimo Teatro Grimani di S. Gio: Grisostomo l'Anno M.DCCIX. In Venezia, M.DCCIX.*

The situation with regard to paper distribution revealed by the evidence so far presented may be summarized thus:

watermark type (4)   'Unicorn': specific to Hanover
watermark type (1)   'Three Crescents N'; used by Handel in Venice, 1709–10, but also in
                     Apollo e Dafne
watermark type (6)   'GVH': used by Hanover B, but also available to Handel in Venice

Wider reference must now be made to the general pattern of paper distribution in Handel's autographs. There is clear evidence for a complete break in Handel's paper supply when he came to England. 'Italian' papers (i.e. of the type used for compositions of Handel's Italian period) are not found in his autographs from *Rinaldo* onwards, except for a brief appearance of other papers of Italian type (not identical to those from the earlier Italian period) in works composed in London during 1724–6.[56] Complementary to this, there are no examples at all of the 'Dutch' papers typical of Handel's works composed in England in any autographs prior to *Rinaldo*. I have not found any examples of these 'Dutch/English' paper types among the Hanover court documents, though they occur frequently in the English public records of the period, so I incline to the view that these paper types were not available, or were not used, in Hanover.

The possibility that there was no comparable break in Handel's paper supply between Italy and Hanover must be considered. In the case of watermark type (6) we may perhaps not be surprised to find some of the same paper in use in both Venice and Hanover, knowing as we do that Kielmansegg (and presumably some lesser Hanoverian court servants) had been to Venice shortly before Handel's arrival at Hanover. Someone may easily have carried a stock of good-quality paper in one direction or the other. Did Handel himself carry unused music paper from Venice to Hanover, however? On the basis of watermark type (1) there is more than a suggestion that he did: this paper is definitely of Italian origin, yet it also appears in the autograph of *Apollo e Dafne* which, because of the associations of the 'Unicorn' paper, can now be regarded as a Hanover work. If this is the case, should we really be looking on 'Italian' papers for other possible compositions from the Hanover period? To attempt an answer to this question it is necessary to look more closely at *Apollo e Dafne*.

It is apparent from the autograph that Handel subjected *Apollo e Dafne* to extensive revisions. These may have been undertaken in several stages, but I think it more likely that there was just one major overhaul. Handel had assistance in this: his hand appears in conjunction with those of two copyists, neither of them identical with Hanover B. The final form of the cantata is clear enough: this version, copied by Hanover B in RM 19.a.6, is the version familiar to us today from Chrysander's edition.[57] The earlier state of the cantata does not survive completely, but elements of it are represented in the autograph thus:

---

56 See Burrows, 'Handlist' (note 43 above). Handel's use of these later Italian papers can be dated
   from their appearance in the autographs of *Tamerlano*, *Rodelinda* and *Alessandro*.
57 *HG* 52B p. 1.

ff. 1–4   Music as *HG* pp. 1–4, followed by 'Spezza l'arco' in G major (9 bars only to end of f. 4',
          subsequent ff. missing)
ff. 13–16 Aria 'Ardi adori' as *HG* pp. 10–11, followed by unset recitative for Apollo beginning 'Son
          medico, e poeta'; composition probably broken off here in an inconclusive state
ff. 21–24 Aria 'Come in ciel', as *HG* pp. 16–17

All of this, it will be noted, is on type (1) paper. Knowing what we do about the associations of this paper with *Agrippina* and the 'Unicorn' paper with Hanover, the obvious conclusion would seem to be that Handel started *Apollo e Dafne* in Venice and carried it with him in an incomplete state to Hanover, where he finished the cantata in a revised form. The changes were no doubt partly dictated by the singers available at Hanover (hence the key change to 'Spezza l'arco' and some other uncertainties in the autograph), but there was also a fundamental literary change as the unset recitative was discarded. On f. 16 and f. 24 unused manuscript pages were filled up as the final version of the cantata developed. One has the impression from the rather haphazard arrangement of pages that in the course of completing the work Handel used up any pieces of manuscript paper that were to hand. The two single sheets of type (1) paper which became ff. 5 and 6 presumably reflect the end of that particular stock. What of the other paper types involved? How many of them were also carried by Handel from Italy? Apart from the 'Unicorn' paper, are we any closer to distinguishing any typical 'Hanover' sources in Handel's works?

There is one clue which takes us some way towards answering these questions, in the rastrography (stave-ruling) of the manuscript lines. The volumes copied by Hanover B have one feature in common: they are all written on music pages ruled with single-stave rastra.[58] The pages are variously ruled with eight, nine and ten staves and the gauge of the lines varies somewhat, but there are two broad types with spans of c10 mm and c11.5 mm respectively, and the consistent exclusive use of single-stave rastra is remarkable enough in itself. It is, furthermore, revealing that whereas Hanover B's manuscripts on paper with type (6) watermark are ruled single-stave, Handel's *Agrippina* movement on paper with the same watermark in RM 20.d.2 is ruled with five-stave rastra.[59] Thus the same paper was ruled differently in Hanover and Venice. Returning to the autograph of *Apollo e Dafne* we can now identify paper types (2), (4) and (5) as originating in Hanover because of their single-stave rulings. Unfortunately these indigenous Hanover papers do not lead us on to a host of other Handel autographs, though reference will be made to them again in connection with the Italian duets. Meanwhile, some attention must be paid to the significance of the remaining papers, types (1) and (3).

Type (1) appears to be an example, rare if not unique in Handel's autographs, of a 'migratory' paper: that is, a paper type which Handel used in more than one location. On the basis of the argument outlined above this migration was largely an

---

58 In addition to the opera collection and Handel copies referred to already, I have examined four other
    MSS copied by Hanover B and fifteen MSS copied by Hanover A: all of them are ruled with single-
    stave rastra. The same is true of the two volumes of duets in Steffani's own hand, RM 23.k.14 and
    RM 23.k.18. In contrast, RM 23.h.15 and RM 23.h.6 (copied by Piva) are ruled with five-stave rastra.
59 Rastra for RM 20.d.2 f. 11=10 @5 90.5.

accident, in that *Apollo e Dafne* had not been finished when Handel left Venice. Nevertheless, if the argument is followed through, ff. 5–6 of the autograph present a strong case for suggesting that Handel used up extra sheets of old Italian stock in Hanover. If so, the possibility must be considered that other compositions on the same paper might also have been composed in Hanover. The same possibility arises with paper type (3), which may have been an indigenous Hanover paper or, assuming Italian origins on the strength of the multi-stave rastra, another migratory one. Table 1 lists the source materials of Handel's works which are written on these paper types. Taking type (3) first, I think it quite likely that the six cantatas and three sonatas involved may have been composed in Hanover. There is no evidence that Handel ever used this paper in Italy, and none of the works concerned are known from the Ruspoli documents or early Italian copies. Although type (3) may have been, like type (1), a migratory paper that Handel brought with him from Italy, it is equally likely that he did not acquire the paper until he arrived in Hanover: in the autograph *Apollo e Dafne* there is no doubt of this paper's specific association with the 'Hanover' revision. Against this may be set the style of the copyist's hand in RM 19.e.7, which is rather Italianate and, indeed, rather reminiscent of the general style of the Ruspoli copyists.[60] This suggests Italian provenance, but it cannot be taken as more than a suggestion. It would not have been surprising to find an occasional Italian musician working in Hanover after Kielmansegg's Venetian visit, and Hanover B himself titled his manuscripts in unimpeachable Italian style. Furthermore the copyist of RM 19.e.7 also copied some Steffani duets,[61] although this might have been done in Italy as easily as in Hanover. For the present, the material on type (3) paper occupies an ambiguous position and may perhaps best be categorized as 'possibly composed in Hanover'.

Paper type (1) is similarly ambiguous in its implications. *Agrippina* is safely tied to Venice, and similarity of rastra may lead to the conclusion that *Dunque sarà pur vero* should be coupled with that opera. On the other hand, the scoring of the accompaniment is suspiciously close to that of *Spande ancor*. It will be noted that most of the cantatas employ the same solo voices as *Apollo e Dafne* (soprano and bass), only *Figli del mesto cor* requiring a different soloist. Again, the cantata and the duet on type (1) paper are not known from any early Italian sources and, to put the matter in its negative aspect, there is no reason why they should not have been composed in Hanover. As to matters of musical style, I have found nothing to distinguish the possible 'Hanover' compositions from Handel's immediately preceding Italian works. Even in *Apollo e Dafne* there is no discernible break between the two versions: Handel evidently expected the same orchestral resources that he had prepared for in the early movements (flute, oboes, bassoon and strings) to be avail-

---

60 Compare with the scribal hands illustrated in U. Kirkendale, *Antonio Caldara: sein Leben und seine venezianisch–römischen Oratorien* (Graz/Cologne, 1966).

61 DSB Landsberg 264/1 ff. 1–2, and index, Landsberg 264/2 ff. 1–94; also Venice Bib. Marciana, Cod. It. IV.768 ff. 27–9 (the same volume also contains copies of Handel Duets nos. 1a, 2, 5, 6, 7 and 10, though not in the same hand). I thank Colin Timms for this information.

Table 1. *Handel sources on paper types (1) and (3)*

source[a]	work[b]	rastra	remarks
A. *composer's autographs*			
watermark type (1), 'Three Crescents N'			
RM 20.e.1	*Apollo e Dafne* (cantata, S, B, orch.)	*10 @10 184*	Begun in Venice 1709–10; ff. 5–6 added in Hanover
RM 20.a.3	*Agrippina* (opera)	*12 @12 188, 12 @12 194*	Composed in Venice, late 1709
RM 20.e.1	*Dunque sarà pur vero* (cantata, S, 2 vn, b.c.)	*12 @12 194*	
Cfm MS 253	*Quando in calma ride* (duet, S, B, b.c.)	*10 @10 185*	See Table 2
watermark type (3), 'without watermark B'			
RM 20.e.1	*Apollo e Dafne*	*10 @5 82.5*	Pages added at Hanover
RM 20.d.11	*Nice che fa* (cantata, S, b.c.)	*10 @5 83*	
Cfm MS 261 pp. 61–76	three instrumental sonatas[c]	*10 @5 83*	
RM 20.d.11[d]	*E partirai, mia vita?* (cantata, S, b.c.)	*8 @4 76.5*	
RM 20.d.11[d]	*Dimmi, O mio cor* (cantata, S, b.c.)	*8 @4 76.5*	
RM 20.e.2[d]	*Spande ancor* (cantata, B, 2 vn, b.c.)	*8 @4 76.5*	
B. *scribal copies on paper with watermark type (3)[e]*			
RM 19.e.7	*Dalla guerra amorosa* (cantata, B, b.c.)	*8 @4 76.5*	
RM 19.e.7	*Figli del mesto cor* (cantata, A, b.c.)	*8 @4 76.5*	

[a] RM = Royal Music Library, British Library; Cfm = Founder's Collection, Fitzwilliam Library, Cambridge.

[b] Line 1 gives title of work, line 2 gives type of composition, voices of soloists and scoring of accompaniment (b.c. = basso continuo).

[c] Sonata in G for treble instrument, probably violin, and b.c. HWV 358, and Sonata in B flat for oboe and b.c. HWV 357 (both ed. T. Best, *HHA* IV/18, Kassel/Leipzig, 1982); Trio sonata in F for recorders and b.c. (ed. C. Hogwood, 1981). The trio sonata lacks the b.c. part in this autograph, but has been completed from a secondary copy now in the Library of Congress, Washington DC; the scribe of this copy is not one of the known 'Hanover' copyists, though the form of his titles is identical to that used by Hanover B.

[d] Watanabe designates the watermark of the paper in these three cantatas as 'without watermark A', but I can find no difference between this and his 'B' type.

[e] Copyist's hand not identical with that of other putative 'Hanover' copyists. In the second cantata, the tempo/style directions on f. 99′ and f. 100′ appear to be in Handel's hand. The 'Ruspoli' version of this cantata is for soprano: the version in RM 19.e.7 was presumably prepared (and possibly transposed) by the copyist to Handel's directions.

able for the completed version.[62] There is some striking solo violin writing in 'Mie piante correte', one of the 'Hanover' movements, but parallels can be found in several earlier works composed by Handel in Italy.

Handel's Italian duets with basso-continuo accompaniment are in a rather different category from the cantatas which have been named so far. They have, of course, some obvious resemblances to the cantatas, in that they are in the Italian language and use similar solo voices: indeed, we can assume that many of the duets were composed for the same singers as the cantatas. But the duets lack the recitatives which give some sort of narrative aspect to the cantatas and, while the cantatas can be related to the forms and structures of opera, the duets are musically more akin to the instrumental trio sonata. The duets are also a more self-consciously 'poetic' medium, employing concentrated imagery within small-scale literary forms: a parallel may be drawn with Shakespeare's sonnets. Handel's music for the duets was probably influenced by comparable works of Steffani's but, as Colin Timms has pointed out, Handel seems to have received this influence in a rather distorted form: the manuscript collection of Steffani's duets that Handel owned omits the solo arias which alternated with the duet movements proper.[63] Handel's duets are specifically associated with Hanover in Mainwaring's *Memoirs*:

Soon after his return to Hanover he made twelve chamber Duettos for the practice of the later Queen, then electoral Princess. The Character of these is well known to the judges in Music. The words for them were written by the Abbate MAURO HORTENSIO, who had not disdained on other occasions to minister to the masters of harmony.[64]

In the absence of corroborative information about her musical activities, it is not possible to make much sense of Princess Caroline's connection with the duets:[65] for the moment, we must regard her as a patron rather than a performer. It may be significant that Mauro was resident near Hanover during 1709–10,[66] though at present not enough is known of his literary style to judge which, if any, of the texts of Handel's duets are his work.

The twenty-two Italian duets with basso-continuo accompaniment published in *HG* 32 can still be regarded as a complete picture of Handel's contribution to this form.[67] Handel's autographs of all but three of these survive, either complete or as substantial fragments. Table 2 lists all of the duets, with a conspectus of paper characteristics of the autograph material. Six duets (nos. 1b, 15–20) obviously form

---

62 Handel may even have expected a larger orchestra to be available in Hanover than in Venice; in his revision of 'Spezza l'arco' he replaced *Basson* with *Bassoni*. For another recent view see below, p. 59.
63 Timms, 'Handel and Steffani' (see note 5 above).
64 *Memoirs* p. 85.
65 Leibniz described the Princess as having 'la voix merveilleuse': see R. L. Arkell, *Caroline of Ansbach, George the Second's Queen* (Oxford, 1939), p. 8. I have found no references to her as a performer, and it must be doubted that she ever performed Handel's duets.
66 Kielmansegg, *Familien-Chronik* (see note 4 above), pp. 446–7.
67 All references to *HG* 32 are to the second edition (1880). The first edition contained only thirteen duets and adopted a different numbering system. Chrysander did not include *Spero indarno*, a duet movement of dubious authenticity for soprano and bass, the earliest source for which is BL Add. MS 5322, probably copied after 1740.

a later group composed in the 1740s, and two (nos. 13–14) date from the 1720s.[68] This leaves ten duets on 'pre-London' paper (nos. 1a, 2, 3, 5, 6, 8–12), which we can assume were composed before 1712. Two other duets for which there is no autograph material seem to belong with this early group (nos. 4 and 7), and thus we arrive at the 'twelve chamber Duettos' referred to by Mainwaring. It is uncertain whether all twelve of these were composed in Hanover, and indeed there is room for doubt as to whether all of them were known there.

The repertory of Handel's duets available at Hanover during his time there can be established from RM 18.b.11, a volume which has already been cited as an example in the hand of Hanover B, and as having the 'GVH' (type 6) watermark. This volume does not carry Hanover court insignia, but its binding matches those of the Steffani opera volumes and there can be little doubt of its Hanoverian origin. The copyist's title to the duet volume is 'Duetti del Sigr Giorgio Federico Handel', and his intention was apparently to produce a library volume of Handel's duets to date. The volume contains Duets nos. 3–12 followed by the Italian trios *Quel fior che all'alba ride* and *Se tu non lasci amore*.[69] The title does not claim that the duets were composed in Hanover, and the true situation is revealed by the presence of the trio *Se tu non lasci amore*, which we know from Handel's autograph to have been composed in Naples in 1708. Although the trios are at the end of the volume, they appear to have been part of the original copying assignment; if the copyist included in his volume trios composed in Italy, then it is possible that some of the duets also originated in Italy. As with the cantatas, there is no easy way to separate duets composed in Hanover from those composed in Italy.

It must be recognized immediately that there is no positive documentary evidence that Handel composed any duets in Italy. None of the duets are named in the Ruspoli papers, and Mainwaring's reference to Hanover is the earliest documentary source for associating the duets with any particular place of composition. On the other hand, Handel's activities under Ruspoli patronage were only one part of his Italian career, possibly a part that has been over-emphasized because of the unusual richness of archival material available. There is, however, sufficient circumstantial evidence to support the possibility that Handel did compose some of the duets in Italy. Handel signed his copy of Steffani's duets 'G F Handel / Roma 1706';[70] he was therefore influenced by these works long before he

---

68 The composition date for Duets 13 and 14 may seem surprising in view of their inclusion in two early manuscript copies, Hamburg, Staats- und Universitätsbibliothek MS MB/1570 and Münster MS 1908. The Hamburg source originally contained only the earlier duets, nos. 13 and 14 being added later, probably in the 1720s. The Münster duet copies MSS 1907, 1908 have no connection with the Ruspoli materials there and, in spite of having titles which are almost identical with the forms used by the Hanover copyist, appear to be independent sources from the third or fourth decade of the eighteenth century.

69 The same repertory of duets, but without the trios, is found in Hamburg MS MB/2767. This copy is also on 'GVH' paper and may thus have originated in Hanover.

70 BL Add. MS 37779; see Timms, 'Handel and Steffani' (note 5 above). Anthony Hicks has suggested ('Handel's Early Musical Development' (see note 10 above), p. 83) that Handel may have used Old Style dates in Rome, and thus he may have acquired his Steffani copy in the early months of 1707.

Table 2. *Handel's Italian Duets with basso-continuo accompaniment*

HG no.	title	voices	source[a]	watermark[b]	rastra	remarks
1a	*Caro autor di mia doglia*	ST	BL	Three Crescents D	10 @10 193	Paper characteristics identical with Duet 18, dated 1742
1b	*Caro autor di mia doglia*	AA	BL	Clausen Cf	10 @2 30.5	Authenticity doubtful[c]
1c	*Caro autor di mia doglia*	SS	–			Text also set by Marcello, so current in Italy
2	*Giù nei Tartarei regni*	SB	BL	Three crescents L	12 @12 188.5	Watermark identical with duet 11. Not identical with *Apollo e Dafne*, type (3)
3	*Sono liete, fortunate*	SA	Cfm	no watermark (lines only)	12 @1 10	Coupled with Duet 3 in an early copy, now Berlin DSB Mus MS autog. G. F. Händel 5 (not Handel's autograph)
4	*Troppo cruda, troppo fiera*	SA	–			
5	*Che vai pensando*	SB	Cfm	Three Crescents J	12 @12 189	Paper characteristics similar to Duets 2 & 6
6	*Amor, gioje mi porge*	SS	Cfm	Three Crescents I	12 @12 189	Similar characteristics to Duets 2 & 5
7	*Va, speme infida*	SS	–			Included in early copies of 'Hanover' duets.
8	*A mirarvi io son intento*	SA	Cfm	GVH/IV, type (6)	10 @1 10	Possibly composed with Duet 6
9	*Quando in calma ride il mare*	SB	Cfm	Three crescents N type (1)	10 @10 185	Paper common to *Agrippina* and *Apollo e Dafne*
10	*Tacete, ohimè, tacete*	SB	Cfm	Three Crescents B	10 @10 185	Rastra different from Duet 9, though similar span. Watermark identical with that of *Chi rapi la pace* (RM 20.d.11 ff. 56–7) – Ruspoli bill 1709. Text from Francesco de Lemene's *Poese diverse* (Milan, 1692 and many subsequent editions)
11	*Conservate, raddoppiate*	SA	Cfm	no watermark (lines only)	12 @1 10	Composed with Duet 3? Italian text altered by Handel
12	*Tanti strali al sen mi scocchi*	SA	Cfm	CV, type (2) (compare GVH/IV, type (6) above)	9 @1 9	

13	*Langue, geme, sospira*	SA	BL	Clausen Cb	10 @2 28	Paper type characteristics of London compositions c.1722. Text G. D. de Totis, *La caduta del regno dell'Amazzoni*, opera set by B. Pasquini, Rome 1690. Handel's textual source may have been the duet setting by Torri, composed before 1718
14	*Se tu non lasci amore*	SA	BL	Clausen Cb	10 @2 28	Composed with Duet 13? Text previously set by Handel as trio (1708)
15	*Quel fior che all' alba ride*	SS	BL	Burrows Cy	10 @2 30–30.5	Dated on completion 1–7–1741 (London). Text previously set as solo cantata, probably within preceding 3 years
16	*Nò, di voi non vo' fidarmi*	SS	BL	Clausen Bk	10 @2 30.5	Dated on completion 3–7–1741 (London)
17	*Nò, di voi non vo' fidarmi*	SA	BL	Clausen Cf	10 @2 30.5	Dated on completion 2–11–1742 (London)
18	*Beato in ver chi può*	SA	BL	Clausen Cf	10 @2 30–30.5	'Beatus ille of Horace' (Handel's title). Dated on completion 31–10–1742 (London)
19	*Fronda leggiera e mobile*	SA	BL	Clausen Cf and Clausen Ci	10 @2 30.5 / 10 @5 89.5	Probably composed with Duet 20. Re-uses themes from *Belshazzar* (1744)
20	*Ahi, nelle sorte umane*	SS	BL	Clausen Ch and Clausen Ci	10 @2 30.5–31 / 10 @5 89.5	Dated on completion 31–8–1745

[a] BL = Composer's autograph in London, British Library RM 20.g.9; Cfm = Composer's autograph in Cambridge, Fitzwilliam Museum MS 253 (30.H.3).

[b] 'Crescent' watermarks follow Watanabe's designations and 'English' watermarks follow those given in Clausen, *Händels Direktionspartituren* (Hamburg, 1972). I have given cross-references to the six 'Hanover' papers (types 1–6) previously described and added one designation of my own (Cy) for an English paper not included by Clausen. It is likely that Watanabe's 'Three Crescents I, J, K and L' are all versions of the same watermark sub-type.

[c] Probably by R. Keiser, and included in his *Divertimenti serenissimi* (Hamburg, 1713).

went to Hanover, and it is reasonable that he might have tried his hand at duets in a similar style during the intervening three years in Italy. If we had to rely on the Ruspoli papers alone for evidence of Handel's Italian vocal chamber music, then we would have no knowledge of the origin of the trio *Se tu non lasci amore*. The forms, style and solo voice ranges of this trio are comparable to those of the duets: some of the duets for two sopranos or for soprano and bass may well have been composed for the same singers. What was good for Naples in 1708 may have been equally successful elsewhere: Handel's duets would have been appropriate for private performances at any of the Italian centres in which he worked.

Once again it is necessary to follow through the evidence of paper types as a possible means of discriminating between works composed in Italy and Hanover. Referring to Table 2, we can immediately associate Duets nos. 3, 8, 11 and 12 with Hanover: all of them have the characteristic single-stave rastra and plausible 'Hanover' watermarks. To these can also probably be added Duet no. 4, which seems to be a companion work to Duet no. 3. It will be noted that these five duets form a cohesive group, in that they are the only ones from the early repertory to employ the combination of soprano and alto soloists. The soprano soloist for these may have been Pilotta who, like Handel, appeared later in the London opera house while still under Hanoverian patronage: she is described in the word-books of Handel's first London operas as 'Virtuosa di S.A.E. d'Hanover'. Assuming that Handel completed the revised form of *Apollo e Dafne* soon after his arrival in Hanover in 1710, the pattern appears to be that Handel found a soprano and a bass available in his first weeks at Hanover, but subsequently lost the services of the bass and gained an alto. It will be noted that in Table 1 there is one cantata for alto solo along with the more numerous ones for soprano and bass. Mainwaring places the composition of the duets during Handel's second period of service in Hanover (1711–12), but I think it more likely that they were composed in 1710–11 before his first visit to London: this is suggested by the occurrence in some of the duets of papers which are identical with sections of *Apollo e Dafne*, and by the complete break in Handel's paper supply which seems to have occurred in 1712.

The autographs of the remaining duets from Mainwaring's 'Hanover twelve' are all written on various forms of the 'Three Crescents' paper. This paper is closely associated with Handel's compositions from his Italian years, and in the case of Duet no. 10 there are clear associative links with the Ruspoli documents which point to an Italian composition. It seems most likely that Handel wrote Duets nos. 1a, 2, 5, 6, 10 in Italy, and that Duet no. 7 belongs with this group. Duet no. 9 poses more of a problem because it was composed on the 'migratory' paper type and employs the same solo voices as *Apollo e Dafne*. It may have been written in Venice, for the same soloists as the first version of the cantata; if it was composed in Hanover this must have been soon after Handel's arrival, as he obviously used up the Italian paper first. One interesting feature of the 'collected Hanover duets' in RM 18.b.11 seems to confirm that some of the duets were earlier compositions. Duet nos. 1a and 2 were apparently unknown to the Hanover copyist: this could hardly have been the case if they had constituted part of a set composed by Handel at Hanover for performance there. Since the autographs of these two duets are written on 'Crescent' paper, it is hardly likely that they are later compositions than those on 'Hanover' papers. The obvious conclusion is that Duets 1a and 2 are pre-existing duets of which the Hanover copyist had no knowledge.

Summarizing the results, it appears on the present evidence that Handel composed five duets (nos. 3, 4, 8, 11, 12) in Hanover, probably in 1710–11, and arrived in Hanover with six others (nos. 1a, 2, 5, 6, 7, 10) which he had composed during the preceding three years in Italy; Duet no. 9 may have been composed either in Venice in 1709–10 or during Handel's first months in Hanover. As will be seen from Table 2, the authorship of only one literary text from these twelve duets can at present be identified. Surmising that Duet no. 10 was composed in Italy, it is perhaps no surprise to find that the text is not by Mauro. Mauro's authorship of the duets composed in Hanover must be borne in mind as a possibility: the texts follow a variety of metrical plans and are not necessarily all by the same author.

After the paragraph on the subject of Handel's duets, Mainwaring's *Memoirs* continue thus:

Besides these Duettos (a species of composition of which the Princess and court were particularly fond) he composed a variety of other things for voices and instruments.[71]

As we have seen, few of these 'other things' can be identified. In the catalogue of Handel's works which accompanied the *Memoirs*, the entry for 'Cantatas' reads 'the greatest part made at Hanover, and other places abroad'.[72] This gives a distorted emphasis. The Italian cantatas possibly composed by Handel at Hanover are greatly outnumbered by those written in Italy, and they form fewer than ten per cent of his compositions in this genre. Taking all of Handel's identifiable compositions from the Hanover period together, they seem to reflect only occasional performances, mainly of Italian cantata-type works. There is some evidence that Handel composed many of his cantatas and duets in pairs, presumably suggesting that two new works of this type were expected for each performance.[73] Even allowing for the loss of some source materials, there is hardly enough in all to suggest a regular and continuous pattern of performances at the Hanoverian court. For the moment, our knowledge of Kapellmeister Händel must rest on five or six Italian duets, perhaps on a similar number of Italian cantatas and three instrumental sonatas, and on the electress's reports of his keyboard-playing.

71 *Memoirs* p. 85.
72 *Memoirs* p. 154.
73 This is also the case with the duets which Handel composed later in London and may also be true of his Italian-period works, though here the pattern is less clear.

Since this volume went to press a significant study of *Apollo e Dafne* has appeared: Hans Joachim Marx, 'Zur Kompositionsgeschichte von Händels Pastoralkantate "Apollo e Dafne" (HWV 122)', in *Göttinger Händel-Beiträge* 1 (Kassel, 1984), pp. 70f. Marx suggests that all the bassoon indications were added in Hanover, on the grounds that no bassoons were available to him in Italy. (In fact, there is a bassoon part in Handel's score of *La Resurrezione*.) In general Marx's study complements my conclusions, but I disagree with his table (p. 72) of paper conjunctions for the autograph, and with the proposition (p. 73) that Handel began the composition of *Apollo e Dafne* in Rome.

Muzio Clementi as an Original Advocate, Collector and Performer, in Particular of J. S. Bach and D. Scarlatti

STEPHEN DAW

(Birmingham)

Just as the significance of the English 'Bach cult' of around 1800 has not always received due recognition,[1] so the role of the English–Italian composer Muzio Clementi has rarely given rise to more than brief comment.[2] What is more, Clementi is not simply a figure significant to any understanding of the English scene or of the 'Bach cult'. His advocacy also of the music of Domenico Scarlatti and other earlier composers revealed him to be broadly discerning and industrious in the pursuit of his art, and he was active over such a wide historical and geographical area that his influence was of real European significance. Although his interest was by no means confined to music of the eighteenth century[3], the aim of the present article is to trace his continuing relationship with the music of Bach, Scarlatti and Handel and, whilst showing that his advocacy of their work displayed unique features,[4] to comment on the significance and influence of his involvement. Those whose business it is to work regularly on early-eighteenth-century composers will need no apology for an essay which seeks to clarify the posthumous but early circulation of their music.[5]

Muzio Clementi (1752–1832) was an energetic and, reportedly, an excitable musician of many talents. His association with the music of the three 1685 composers was reflected in his work as a performer, composer, celebrated extemporizer, collector of manuscripts and publisher; in addition, it could be claimed that his work as senior partner in the piano-manufacturing firm of Clementi & Collard (between

---

1 Cf. H. F. Redlich, 'The Bach Revival in England 1750–1850', *Hinrichsen's Musical Year Book* 7 (1952), pp. 287–300.

2 E.g., in Leon Plantinga's well-proportioned study (Plantinga 1977: see References below) four first editions of Bach are mentioned only in footnotes; in Alan Tyson's invaluable thematic catalogue (Tyson 1967) there are no BWV or Kk numbers. Earlier studies are even less thorough.

3 He also published much later music, notably Beethoven's and including some first editions.

4 Not least his promoting of all three of them.

5 The usefulness of source studies as they concern later collectors and copyists is obvious; with regard to J. S. Bach, Hans-Joachim Schulze repeated the call for such work in 1975 ('Die Bachüberlieferung – Plädoyer für ein notwendiges Buch', *Beiträge zur Musikwissenschaft* 17 (1979), 45–57).

1798 and 1832)[6] was quite strongly influenced by the rich harpsichord styles of Scarlatti and the Bach family.[7] In all of these areas, his interest continued for many years and in ways that demonstrate clearly a continuing interest in Bach, Handel and Scarlatti.

There follows a calendar of Clementi's interest in these composers, such as may be clearly established from his activities as a performer and as a publisher: perhaps it should be emphasized that many further details of the programmes which Clementi performed may yet materialize,[8] and that further details regarding his sources and his editing revisions as a publisher[9] will no doubt appear in the future.

Calendar of Clementi's reported performances of music by J. S. Bach, Domenico Scarlatti and G. F. Handel, and of his publication of their music

1 Between c1767 and 1774 or later, Clementi is reported to have practised the music of 'Corelli, Alessandro Scarlatti, Paradies[10] and Handel' and to have studied it as part of his self-instruction (as a performer?) and to help in the forming of his good taste (as an extemporizer and as a composer?). It seems perfectly possible that for 'Alessandro Scarlatti' we should read 'Domenico Scarlatti', some of whose music was already available and popular in England. Handel's music would be regarded as prescribed material at this time for any aspiring musician in England.

2 In the winter season of 1780–1 during his visit to Paris (or possibly on an untraced later visit c1783–4), Clementi played, after sonatas of his own, Scarlatti's Sonata in A major Kk 113.[11]

3 By October 1784, during his reported sojourn in and near Bern, Clementi's performances of Scarlatti's music drew from an anonymous hearer the following remarks:[12]

When you witness his playing of rapid octave passages for one hand, it will be clear that these are not easy; but he always achieves more than is written – even octave trills – and every note is quite distinctly audible. He plays with an inimitable rapture, with a continual flexibility of volume and timing (between *lentando* and *rubando*) that it would be impossible to convey in notation.

In some places, he applies his own special fingering; trills that follow one another he executes marvellously, using such fingerings as 3 & 1, 4 & 2 and 5 & 1. I have never heard any-

---

6 The pianos were often labelled 'Clementi', but the firm's main piano-maker was William Collard. Clementi's partners in the firm changed frequently, as did the firm's functions – music publishing from the last years of the eighteenth century, the sale of popular woodwind instruments c1810, etc.

7 The advanced keyboard writing in W. F. Bach's *Polonaisen* and in some of C. P. E. Bach's clavichord works may well have exerted some such influence.

8 His activities as a performer were prodigious in the years between 1775 and about 1803. But detailed impressions of his repertoire and performance practice cannot yet be given.

9 Similarly, the sources for much of his *Practical Harmony* cannot yet be identified.

10 I.e. Pietro Domenico Paradisi (c1707–91), whose music became fashionable in England after he settled there in 1747.

11 Tyson 1967 p. 47. This sonata had been published by John Johnson, London, by 1760 (cf. R. Kirkpatrick, *Domenico Scarlatti* (Princeton, N.J., 1953), p. 408).

12 Slightly modified from the translation in Plantinga 1977 pp. 70ff, 108.

body play the sonatas of Domenico Scarlatti as he does; up to now, I feel that I only half knew them.

4 On 6 June 1791, Clementi published his own edition of *Scarlatti's Chefs d'Oeuvre, for the Harpsichord or Piano-forte; Selected from an Elegant Collection of Manuscripts, in the Possession of Muzio Clementi* (London, 1791). This collection contains the first English edition (and very probably the very first edition) of the following Scarlatti sonatas:

Clementi no.	Kk	Key	Source (primary, according to Kirkpatrick)
1	378	F major	[1754?] Venice VIII, 21
3	380	E major	[1754?] Venice VIII, 23, in F
4	490	D major	[1756?] Venice XII, 7
5	400	D major	[1754?] Venice IX, 13
6	475	E♭ major	[1756?] Venice XI, 22
7	381	E♭ major	[1754?] Venice VIII, 24, in E
8	206	E major	[1753?] Venice III, 1
9	531	E major	[1757?] Venice XIII, 18
10	462	F minor	[1756?] Venice XI, 9
11	463	F minor	[1756?] Venice XI, 10

Clearly there is no direct relationship between Clementi's selection and the Venice albums; nor is there any other known source which shows any positive concordance with Clementi's publication; it would seem that his 'elegant collection of manuscripts' is lost. Of the twelve numbered pieces in the collection, no. 2 is anonymous (probably not by Clementi, to whom pastiche did not come easily), and no. 12 in F major is now attributed to Antonio Soler (no. 5 in S. Rubio (ed.), *Sonatas por instrumentos de tecla*, 7 vols. (Madrid, 1958–62) and was apparently misattributed by Clementi. This publication is further discussed below.

5 On 26 October 1801 Clementi registered at Stationers' Hall the first edition of his *Introduction to the Art of Playing on the Piano Forte*, which includes pieces chosen for study purposes by many composers, including the following attributed to Handel, 'Scarlatti' and 'Sebastian Bach':

Lesson no.	work
III	'Air, in ATLANTA; by HANDEL'
IV	'Air; in SAUL; by HANDEL'
V	'Dead March, in SAUL; by HANDEL'
VIII	'Air, in JUDUS MACCABEUS, by HANDEL'
IX	'March, in JUDUS MACCABEUS, by HANDEL'
XV	'LESSON XV by SCARLATTI', marked 'Larghetto' (Kk 34)
XXV	'LESSON XXV by HANDEL', marked 'Allegro'
XXVI	'MINUET in SAMSON by HANDEL'
XXX	'MINUETTO by SCARLATTI' (Kk 42)
XXXIII	'GAVOTTA in OTHO by HANDEL'
XXXV	'LESSON XXXV by SCARLATTI', marked 'Allegro' (Kk 35)
XXXVII	'MINUET in ARIADNE by HANDEL'
XXXVIII	'MARCH in the OCCASIONAL ORATORIO by HANDEL'
XLIII	'MINUET by SCARLATTI' (Kk 40, 'minuetto')
XLVIII	'POLONOISE and MINUET by SEBASTIAN BACH' (from BWV 817, Polonaise and Menuet; first edition)

There are also short preludes 'by the Author' to accustom the pupil's fingers to the feel of the keys of which all of the Lessons represent examples; although these are all short, they are not so inadequate for their professed purpose as some have stated, if they are used in combination with the scales and shakes also specified. More important to our study is the little Prelude in E major which precedes the Bach movements (p. 62); this can hardly be described alongside its fellows as 'by the Author' (Ex. 1). It is so obviously derived from another Bach movement as to demonstrate a certain familiarity with it (Ex. 2). For further discussion of the provenance of all of these sixteen movements, see below. The Bach Polonaise appears to be published here for the first time; and although the Minuet had been published earlier, this is its first appearance in print alongside the Polonaise.[13]

Ex. 1.

Ex. 2. J. S. Bach, Gavotte from French Suite no. 4, BWV 815 (Fassung B)

6 Shortly after publication of the above, or simultaneously with it, Pleyel of Paris published his own edition of *Scarlatti's Chefs d'Oeuvre* (no. 4 above) under the title *Méthode Pour la Pianoforte par Muzio Clementi contenant . . . Cinquante Leçons doigtées par les Compositeurs les plus célèbres, tels que Handl [sic] . . . Bach . . . Scarlati [sic] . . . &c.*[14]

7 On 23 November 1801, Clementi published Volume 1 of *Clementi's Selection of Practical Harmony for the Organ or Piano Forte* (Tyson 1967 Wo 7, I). This volume includes the following music by Handel and Bach:

Clementi's pages	composer	work
36	Handel	'Fuga a 2' in B minor (arranged from Sonata Op. I No. 9, with adjusted conclusion)[15]
132–7	J. S. Bach	'Preludio: Gravement' (BWV 572)
138–45	J. S. Bach	'Suite in G' (BWV 816), with all movements of the A major version (*NBA* V/8 pp. 40–51) present in the following order: Gavotte, Courante, Loure, Allemande, Sarabande, Bourrée, Gigue

13 For details regarding the complex revised editions of Clementi's *Introduction*, see the New Introduction and the List of Editions in Rosenblum 1974.

14 Rosenblum 1974 p. xxxiv.

15 The Hicks nos. (see List of Abbreviations) are currently the most practical vehicle for reference to Handel's music, particularly keyboard music. The author would also like to express here his grateful appreciation to Anthony Hicks for expert assistance in the preparation of this essay.

8 On or around 20 February 1802 Clementi published Volume 2 of *Clementi's Selection of Practical Harmony for the Organ or Piano Forte* (Tyson 1967 Wo 7, II). This volume includes the following music by J. S. Bach, Handel and D. Scarlatti:

Clementi's pages	composer	work
65	J. S. Bach	'TOCCATA . . . FUGA in D minor' (BWV 913) marked Presto/Adagio/ FUGA
74, 76, 78, 80, 83, 86, 89, 92, 94, 96, 98	Handel	Eleven Fugues: *Six Fugues* (1735) in the order nos. 1, 6, 3, 5, 2, 4, and five from the *Suites de Pieces* (1720) in the order nos. 4, 6, 3, 2, 8
132	Scarlatti	'Fuga 1' (Sonata in D minor, Kk 41)
135	Scarlatti	'Fuga 2' (Sonata in G minor, Kk 30), headed 'The following, by Domenico Scarlatti, is the celebrated CAT'S FUGUE', and 'Moderato'

Only the Bach item appears to be first edition; for further information on Clementi's putative sources and editing technique, see below.

9 By autumn (after 14 July) 1802, Clementi, accompanied by his pupil John Field, left England for the second and most extended of his several continental tours. His journeys took him to Paris, Vienna, St Petersburg, Berlin, Dresden, Prague, Vienna (2),[16] Zurich, Leipzig, Berlin (2), Leipzig (2), Venice, Florence, Rome, Naples, Rome (2), ?Leipzig (3), Berlin (3), Riga, St Petersburg (2), Vienna (3), northern Italy (2), Rome (3), Milan, Vienna (4), ?Prague (2) and northeastern Europe (Rostock perhaps, or another Baltic port that would be safe in the prevailing political state of Europe). His absence from England lasted until the late summer of 1810. To judge from the preserved correspondence, Leon Plantinga is correct to assume that the purpose of the tour was not principally to perform, since after 1804 there are no reports of Clementi's performing in public;[17] the aims of the tour seem to have been divided between business (mainly the negotiation of pianoforte sales by his joint company, but also the assembling of music for publication under his own imprint) and personal expeditions (his first marriage, visits to his homeland). Perhaps most significant of all is the remark made at that time by William Gardiner that Clementi's objective was 'avowedly to collect MSS for his work on practical harmony'.[18]

10 Probably during 1802, Clementi's firm published *Ten Select Voluntaries, for the Organ or Harpsichord (never before publish'd) Composed by Mr Handel, Dr Green &c. Book II.*[19] This volume followed a publishing tradition of miscellaneous organ albums that dated back, through the recently acquired firm of Longman & Broderip, to Longman, Lukey & Co. in 1771. Until further information comes to light regarding Clementi's published series – which may not have been

---

16 I.e. second visit to Vienna, and so forth ('?Leipzig (3)' indicating a possible third visit to Leipzig).

17 Plantinga 1977 pp. 211ff.

18 *Ibid.* p. 158.

19 It seems that this was the second of four printed or projected volumes, of which others have not yet been traced. Cf. W. C. Smith and C. Humphries, *Handel: A Descriptive Catalogue of the Early Editions* (Oxford, 1970), p. 254. The author would like to thank Malcolm Jones for valuable assistance with regard to early editions of Handel.

completed, as only the one 'Book II' has been reported – we may be correct in assuming that the whole project was effectively a reprint from late-eighteenth-century sources. In these, both a set of 'Rules for Tuning' published by Longman & Broderip in *c*1780 and a frequently encountered set of '6 Fugues or Fughettas' – both attributed to Handel – are today regarded as spurious.[20] In all probability neither Clementi's editors nor the public who might purchase the series will have been aware of this lack of authenticity.

11 During Clementi's tour of 1802–10, the following continental editions of his *Introduction to the Art of Playing on the Piano Forte* (see item no. **5** above), and containing the 'Lessons' by Handel, Scarlatti and Bach from the first London edition, were issued:

by Hoffmeister & Kühnel, Leipzig etc., 1802 (text in German)

by Cappi, Vienna, 1806 (text in German)

by Cappi, Vienna, later 1806 (text in French)

by André, Offenbach (André's first full edition), 1809 (text in German, probably derived from revised reprints 2–4 issued in London during the period 1801–11[21] and apparently treated as second, third and fourth editions). André's edition is known to have sold in European Russia.

12 About 1810, *Scarlatti's Chefs d'Oeuvre* (see no. **4** above) was reissued by Clementi, Collard, Davis & Collard.

13 On 18 February 1811, two new publications were announced in the *Morning Post*:[22] Volume 3 of *Clementi's Practical Harmony* (Tyson 1967 Wo 7, III) and the simplified and radically altered fifth edition of *Clementi's Introduction to the Art of Playing on the Piano Forte*. The former was devoted exclusively to music composed by members of the Bach family, and included the following works of J. S. Bach:

Clementi's pages	work
52–5	'Fuga' in C minor (BWV 575): this is the first edition,[23] but the composer named as C. P. E. Bach
115–21	'Fuga: Allegro' in A minor (BWV 944.ii): first edition
122–3	'Fuga: Allegro' in C major (BWV 953): first edition

The fifth edition of the *Introduction* omitted thirty-five of the original 'Lessons' and was restricted to five major keys (C, F, G, B♭ and D) and three minor (A, D, and E); the little derived Prelude in E major was omitted along with most of its companions. Still included were five Handel arrangements, which had originally served

20 Cf. T. Best, 'Handel's Harpsichord Music: A Checklist', in C. Hogwood & R. Luckett (eds.), *Music in Eighteenth-Century England: Essays in Memory of Charles Cudworth* (Cambridge, 1983), pp. 171–87.

21 Rosenblum 1974 p. xxxvii.

22 Tyson 1967 pp. 84, 103.

23 Cf. D. Kilian's note in *NBA* IV/5-6 *KB* p. 272.

as Lessons III, VIII, XXXIII, XXXVII and XXXVIII – two Airs, a Gavotte, a Minuet and a March. There was no Scarlatti or Bach henceforth in English editions of the *Introduction*; but see item no. **14** below.

14 On 9 April 1811 Clementi announced in the *Morning Post* the publication of the *Appendix* to the fifth edition of *Clementi's Introduction to the Art of Playing on the Piano Forte*. This was designed as a continuation ('calculated for the greatest improvement') of studies commenced in the fifth edition, which had become less rapidly demanding than its predecessors.[24] It contained the following Lessons in the *Introduction*, as well as the Prelude in E major:

by Handel: IV, V, IX, XXV, XXVI

by Scarlatti: XV, XXX, XXXV, XLIII

by J. S. Bach: XLVIII (both movements)

There were additional pieces, but none of these were the work of Handel, Scarlatti or J. S. Bach.

15 Between 1812–14 and 1818–19 Clementi issued the seventh and eighth editions of his *Introduction* (the sixth edition of September 1811 had been a Spanish translation of the fifth, published in London but dedicated to the Spanish Nation – then suffering under the rigours of the Peninsular War). In these editions, the number of Handel arrangements present in the fifth edition was reduced; in the seventh edition, the original Lesson XXXVIII (*March in the Occasional Oratorio*) was removed, leaving Lessons III, VIII, XXXIII and XXXVII only; in the eighth edition, only the original Lesson VIII (*Air in Judas Maccabaeus*, 'See, the conquering Hero comes') was left. As the same piece also remained in the preserved tenth edition (1821–2), we are presumably safe to assume that it was included in the unlocated ninth edition.[25]

Around 1815, Carli of Paris issued the first known foreign edition to include music derived from both the *Introduction* and the *Appendix*; his sources were the eighth edition of the *Introduction* and the 1811 *Appendix*, which continued to be advertised in editions seven and eight.[26]

16 Around 1815 Clementi published Volume 4 of *Clementi's Selection of Practical Harmony* (Tyson 1967 Wo 7, IV); although it contained no music by the 1685 composers, its contents still emphasized fugal techniques. A report published in the *Musical Souvenir* for 1831, which states that all four volumes appeared between 1811 and 1815,[27] may indicate that Volumes 1 and 2 were reprinted during that period.

17 Around 1820–1 Clementi revised the 1811 *Appendix* (see item no. **12** above) to form the Second Part of *Clementi's Introduction to the Art of Playing on the Piano Forte, being an Improvement upon his Work formerly called An Appendix; containing Preludes, Scale-Exercises, National Airs, Variations, Two Masterly*

24 Cf. Rosenblum 1974 pp. xxiff.
25 *Ibid*. pp. xxiv-xxviii.
26 *Ibid*. pp. xxxivff. Carli's title began *Méthode complette* . . .
27 Tyson 1967 p. 103.

Fugues of Sebastian Bach, with other Pleasing and Instructive Pieces . . . Op. 43.
Apart from the music drawn from the *Appendix*, there were thirteen new Lessons
in the Second Part, including Bach's 'two masterly Fugues' and a Fugato by
Handel; the latter occupies p. 46 of the volume (in which the Lessons are no longer
numbered). The preceding entry is the *Minuet from Samson*.[28] The headings of the
Bach fugues, which conclude the volume, are not without significance. The first, on
Clementi's p. 120, is headed 'Fuga by J. S. Bach; from an Original MS: of the
author'; the music follows the Bach autograph of BWV 870 (Fugue in C major,
WTC Bk 2) which has been established as the probable direct source.[29] The second
fugue (a version of the Fugue in C sharp minor, *WTC* Bk 2) corresponds to no
other preserved copy, and is headed 'Fuga by J. S. Bach' without further detail.
Although it is possible that an autograph of J. S. Bach or a copy, now lost, in the
hand of Anna Magdalena Bach was originally part of Clementi's portfolio of MSS
for Book 2 of the *WTC* and was thus the source for this edited version, no information is yet forthcoming; nor on the method by which he may have obtained it. There
are today three preludes and their associated fugues missing from the extant
portion of that portfolio, now held by the Reference Division of the British
Library.[30]

The Handel Fugato constitutes an arrangement of the fourth movement
(Allegro) of Handel's Concerto Grosso Op. VI No. 1 in G major, which is a
concerto-fugato in three parts. Clementi's arrangement (whether made by him or
derived from an intermediary source) is interesting for its fidelity to the contrapuntal essentials of the original (without additional continuo harmonies or other
'improvements'). It is also unique among Clementi's preserved Handel editions in
that it includes plentiful dynamic indications; some of these seem to be drawn
directly from Handel's own editions, but others have been added to indicate solo–
ripieno contrasts (*piano/forte*) or even occasionally to serve as more subjective
suggestions.[31]

18 In 1822, according to a claim he made later, the French pianist Camille Petit
overheard Clementi playing at his home, 1 High Row, Kensington. He reported that
Clementi first played some exercises, then the Prelude and Fugue (presumably
including the Largo) of Handel's Suite in F sharp minor (Hicks 205–6).[32]

19 In late September 1826, the eleventh edition of *Clementi's Introduction to the
Art of Playing on the Piano Forte . . . Op. 42* was published; a tenth edition, also
headed 'Op. 42', had been issued in or before 1823. The eleventh edition excluded

---

28 Rosenblum 1974 pp. xxxiiff.
29 Cf. W. Emery, 'The London Autograph of "The Forty-eight" ', *ML* 34 (1953), pp. 106ff; also
    D. Franklin & S. Daw (eds.), *J. S. Bach: Das wohltemperirte Clavier, Teil 2*, facsimile edn (London,
    1980), Introduction.
30 Franklin & Daw, *op. cit.* (see note 29).
31 These comments spring from a comparison of Clementi's edition with that edited as Op. VI No. 1 by
    H. F. Redlich & A. Hoffmann (Kassel, 1965).
32 Cf. Plantinga 1977 p. 282 note 71.

the one remaining Handel 'Air'; this was almost certainly the last edition of this work in which Clementi would have been involved personally.[33]

20 On 17 December 1827, at a banquet held in his honour at the Albion Hotel, London, Clementi was persuaded to play the piano in public for the first time in many years.

He extemporised on a theme from Handel, and completely carried us away by his fine playing. His eyes gleamed with youthful fire; those of many of his hearers were dimmed with tears of emotion. Amidst shouts of applause, and the heartiest congratulations, he resumed his seat.[34]

If we search for the influence that the three Baroque masters exercised on Clementi's work as a composer, we shall not find it pronounced in the case of his structures, at least so far as his fugal works are concerned. These nearly all had their origin in his early compositions, designed for publication in France, and may well have reflected some fashion of the 1780s. Clementi clearly was familiar with the manner of fugal writing in the Handelian idiom, but his notion of structure, of drama and of the texture of successful counterpoint was crude. There is also little personality about his fugal writing, even if we compare it to the works of the younger Bachs, Albrechtsberger and Gottlieb Muffat[35] included in his own *Practical Harmony*. There is no certainty whatsoever that Clementi had encountered any of the *WTC* before he began music publishing in 1798, and resemblances noted by Leon Plantinga between the writing of Clementi and J. S. Bach[36] might well be traced between Clementi and Handel or Handel and Bach. To agree that some similarities do exist is not to admit that these have any real significance.

Clementi's canons, including some of those in his *Gradus ad Parnassum* (Op. 44; Part 1 March 1817, Part 2 April 1819, Part 3 November 1826) are generally more successful as counterpoint, but they do not necessarily display any real early-eighteenth-century influence on him. If some of their easy grace reminds us of Domenico Scarlatti, there were probably other Latin sources for this style.[37]

Clementi's compositions in the sonata style present interesting problems to players of the modern piano – even more than Beethoven's – for he was sensitive both to the instruments of his time and to the artistic ideals of the period around 1800. Even his late piano music often contains the kinds of texture that one feels Domenico Scarlatti might have devised had he composed for the piano. The upper and lower registers of the instruments are used alternately or simultaneously in close chords, which are obviously intended to sound distinct as well as contrasted; the middle register is frequently filled with notes (the textures may even look

---

33 Cf. Rosenblum 1974 p. xxviii.
34 Charlotte Moscheles, *Life of Moscheles*, trans. A. D. Coleridge (London, 1873), quoted Plantinga 1977 p. 247.
35 Clementi published these in Volume 2 of his *Practical Harmony* as works by Frescobaldi, but they have been shown by Susan Wollenberg to be by Gottlieb Muffat; see Plantinga 1977 p. 188.
36 Plantinga 1977 pp. 154, 207.
37 It should not be forgotten that Clementi was already musically versatile before he first left Italy.

Brahms-like), but the nature of the writing makes it clear that Clementi expected a precise and defined effect. That in the early nineteenth century this sensitive response to instrumental timbre was a conservative feature, and one indebted to Clementi's obvious affection for music of the early and mid eighteenth century, seems highly probable. The pianofortes made by W. F. Collard and his assistants for Clementi clarify all this:[38] it is hardly surprising that, well restored, they are ideally suited to Clementi's own music. But one may also think that of all pianofortes ever manufactured, a good Clementi square or grand of the period up to about 1825 is the best equipped to project the life and the emotion of Domenico Scarlatti's sonatas.

We have no record of Clementi's playing of music by J. S. Bach or any other Bach apart possibly from Johann Christian (which he would have played as an orchestral pianist in London); however, the evidence from his publications that he especially valued Bach fugues as teaching pieces finds support in reports of two of his most significant pupils. John Field, while still a pupil in 1802, is twice reported as having played music of J. S. Bach with great distinction;[39] and we are told that Ludwig Berger was impressing Berlin audiences with his Bach playing before he accompanied both Field and Clementi to St Petersburg in 1805.[40] The report of Clementi's lesson–interview with J. A. de Méreaux,[41] published at Paris in 1867, is taken by Plantinga at face value as representing an historical account of Clementi's practising routine while still a young man at Peter Beckford's house in Dorset. However, when one knows that the origin of this report is a single lesson given to Méreaux in Paris in 1820, it is easy to see how it might really be an indication of Clementi's views regarding the training of pianists in 1820, which he presented perhaps in such a way as to imply that he wished his eager French pupil to follow his youthful example.[42] When Méreaux wrote, so much later, that

he devoted eight hours each day to the harpsichord . . . Sometimes he was obliged to practise for twelve or fourteen hours on end in order to keep up with the daily target he had set himself. It was the works of Sebastian and Emmanuel Bach, of Handel and Scarlatti that he studied continually; he did this from two different standpoints, that of finger technique and that of instrumental composition

he was probably paraphrasing remarks of Clementi that one may conjecture went originally as follows:

When I was young, I practised for long hours, making up time missed: to succeed as a keyboard-player requires such devotion.

Perhaps he then specified the hours that he considered necessary and went on:

I have found the works of Sebastian and Emanuel Bach, of Handel and Scarlatti invaluable; one should give them continuing attention from each of two points of view . . . etc.

38 There is need for a thorough study of the activities of both Collard and Clementi, large numbers of whose instruments are preserved.
39 Plantinga 1977 pp. 154, 207.
40 *Ibid*. p. 209.
41 *Ibid*. p. 7 (and source cited).
42 The slight imprecision characteristic of the French language in reporting the past might easily have led to this ambiguity.

This interpretation is supported by the strong evidence of Clementi's publications between 1801 and 1811.

As an editor of music by Scarlatti, Handel and Bach, Clementi appears to have been quite careful and diligent: his editions contain few errors in notation, he avoided works more recently put into print by others, and he seems to have gone to some trouble to find good music from the past to publish. We cannot be certain of his methods as an editor, since the bulk of his manuscript collection has not been traced; his edition of the C major Fugue from Book 2 of the *WTC*, for which we do have both source and edition, is very good (his only addition is the tempo indication 'Allegro'). His *Scarlatti's Chefs d'Oeuvre* is an early example of a romantic, interpretative edition; even if we are instinctively repelled by his (obviously added) expression marks in Kk 206, at least they convey something to us of his youthful performance style, which was so admired in Bern. The expression marks in this sonata include *pp, p, dim, cres, espressivo, espr:, fz* and *rinf*.

Several efforts by recent scholars to trace the date and place of the sale of Clementi's music after (or before?) his death have remained unsuccessful. We know that there was a sale, and that he gave a direction in his will that William Horsley should assist his wife Emma in the 'arranging' of his manuscripts. However, apart from a parcel containing the *WTC* portfolio and a book of fugues by Pachelbel,[43] bought by John George Emett (1787–1847), we do not know of any manuscripts which were sold there – even of his own compositions. Perhaps discoveries may yet be made.

There is an interesting similarity between the works of J. S. Bach published in Volumes 1, 2 and 3 of *Clementi's Practical Harmony* (BWV 572, 816, 913, 944.ii and 953) and a catalogue issued in December 1781 by the Hamburg music and book dealer Johann Christoph Westphal.[44] Westphal's list groups the following:

Bach J. S.	6 Clavier Suiten	perhaps BWV 812–817, not BWV 806–811?
–	1 Clavier-Solo, C dur	perhaps BWV 953?
–	Fantasie Chromatique	BWV 903 or 903.i only
–	Piece d'orgue a 5. avec le Pedale [*sic*]	BWV 572
–	Partite diverse über O Gott du frommer Gott	all or part of BWV 767

We must remember that Clementi also showed some familiarity with the Suites BWV 817 and 815 in his *Introduction to the Art of Playing on the Piano Forte*.[45]

In Volumes 1 and 2 of *Practical Harmony* we encounter twelve fugues attributed to Handel. Although there are several publications from around 1800 which claim to contain large quantities of fugues by that composer, Clementi's series stands out in that it really does contain Handel's authentic keyboard fugues. They were well

---

43 That Emett bought the Pachelbel volume was recorded by his daughter Sarah (see Emery, 'The London Autograph' (note 29 above)); this may well have been the volume, principally of Pachelbel Magnificat fugues, which is today in the British Library (Add. MS 31221).

44 Printed in *Dok* III p. 269.

45 The six suites were issued in their entirety by Forkel in Vienna and Leipzig (1802–3). The Menuet of BWV 817 had been published alone by Hummel (Amsterdam), probably in an anthology of 1767 (cf. A. Dürr, *NBA* V/8 *KB* pp. 87ff).

edited (and, where relevant, well arranged). The six fughettas (or *Fugues faciles*) which are now known not to be by Handel are excluded from *Practical Harmony*, which may indicate that Clementi saw them as inauthentic; after all, the separate publication which his firm did issue and which apparently did contain them (item no. **10** in the Calendar above) may well have been based on an earlier one supervised by Longman, and probably appeared while Clementi was abroad. The Handel arrangements (and the attractive G major harpsichord Allegro) in the *Introduction* have no known direct source, and it is likely that some if not all of the arrangements were Clementi's own; they will have sounded very neat on early grand and square pianofortes.

The Scarlatti *Chefs d'Oeuvre* derive from manuscripts that are lost and that perhaps ascribed all twelve sonatas to Scarlatti. This source seems to have been independent of other English editions, and it has presumably disappeared. The remainder of the pieces by Scarlatti with which Clementi may be associated are quite different: they were available in print, and presumably most of them were quite well known until at least the 1790s.

Considering his obvious interest in German music and in fugue,[46] it seems surprising that so little in the way of music by German composers survives in Clementi's own handwriting. Indeed, the only copy from Clementi's hand of a work entirely by another composer that we have traced has survived by a lucky chance. This is SPK Mus MS Bach P 1165, a copy of Bach's Duet no. 4 in A minor (BWV 805), the last movement before the closing fugue of *Clavierübung III*. It is headed 'Fuga di Seb. Bach' by Clementi; the copy is carefully authenticated by his close associate J. B. Cramer, who apparently gave it to 'his friend' the collector Aloys Fuchs at Vienna on 5 January 1837. The manuscript (see Plates A and B) was copied either from an original print or from a manuscript copy; a date between 1802 and 1805 seems probable, i.e. it was copied at Berlin or elsewhere in Germany. In view of Clementi's first marriage to the daughter of a Berlin cantor (Johann Gottfried Georg Lehmann of the Nicolaikirche), and of that cantor's known connection with Wilhelm Friedemann Bach, it seems highly probable that Clementi found much of his Bach-family material for Volume 3 of *Practical Harmony* in Berlin. It has even been suggested as a possibility that Cantor Lehmann may have presented his distinguished son-in-law with the British Library *WTC* manuscripts.[47] Another obvious source for research at that time into the Bach family's music would have been the Amalienbiliothek, which Carl Friedrich Zelter had newly catalogued in 1802;[48] the presence of a number of pieces by J. P. Kirnberger in Volume 1 of *Practical Harmony* even perhaps suggests that Clementi made an earlier visit to Berlin in 1782–5, although we do not know of a visit to northern Germany so early.

46 Cf. Leon Plantinga, 'Clementi, Virtuosity and the "German Manner"', *JAMS* 25 (1972), pp. 303–30.
47 For information on Lehmann, the author wishes to record his thanks to Don Franklin (Pittsburgh) and Hans-Joachim Schulze (Leipzig).
48 See E. R. Blechschmidt, *Die Amalien-Bibliothek: historische Einordnung und Katalog* (Berlin, 1965), p. 30.

Plates A and B. Clementi's copy of BWV 805 (SPK Mus MS Bach P 1165)

Clementi's contribution to the study of the music of Bach, Handel and Scarlatti should not be overrated, but neither should it pass unnoticed. In a sense, he showed in his didactic works that he belonged to a musical tradition that they would have acknowledged too. With regard to his *Gradus ad Parnassum* a contemporary critic, writing in the *Repository of the Arts* in 1827, remarked:

[The *Gradus*] will form a guide to the students of every country, in the present as well as the future ages; like Bach's works it will stand as a record of the attainments in pianoforte playing, and, indeed, of the harmonic knowledge possessed by the living generation.[49]

This reviewer perceived that Clementi, like Bach, recognized a relationship between theory and practice; that he realized the two could be fruitfully blended in music that had vigour as well as stature. Because of this recognition, the music of the past, with its special ingenuities of counterpoint and motif, retained its power and its purpose for Clementi. Because of this, there was a need for beginners on the pianoforte to play good music in order to develop themselves technically. Clementi's life history, his compositions and his attitudes to music of others stand as a witness to his age – and a most revealing one – for future generations.[50]

References

Plantinga, L. B., *Clementi: His Life and Music* (London/New York, 1977)

Rosenblum, S. P. (ed.), *Clementi's Introduction to the Art of Playing on the Piano Forte*, facsimile edn (New York, 1974)

Tyson, A., *Thematic Catalogue of the Works of Muzio Clementi* (Tutzing, 1967)

49 Quoted more fully in Plantinga 1977 pp. 270, 284.
50 The author wishes to record his thanks to Alan Tyson for so effectively stressing these points in his private communication of 9 September 1982.

Handel's Early London Copyists

WINTON DEAN

(Godalming, Surrey)

Since Chrysander published his biography and embarked on his monumental edition more than a century ago Handel scholarship has been a grossly neglected area, not least in Britain, which should have taken the lead. Although the vast majority of the manuscript sources are in this country, until very recently no attempt has been made to subject them to a systematic examination or even to draw up an adequate calendar of their contents. The fact that Handel scrupulously dated his principal autographs – which with minor exceptions are all assembled in two places, the Royal Music collection in the British Library and the Fitzwilliam Museum in Cambridge – has led to the easy but quite erroneous assumption that no problems of chronology arise. Handel constantly revised and altered his works, especially for revivals in the theatre, with the result that a great deal of music, much of it unpublished, is scattered among early copies. An investigation of the copyists, their identity, habits and dates of operation, is obviously an essential preliminary to the assessment of this material. Yet the only published work of any consequence in the field has come from a Danish and a German scholar.

Until the appearance of Jens Peter Larsen's book *Handel's 'Messiah': Origins, Composition, Sources* (London, 1957), nearly all eighteenth-century Handel copies were ascribed almost automatically to his amanuensis John Christopher Smith, or sometimes to the two Smiths, father and son. Larsen demolished this never very convincing assumption and demonstrated the existence, during the 1730s and later, of a circle of copyists working more or less under Smith's guidance, whom Larsen designated S1 to S13. At the same time he allotted symbols to a number of other copyists according to the libraries where their work is preserved: RM1 to RM10 (Royal Music Library), BM1 to BM6 (British Library, Additional Manuscripts), Hb1 and 2 (Hamburg Staats- und Universitätsbibliothek), Lenn 1 and 2 (Barrett Lennard collection in the Fitzwilliam Museum) and Fitz 1 (other Fitzwilliam manuscripts). He recognized the existence of many more. Hans Dieter Clausen, in his comprehensive study of Handel's performing scores, *Händels*

Direktions-partituren ('*Handexemplare*') (Hamburg, 1972), added twelve more Hamburg copyists, whom he numbered H1 to H12.

Every Handel scholar is indebted to the pioneering work of Larsen and Clausen, which established an essential foundation on which we can build. It could not be final, for the very good reason that they did not have access to all the manuscripts, especially of the early works. Clausen, though aware of the British Library and Fitzwilliam holdings, restricted himself to the Hamburg scores, where the identification of copyists was only one among many considerations. Larsen used the principal public collections (British Library, Royal College of Music, Fitzwilliam, Tenbury, Hamburg), but was denied access to the bulk of the Aylesford collection copied for Handel's friend Charles Jennens (then owned by Sir Newman Flower, since 1965 in the Henry Watson Music Library, Manchester), and was unaware of the private collections of Gerald Coke and the Earl of Malmesbury. As it happens these two contain many key manuscripts, in several instances the earliest surviving copies of works whose autographs are missing or defective.[1] Some were dated by the original owners; others can be given a surprisingly precise date from internal evidence. Further unexamined early copies can be found in places as far apart as Oxford, Hereford, Berlin, Munich, Vienna, Washington and Tokyo – a list by no means exhaustive. Detailed inspection of this material, quite apart from yielding a substantial amount of unknown music, exposes a totally unfamiliar picture of Handel's copyists and the way they worked.

Although the present study is necessarily limited in scope, the whole field is so little mapped and so enveloped in a fog of obscurity and ignorance that some preliminary clearing of the ground may be helpful. In the first place, there have inevitably been a few false identifications. Larsen's and Clausen's lists each contain two duplicates. RM5 and RM6 are the same person; so are RM7 and RM9, H6 and H9, and H11 and H12. Secondly, the widening of the search has helped to distinguish those copyists who were closely linked with Handel's immediate circle from those who were not, and to define the periods during which each one was active. For the present commemorative volume, I had first intended to cover the years up to 1725, but soon found that this would take up more space than was likely to be available. Nevertheless it may be useful if I indicate which of the copyists enumerated by Larsen and Clausen were active before 1725, and their relative importance. All the S series except S2, RM5–10, BM2–6, Hb1 and 2, Lenn 1 and 2, Fitz 1 and H6–12 are later – some of them much later. So far as is known, RM3 and BM1 copied only a single Handel score each, and RM2 two; there is little to connect them closely with the composer. H4 was rather more prominent, but was not in action for long. On the other hand RM1, RM4, H1, H2, H3 and H5 – and of course Smith – were important copyists, at least for a time, not only in the number of manuscripts that contain their work but in their relationship to the source, Handel himself. So were

---

1 I owe a huge debt to Mr and Mrs Gerald Coke and to Lord and Lady Malmesbury for allowing me on numerous occasions to disturb their households and for making me so welcome in their libraries. Without their co-operation much of my work, in this study and elsewhere, would have been stillborn.

several others either wrongly identified or not mentioned by Larsen and Clausen. I hope elsewhere to describe and classify their work, designating them by the letters of the Greek alphabet in the order in which they appear among the sources. Only those having a demonstrable or likely link with the composer will be included in the series. I am conscious that any conclusions reached will always be subject to revision in the light of further evidence or reinterpretation.

Handel scholars have for some time been aware of two puzzles posed by the early Smith copies. One is the year of Smith's arrival in England, and therefore the earliest possible date for any manuscript copied by him. According to Coxe's *Anecdotes of George Frederick Handel and John Christopher Smith* (London, 1799), p. 37, Handel, who had known Smith in his youth at Halle, visited him in 1716 at Ansbach, where he was engaged in the wool trade, and invited him to act as his treasurer and secretary; Smith at once threw up his job and accompanied Handel to London, leaving his family in Germany till 'the fourth year of his residence in England'. This has been questioned, especially as Smith in a letter to the fourth Earl of Shaftesbury on 28 July 1743 spoke of Handel's having 'many proofs of my fidelity this 24 years'.[2] The second puzzle is the startling change that Smith's handwriting appears to have undergone towards 1720. Larsen does not give a facsimile of this 'Smith Mark I' (his first facsimile in fact shows H1's hand), but he reproduces four versions of the C clef on p. 263, and Clausen gives a rather fuller illustration on his p. 269. Some of the discrepancies must raise a suspicion that more than one copyist is involved.[3]

That suspicion can now be enlarged into a fact. The principal Mark I manuscripts relied on by Larsen and Clausen (dated around 1720 by the former, 1716 or 1717 by the latter) are RM 19.e.4 (*Il pastor fido*) and RM 19.d.5 (*Rinaldo*) in the British Library, and MA/1003 (*Amadigi*) and MB/1570 (Italian duets and trios) in Hamburg. The last is a composite manuscript containing several hands of different dates. The Mark I hand can be found in a number of other manuscripts, listed in full below; there are at least nineteen, some written in association with other copyists. Internal evidence proves conclusively that two of them antedate by several years the earliest possible time of Smith's arrival in London. RM 19.e.4 must have been copied in October 1712, for its first state reproduces the score of *Il pastor fido* before Handel finished the autograph on the 24th of the month. It contains, as insertions, several pieces sung at the first performance on 22 November 1712, as we know from the printed libretto; they are likewise insertions in the autograph. The earliest of the three scores of *Teseo* in Gerald Coke's collection, in the same hand, provides striking confirmation. Handel finished and dated the autograph of this opera on 19 December 1712, and first performed it on 10 January

2 Betty Matthews, 'Unpublished Letters Concerning Handel', *ML* 40 (1959), p. 263.
3 In his article 'Probleme der Händel-Überlieferung', *Mf* 34 (1981), pp. 137–61, which is partly a review of Clausen's book, Larsen acknowledged the possibility of error here. Of the four facsimiles on his p. 263 only *b* and *c* show Smith's C clef; of Clausen's examples on p. 269 only the three bottom lines represent Smith.

1713. The Coke copy contains words and music (subsequently cancelled or folded over) for a character, Medea's confidante Fedra, who was reduced to a mute not only before the first night but before the libretto was sent to the printer. The manuscript can thus be dated within very narrow limits to the last days of December 1712. Fedra's words and music are found nowhere else, since the scenes in which she appears are missing from the very fragmentary autograph.

The Handel manuscripts in the Earl of Malmesbury's collection belonged originally to Elizabeth Legh of Adlington Hall, Cheshire, a friend of the composer and a passionate admirer of his music, who from about 1715 until her death in 1734 ordered copies of all his works and had them specially bound in leather with her coat of arms stamped on the cover. They are still in their original condition. Not only that: Elizabeth Legh added numerous annotations and comments, including indexes for each volume and not infrequently the dates when she acquired them. In two instances she supplied the name of the copyist as well. Her score of *Teseo*, in the Mark I hand, bears the note in her writing: 'transcribed by Mr Linike June 1717'.

Who was this Linike? With Elizabeth Legh's invaluable clue we can discover a fair amount about him. He was probably of German origin, and perhaps related to the Weissenfels family of that name, of which three members – Ephraim, Christian Bernhard and Johann Georg – appear in *The New Grove*. None of these can be our man: the dates do not fit, although the best-known of them, Johann Georg, who in November 1725 adapted and conducted the first Hamburg production of Handel's *Giulio Cesare*, was in England for a time from 1721. The man we are seeking was a London musician who signed himself 'D. Linike', establishing the authentic form of a name on which other people, true to contemporary practice, bestowed an astonishing variety of spellings: Lynike, Linikey, Leneker, Lenniker, Liniken, Linikin, Lunecan, Lunican, Lunicon, and even Unican. The contexts leave no doubt that this was all one man.

He was primarily a viola-player, though he may well have earned more money as a copyist. We first encounter him in a list of twenty-three musicians who applied for jobs when John Vanbrugh was planning to establish an opera orchestra at his newly built Queen's Theatre in the Haymarket about November 1707.[4] Linike asked for £1 a night. He was not among the first two choices (the orchestra, numbering twenty-five to thirty, never included more than two viola-players), but he is rated at 8 shillings a night in an estimate dating from January 1708, shortly before Vanbrugh's season opened. This fee was confirmed later, and was apparently raised to 10 shillings about 1709/10. There is documentary evidence that Linike was a

4 Judith Milhous and Robert D. Hume, *Vice Chamberlain Coke's Theatrical Papers 1706–1715* (Carbondale, Illinois, 1982), p. 31. All information about Linike's activities during these years is taken from this authoritative source. I am indebted to the editors for allowing me to see their proofs in advance of publication, and for a facsimile of Linike's signature. For the 1720 reference, see the same authors' 'New Light on Handel and the Royal Academy of Music in 1720', *Theatre Journal* 35 (1983), pp. 158–61.

member of the orchestra for at least six seasons, and he almost certainly continued until the Haymarket opera closed in the summer of 1717. When the Royal Academy of Music was planning to reopen it in the spring of 1720 we find his name on a roster drawn up by the Duke of Portland on 15 February. Five salary levels appear among the thirty-four (later thirty-two) musicians listed; Linike, the senior of two violas, is placed in the fourth. His proposed salary of £40, apparently covering a total of ninety performances in two seasons, is less than he had received ten years earlier.[5] His activities of course were not confined to the theatre. During the 1711/12 season he was paid four guineas for playing at private concerts for the Duchess of Shrewsbury, the Italian wife of the Lord Chamberlain.[6] It is his receipt for this sum, dated 24 June 1712, that bears his only known signature.

The earliest reference to Linike's activities as a copyist occurs in a document written by Heidegger on 5 May 1711:[7]

Mr Collier agrees to pay to Mr Lunecan for the Copy of Rinaldo this day the sum of eight pound and three pound every day Rinaldo is playd till six and twenty pound are payd and he gives him leave to take the sayd Opera in his custody after every day of acting it till the whole six and twenty pound are payd.

Collier, the business manager at the Haymarket, was in debt to tradesmen and evidently still owed money to Linike for the score (and parts?) used at the first performance of *Rinaldo* on 24 February that year. This suggests that Linike was the regular theatre copyist at the Haymarket; he was well paid for the job. It is significant that it should have been undertaken by viola-players, who were among the lowest-paid members of the orchestra; another of them, W. Armstrong, received £9 9s 5d on 13 July 1708 for copying a score of Bononcini's *Camilla* for the Duke of Bedford.[8] The temptation to identify the score mentioned by Heidegger with RM 19.d.5 must be resisted. Both the contents of that copy and Linike's handwriting point to a later date, probably about 1716.

Confirmation that Linike was the principal Haymarket copyist comes from the theatre accounts for the 1716/17 season,[9] which record six payments totalling £17 13s 0d 'to Mr Linike for copying Musick'. For similar services 'Mr Davies' received £8 15s 6d, and 'Mr Smith' (probably yet another viola-player – not Handel's amanuensis) £1 1s 6d. Further copying bills with no recipient named amounted to £29 0s 6d; they included the score of a new opera, probably *Tito Manlio*.

Another document connects Linike closely with both Handel and Smith. The autograph of the Chandos Anthem *O be joyful in the Lord* has an inscription on the outside of the fifth gathering (RM 20.d.8, f. 120), upside down on the page: 'For

---

5 Milhous and Hume, in *Theatre Journal* 35 (1983), based on Portland Papers on deposit in Nottingham University Library.

6 This document is wrongly dated in Milhous and Hume, *Coke's Theatrical Papers*, pp. 191–3; it cannot refer to the 1712/13 season, because one of the singers listed was then no longer in London.

7 Milhous and Hume, *Coke's Theatrical Papers*, p. 176; also (less accurately) in Deutsch *Doc* p. 40.

8 Gladys S. Thomson, *The Russells in Bloomsbury* (London, 1940), p. 129.

9 In the Hampshire Record Office; I owe this reference to Lowell Lindgren. See also S. Rosenfeld, 'An Opera House Account Book', *Theatre Notebook* 16 (1962), pp. 83–8.

Mr Smith to be left att Mr Linikey's att ye White Hart in ye Hay Market with Speed'. This anthem was probably composed in September 1717. Although the sentence is not in Handel's writing, it seems likely that the message concerns the copying of the score soon after composition; and the form of words suggests that Smith in his secretarial capacity was to give it to Linike to copy. This agrees with other evidence that Smith was not yet acting as Handel's copyist. As we shall see, there are grounds for supposing that he embarked on this service under Linike's supervision.

Linike's name occurs in several press announcements quoted in *The London Stage*.[10] It was customary for leading singers and instrumental players to enjoy benefit concerts, usually in the spring of the year; the receipts, after payment of expenses, went to the beneficiary. Benefits were announced for 'Lenniker' at Hickford's Room on 3 May 1717, for 'Leneker and Mrs Smith' (wife of John Christopher?) at the same place on 18 February 1719, for 'Linike' at the New Haymarket Theatre on 27 March 1724, and for 'the Widow Linike' at Hickford's on 16 March 1726. Linike presumably died during the winter of 1725–6. The programmes consisted of vocal and instrumental music, 'by the best Hands in the Opera' in 1717. Some of Linike's orchestral colleagues are named in the bills: Matthew Dubourg (violin), Pietro Chaboud (German flute and bass viol) and Jean Christian Kytch (oboe). Dubourg played 'several new Solos and Concertos' for Linike in 1717 and 'a new Concerto, Compos'd by Mr Hendel' in 1719.

The Handel manuscripts copied by Linike cover the years 1712–21. Since a number of them, including the earliest and latest, are firmly dated, it is possible by tracing the development of his handwriting to supply approximate dates for the rest. Table 1 lists all those so far discovered; further research may well reveal others. The surest pointers to dating Linike copies are the C clef and the crotchet rest; the detached semiquaver is sometimes a help, though Linike occasionally reverted to his early practice in later copies. As Plates A, B and C show, his treble and bass clefs are remarkably constant throughout. The former has a fair rounded figure with a straight stem and no curl at the bottom; the latter is distinctive, with its tail curled neatly round like a seated cat. The C clef, on the other hand, passes through three distinct phases. In the earliest copies up to and including no. 9 it is of a 'comfortable armchair' type, with two short horizontal lines above and two longer ones below, all more or less parallel and at right angles to the downward stems. By 1717 (nos. 10–18) it has grown more flexible, with the short lines in the upper quadrant no longer parallel and modified by an upward curl.[11] In the 1721 copy (Plate C) it is still more schematic. The crotchet rest in the earliest copies is almost a right angle made up of a horizontal and vertical line, but this soon changes to a more sloping form with a hook emerging by degrees at bottom left and progressively

10 Emmett L. Avery (ed.), *The London Stage 1660–1880* (Carbondale, Ill., 1960), vol. II: *1700–1729*.
11 Larsen's C clef type *a* (p. 263) and Clausen's top four lines (p. 269) all show Linike's hand. Larsen's *d* is RM 1.

Table 1. *Linike Copies*

date	source	work	remarks
1 Oct. 1712	RM 19.e.4	*Il pastor fido*	copied before completion of autograph
2 late Dec. 1712	Coke	*Teseo*	copied before printing of first libretto
3 (1713)	BL Add. MS 5323	Utrecht Jubilate & Te Deum	probably earliest copy
4 (1715)	Coke	*Amadigi*	earliest surviving copy
5 ?1715	Munich, private collection	*Teseo*	unfoliated; p. [1] only; rest RM1, except last two pages added later (S2 and Jennens); ex-Aylesford
6 c1715–16	BL Add. MS 16024	*Il pastor fido*	appendix RM1
7 c1716	RM 19.d.5	*Rinaldo*	much amended by Handel
8 c1716	Washington, L. of C. (Landon)	*Amadigi* arias etc.	ff. 15–38; additions by Smith (ff. 1–14, c1719) and another (a source recently acquired by the Library, not yet with call number)
9 c1716	Hamburg MA/1003	*Amadigi*	amended by Handel
10 June 1717	Malmesbury	*Teseo*	dated by Elizabeth Legh; one insertion RM1
11 c1717	Malmesbury	Ode for Queen Anne's Birthday	dated; pp. 1–100; later additions Newman, Smith and Hb1
12 1717	Hamburg MB/1570	Italian duets	dated 1717 and 1718 (i.e. before 25 March 1718); pp. 9–12, 14–20, 76, 91–109; with *Alpha*, *Beta*, RM1 and RM4
13 1717/18	Malmesbury	pieces for harpsichord	pp. 18–19, 61–80, 129; with RM1; incorporated later in composite volume dated 30 August 1722
14 (1717/18)	Malmesbury	overtures etc. for harpsichord	dated; ff. 1–8, 61–121; with RM1 and *Beta*; later additions
15 1718	Bodleian MS Mus d 61	Italian cantatas	ff. 1–40, followed by one cantata in later hand
16 c1718–19	BL Add. MS 31574	Italian cantatas	ff. 1–76; with RM1
17 c1719	Bodleian Tenbury 881	Chandos Anthems: *As pants the hart* and *Sing unto the Lord*	
18 c1719	Hereford Cathedral Lib. R.X.XVI	Chandos Anthems: *Have mercy on me* and *O be joyful*	
19 6 June 1721	Berlin Amalienbibliothek 439b	*Muzio Scevola* (without recits.)	dated by copyist at end

Plate A. Linike's handwriting, October 1712: *Il pastor fido* (BL MS RM 19.e.4, f. 71ʹ)

Plate B. Linike's handwriting, June 1717: *Teseo* (Malmesbury MS)

Plate C. Linike's handwriting, June 1721: *Muzio Scevola* (SPK MS Am. B. 439b)

lengthening. There are signs of this in nos. 4 and 5; it becomes more pronounced from no. 6 onwards, but reverts towards its original slope and a smaller size in no. 19. The semiquaver in nos. 1 to 4 is as *a* below; from 1716 it becomes *b* or *c*, but

occasional examples of *a* occur as late as no. 16 and even no. 19. Linike's notes are always clear; so as a rule are his words, which have a forward slant and a certain resemblance to Smith's. However, identification of copyists by their verbal texts needs to be approached with caution, for two reasons: many of them wrote a very similar cursive hand, and in a fair number of manuscripts music and words were the work of different scribes. The calligraphic Act and Scene headings usual in opera full scores are so similar as to suggest that they either were written by the same man (regardless of who did the bulk of the music copying) or were expected to conform to a prescribed pattern.

As already mentioned, Larsen established the existence of a Smith circle of

84

copyists during the 1730s, with S1 and S2 taking a leading part, aided on occasion by S3 and S4. This is fully confirmed by evidence unknown to Larsen, with the proviso that S2 was working from about 1722/3 and S1 probably by 1728. The manuscripts newly studied reveal that there were at least two earlier circles, one (c1715–19) based on Linike and another (c1720–5) based on Smith. During this second period, the early Royal Academy years, there was evidently a great demand for copies and heavy pressure on the scriptorium, with the result that a surprisingly large number of manuscripts show the work of three, four or even five different hands. They collaborated in various ways. Sometimes they took an act each; sometimes one would break off in the middle of a page and another would carry on. Occasionally the changeover was so frequent, no doubt when pressure was greatest, as to suggest that a second copyist had to take up his pen however briefly when the first for whatever purpose left the room.

The activities of the Linike circle are most clearly observed in the volumes copied for Elizabeth Legh, which include two now in the Bodleian (MSS Mus d 61 and 62). A volume of harpsichord pieces in the Malmesbury collection, dated 1718 on the title-page but inscribed by the owner 'Elizabeth Legh her book 1717' (presumably Old Style, i.e. up to 25 March 1718), shows five copyists in action: *Alpha*, Linike, *Beta*, RM1 and RM4. *Alpha* wrote only the first seven pages (p. 8 is blank) and may not have been a member of the circle; I have not found his writing elsewhere. The other four worked closely together, taking turns; each on occasion filled the verso of a leaf whose recto shows the hand of one of the others. Another harpsichord volume in the same collection, mostly arrangements of overtures and instrumental pieces from the operas, is inscribed 'Eliza: Legh August yᵉ 30, 1722'. That date however is misleading. The core of the volume – pp. 1–10, 17–80 and 121–30, of which 10, 17 and 130 are blank – belongs to 1717–18; this is confirmed by the paper, the rastra and the copyists.[12] In the summer of 1722 Elizabeth Legh evidently had these pages bound up with more than 150 others, of which the majority carried freshly copied music but about 45 were left blank; these in due course were filled with music written on three subsequent occasion, in 1724, 1726 and 1727, the volume being returned each time to the scriptorium. The original 1717–18 section was copied by RM1 and Linike in conjunction. They shared a series of instrumental excerpts from *Rinaldo* (others were added in 1722 by H1 and Smith on the inserted pp. 11–16) and the overture to *Agrippina*, mangled as *Argripini ed Nerone*. RM1 contributed the overtures to *Teseo, Il pastor fido* and *Amadigi* and two sinfonias from the last opera, Linike the concerti grossi Op. III No. 4 (also known as the second overture in *Amadigi*) and Op. III No. 2. Bodleian MS Mus d 61, a volume of Italian cantatas (some unpublished) dated 1718, likewise shows Linike, RM1 and *Beta* working together, and has later additions at the end.

The three copyists (apart from *Alpha*) associated with Linike in these

---

12 I am grateful to Terence Best for help with the paper and rastra, and for much stimulating discussion of all the problems involved.

Plate D. Hand RM4, c1717/18: *Amadigi* (BL Add. MS 47848, f. 38)

manuscripts of about 1718 all occur elsewhere: see Tables 2, 3 and 4. RM4 (c1717–21) has a neat and regular hand with little variation in clefs, notes or words (he was evidently hurried when he copied the few pages from *Muzio Scevola*); his bass clef is individual, his C clef not unlike Handel's (Plate D). Although his copies are not numerous, three of them are of substantial works in complete volumes. The other two copyists are decidedly eccentric. *Beta*'s peculiar hand, with a dejected C clef of geriatric aspect (Plate E), is found in four manuscripts, none of them devoted to a single work and all of about the same date. The two RM volumes are composites assembled years later from copies of various periods; the paper and rastra of *Beta*'s contributions suggest a date about 1717 or a little earlier.

RM1 was much more actively associated with Linike and Handel (and later with Smith and others); he appears in two dozen manuscripts covering the years 1713(?) to 1725, and worked alone and in collaboration. His hand is so erratic as to suggest at first glance the work of several different men, but a comparative study of the large amount of material available leaves no doubt that we are dealing with a single individual, albeit a graphological freak (Plates F, G and H). All three clefs are subject to extremes of irregularity, depending perhaps on the speed with which he

Plate E. Hand *Beta*, 1718: Italian cantata (Bodleian MS Mus d 61, p. 169)

wrote; he often gives the impression of being in a tearing hurry. If the general appearance of his copies is untidy, with casually written key signatures and ill-formed words, the notes at least are legible. The crotchet and quaver rests are small and uneven. When he tries hard he can be reasonably neat, for example at the start of long jobs like the Manchester *Amadigi* and the RM *Teseo*; but the cloven hoof begins to show before long. After he has been copying for a time his clefs begin to run amok, the downward stroke of the treble sometimes completely missing the lower loop and the C clef describing all manner of contortions. He even supplies different clefs for more than one system with a single stroke of the pen. His bass clef nearly always has a somewhat hunchbacked appearance, and is peculiar in other respects. Nothing is predictable about the placing or even the presence of the two dots of the F clef; in a key with one flat they can appear before the flat or after it or be missing altogether, and all three forms are found on the same page (Plate H). A

Table 2. RM4 Copies

date	source	work	remarks
1 ?1717	Coke	*Rinaldo*, 4 arias	for 1717 revival
2 c1717	RM 19.d.3	*Brockes Passion*	
3 1717/18	Malmesbury	pieces for harpsichord	pp. 110–57 and 4 unnumbered; see Linike copy 13
4 c1717–18	BL Add. MS 47848	*Amadigi*	
5 1718	Malmesbury	Utrecht Jubilate & Te Deum	dated by Elizabeth Legh
6 (1721)	RM 19.c.8	*Muzio Scevola*	ff. 1–9 (Amadei); with RM1, H2 and another

Table 3. *Beta* Copies

date	source	work	remarks
1 c1717	RM 18.b.8	pieces for harpsichord	ff. 1–4, 33–57 of composite volume
2 c1717	RM 18.b.4	sonata for 2 keyboards	ff. 12–20 of composite volume
3 1717/18	Malmesbury	pieces for harpsichord	pp. 13, 158–96; see Linike copy 13
4 1718	Bodleian MS Mus d 61	Italian cantatas	pp. 156–258; see Linike copy 15

Table 4. RM1 Copies

date	source	work	remarks
1 ?1713	RM 19.e.6	*Teseo*	amended by Handel; ? used in performance
2 ?1715	Munich, private collection	*Teseo*	unfoliated; for p. [1] and later addendum see Linike copy 5
3 c1716	Manchester MS 130 Hd4 v.46	*Amadigi*	
4 ?1716	BL Add. MS 16024	*Il pastor fido*	
5 c1716–17	Washington L. of C. (Littleton)	*Amadigi*	appendix (ff. 94–104) to Linike copy 9

No.	Date	Location	Work	Notes
6	1717	Malmesbury	*Teseo*	insertion (pp. 221–3) in Linike copy 10
7	c1717	Boston Museum of Fine Arts (Edwin M. Ripin MS)	pieces for harpsichord	pp. 1–103; later additions by S1, Smith and others
8	1717/18	Malmesbury	pieces for harpsichord	pp. 21–75, 77–90; see Linike copy 13
9	(1717/18)	Malmesbury	overtures etc. for harpsichord	pp. 1–9, 21–59, 121–8; see Linike copy 14
10	1718	Bodleian MS Mus d 61	Italian cantatas	pp. 9–60, 122–55; see Linike copy 15
11	1718/19	Malmesbury	*Acis and Galatea*	dated 1718 (? Old Style); pp. 1 – part of 60 (rest Smith)
12	March 1719	Malmesbury	Te Deum in B flat	dated 25 March 1719; p. 1 only (rest Smith)
13	c1719	Bodleian Tenbury 881	Chandos Anthem: *I will magnify thee*	ff. 77–119; see Linike copy 17
14	c1719	Bodleian Tenbury 882	Chandos Anthems: *Let God arise*, *My song shall be alway*, *O come let us sing*	ff. 1–56 recto, 93–146; last two anthems partly Smith
15	c1719	Bodleian Tenbury 883	Chandos Anthem: *The Lord is my light*	no foliation: two other anthems Smith
16		RM 19.e.7	Chandos Anthem: *O praise the Lord with one consent*	ff. 1–47 of composite volume
17		Coke	*Amadigi*, second copy	overture only; rest later
18	(1720)	BL Add. MS 31562	*Radamisto* (without recits.)	ff. 44 verso–81, 107 verso–113 (clefs only); rest Smith and another
19	(1720)	Fitzwilliam MS Mus 72	*Radamisto*	no foliation, part of Acts II and III, rest Smith and another; later additions S2 and one more
20	?1720/1	RM 19.d.12	aria from Bononcini's *Astarto*	pp. 66–8 of composite volume
21	(Apr. 1721)	Tokyo, Nanki Library	*Muzio Scevola* (incomplete)	last two movements of Act I overture (Amadei), 3 pages; with H2, H1 and another
22	(1721)	RM 19.c.8	*Muzio Scevola*	ff. 43–7 recto (Amadei); see RM4 copy 6
23	c1722	DSB Mus MS 9042	*Acis and Galatea*	ff. 1–26;[a] rest Smith
24	mid-1720s	Malmesbury	*Rinaldo*	second appendix (pp. 357–89); rest Smith and S2
25	(1725)	RM 19.c.7	*Giulio Cesare*	with 1725 additions at end

[a] Illustrated as Kp4 by Wolfram Windszus, *Aci, Galatea e Polifemo*, diss., University of Erlangen (Hamburg, 1979), p. 143.

Plate F. Hand RM1, ?1713: *Teseo* (BL MS RM 19.e.6, f. 74ʹ)

Plate G. Hand RM1, c1719: Chandos Anthem 5A (Bodleian MS Tenbury 881, p. 101)

Plate H. Hand RM1, 1725: *Giulio Cesare* (BL MS RM 19.c.7, f. 67)

few extra examples will serve to illustrate some of the wilder fantasies of this Protean clefomaniac.

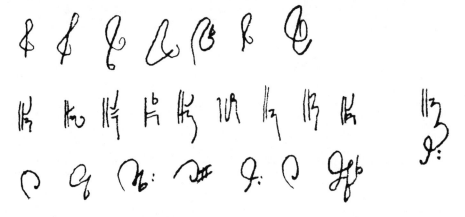

A feature of some RM1 copies is his placing of the clef at the very beginning of the staff, or even partly in the margin, where it is apt to be cut off by the brace (Plate G). That he was closely associated with Handel there can be no doubt. RM 19.e.6 has a number of annotations and corrections by the composer, and may have been used in the 1713 performances of *Teseo*. RM1's career continued throughout the

Linike and first Smith periods. The gyrations of his hand make it of little use for dating, but the music he copied generally supplies a limit.

One more early copyist, Thomas Newman, demands a mention. Again Elizabeth Legh identifies him, writing on the title-page of the Malmesbury score of *Il pastor fido*: 'Transcribed by Mr Newman Feb^r 1715' (this may be 1716 New Style). Newman also copied the Malmesbury *Amadigi* (dated 1716 by Elizabeth Legh), a keyboard fugue in E minor in DSB Mus MS 9171 ('Fuga di Sr Hendel 1717'), and two Italian duets in Hamburg MB/1570. His writing is neat and clear, with a small 'armchair' C clef and a very distinctive crotchet rest (Plate I). Although no document connects Newman with Linike, the fact that he copied two complete operas for Elizabeth Legh places him close to the source of supply. We know a little about his career. He was a theatrical prompter, listed in *The London Stage* as attached to Drury Lane in the seasons 1702/3, 1704/5, 1707-9 and 1710-14, and to the Haymarket in 1706/7 and 1709/10. He may have worked at the Haymarket in 1705/6 as well, for the Lord Chamberlain's papers at the Public Record Office contain a complaint from Christopher Rich, dated 9 December 1705, accusing Vanbrugh of trying to entice Newman away from Drury Lane, where Rich was the notoriously unpopular and stingy manager.[13] Several of Newman's copying bills survive in the Folger Shakespeare Library (Washington), the Pierpont Morgan Library (New York),[14] and the British Library (Egerton MS 2159 f. 36), the last with a letter complaining about tardy payment. They all date from about 1713-15; they are not concerned with music, but the hand appears to be the same as in the scores.

It remains to discover when and how Smith entered the picture. The earliest identifiable copy with his hand is the Malmesbury *Acis and Galatea*,[15] described on the title-page as 'An English Opera Composed by George Frederick Handel Esquire, London, Anno 1718' and by the owner 'Elizabeth Legh her Book 1718' (again this could mean early 1719 New Style). Smith took over from RM1 after the top system on p. 60 and copied till the end of the work (p. 259). A score of the B flat Te Deum in the same collection, dated 25 March 1719, shows Smith again collaborating with RM1. Here RM1 wrote the first page only and Smith the rest. This suggests that he was learning his business, RM1 giving him a start. Smith himself followed the same procedure later, for example in the Bodleian *Giulio Cesare* (MS Mus d 220, c1725), where Smith began and three other copyists continued, and the Malmesbury *Brockes Passion* (probably late 1720s), where Smith wrote the first page and S1 the remainder.

If Tenbury MSS 881-3 (nine Chandos Anthems; now in the Bodleian) were all copied at the same time, which seems overwhelmingly probable, we find Smith

13 Allardyce Nicoll, *A History of English Drama 1660-1900*, 6 vols. (Cambridge, 1952-9), II, p. 289.
14 I am indebted to Judith Milhous for photocopies of the bills in American libraries.
15 This score confirms an earlier conjecture that Handel composed the work for only five singers. Each choral part bears the name of a character: 'Canto' = Galatea; 'Basso' = Polypheme; Tenors 1, 2 and 3 = Acis, Damon and Coridon respectively. 'Would you gain the tender creature?' is for 'Coridon. 3 Tenor'.

Plate I. Newman's handwriting, February 1715 (O.S.?): *Il pastor fido* (Malmesbury MS)

working with Linike and RM1. Two of the anthems in MS 882 are divided between RM1 and Smith. The date is probably 1719. It is worth noting that these three Tenbury manuscripts and Hereford Cathedral MS R.X.XVI of about the same date give the complete series of Chandos anthems without duplication. Tenbury MS 884 ('Opera of Amadis & Other Songs'), an *Acis and Galatea* in the Coke collection, a fragment of Act I of *Agrippina* in RM 19.d.12 (ff. 1–17), a duet from *Amadigi* in BL Add. MS 31571 (ff. 1–10), and the first fourteen leaves in the Washington Landon songs from *Amadigi* (see Table 1) – all the unaided work of Smith – belong to the same period and probably the same year. At least four copies show Smith's work in 1720: in Bodleian MS Mus d 62 (Italian cantatas, dated) he collaborates with H1 and S2, the earliest known appearance of either (S2's contribution may be a rather later addition); in the Malmesbury *Radamisto*, likewise dated, he takes turns with another newcomer, *Gamma*; in Fitzwilliam Mus MS 72 (*Radamisto*, datable from internal evidence) he works with RM1 and yet another, *Delta*; towards the end of that year he writes the performing score for Handel's first revival of the same opera[16] on 28 December (Hamburg MA/1043). He probably copied the whole of it, though this cannot be proved owing to the removal of many pages at subsequent revivals.

In all these pre-1721 copies Smith's hand shows certain individual features. His treble clef, taller, narrower and usually more sloping than Linike's, lacks the characteristic little tail at the bottom of the stem familiar throughout his later work. We can actually watch him starting to develop this appendage in BL Add. MS 16108, a *Muzio Scevola* copy (containing several hands, like most copies of this opera) dating mostly from about April 1721, and in the keyboard volume Drexel MS 5856 in New York Public Library. Occasionally, for example on some pages of Tenbury 884 and Washington Landon, Smith's C clef is close to the second state of Linike's, that in use from about 1717 (Plate B), though more often it approximates to its later shape. Most remarkable however is the bass clef, which is found in two totally different and unrelated forms in the same manuscripts and often on the same page (Plate J). One is virtually identical with Linike's; the other is the common type used by Smith himself later and by most other copyists of the time. The choice of one or the other is purely arbitrary. The Linike type, through always outnumbered, occurs sporadically throughout the 1719 copies, notably the Malmesbury and Coke scores of *Acis and Galatea* and the Tenbury *Amadigi*. There are, for example, twenty-eight instances in the 200 pages of the Malmesbury *Acis and Galatea* written by Smith, and seven in the seventeen folios of the *Agrippina* fragment in RM 19.d.12. In 1720 it begins to die out. Two specimens appear suddenly on p. 41 of the Malmesbury *Radamisto*, just before Smith gives way to *Gamma*; six in the Fitzwilliam *Radamisto*; nine (five in one aria) in the December performing score of that opera; five (four in one aria) in the Hamburg *Floridante*

---

16 The original performing score used in April 1720 is lost, and the first version of the opera has never been published. Chrysander's first version reflects Hamburg MA/1044, copied by H1 after December 1720.

Plate J. Smith's handwriting, c1719, showing both types of bass clef: *Amadigi* (Bodleian MS Tenbury 884, p. 100)

(1721); three in Drexel MS 5856; none in the Smith sections of Bodleian MS Mus d 62. Single isolated specimens occur in the Hamburg scores of *Ottone* (Act III only) and *Flavio*, and in the Malmesbury copies of the same operas (1724 and 1723 respectively). The last three were partly copied by others.

What conclusions can we draw from this? First, that Smith, who was not originally a copyist or even a musician (or of course an Englishman; several of these early copies contain jottings by him in German), was enlisted in the Linike circle about the end of 1718. He was already Handel's friend and trusted secretary, and by 1720 was concerned in a music shop in Coventry Street off the Haymarket.[17] It was becoming apparent that Handel's large output and the growing demand for copies, both for performance and for sale to patrons (accentuated by the failure of Walsh or any other publisher to print anything more than a few truncated arias in the nine years between *Rinaldo* and *Radamisto*), required the services of more and more scribes. Although there was no opera between 1717 and 1720, Linike was doubtless busy playing in concerts; in any case, like Smith later, he could not carry the full load of work. My second conclusion is that Smith, perhaps at Handel's suggestion, learned the copyist's trade under the guidance or tuition of Linike, whose idiosyncrasies in such matters as clef-formation he would naturally begin by imitating. His musical hand soon developed greater assurance and characteristics of its own. By 1720 he was ready to succeed Linike in command of Handel's scriptorium, a position he occupied until his death in 1763. We may be thankful that he modelled his style on Linike and not on RM1.

17 He and Richard Meares issued the first volume of Handel's *Suites* for harpsichord and the score of *Radamisto* in November and December that year.

The 'Dotted Style' in Bach, Handel, and Scarlatti

DAVID FULLER

(State University of New York at Buffalo)

It must be said at the outset that this is not yet another article about overdotting. The reader, exasperated by twenty years' controversy on that subject, may well ask what more could usefully be written. The concern here is rather with persistent dotting considered as a rhythmic genre. Although for simplicity's sake the title speaks of 'the dotted style' in the singular, persistent dotting characterizes many styles, even in Bach, Handel, and Scarlatti, to say nothing of Allegri, Haydn, and Meyerbeer.

Our purpose is to explore informally some of the relationships among these styles, with a view to forming hypotheses about what persistent dotting meant to the three composers of 1685. Since their contemporaries and immediate forebears occasionally labeled dotted movements *alla francese* or *in stil francese*, the question arises whether all persistent dotting in the late Baroque period was felt to be French. And if so, then did Bach, Handel, Scarlatti, and their countrymen distinguish persistent, uninterrupted dotting from, on the one side, the more varied rhythms of French overture style and from, on the other, the dotted effects produced by performers' un-equalizing of equally notated values (either for expressive purposes or to agree with triplets)? No composer of stature in the early eighteenth century can possibly have been anything but thoroughly familiar with the French overture and its varieties, or with the practice of altering even notes to fit with triplets in order to avoid the effect of 'two against three', which was not only difficult to play but was sometimes considered undesirable. But it is far from clear how much non-French musicians knew about the conventional, and to a large extent codified, dotting in performance of evenly written passages that we now loosely call *notes inégales*. Ultimately, these researches will have a bearing on the knotty question whether Bach, Handel, and Scarlatti ever failed to write out dotting when they wanted it; here, however, our attention will be directed to written dotting. Even this is not without its ambiguities and problems of interpretation, as we shall see, but our purpose is to argue questions not of performance but of rhythmic style in composition.

99

DAVID FULLER
The 'Dotted Style'

Bach's *Art of Fugue* furnishes us with a paradigm of our stylistic problem – and indeed, this investigation grew out of the author's attempt to ascertain, by learning to play *Contrapunctus* 6 (*in Stylo Francese*) in various ways, whether any alteration of the written values was needed or even plausible. I must thank Peter Williams for pointing out to me that much of the dotting and the little *tirades* of thirty-second notes that give this piece its air of a French overture were additions in the manuscript to an originally simpler rhythmic state; and I am indebted to Christoph Wolff for suggesting that the purpose of the changes seems to have been to improve the harmony. The latter's researches also point strongly to the conclusion that although the heading 'in French style' appears only in the posthumous engraving, Bach himself was responsible for it.[1] One can imagine Bach conceiving the happy solution to contrapuntal problems of overlaying his fugue with the character of an overture, and then adding a justification *post facto* as if he wished to convey the impression that that had been his idea all along.

Contrapunctus 2 (no. 3 in the fair-copy score, DSB P 200) is very different. From bar 4 to the final chord eighty bars later, the alternation of dotted eighths with sixteenths is never interrupted, nor is it ever overlaid with other values that would fill the pauses on the dotted notes, as happens so often in *Contrapunctus* 6. This is what we might call the 'pure' dotted style, dotting in its most straightforward form. There is no heading to point out a French connection; what was Bach thinking of? Jig rhythm (e.g. alternating quarters and eights in 6/8 time)? A gentle lilt? A literal reading? The relentless jerking that would be produced by consistent overdotting?

The three-part mirror fugues and their arrangement for two keyboard instruments with an added free voice present us with a whole packet of problems. The subject of the fugues (or rather of one fugal 'substance' manifesting itself in four fugues) consists mostly of triplets, but much of the rhythm in the body is dotted. In the three-part originals, which are notated in 2/4 time in the manuscript, and in **C** (with note-values doubled) in the print, the quadruple division of the beat is almost uniformly dotted throughout, while in the duet arrangements dotting is abandoned for extended passages of 'straight' sixteenths.[2] In the originals, these passages (here dotted) have no triplets against them in another voice, so that pure dotted rhythm reigns for considerable spaces (passages of eight, four, six, and eight bars). All are episodes based on the tail of the subject, and that tail consists of a bar of dotted figures in the originals and of even notes in the arrangements; thus there is perfect logic in the alteration of the dotted episodes to undotted ones in the duets. But the added free voice of the duets introduces triplets against the even notes of the episodes. Thus these fugues present us with a compendium of conflicts between

1 C. Wolff and others, 'Bach's 'Art of the Fugue': An Examination of the Sources', *Current Musicology* 19 (1975), p. 45
2 'Straight eighths' in the terminology of modern American jazz musicians is the exact equivalent of the eighteenth-century French *croches égales*, that is, a call for undotted execution where dotted execution might be expected.

100

triplets, dotted figures, and even values – sometimes more than one conflict at a time. Ex. 1 shows the subject with its dotted and straight tail and a passage (Ex. 1c) from the body of the duet version of the *rectus* fugue (the reader should be

Ex. 1

a Subject of three-part mirror fugue, *rectus* (as in P 200)

b Subject of duet arrangement of same fugue

c Passage from episode of duet arrangement (the first half of bar 46 shows considerable hesitancy in rhythmic notation in the various sources of both *rectus* and *inversus*, *a 3* and *a 4*)

reminded that although each three-voice fugue is a literal inversion of the other, the free fourth voice in the duets does not invert and is different in *rectus* and *inversus*; moreover, it migrates from one hand to another of the two players, wherever there is room or need for it).

Many of these conflicts are matters of interpretation that do not directly concern us, but the general question of whether dotting in a context of triplets constitutes the 'dotted style' is important in determining how wide our net must be cast, since a very substantial repertory of music, from the late seventeenth century to the early nineteenth, uses dotting as a way of notating rhythms meant to coincide with the first and last notes of ternary groups. Not every contemporary of our three composers was in agreement how to play dotted notes against ternary groups, nor is there any reason to believe that any single composer was always consistent in the matter. It can be proved by reference to instances of single note-heads whose stems run both to triplet-beams and to the short notes of dotted figures, that Bach some-

101

times assimilated dotted to triplet rhythm (or the other way around; see note 5). But J. F. Agricola is our witness that Bach also taught his students to distinguish between simultaneous dotted and ternary rhythms by playing the short note of the dotted figure after the last note of the triplet unless the music was very lively.[3] If this rule always held in Bach's music, then the triplets of the mirror fugues would not exclude them from the 'dotted style', since true dotted rhythm would be preserved. But since it manifestly does not hold everywhere, it cannot help us much with the classification of these pieces.

It can be argued that in this case the dotted figures were meant to be assimilated to the ternary motion. In the duet versions Bach seems to have made a rule for himself that the even rhythm of the tail of the subject was to prevail so long as neither of the other two fugal voices had triplets, but that it would give way to dotted figures under the influence of triplets in another fugal voice. The passage in the first player's left hand does yield in this manner – though half a bar late – and alters the rhythm in a sequence to do so, as can be seen in Ex. 1c. If the dotting were not to coincide with the triplets anyway, there would be no particular reason to introduce it in such a disruptive way. What is particularly odd, however, is that the triplets contributed by the free fourth voice come and go without effect on 'straight' notes against them.[4] If we are correct about the ternary meaning of the dotted figures, then we can hardly avoid the conclusion that two-against-three conflicts must exist between the 'straight' notes and the triplets of the free voice, and that fact, as well as the predominance of triplet rhythm assured by the added voice, would exclude the duets from consideration as examples of the 'dotted style'.

There are many instances scattered throughout late Baroque music, but particularly in arias, where the 'dotted style' seems to be comfortably established, only to be cast into question by the appearance of triplets later on, often in vocal divisions (melismas). As one example for dozens, we may cite Narciso's air 'Spererò poichè mel dice quel bel labro' from Act II Sc. 16 of Handel's *Agrippina* (1709), in which the continuo is dotted throughout but the voice introduces a passage of triplets. In view of the gentle nature of the text, one is tempted to assume that all the dotting should be softened to triplet rhythm. But though ternary rhythm may modify the written dotting, the predominant motion is alternating long and short values notated as dotted figures, not ternary groups of notes. A much more equivocal example is 'In mille dolci modi' from Act II Sc. 13 of *Sosarme* (1732). The *HG* score shows few bars of continuous dotting, the little that is established in the ritornello

3 *Allgemeine deutsche Bibliothek*, 1769, III p. 757, and 1775, III p. 810. Agricola is protesting the abandonment of such meters as the 18/16 of Bach's *Goldberg Variation* 26, against which, if he is to be believed, the dotted-eighth-sixteenth figures in 3/4 time in the other hand should be played as written (Agricola does not, however, mention this piece). His point is that the object of writing dotted figures against triplets in duple meter is to preserve a distinction between that kind of rhythmic clash and the smooth coordination of alternating quarters and eighths against continuous eighths in 3/8 time (or some multiple). He refers to the 'ältern französischen Clavierspieler' ('older French keyboard-players') as well as to J. S. Bach in support of his view.

4 In the first half of bar 40, *rectus* has dots, while *inversus* has 'straight' eighths against a fugal voice in triplets. If our inference is correct, then the error is in the *inversus*, which should be dotted.

being softened to triplets upon the singer's repetition of the same material (see Ex. 2a–c). But what if all those triplets were to be assimilated to the duple division of the beat, as bars 3–5 of the ritornello already have them? Another version of the same song, written out for a musical clock and thus perhaps more accurately indicating the sounding rhythm, shows such assimilation until the first extended melisma on '-rò', which remains in triplets[5] (see Ex. 2d–e). The mere presence of

Ex. 2 Handel, 'In mille dolci modi', from *Sosarme* (*HG*, and Squire, 'Handel's Clock Music' (see note 5))

a Instrumental ritornello
b, c First vocal phrase, for musical clock and for voice.
d, e Later passages, for voice with violins *obbligati* and for musical clock

triplets in a dotted piece may well have no mitigating effect on the dotting if the two rhythms are kept separate, as, for example, in the duet in *Amadigi* Act II Sc. 4.

It sometimes happens that triplets appear just at the final cadence (or at the cadence of each strain) in an otherwise dotted piece. Two of Scarlatti's sonatas illustrate what one might call these 'last-minute' triplets. In Kk 238, they appear in the first strain after nineteen bars of almost continuous dotting, and in the second

5 W. Barclay Squire, 'Handel's Clock Music', *MQ* 5 (1919), p. 544. On the question of the assimilation of triplets to duple meter, see M. Collins, 'The Performance of Triplets in the 17th and 18th Centuries', *JAMS* 19 (1966), p. 281.

after fifteen (the final seven bars are repeated and a codetta of three bars is appended, so that the cadential triplets are heard three times in the second strain). Ex. 3 shows how they are introduced, and incidentally provides good and typical

Ex. 3 D. Scarlatti, Sonata Kk 238 after Parma MS (facs. *Complete Keyboard Works*, ed. R. Kirkpatrick, vol. 9 (New York, 1972))

reason to distrust details of dotting in eighteenth-century scores (the alignment of notes is as it is in the Parma manuscript, which is reproduced in the facsimile edition). In Kk 256, the dotting is less continuous, but the triplets (in a melodic formula very similar to that in Kk 238) are delayed further, not appearing until the final bars of the second strain. Should these triplets throw all the dotting into soft focus? Or are they meant as a rhythmic contrast to a prevailing dotted vigor? One is reminded of the Allemande in Rameau's A minor harpsichord suite of c1728, which moves mainly in sixteenths until the codetta of each strain, whereupon it breaks into a *batterie* of triplets. Many harpsichordists find these a justification for unequalizing the sixteenths throughout the piece, producing *notes inégales* (a liberty that they are usually too timid to apply without such an excuse). But triplets or no triplets, real *notes inégales* are demanded in Rameau's allemande, if dozens of French theorists are to be believed. What we shall probably never know is *how* unequal they should be according to *le bon goût*, and thus how aggressive, how 'dotted'-sounding.

I would not claim that Scarlatti's triplet closes were copied from Rameau; the formula he uses is a common one of the *galant* style. But these sonatas, along with Bach's *Art of Fugue* and Handel's airs, bring up the question of the relationship between what is called here the 'dotted style' and the French convention of inequality. Inequality is usually defined as the alteration in performance of evenly written notes to long–short pairs, but, as I have tried to explain in the article 'Notes inégales' in *The New Grove*, it is rather a matter of rhythmic style, notated or not. French inequality is often written out in dotted figures, and there is no need to adduce unwritten *notes inégales* to supply a comparison with the 'dotted style'. Furthermore, contrary to what is now often said, French inequality ran the gamut from barely perceptible to extremely dotted.[6]

Unnotated inequality cannot in any case be counted as part of the 'dotted style' as discussed here because it is a style of playing, not of composition, even though the composer might have relied on it. French written dotting, though it may differ not at all in sound or theory, can be so counted. There is not a great deal of this written dotting because not much was needed, and it may well be that the greater part is contained in Nicolas Gigault's extraordinary *Livre de musique pour l'orgue*, published in the birthyear of Bach, Handel, and Scarlatti. Its 180 shortish pieces contain enough dots to have supplied all Europe, and the composer in his preface invites the player to add yet more 'pour animer son jeu plus ou moins'. In some, the dotting continues almost without interruption in both hands from beginning to end, and not more than a handful are without substantial passages of dotting (Ex. 4). Yet none of his fugues is more obsessively dotted than *Contrapunctus* 2. If the

Ex. 4 N. Gigault, *Fugue à 2 du 3e et 4e ton* (*Archives des maîtres de l'orgue*, vol. 4 (Paris, 1902), p. 119)

treatise cited in note 6 is to be believed, the dotting in the example should be very sharp. Nothing in sound or sight distinguishes it from the most extreme of foreign 'dotted styles'. There are other examples, doubtless milder; we need go no further than François Couperin, whose 'Terpsichore', 'Olympique', 'Mézangère', 'Invalides', 'Attendrissante', 'Fidélité Audacieuse' and 'Guirlandes' (part 1), to choose only pieces from the four harpsichord books, are dotted throughout.

All these are very different from French overture style. There are those who cry 'French overture' at the least sign of a dot, but if the purity of the dotted style is measured by the persistence with which it pounds away at a single rhythmic figure, then the French overture must be regarded as a special case and far from pure. First of all, it is only the first strain of an overture that we refer to when we speak of its rhythmic style. Ordinarily, that part is characterized by interruptions and variety in the dotted figures, some of which have *tirades* of different lengths after the dots, and not all of which are on the same metrical level (that is, there are apt to be dotted quarters as well as dotted eighths, and perhaps other values as well).[7] Real

---

6 'Il faut etremement [*sic*] pointer le duo car ces [*sic*] en cela ou est sa beauté' (W. Pruitt, 'Un traité d'interpretation du XVIIe siècle', *L'orgue* 152 (1974), p. 107).

7 J. O'Donnell, 'The French Style and the Overtures of Bach', *EM* 7 (1979), p. 190, makes a case for a much faster tempo in the first strains of French overtures than we are used to. This would alter considerably our perceptions of the dotting and any possible exaggeration of the rhythms.

French overtures, especially those by Lully, often look plainer than their foreign imitations, which may better reflect actual executions by the Lullian orchestra, and both French and foreign examples may diverge considerably from this model.

Contrast between the first and second strains is of the essence of an overture – at the very least, a contrast in texture, usually between florid homophony and fugato or informally imitative polyphony. Occasionally, one finds persistent dotting in the second strain, as in the overture to Handel's *Almira* (Hamburg, 1705). Perhaps Steffani's overture to *Le rivali concordi* (Hamburg, 1693) was the link between Handel and the overture to Lully's *Amadis* (1686), in both of which the second strain is similarly dotted. In any case, Handel used the same treatment in *Floridante* (1721) and elsewhere (for example, in the seventh of the eight *Suites de pièces*): see Ex. 5. This *is* the 'dotted style', and its single-minded drive is quite

Ex. 5 a Lully, *Amadis*
      b Steffani, *Le rivali concordi*
      c Handel, *Almira*
      d Handel, *Floridante*

different from the pompous effect typical of first strains. Graham Pont has found impressive evidence that in the performance of Handel's overtures, at least, such alterations to the written rhythms of the first part as were introduced in performance preserved the principle of variety and unpredictability.[8]

The question whether Bach intended the rhythms of *Contrapunctus* 6 to be similarly altered raises points not ordinarily encountered in real overtures, however. Here, the analogy of the fourth of the *canones diversi* in the *Musical Offering* (*per Augmentationem, contrario Motu*) is illuminating. In both that piece and *Contrapunctus* 6, the *tirade*-like figure of three thirty-seconds is notated strictly, the preceding eighth note being tied to the first of four thirty-seconds, while in other fugued pieces in French overture style, the *Fughetta super 'Wir glauben all an einen Gott'* (BWV 681), the fugue in the First French Suite (BWV 812), and the D major Fugue BWV 850 (*WTC* Bk 1), a simpler but inexact dotted eighth is used before the thirty-seconds. In the canon, the *tirade* is augmented (its values doubled) along with the rest of the melody, and unless the written values are strictly adhered to, the listener will be confused trying to follow the rhythmic manipulation and the counterpoint will be thrown off. The inexactness of a dotted eighth followed by three thirty-seconds invites liberty in the rendition of the rhythm. In *Contrapunctus* 6, although the *tirades* are not augmented, the subject is diminished (as well as inverted), and the careful notation of the *tirades* may be a signal that they are to be played in strict time and the dotting rendered literally. Although synchronizing all the eighths with sixteenths in other parts (thus double-dotting all the dotted quarters) eliminates much dissonance and smooths out the harmony beyond whatever improvement Bach had intended by the dotting he added, the delight of hearing the subject combined with itself exactly reproduced at different speeds is sacrificed.

Uses of the 'Dotted Style'

In vocal music, persistent dotting in the accompaniment is usually relieved in one way or another by the voice parts – the first and last sections of 'Surely he hath borne our griefs' from *Messiah* come immediately to mind. But it is also true, especially in Handel, that dotting written out for instruments may have been supplied by solo singers when unwritten, as I have suggested for 'In mille dolci modi',so that the interruptions of the dotted effect were fewer than the page implies. It is rare, however, even in accompaniments, that the dotting is not interrupted; this often happens under the influence of the text. The text also engenders imaginative uses of dotting. The most characteristic function is to depict anger or savagery of some kind, as in, for example, 'O numi tiranni' from Domenico Scarlatti's *Tetide in Sciro* (1712), with its dotted octave leaps not only in the accompaniment but for the

---

8 'French Overtures at the Keyboard: "How Handel rendered the playing of them" ', *Musicology* 6 (1980), pp. 29ff. See also the same author's 'Handels' Overtures for Harpsichord or Organ', *EM* 11 (1983), pp. 309ff.

singer, or in Bach's remarkable 'Seht, wie reisst, wie bricht, wie fällt' from Cantata 92 at the words 'Let Satan rage, storm, roar' ('Lasst Satan wüten, rasen, krachen': see Ex. 6). But one of Bach's most consistently dotted arias has the text 'Only the

Ex. 6

Laßt Sa-tan wü-ten, ra-sen, kra - - - - chen,

presence of the Most High can be the source of our joy' ('Des Höchsten Gegenwart allein Kann unsrer Freuden Ursprung sein': Cantata 194, part 2). A few triplets with dotted figures against them suggest that jig rhythm may have been intended for this aria. If dotting can express joy, it can also express sorrow (the *Trauerode* BWV 198, or 'My beloved Jesus is lost' ('Mein liebster Jesus ist verloren') in BWV 154), the toiling of the soul along the arduous road to salvation (Cantata 58), or the fear of death (Cantata 60).

One of the most extraordinary instances of heaping rhythm upon rhythm expresses the wavering of an uncertain faith in the aria 'Wie zweifelhaftig ist mein Hoffen' in Cantata 109. There is hardly a bar without rhythmic conflict, the dominant one being the simultaneous dotting of the eighth and sixteenth. But there are also triplets, even notes, short *tirades*, and quick dactyls (these last are found only in the instrumental parts, while the triplets occur only in the singer's part; possibly one figure is meant to be assimilated to the other): see Ex. 7. The complexity of this piece goes far beyond the 'dotted style', of course, yet its character is determined by dotting.

In Eurilla's aria 'Occhi belli' from *Il pastor fido* (1712) Act II Sc. 2, Handel puts dotting to yet another use, creating a delicious color by directing the violin and bass to play pizzicato (the dots are replaced here by rests) and the harpsichord *arpeggiato*. 'Io non ti chiedo più, oh sposo amato' from *Silla* (1713) Act III Sc. 2, which became 'O caro mio tesor' in *Amadigi* (1715) Act I Sc. 7, has double-dotting throughout, the second dot being replaced by a rest (in *Amadigi* the voice part is single-dotted). It is hard to see how either text justifies such rhythmic piquancy. At the furthest reach from both *Contrapunctus* 2 and 'dotting for savagery' are the seven bars of dotted undulation that precede the opening arioso from *Esther* (1732), 'Breathe soft, ye gales! Ye rills, in silence roll!' The effect, with violins *divisi a 5* accompanied by viola, harpsichord, harp, and theorbo and alternating with the wind band, is calculated to soothe even Satan's dotted rage. Handel's precedent must have been the *sommeil* scene of French opera. A much more characteristic Handelian use of dotting is the *pomposo* style – so indicated – in the introduction to the first aria and chorus of *Theodora* (1749).

Sometimes dotting can take on a frankly pictorial meaning, as in Bach's aria 'Wirf, mein Herze, wirf dich noch in des Höchstens Liebesarme' (Cantata 155), where dotted leaps hurl the Christian's heart up into God's loving arms like a clay

108

Ex. 7

pigeon from a trap. Repeated chords in dotted rhythm can be used to suggest flagel-
lation, as in the middle section of 'He was despised' (*Messiah*) at the words 'He gave
His back to the smiters', where 257 chords in unbroken dotted succession leave no
doubt what is intended.

But obsessively persistent dotting is found more often in instrumental than in
vocal music. In the case of Scarlatti's Sonata Kk 8, as published in the *Essercizi*
(1738), the dotting, wholly uninterrupted from beginning to end, even at the double
bars, and covered only by a few written-out slides, appears to have been the result
of second thoughts about the piece; a version considered by Sheveloff to be earlier
has much less dotting.[9] The difference may, however, be only a matter of notation,
since with the exception of three pairs of beamed even eighths, all dotting that can be

9 J. Sheveloff, 'The Keyboard Music of Domenico Scarlatti', Ph. D. diss, Brandeis University, 1970.
the 'earlier' version was included in Roseingrave's edition (1739) along with the 'later' one, which was
marked *allegro differente* (W. Gerstenberg, *Die Klavier-kompositionen Domenico Scarlattis*
(Regensburg, 1933), p. 31n).

Ex. 8 Sonata Kk 8

a in *XLII suites de pièces pour le clavecin*, ed. T. Roseingrave (London, 1739)

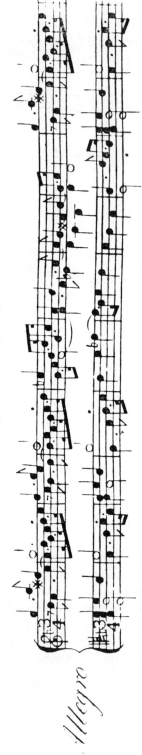

b in *Essercizi per gravicembalo* (London, 1738)

notated without recourse to double-stemming and ties is written out in the earlier version, while the rest, more troublesome to notate, may have been expected to be supplied by the player (Ex. 8). The very peculiar Kk 92 is dotted nearly as uninterruptedly as Kk 8, and its dense, mostly four-part texture seems to have come out of the same compartment of Scarlatti's creative font as Kk 8. It lacks the refinement of Kk 8 in either version, however – indeed, certain passages seem quite irrational.

In Bach's instrumental music, only the dotting of *Contrapunctus* 2 is comparably persistent, but the E flat Prelude for organ in *Clavierübung III* (the so-called 'St Anne' BWV 552.i) has ninety-seven dotted bars in its four ritornellos, in sixty-nine of which a steady dotted pattern is maintained. The dotting in the last movement of Handel's concerto grosso Op. VI No. 12 is sufficiently mixed with triplets to suggest that the whole piece should be played in jig rhythm. Dotted sixteenths are a favorite in his introductory movements; four of the Six Sonatas for two Oboes and Continuo begin this way, as well as many other works such as the sixth and eighth harpsichord suites (1720 Collection). All three of our composers used the Italian dotted *grave* in its typical function as a slow interlude in sonatas and concertos: Scarlatti in the sixth, seventh, thirteenth, and seventeenth orchestral *sinfonie* and in the sonata Kk 91 (a four-movement piece for melody instrument and continuo); Handel in his concerto grosso Op. VI No. 2, Bach (second-hand) in the Concerto for Four Harpsichords after Vivaldi (BWV 1065).

The History of the 'Dotted Style'

Dotting is as old as mensural notation, but persistent dotting as a characteristic of rhythmic style appears only in the sixteenth century, and there first as a way of enlivening diminutions in instrumental and vocal music. Since it was usually unwritten, it belongs to the history of performance. One of the earliest manifestations of written dotting sufficiently prominent to merit its being called a style is in Lorenzo Allegri's *Primo libro delle musiche* (1618), a collection of ballet suites written for entertainments at the Florentine Medici court between 1608 and 1615.[10] Several of the pieces, all in duple meter, are dotted. Thus the style was established at the beginning of the seventeenth century as a feature of dance music in an Italian court with strong French ties – in a city that would later give Lully to the world. Was it considered to be Italian or French? Occasional instances of dotted melodies can be found in French ballet music of the same time, but they are very few (we are not, of course, speaking of the ubiquitous courante and other dotted triple-time dances). The possibility that Allegri's notation reflected the French way of performing undotted music cannot be ruled out. Dotting can also be found as a feature of Italian *gorgia* and other special styles (Monteverdi's *stile concitato*), and in occasional passages of Italian string sonatas of the first half of the century – probably in imitation of vocal diminutions (a few examples can be found in Frescobaldi). But in Italy, dotting appears to be going out of fashion towards mid-

10 *Ballet Suites for String Orchestra and Basso Continuo*, ed. H. Beck (London, 1967).

century, and when it reappears it is as a conscious import from France. Beginning in the 1660s, the fashion for dances and sonatas *in stil francese* burgeoned among Italian string composers such as Uccellini, Colombi, G. M. Bonocini, G. B. Vitali, and later Albinoni.[11] This new wave coincided with the peak 'dancing years' of Louis XIV and the beginning of French cultural and political ascendancy in Europe. Roger North reports the same for England, where French musical styles cannot have been such a novelty – Charles I's queen was the sister of Louis XIII and brought her musicians with her, and English lutenists devoured French ideas. According to North, 'During the first years of Charles II all musick affected by the *beau-mond* run into the French way.'[12] Although much more was meant by *stil francese* or 'the *French way*' than dotting – it probably had as much to do with dance types and the homophonic orchestral style as with rhythm – dotting was certainly part of it, and written dotting became more and more prominent in Italian string music. The Corellian ensemble *allemanda* (Op. II and Op. IV, 1685 and 1694) is often dotted throughout, and the first two movements of the concerti grossi Op. VI Nos. 3 and 7 amount to French overtures. The second-rate sonata of doubtful attribution in the new complete Corelli edition vol. V (Cologne, 1976), pp. 86–9, has a whole movement in 'pure' dotted style.

Whether or not it was under the influence of the new frenchified dance music, arias in dotted style crept into Italian opera in increasing numbers from the 1670s on. Jacopo Melani's *Ercole in Tebe* (1661), composed for the wedding in Florence of a French princess with a Medici, already contains a *ballo* with a good deal of dotting; Melani had visited Paris in 1644.[13] An early example of almost unbroken dotting in an opera aria is Legrenzi's 'Se baciar felice amante potrò' from *Totila* (1677) Act I Sc. 19 (it may be noted that Legrenzi was also a distinguished composer of string sonatas). Airs of this kind – quite unlike anything in French opera, it should be pointed out – continued to appear: in Stradella's *Moro per amoro* (n.d.), 'Sono care quelle pene' (Act III Sc. 2); Pasquini's *L'Idalma* (1680), two arias; Steffani's *Le rivali concordi* (1693), 'Chi mi piace' (Act III Sc 13) and a few others: Albinoni's *Zenobia* (1694), two arias; Pollarolo's *Gl'inganni felici* (1696); and, above all, the operas of Alessandro Scarlatti. In a *da capo* aria in 3/4 time (*Marco Attilio Regolo*, 1719, no. 107), the *A* section, written in continuously dotted eighths, is marked *Allegro alla francese*, and the *B* section, in even eighths, is simply *Allegro*. Since there is no change in tempo, the only possible inference can be that Scarlatti (or his copyist) made an explicit connection between dotting and the French style.

We remarked earlier that only a handful of Gigault's organ pieces were quite without dotting. One of these furnishes us with a perfect counterpart to Scarlatti's aria: It is headed *Fugue du 1er ton poursuivie à la manière italienne, a 4 parties*. In fact, ten of its sixty-eight bars have traces of dotting, but for Gigault that amounts

11 W. Klenz, *Giovanni Maria Bononcini of Modena* (Durham, N.C., 1962).
12 *Roger North on Music*, ed. J. Wilson (London, 1959), pp. 185, 350.
13 These citations were made possible by the series of facsimile publications of the Garland Press: *Italian Opera, 1640–1770*, ed. H. M. Brown.

to none at all. If for Scarlatti the presence of dotting signaled French style, the lack of it signaled Italian style for Gigault.[14] It is curious that Italian dotting seems not to have penetrated keyboard music to any great extent. In the seven volumes devoted to Bernardo Pasquini in the *Corpus of Early Keyboard Music*, for example, persistent dotting is found in only one allemande (out of fifteen) and three courantes (out of twelve) – and these, perhaps, under French influence.

Dotting is not characteristic of early-seventeenth-century Germany music. More or less completely dotted strains (not usually the first) can be found here and there in the *Neue musicalische Intraden* of Melchior Franck, dated 1608 (when Allegri is supposed to have begun writing his Florentine ballet suites – it is worth noting that Allegri, who was known as 'Lorenzino todesco', may have been born a German). There is a section in true dotted style in the Capriccio no. 3 in Froberger's autograph manuscript of 1656: that is, there are twenty-six bars of eighth-note dotting in common time broken only by some *tirade*-like scales. (Froberger had visited Paris four years earlier.) Scattered through his suites are also a few more or less dotted allemandes and gigues, but these were almost certainly written under the influence of French lute music, which was copiously dotted – or, if not, apparently was played as if it had been.

The Italian fashion for French dances in the 1660s can be observed also in Austria, in the *Balletti francesi* supplied by Johann Heinrich Schmelzer for Cesti's *Nettuno e Flora* (1669). A 'Margarita' in this set is completely dotted. A gigue for Cesti's *Pomo d'oro* (1667) is notated in common time and dotted almost throughout. Other instances may be found of partial dotting. What is very likely an influence from Italian sonatas shows up in dotted introductory movements to Johann Pezel's sonatas (*Musica vespertina*, Leipzig, 1669, and *Hora Decima*, Leipzig, 1670).

The French overture, and suites of dances attached to it, came to Germany in an explosion of imitations beginning with the *Composition de musique* (1682) by J. S. Kusser (who had lived with Lully for six years) and continuing with publications by J. C. F. Fischer, Georg Muffat and a host of others. One of Fischer's overtures seems to have been modelled directly on Lully's for *Amadis*, with its vigorously dotted *reprise* (the similar ones by Steffani and Handel, both written for Hamburg, have already been mentioned). French keyboard music was well known in Germany in the late seventeenth and early eighteenth centuries; two of the suites in the manuscript transmitting those by Buxtehude are by Lebègue (Copenhagen, Kongelige Bibliotek, MS mu 6806.1399), and Bach's knowledge of De Grigny, Couperin, Le Roux, Dandrieu, Marchand and others is documented. But with the notable exception of Gigault, French dotting was usually left to the player and could be transmitted only by live performance or by the compositions of foreigners that imitated this manner of performance.

Contrapunctus 2 is so very striking and so little characteristic of Bach fugues

---

14 Gigault was probably referring to the kind of counterpoint in which the fugue was composed, but he must have felt that the lack of dotting went with it.

that it is surprising to find precedents. It seems possible that these were inspired by the fugal *reprises* of French overtures. The earliest is a fugue on the Magnificat by Pachelbel dating from not later than 1701.[15] But the connection is much more explicit in a Praeludium by Georg Böhm in the form of a French overture, found in the Möller MS (SPK Mus MS 40644, written in the first decade of the eighteenth century largely by Johann Christoph Bach). Though the reprise is not a true fugue, its appearance in a 'prelude', a common seventeenth-century designation for a multi-sectional piece containing fugues, is strongly suggestive. An extended and completely dotted formal fugue by Zachow occurs in the same MS as the last piece in a suite. Another dotted fugue is found in J. C. F. Fischer's *Ariadne musica*, one of the models for the *WTC*. There is a striking family resemblance between the subjects of these last three (see Ex. 9).

One might suppose that English virginal music, with its immense variety of figuration, would exploit dotting as well, but only the occasional passage is found. More dotting is observable in Simpson's model divisions (1659), but here as in keyboard music the dotting is no more than a survival from Renaissance diminution technique. This is in a striking contrast with later English music, which is prodigal with dots. Purcell dotted eighth notes more often than not, in 3/4 meter, obviously in imitation of French *notes inégales*. The majority of his harpsichord allemandes are dotted, as are those of many other English keyboard composers. There is no reason to doubt North's attribution of this style to French influence. For several years after the Restoration, the music at court was in the hands of French musicians, and their style must have been not only familiar but, because of its social status, highly influential. Whether the English unequalized rhythms that were written 'straight' is an open question, but that they wrote down rhythms derived from French performing style is undeniable.

It is not possible to make the same easy and rapid survey of Spanish music as of other European music. During Scarlatti's active years in Spain, the overwhelming foreign presence there was Italian. But in Spain, as elsewhere in Europe, there was a lively fashion for French dances. A dancing manual by Bartolomé Ferriol y Boxeraus, *Reglas útiles para los aficionados a danzar* (Capua, 1745),[16] has an air from Campra's *Hesione* with diminutions that are entirely dotted. Such dotting, however, is not especially characteristic of the manual as a whole.

In the eighteenth century, the dotted style gradually waned, but it never entirely disappeared. Sonatas by Marcello and Haydn (Hob. XVI/21) contain dotted movements; the style can be found in Galuppi, frequently in English keyboard music, here and there in Mozart. In the early nineteenth century, it received a new lease on life with one of the most savagely and obsessively dotted of all pieces, Beethoven's *Grosse Fuge*. Nothing in Bach, Handel, or even Gigault outdoes the dotting in the

15 For these references I am indebted to Paul Walker, who is preparing a dissertation on the German fugue before Bach.
16 Maurice Esses, 'The Impact of French Dancing on Spanish Society during the Eighteenth Century', paper delivered at the Fall 1983 meeting of the New York - St Lawrence Chapter of the American Musicological Society, University of Toronto.

Ex. 9 a Pachelbel, Fugue on the Magnificat (BL Add. MS 31221, f. 50'; *DTÖ* 17, p. 82)

b Böhm, Praeludium (SPK Mus MS 40644; *Sämtliche Werke*, rev. edn by G. Wolgast (Wiesbaden, 1952))

c Zachow, *Fuga finalis* from Suite in B minor (*Gesammelte Werke für Tasten-instrumente*, ed. H. Lohmann, Wiesbaden 1966); cf. the final fugue of Handel's Concerto Grosso Op. VI No. 12 (HWV 330.v)

d Fischer, Fugue no. 19 from *Ariadne musica* (1702), ed. E. von Werra (1901/1965)

episodes of the second movement of Schumann's C major Fantasy Op. 17, and the monotonous 6/8 of grand opera is often condensed to persistent dotting. Marches were dotted in the nineteenth century as they had been before.

The Meaning of the 'Dotted Style' for Bach, Handel, and Scarlatti

We can trace (very tentatively, to be sure, since only a fraction of the total repertory has been taken into account) certain patterns in the history of dotting. Except for processional pieces and stately dances, dotting seems to have been chiefly a matter of performance or special effect before the middle of the seventeenth century. After about 1660 and almost certainly under the influence of French performing style, persistent dotting became a widespread mannerism which was eventually channeled into certain especially receptive genres. One of these was the sonata, another the ballroom dance, another the Italian opera aria (perhaps a tributary of the sonata), another the overture. But the two halves of the overture were independent, as far as dotting was concerned, and led in different directions. The first retained its overture identity, while the second may have been the model for a few dotted fugues. The richest variety was in the aria, which used dotting for a wide range of expressive and pictorial purposes. In England, dotting must have been perceived – at least in Purcell's day – as the written rendition of French performing style. But it is unlikely that the French label would have been attached to all dotting in Italian arias, in spite of Alessandro Scarlatti's example. Rather, it must have been just another rhythmic resource, even though ultimately it might be traceable via the sonata to French inequality.

If any general perception of a national origin for dotting existed for Bach, Handel, and Scarlatti, it was probably that dotting in vocal music was Italian-international and that dotting in instrumental music was French. Cutting across this generalization must have been others concerning specific styles. Varied dotting in a homophonic texture, embellished with *tirades*, was associated with the first strain of the French overture (or perhaps simply of the overture, since the majority must have been German). The dotting of continuous, mainly conjunct eighths in 3/4 time was the written equivalent of French *notes inégales*, as Alessandro Scarlatti's heading in *Marco Attilio Regolo* acknowledged. Dotting of the eighths in gavottes and other characteristically French dances must also have been understood as written inequality. Dotting of introductory movements not in the style of the first part of a French overture was probably thought of as more Italian than anything else. This was true not only of movements in dotted eighths or quarters in the manner of many of Corelli's preludes and allemandes, but also of those in dotted sixteenths like the introductions to Handel's Sonatas for Two Oboes and many other pieces. None of Bach's sonatas begins with such a movement, but the Sinfonia to the C minor Partita BWV 826 appears to be a conscious reference to this Italianism.

To return to the *Art of Fugue*, we can be reasonably sure that Bach knew at least three precedents for his *Contrapunctus* 2, and they were all German: the fugues by

116

Fischer, Böhm, and Zachow referred to above. What differentiates *Contrapunctus* 2 most sharply from these is its subject, dictated by its place in the cycle. Bach might have perceived persistent dotting to be French in a general way, but it was not necessary for him to make the synthesis of French rhythm and German polyphony to produce the piece. *Contrapunctus* 6 was an overture (French or German), and the mirror fugues were probably not considered to be dotted at all. It is hard to believe that either Bach or Handel was much concerned about the pedigree of this or that dotted style in vocal music unless it was because some special symbolism was intended, like that in Cantata 61 for the first Sunday in Advent, where an overture suggests the beginning of the liturgical year. Otherwise, dotting was just another expressive or pictorial resource.

Scarlatti used the dotted style in his sonatas very little – but for his birthday he might not be in this essay at all – and his vocal music is difficult of access, so that generalizations are impossible. We have his father's extensive use of dotting and his acknowledgement of the connection to French style in one instance. But it is worth noting that the three most copiously dotted sonatas, Kk 8, Kk 92, and Kk 238, are all full-voiced, serious pieces with no trace of the bravura brilliance so characteristic of his style. Perhaps they recall Corelli's preludes or allemandes as much as anything. Some of Couperin's dotted allemandes are in the same vein.

What makes the dotted style interesting to write about is that it is at the same time so aggressive and so nonessential – some would say gratuitous. The 'dotted style' is not a complex of rhythmic patterns but a uniform modification of steady, patternless, motor rhythm. Except for polyphonic rarities like *Contrapunctus* 6, a piece in the true 'dotted style' can be undotted and played 'straight' with no effect on the structure or relationships of its parts. Conversely, an undotted piece in steady motion can be dotted – but why? Aside from some symbolic purpose, the ordinary reasons are to increase energy or make the piece more graceful, but the method seems somehow mechanical or cheap, and persistent dotted rhythm faintly embarrassing. One often hears musicians finding ways to soften it, if indeed they can be persuaded to play dotted pieces at all. Yet three of the greatest composers of the eighteenth century occasionally took the considerable trouble to write hundreds of extra dots and flags, and it is our job to figure out what they meant by it.

The Mietkes, the Margrave and Bach

SHERIDAN GERMANN

(Boston, Massachusetts)

The unsigned white harpsichord at Schloss Charlottenburg in Berlin stands in the center of a complicated network of relationships, each line of which is delicate in itself; but in their aggregate, these lines form a stronger pattern of relationship between Johann Sebastian Bach and an existing harpsichord than any that could be found in the past. As a musical instrument, it has received little attention until recently, though its decoration has long been praised by writers on chinoiserie. But it is an important instrument not only because of its possible connection with J. S. Bach, but because (with the very similar black harpsichord also at Charlottenburg) it fills an important gap in our knowledge about German harpsichord-building.

In trying to answer the tantalizing question of what instruments J. S. Bach preferred, some writers have urged the superior claims of the Saxon school of harpsichord-building, supported by his relationship with the organ-, piano- and harpsichord-builder Gottfried Silbermann of Freiberg, by his performance on several Silbermann pianos, and by C. P. E. Bach's love for his Silbermann clavichord.[1] Silbermann harpsichords seem to have had a greater reputation in their own time than the instruments from Hamburg (perhaps a carryover from the fame of the Silbermann organs).[2] That Bach, at the end of his life, helped Silbermann sell his pianos is well known, as is his famous encounter with Frederick the Great in 1747 at Potsdam, during which he played and approved the king's Silbermann pianos.[3]

---

1 Since C. P. E. Bach later gave the Silbermann clavichord away, we must assume he found another instrument even more to his liking; cf. Russell 1959 pp. 104–5 note 2. However, see also O. Fleischer, *Führer durch die Sammlung der Königlichen Hochschule für Musik in Berlin* (Berlin, 1882), p. 111; Hirt 1968, pp. xvi–xviii; and Ernst 1955 pp. 18 and 35–6.

2 Hubbard 1965 p. 173.

3 Hirt 1968 pp. xvi–xviii; *BR* pp. 176, 259, 305–6; A. Yorke-Long, *Music at Court: Four Eighteenth-Century Studies* (London, [1954]), pp. 131–3; and P. Williams, 'J. S. Bach's *Well-tempered Clavier*: A New Approach', part 1, *EM* 11/1 (January 1983), p. 50n, and correspondence *EM* 11/3 (July 1983), p. 419.

119

But we have no reason to think that Bach owned or played any specific harpsichord by Silbermann.[4]

Some (especially organists) have pressed the appropriateness for Bach of harpsichords of the Hamburg type, usually with emphasis on the largest and most organ-like harpsichords with 16′ stops. Raymond Russell strongly praised the quality of the Hass instruments in comparison with the more famous Silbermanns, as did Frank Hubbard albeit with musical reservations.[5] In particular, the so-called 'Bach Disposition' (with upper manual $1 \times 8'$, $1 \times 4'$ and lower manual $1 \times 16'$, $1 \times 8'$, coupler), found on a harpsichord structurally similar to the Hass/Hamburg type, had a great vogue in the first half of this century,[6] until the authenticity of the disposition was demolished by Georg Kinsky, Friedrich Ernst, Raymond Russell, and Frank Hubbard.[7] In any case, Bach was in Hamburg well before the two surviving dated 16′ Hass harpsichords were built, in 1734 and 1740, so we have no reason to think he knew such instruments. The supposed 'Bach Disposition' had given rise to a vogue for 16′ instruments which has no firm historical basis. But in recent years the pendulum has swung back in favor of the simple, classic $2 \times 8'$, $1 \times 4'$ harpsichord, with a widespread and growing conviction that the 16′ and 2′ stops usually add little to the resources of a good harpsichord and can possibly impair its resonance, muddy the tone, or obscure contrapuntal clarity with too many partials.

Since around 1950, attention has been focused – sometimes with musically illuminating results – on performing early keyboard music on the specific type of instrument each composer may be thought to have used. Restoration and copying of representative examples (especially French, Flemish and Italian) has proceeded apace; but German harpsichords seem until very recently to have been comparatively neglected in this re-examination.

Judging by their survival rate there, Italian and Italianate (often South German but strongly influenced by the Italian style) instruments must have been parti-

---

4 The only hint of this is the 'large veneered harpsichord' mentioned in the inventory of Bach's estate in 1750, which might suggest an instrument from Central Germany more strongly than one from North Germany (which were normally painted) or South Germany. But the few surviving instruments by the Silbermann family suggest that they did not use fancy wood veneers (as, for instance, Friederici did), but rather plain walnut or oak (either solid or, on the spinets, plainly veneered to appear solid) or even painted false graining on plain hardwood to imitate ordinary walnut grain. A better guess for the authorship of this instrument, which was to remain in the family and therefore probably had sentimental as well as musical value, would be J. S. Bach's cousin Johann Nicolaus Bach. He was well known as a part-time builder of keyboard instruments, and his *Lautenklavier* (a gut-strung harpsichord) was praised by Adlung. Two *Lautenwerke* are also mentioned in Bach's estate, with his five harpsichords and one spinet. See the inventory of J. S. Bach's musical instruments in *BR* and in Russell 1959 p. 183.

5 Russell 1959 pp. 99–104, and Hubbard 1965 p. 173.

6 See C. Sachs, *Sammlung alter Musikinstrumente bei der staatlichen Hochschule für Musik zu Berlin* (Berlin, 1922), No. 316.

7 Kinsky 1924 pp. 134–7, Ernst 1955 pp. 68 and 74–5; Russell 1959 pp. 107–8; Hubbard, 1965 pp. 184–5, 331–3.

cularly widespread in Germany,[8] and the political disunity of the German region was paralleled by a wide diversity of types of German harpsichords. Yet it would be difficult to accept the premise that no light could be shed on Bach's music (as well as other German music) by hearing it played on an instrument which the composer might reasonably be supposed to have approved or even preferred. It may be partly the difficulty of deciding what that instrument should be, among an embarrassment of choices, that has prevented German instruments from enjoying their share of the harpsichord revival until very recently. But it has long been known that Bach purchased a large and unusually expensive harpsichord from Michael Mietke of Berlin, and travelled to Berlin in early March of 1719 (*Dok* II pp. 73–4) to take possession of it and bring it back to the court at Cöthen. This was little help in settling the question of what Bach's preferred harpsichord might be like, since virtually nothing was known until recently about Mietke's instruments. But in the last few years it has become clear, through a complicated web of circumstantial evidence, that the two harpsichords at Schloss Charlottenburg are almost certainly by Mietke. By stretching that web a little farther, we may be able to establish something between a possibility and a probability that Bach actually knew and played the white Charlottenburg harpsichord.

The network of relationships is built by establishing or exploiting known connections between people, places and things. Because the relationships interact with each other in backtracking patterns, they do not lend themselves to verbal expression and are more easily summarized in graphic form, as shown in Fig. 1. Circles represent people or places, with the white Charlottenburg harpsichord standing in the central circle. The solid numbered lines show known, factual, and provable relationships; the dotted numbered lines show highly probable connections; and the line of small circles (no. 26) shows a possible or probable connection. The numbered paragraphs below refer to the numbered lines on the diagram.

1. The white harpsichord is decorated by Gerard Dagly, who was probably the greatest japanner in Europe. The attribution is well established through stylistic and motival analysis, and is virtually unquestioned though none of his surviving pieces is signed.[9]

2. Dagly was court decorator, lacquerer and cabinet-maker to the Brandenburg court from 1687 to 1713.[10] Normally his court furniture was not signed. From 1696 he was *Kunstkammermeister*, superintendent of all decorations at all the Berlin palaces, and in particular was in charge of the large collection of oriental porcelain at Schloss Charlottenburg, which inspired his striking imitation of white porcelain on the unusual white ground of the harpsichord.

3. The white harpsichord has a history of association with Schloss Charlottenburg, appearing sporadically in reports and inventories from 1705 onwards.[11]

8 See Ernst 1955 pp. 32–3, and Williams, 'J. S. Bach's *Well-tempered Clavier*: A New Approach', part 1 (see note 3), pp. 48–52, for an interesting discussion of Bach's music in relation to Italianate harpsichords.
9 There is a considerable literature about this instrument because of the superb quality of its decoration. See Appendix A.   10 Huth 1971 p. 66.   11 Kühn 1970, I pp. 61, 72.

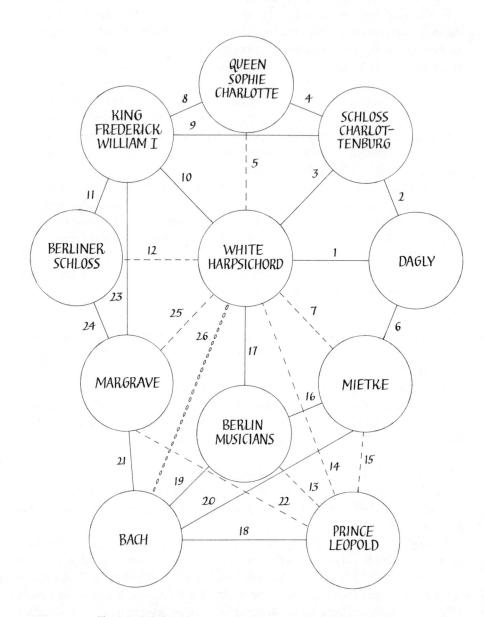

Figure 1. Relationships around the white Charlottenburg harpsichord

4. The Electress (later Queen of Prussia) Sophie Charlotte caused Schloss Charlottenburg to be built from before 1695 to 1713, when all building was stopped by her pathologically philistine son Frederick William I. She made it one of the great cultural centers of Europe, with particular emphasis on philosophy (she was a close friend of Leibnitz) and music. She was herself an accomplished musician, sometimes conducted orchestral performances and was known as a fine player of the harpsichord, on which she was taught (probably on this very harpsichord) by one of her court musicians, G. Buononcini. Her head musician among the Italians she attracted to the court was Attilio Ariosti. She and King Frederick I encouraged Dagly and the other court artists and musicians to make the furnishings and the artistic life of Schloss Charlottenburg celebrated throughout Europe.[12]

5. A report by the palace steward in 1760, reporting on damage after the four-day sack of Schloss Charlottenburg by the Russians during the Seven Years' War, refers to the 'lacquered harpsichord' which was formerly the property of Queen Sophie Charlotte.[13] Thus it is virtually certain that our white harpsichord was personally owned by her. The instrument is reported to have been used later by Princess Amalie, Frederick the Great's youngest sister, and was mentioned again in an 1800 inventory of Schloss Charlottenburg.[14]

6. Dagly is known to have decorated harpsichords for Michael Mietke.[15] This is not surprising, since Mietke was established in Charlottenburg before 1680, and was the court instrument-builder from 1697 to at least 1713;[16] and Dagly was the court decorator, also working and living in Charlottenburg. It is to be expected that Sophie Charlotte should commission Dagly, the court decorator, to japan her own harpsichord which was made by Mietke, the court builder. (Or her husband may have commissioned the work as a gift.) That it is unsigned only increases the probability, for Dagly, like Mietke and other Royal purveyors, did not sign pieces destined for the court.

7. Thus we may assume that the white harpsichord was almost certainly built by Mietke.[17] We may add to these reasons the fact that when seeking for the builder of an instrument owned by the queen and clearly of the Berlin school[18] there is not a large field for selection.

8. After Sophie Charlotte's death, the harpsichord will have been used often in the brilliant concert life at Charlottenburg and the Berliner Schloss. Though Frederick's love of the arts was not as profound as his wife's, he seems to have

12 *Ibid.* pp. 1–4.
13 *Ibid.* pp. 61, 72.
14 Krickeberg 1976 p. 15; Kühn 1970, I pp. 61, 72, 97.
15 Stengel 1958 p. 76.
16 Boalch 1974 pp. 113 and 197; Haase & Krickeberg 1981 p. 48 and illus. 13; and Sachs 1910 pp. 186–7.
17 Krickeberg 1976 p. 3; S. Germann, 'Five Schools of Harpsichord Decoration', *Journal of the American Musical Instrument Society* 4 (1978), pp. 92–5; Germann, 'Regional Types of German Harpsichords', paper read at American Musical Instrument Society, New York, 1980; Haase & Krickeberg 1981 p. 48.
18 Its close structural relationship to the much later instrument of 1792 by the Berlin builder Oesterlein establishes that one may speak of 'the Berlin school'. See Haase & Krickeberg 1981 p. 48 and illus. 13.

adored all the splendid ceremonies and royal luxuries to which music could contribute.

9. When King Frederick I died in 1713, their son Frederick William I ('the Soldier King') inherited Schloss Charlottenburg and the white harpsichord with the other royal furnishings.

10. He detested his parents' cultivated way of life, particularly the virtuoso concert music and other Frenchified elegancies for which his mother had been so greatly admired.[19] He immediately dismissed the court artists, painters, decorators, musicians, sculptors, and architects, and called a halt to all building projects except those for military and government functions.[20] The result was a mass emigration from Berlin of artists of all kinds, including Dagly.

11. The new king used Schloss Charlottenburg as little as possible, except for important state occasions and ceremonial family reunions. He also reduced the time he spent in the Berliner Schloss, preferring Potsdam and Wusterhausen, the crude hunting lodge near Berlin. However, though he kept chained eagles, loose bears and hunting animals in the rooms at Wusterhausen and Potsdam, to the terror of unwarned guests,[21] his reputation for boorish living has sometimes been exaggerated. He did in fact keep the palaces and their furnishings in good repair, and he was aware that his authority as king was supported by splendid spectacles on state occasions.[22] But he disliked all kinds of waste, and what he had no use for he sold, lent, or gave away, rather than let valuable things deteriorate through neglect.[23]

12. The white harpsichord may have remained at Schloss Charlottenburg (ignored until Frederick the Great's accession in 1740) from the death of Queen Sophie Charlotte until modern times. But at least during her lifetime it was moved regularly and normally wintered in the Berliner Schloss. Though a careful inventory of the contents of Schloss Charlottenburg was taken at her death in April 1705, there is no mention of any musical instruments. This is surprising, considering the active musical life at the palace. But it may be assumed that the musical instruments were still in the Berliner Schloss for the winter months, for even Sophie Charlotte spent only the summers at Charlottenburg.[24] Therefore we may presume that from 1705 until there was some reason to move it, the white harpsichord remained in the Berliner Schloss.

19 Hodgetts 1911 pp. 100–101.
20 Hodgetts 1911 p. 92; Huth 1971 p. 70. 'He reduced his Household accordingly, at once, to the lowest footing of the indispensable, and discharged a whole regiment of superfluous official persons, court-flunkies, inferior, superior and supreme, in the most ruthless manner' (Thomas Carlyle, *History of Friedrich II of Prussia*, I (Centenary Edition, London, 1899), p. 307). The fact that Dagly was referred to at court as 'the Frenchman' may have caused him to be among the first to feel the Francophobic boot.
21 Mitford 1970 p. 36; H. Huth, 'Die Wohnungen Friedrichs der Grossen', *Phoebus*, 2/3 (1949), pp. 107–8; Kühn 1970, I p. 4. See Hodgetts 1911 p. 75, and pp. 99–100 for the dislodging of a bear from a chambermaid's bed.
22 Kühn 1970, I p. 4; Hodgetts 1911 pp. 102–8. Kühn & Börsch-Supan 1980 pp. 16–17.
23 Kühn & Börsch-Supan 1980 pp. 16–17.
24 Kühn 1970, I. p. 31.

13. As a youth, Prince Leopold of Anhalt-Cöthen attended the *Ritterakademie* in Berlin from 1707 to 1710. As an enthusiastic musical amateur he may be presumed to have formed connections with the musicians at the court. Despite Sophie Charlotte's death, Berlin continued to be a musical center,[25] though it was now focused less on aesthetic interests and more on state and ceremonial occasions. When Prince Leopold later set up his own court at Cöthen, he took advantage of the large body of unemployed court musicians from Berlin (sacked by the new King Frederick William I in 1713)[26] by hiring several of them, starting in 1715 with Augustus Stricker as Kapellmeister. He probably had known many of these musicians when he was a passionate amateur of music in Berlin in his *Ritterakademie* years.

14. It is likely that Prince Leopold was familiar with the white Mietke harpsichord from hearing it at state occasions and palace concerts during 1707–10.

15. It is also possible that he knew Michael Mietke himself, for the latter was employed by the court to tune and maintain as well as build the court instruments.[27]

16, 17. The ex-Berlin musicians were certainly familiar with the builder Mietke (at least in his capacity as tuner of the court instruments) and particularly with the white Mietke harpsichord, with which they had undoubtedly been used to play.

18. J. S. Bach was Kapellmeister to the court of Prince Leopold at Cöthen from December 1717 until April 1723, and described the prince as truly loving and understanding music (*Dok* I p. 67). They had a relatively close relationship, at least at the beginning of his term of office, when the prince served as godfather and namesake to Bach's son (*Dok* II p. 73). Bach's salary was the second highest of any court official.

19. If the six or more musicians from Berlin who served under Bach came to Cöthen with strong opinions about Mietke harpsichords, Bach must have aware of it, and rather more forcibly aware of Prince Leopold's views on Mietke instruments. It is likely that the prince's musical taste and aspirations were formed during his stay in Berlin as a musically enthusiastic youth,[28] and that what was good for the king in Berlin was good for the court at Cöthen. Given the esteem in which the prince clearly held J. S. Bach, it is reasonable to assume that if Bach had not approved the choice of a Mietke harpsichord, the prince would have valued his advice enough to follow it. However, it is perfectly possible that Bach was unaware of Mietke harpsichords until he arrived at Cöthen, and that he found there ex-Berliner Mietke-supporters eager to persuade him at least to consider a Mietke harpsichord for Cöthen.

20. Whatever the first cause, Bach did travel to Berlin in March 1719 for the purpose of receiving and bringing back to Cöthen a new, large, and unusually expensive double-manual Mietke harpsichord.[29]

25 Besseler 1956 pp. 25–6; Kühn 1970, I p. 2–4; Kühn & Börsch-Supan 1980 p. 15.
26 Nelson 1970 p. 57. Those who escaped to Cöthen were fortunate: the king conscripted into the army many of those who did not.
27 Sachs 1910 p. 186.
28 Besseler 1956 pp. 25–6.
29 See also H. Wäschke, 'Die Hofkapelle in Cöthen unter Johann Sebastian Bach', *Zerbster Jahrbuch* 3 (1907), p. 33; F. Smend, *Bach in Köthen* (Berlin, 1951), p. 17; and *BR* p. 431.

21. Bach's connection with the Margrave Christian Ludwig of Brandenburg is known only from Bach's own dedication of the Brandenburg Concertos to the margrave on 24 March 1721. At the beginning of the rather formal document, written in court French, is the oddly informal phrase 'As I had a couple of years ago the honor of appearing before Your Royal Highness. . .' ('Comme j'eus il y a une couple d'années, le bonheur de me faire entendre à Votre Altesse Royalle': *Dok* I p. 216). This suggests strongly that Bach met and played for the margrave approximately in the spring of 1719. Spitta was puzzled about where they could have met (Spitta I p. 736) and speculated on distant watering places, unaware of Bach's trip to Berlin in March 1719, which fits the 'couple of years ago' of the dedication perfectly.

The margrave spent half his time 'on his estates in Malchow'[30] and half in Berlin. There has evidently been some confusion between the town of Malchow in Mecklenburg, some seventy-five miles north of Berlin, and the small Berlin suburb of Malchow (now part of the city) only five miles from the Berliner Schloss, a confusion which was resolved by Besseler.[31] In effect, the margrave normally spent his summers on the edge of Berlin, and his winters in the center of Berlin. It is logical to assume that Bach met and played for the margrave at his winter residence in the Berliner Schloss on the occasion of picking up the new Mietke harpsichord.[32]

22. It is likely that this was no chance meeting but was deliberately arranged. Since both Prince Leopold and the margrave were enthusiastic music-lovers, they were probably acquaintances from Leopold's days in Berlin ten years earlier. And the phrase 'appearing before Your Royal Highness, by virtue of Your Highness's commands ('de me faire entendre à Votre Altesse Royalle, en vertu de ses ordres') supports the possibility that Prince Leopold may have written to the margrave to suggest such a meeting.

23. Margrave Christian Ludwig of Brandenburg was the youngest son of the Great Elector and therefore the uncle of Frederick William I (see Fig. 2). He was a passionate amateur of music, with his own orchestra, on which he spent the bulk of his fortune (Spitta I p. 128).

24. Though the king was extraordinarily insensitive to the arts, he seems not to have been lacking in family feeling, and it is therefore not surprising that the winter residence of his uncle was the Berliner Schloss, where he and the other 'cousin margraves' grew up.[33] His nephew disliked the palace anyway and was no doubt glad to find a use for rooms too formal for his own taste.

25. Since the new King Frederick William I spent a minimum of time at Charlottenburg, it is reasonable to suppose that he would have left Sophie Charlotte's musical instruments in the Berliner Schloss, where he spent more time and where they would more frequently be useful. As established in no. 12 above, there is a strong possibility that the white Mietke harpsichord already lived in the Berliner

30 This was pointed out notably by Spitta (II p. 128), in which he was followed by later biographers.
31 Besseler 1956 p. 25.
32 Besseler argues that Bach must have traveled to Berlin by the autumn of 1718 to order the harpsichord in person, and that he must have met the margrave then. But though Bach may have been in Berlin then, this is no reason to think he did not play for the margrave in March 1719, a date that fits perfectly the 'a couple of years ago' of the Brandenburg dedication page. Therefore it seems needless to presume that the meeting occurred on a separate trip.
33 Besseler 1956 pp. 25–6; Carlyle (see note 20), I p. 9.

A simplified genealogy of the Brandenburg-Hohenzollern line
(only persons mentioned in the text are included)

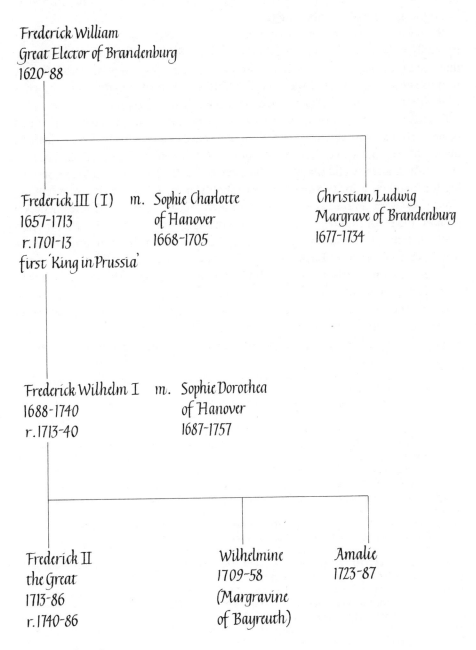

Frederick William
Great Elector of Brandenburg
1620-88

Frederick III (I)   m. Sophie Charlotte   Christian Ludwig
1657-1713   of Hanover   Margrave of Brandenburg
r.1701-13   1668-1705   1677-1734
first 'King in Prussia'

Frederick Wilhelm I   m. Sophie Dorothea
1688-1740   of Hanover
r.1713-40   1687-1757

Frederick II   Wilhelmine   Amalie
the Great   1709-58   1723-87
1713-86   (Margravine
r.1740-86   of Bayreuth)

Figure 2.

Schloss, having been left there after Sophie Charlotte's illness during the winter of 1705, and the indifferent Frederick William having had no reason to move it. He may have put the white harpsichord at his uncle's disposal. Possibility becomes probability when we consider that the king himself detested indoor music,[34] while his uncle loved music passionately; the king had a fancy harpsichord for which he usually had no use; and he habitually lent things or gave them away in order to avoid the expense of maintaining them.[35]

26. Since the margrave was living in the Berliner Schloss, and since Bach very probably played for the margrave in the Berliner Schloss, there is a good chance that the performance was on this white harpsichord. Bach was in Berlin for the purpose of buying a Mietke and would be unlikely to be knowingly under the same roof with another Mietke harpsichord without seizing the opportunity to play it.

Clearly the Brandenburg Concertos were written over some period of time,[36] and some early parts of this music may already have been in Bach's head when he played for the margrave. But by 24 March 1721, when he dedicated the six concertos, Bach already had the Mietke harpsichord at Cöthen and had been composing for it and on it for two years. Very probably at least some of the Brandenburg Concertos were among the works composed on and for the Cöthen Mietke; perhaps the Fifth Brandenburg Concerto ('the first harpsichord concerto'), apparently the last of the group to be composed, was written for the inauguration of the new Mietke harpsichord Bach had purchased in Berlin early in 1719.[37]

A less circumstantial reason to think that Bach particularly valued Mietke's harpsichords is found in the well-known remarks of Bach's pupil Agricola (1768) in which he quotes Bach's preferences about manual size.[38] This is usually interpreted only in relation to the length of keys on organs. But the reference to harpsichords, and to the width of keys as well as their length, even to specific praise for the narrow

---

34 Except church and organ music. See Hodgetts 1911 p. 91, and pp. 111–12 for the only recorded occasion when the king showed affection for the sound of a harpsichord: 'The King at his reviews was enabled to make the regiments fire in battalions, divisions and platoons, with an expedition and accuracy which surpassed every expectation; just as if he were playing on so many harpsichords.'

35 For instance, he gave the opera house which Sophie Charlotte had built at Charlottenburg to the citizens, who made it into a school; and some of the outlying parts of the property of Schloss Charlottenburg were given to the city for farmland (Kühn & Börsch-Supan 1980 pp. 16–17). He gave Sophie Charlotte's collection of music (formed partly under the direction of her court musicians, Attilio Ariosti and Buononcini, including the Op. V that Corelli had dedicated to her) to the Royal Library, from which it passed to Princess Amalie, sister of Frederick the Great (see Kühn 1970, I p. 2).

36 Besseler 1956 p. 26, and 'Zur Chronologie der Konzerte J. S. Bach', *Max Schneider-Festschrift* ed. H. Besseler (Leipzig, 1955), pp. 115–28, and *Vorwort zur neuen Taschenpartitur der Brandenburgischen Konzerte* (Kassel and Leipzig, 1956).

37 H. Besseler, *NBA* VII/2 *KB* (1956), p. 18; Wolff, *The New Grove Bach Family* (London/New York, 1983), p. 157. This supposition is supported by the good fit to the original range of the two Charlottenburg harpsichords, which extended only to c''' in the treble: though the Fifth Brandenburg Concerto is in D major, its solo part does not go above c''' . I am indebted to Peter Williams for pointing out the significance of the range of the concerto.

38 J. F. Agricola, notes on Jacob Adlung, *Musica mechanica organoedi* (Berlin 1768), II pp. 23–4; quoted in *Dok* III p. 193, translated in *BR* pp. 258–9.

keys on instruments from Brandenburg (of which the Mietkes are the only known harpsichords from Bach's period), has been generally overlooked. In both respects the two harpsichords at Charlottenburg fulfill his criteria admirably, especially the white. Its octave span of $6\frac{5}{32}$ inches (156.5 mm; *Stichmass* 469.5) is even narrower than the average French. The sharp length is only $2\frac{13}{16}$ inches (72 mm), and the key heads of $1\frac{3}{8}$ inches (35–36 mm) are almost the shortest measured on harpsichords from any country.

Sebastian Bach had another opportunity to meet the white harpsichord, when he visited his son Carl Philipp Emanuel Bach in Berlin in 1741. In his autobiography, Emanuel writes that in 1740 he had the honor of accompanying, in Charlottenburg and alone at the harpsichord, the first flute solo which Frederick played as king.[39] The instrument that Emanuel played may well have been the white harpsichord. Though it was most likely in the Berliner Schloss during at least the early years of Frederick William's reign, it had been brought back to its original home at Schloss Charlottenburg some time before 1760, when it was listed in the palace steward's report.[40]

Frederick had moved into Schloss Charlottenburg on the day of his accession, in May 1740, and for several years it was his major residence. He relished his freedom from his father's philistine despotism, and immediately established the intellectual and musical court which he had always longed for, and for which he had admired his grandmother Sophie Charlotte. If the white harpsichord was not already back at Charlottenburg (perhaps brought there by Frederick William to serve at some ceremonial functions, such as the Treaty of Charlottenburg in 1723), Frederick would very probably have brought it there in 1740, as the most beautiful of the royal keyboard instruments, and because it had been his grandmother's.[41] It seems likely that this was the harpsichord that Emanuel Bach played for that first royal flute sonata.

There is still another connection between Bach and the white harpsichord. Frederick's sister Princess Amalie is reported to have used it in her suite in Charlottenburg. She acquired Sophie Charlotte's music collection (which Frederick William had given to the Royal Library; a list of it still survives) and also acquired a large collection of J. S. Bach's manuscripts through his pupil Kirnberger, who was her teacher and court musician. Her collection included the fair copy MS ('dedication copy') of the Brandenburg Concertos, which came into Kirnberger's possession after the death of the Margrave Christian Ludwig in 1734.[42] Amalie was a fine musician and studied with one of Bach's foremost pupils, so there can be little doubt that she and Kirnberger will have played some of Bach's music, even the

39 Wolff, *New Grove Bach Family*, p. 257.
40 Inventory of the Kastellan Daun, 1760, and of 1800 (Kühn 1970, I pp. 61, 72).
41 Though Frederick the Great never knew her, Sophie Charlotte remained a legend in the family, admired by Frederick's mother, Sophie Dorothea, who tried to imitate her cultivated soirées whenever her husband was out of town. Sophie Charlotte was a strong influence on her grandson's attitude to cultural life at court, and undoubtedly he instantly chose Charlottenburg as his main residence because of her influence. See Kühn 1970, I p. 4, and Hodgetts 1911 p. 104.
42 Kühn 1970, I p. 2; *BR* pp. 332, 347, 372 (Amalie's purchase of four hundred chorales by J. S. Bach, bought from C. P. E. Bach while he was in Hamburg, also demonstrates her esteem for Bach's music); Schweitzer 1911, I pp. 234–5, 405; Besseler 1956 pp. 27–8.

Plate A. The white Mietke harpsichord

Brandenburg Concertos (in copies or adaptations from the clean score), on the white harpsichord.

Neither of the Charlottenburg harpsichords has received much musical attention in print until very recently, though Friedrich Ernst wrote, 'There could be no better evidence from the time of Bach at our disposal than these instruments'; they 'reveal unmistakable signs of a workshop which was influenced by Italian models (Silbermann?)'.[43] He was aware that Bach had gone to Berlin to buy a harpsichord, but

43 Ernst 1955 pp. 71–2. Kinsky called the white harpsichord a 'Forte-piano by Gottfried Silbermann, Freiberg, around 1745' in *A History of Music in Pictures* (London, 1930), p. 235. Oddly, while refuting the Berlin 'Bach Harpsichord's' association with J. S. Bach, he postulated Michael Mietke as its builder – the one builder who later could be associated with Bach, though he could not have built that much later harpsichord no. 316 (Kinsky 1924 pp. 134–7). The black harpsichord was restored to playing condition under Ernst's direction in 1958.

Plate B. The black Mietke harpsichord

failed to make the obvious connection with Mietke, believing that the Cöthen harpsichord would have been a small, lightly built long-cased single-manual $2 \times 8'$ (or possibly $2 \times 8'$, $1 \times 4'$) harpsichord. Only recently have these Charlottenburg instruments been associated with Mietke.

Its japanned decoration can serve to date the white harpsichord. Dagly left Berlin in 1713, when Frederick William I, with his triple-barreled hatred of the arts, of the French, and of spending money, made an instant clean sweep of court officials, starting on the day of his accession. This gives us a *terminus ad quem* for the date of the white harpsichord; and an even earlier one is provided by a report by the palace steward's inventory of 1760. He refers to the harpsichord which had belonged to Queen Sophie Charlotte at Schloss Charlottenburg, and there can be no reasonable doubt that this is the harpsichord. Since she died in February 1705 after a long illness, the harpsichord must have been built by 1703.

The decoration also provides the *terminus a quo*. A vignette on the bentside near the tail, showing a group of noblemen followed by a servant holding a tall double fan on a pole, is derived from an engraving first published in Amsterdam in 1702 by Peter Schenck the elder.[44] Therefore the white harpsichord can be dated 1702–4. It is most likely that it was built by 1702, and decorated by 1702–3, in order for Sophie Charlotte to have had it long enough for her ownership and use of it to be remembered. Since Dagly is known to have lacquered directly for Mietke, we may assume that the harpsichord was decorated in the year its construction was finished. Telemann attended Buononcini's famous 1703 production of his *Polyphemo* in Berlin, in which most of the singers were noble, and most of the instrumentalists

44 Huth 1971 p. 71 and pl. 6d.

131

were concertmasters and kapellmeisters.[45] In the middle of the orchestra sat Queen Sophie Charlotte herself playing continuo at the harpsichord, and we have no reason to think that she did not perform on her splendid white Mietke.

The japanned decoration may also supply an approximate date of 1703–13 for the black Charlottenburg harpsichord, for it must have been japanned before 1713, when Dagly's shop closed (see Appendix A). Its original range was more extended than that of the white harpsichord, so it is probably later than 1703. Being destined for the court, the white instrument is not signed. The black now has no signature, but if there ever was one it would probably have been signed and dated in ink on the front of the soundboard, as was done on the later Hamburg harpsichords. Neither instrument has a painted soundboard, but it is not impossible that former sound-board paintings have been removed, in which case the signature and date would be lost with the paintings. All the rest of the painted decoration points back to the French and forward to the Hamburg school in such a straight line that one would expect a painted soundboard as part of the overall aesthetic.

The white harpsichord has received, on account of its superb decoration, far more attention in print than the black, but the black is musically at least equally important, being a double, and substantially less altered. It has no historical connection to Schloss Charlottenburg,[46] and no provenance that can connect it specifically with J. S. Bach. Therefore it stands outside the discussion connecting Bach with Mietke. But that connection once established, it is very important in understanding the musical qualities of Mietke's instruments, for it is a valuable point of reference for the more extensively altered white instrument.

Both instruments were significantly altered, probably before 1750. The scales were originally quite short (the black was around $11\frac{5}{8}$ inches and is now around $13\frac{3}{16}$; the white was and is even shorter), and the compass of both was smaller. On both instruments, the black endblock scrolls are carved in unusually shallow relief, in a similar style but slightly differing design. Their relief borders suggest that those on the white harpsichord are original but were cut off at the ends when the keyboards were enlarged, whereas the black harpsichord had new endblocks made in a similar style during the enlargement, for their symmetry is unimpaired. In their present

45 G. P. Telemann, autobiography in J. Mattheson's *Grundlage einer Ehrenpforte* (Hamburg, 1740) and E. L. Gerber, *Allgemeine Musikalische Zeitung* 8 (1805–6), p. 387.

46 Private communication from Dr Helmut Börsch-Supan, 22 March 1980. However, Ernst (1955 p. 71) says that according to tradition the black harpsichord also had belonged to Sophie Charlotte, though he doubted this, since he dated both instruments around 1725. On the other hand, A. J. Hipkins in *Musical Instruments, Historic, Rare and Unique* (London, 1888), while discussing chinoiserie on harpsichords, refers to the white harpsichord as Queen Sophie Dorothea's instrument, 'until lately preserved in her palace at Charlottenburg, but now in the Hohenzollern Museum'. Probably he means Sophie Charlotte, not Sophie Dorothea; yet it is the black harpsichord, which may have been owned by Sophie Dorothea, which was at the Hohenzollern Museum (formerly Schloss Monbijou; see below). Either he confused the white and the black instruments, or he confused their ownership and location. But the possibility that the black harpsichord was also owned by Sophie Charlotte is interesting, for if it was hers it has as much chance as the white of having been at the Berliner Schloss in 1719, and therefore of being the harpsichord J. S. Bach played for the Margrave.

states, both the black and white harpsichords are musically significantly different from what they were in J. S. Bach's time. Instead they represent the compass and scale and pitch they probably had in the time of C. P. E. Bach in Berlin, and with their short scales, double bentsides, shove couplers and box slides they may represent the typical Berlin harpsichord described by Sprengel.[47]

But if the way they play has been changed, the way they were built remains. At first glance, one is struck by their seeming eclecticism. They seem to share in almost equal quantities features we usually associate with all three major regional schools of German harpsichord-building: the Hamburg school, the South German and the Saxon. But the Charlottenburg harpsichords are from the very first years of the eighteenth century and thus precede most surviving instruments from the Hamburg and Saxon schools. The borrowing, if any, was in the other direction.

Italian and, more directly, South German influence is suggested by the use of cap moldings (especially on the nameboard), plain wood veneer with inset, overhanging top molding around the soundboard within the painted case, and boldly Baroque broken curves on the key brackets (all of which suggest the 'false-inner/outer case' illusion so commonly found in those regions), the carved black endblocks, the gilt molding on the top edge of the lid, the case bottom molding, the molded bridges and scrolled bridge ends, and the moldings around the wrestplank and gap. Technically, the original short scales, the expanded gap in the base, the thin cases, the knee-like framing, the box slides, and the bottom built inside the case walls also suggest southern influence.

Some features remind us of the Hamburg school: their large size, round tails on double-curved bentsides, elaborate chinoiserie case decoration, white case color, combination of decorative wood (walnut and maple) with painted decoration, black arcaded key fronts, fire-gilt hinges, stop levers on the wrestplank, elaborately shaped jackrail support blocks, seven- or eight-legged Baroque baluster stands with low shaped stretcher, the cut-back in the apron as a courtesy to the player's knees, the very high, massive bridges and nuts, and the lack of a rosehole in the soundboard. We see these features grouped together more often on Hamburg instruments than elsewhere, though the indirect source for many of them must be France.

Characteristics often associated with the Saxon school (but probably coming to Berlin and to Central Germany also from the French school) are seen in the flat case top, the narrow octave span of $6\frac{5}{32}$ inches, the short key heads with black naturals, white-topped sharps, and black arcades, the simple, classic dispositions, and the plain, unpainted soundboards.

But the single strongest visual connection is with late-seventeenth-century French instruments, as exemplified by the Desruisseaux of the 1670s in the Paris Conservatoire; and many of the most striking characteristics of the Charlottenburg instruments can be traced more directly to such French instruments than to any of the regional types of German harpsichords. The most notable feature, the double bentside, was made in France before Hamburg, though surviving examples are very

47 Hubbard 1965 pp. 268–9, 275–6, and 278.

rare.[48] The light construction, with relatively thin cases around inset bottoms, and rather large bottom and cap moldings, first suggests South German and Italian instruments, as does the lining of the case interior with plain wood above the soundboard (the black with walnut, the white with maple) which also forms the scroll inside the cheeks. But all these features, even the lack of a rose, are also found in seventeenth-century French instruments, especially in spinets and ottavinos and a few harpsichords with round tails and cheek scrolls.[49] The Charlottenburg harpsichords strongly suggest the native sevententh-century Parisian school before its course was changed by the vogue for rebuilding Ruckers harpsichords. The French characteristics diffused in the various German regional schools seem more concentrated in the Charlottenburg harpsichords than elsewhere in Germany.

This may not be a coincidence, for the first years of the eighteenth century were precisely the time when the former Elector of Brandenburg was consolidating his new position as Frederick I, first and self-crowned 'King in Prussia', by surrounding himself with all possible pomp and making his palaces in Berlin and Charlottenburg the most direct imitations in Europe of the court of Louis XIV.[50] All things French were aped, and artists and craftsmen were imported from France to glorify the court. It was said that as early as 1680 Mietke adopted the French style of construction and charged 300 Thaler for his instruments as French imports, until he was caught at it and had to lower the price to the 60 to 80 Thaler suitable for the home-grown product.[51] He may well have been trained in France, or by an expatriate French builder.

48 A typical instance of the automatic association of double bentsides with Hamburg instruments is found in Russell 1959 pl. 62, with reference to a design by Thornhill for the lid of a harpsichord of Handel: 'The double curve lid narrows down the probable makers to one of the Hamburg families (Hass or Zell) and to the Hitchcocks. Handel may have possessed a German harpsichord . . .' But the proportions are wrong for Hass or Hitchcock. An artist might be casual about the exact proportions of a lid in his preliminary sketches, but not in a finished sketch like this, where he has to take careful account of the amount of headroom his figures have below the diagonal of the bentside edge. His scale at the bottom of the drawing shows his concern for accuracy. The double curve of the bentside lacks Hass's straight section and shallow curve, broad in the alto, and the pointed tail curve. (Furthermore, wishful thinking would cause Thornhill to err in the direction of making the bentside edge higher, not lower, as he seeks room for a rational horizon and clearance for standing figures.) The sketch does not match the Hitchcock proportions either, being too broad in the tenor and bass. The proportions do match well the 1683 Haward at Hovingham Hall, the Zells of 1728 and 1741, the Desruisseaux of the 1670s, and the Charlottenburg harpsichords.

49 Most of these features are found in such instruments as the Desruisseaux of the 1670s and the Richard 1693 and 1690 spinets (all in the Paris Conservatoire de Musique), an anonymous single harpsichord in the collection of Tony Bingham in London, the Dufour harpsichord of 1683 in a private collection in Germany, and a Rastoin spinet of 1689 (formerly Salomon Collection). Of these, only the Desruisseaux and the Dufour have a rose, so we also have seventeenth-century French authority for roseless soundboards.

50 It was said that he rose very early just to have more time to enjoy the pleasure of being king (Ergang 1941 p. 21).

51 Loesser 1954 p. 15, an anecdote with no source cited but obviously drawn from C. F. Weitzmann, *Geschichte des Clavierspiels und der Clavierliteratur* (Stuttgart, 1879), p. 252 (quoting a handwritten annotation, by a contemporary of Mietke's, in Weitzmann's own copy of Mattheson's *Das neueröffnete Orchestre*, 1713). I am grateful to John Koster for tracking down this elusive reference.

There is another builder, Johann Rost, who merits some consideration for the honor of having built the two Charlottenburg instruments. A harpsichord 'of the year 1706 built by the famous Rost' was advertised for sale in 1748, and the Queen of Prussia paid Johann Rost on 26 February 1720 for repairing a harpsichord.[52] He must have been an independent harpsichord-maker working in Berlin at the same time Mietke was the court harpsichord-builder in the town of Charlottenburg. He died before 1747, according to a public announcement of that date.[53] The possibility of his authorship of the two harpsichords is considered in Appendix B, but there is enough circumstantial evidence to make this conclusion unlikely. Nevertheless, Rost is interesting in another context. The harpsichord which the queen paid Rost to repair or refurbish in 1720 was probably another Mietke. He had died only a few months before in 1719, and she would naturally have turned to the other harpsichord-builder in Berlin for repairs and maintenance work on any harpsichord she already owned.

The extraordinary family life and finances of the royal family bear on the queen's possible relationship with Mietke and Rost. Her own private residence was Monbijou, a small palace in Berlin,[54] which had been given to her on her marriage by her father-in-law, King Frederick I. As her marriage with Frederick William I became increasingly stormy and chaotic, she led as separate a life as possible at Monbijou, especially while he was away on military activities. She spent as much money as she could get her hands on[55] in an attempt to hold a cultured and civilized court such as she had known in Hanover and such as Queen Sophie Charlotte, her admired aunt and mother-in-law, had held at Schloss Charlottenburg. Though her husband would not permit such a 'frivolous' expense as a permanent court orchestra, she held concerts and balls with impromptu groups whenever possible, and for these a harpsichord was indispensable.

If Sophie Dorothea ordered a harpsichord before Mietke's death in 1719 (or picked one up second-hand) it would still probably be by Mietke, the court builder. Or she may have received a Mietke as a gift (like Monbijou) or inheritance from her

52 In 1720 this was not Queen Sophie Charlotte, but Sophie Dorothea, wife of Frederick William I. See Stengel 1958 p. 76.

53 Stengel 1958 p. 75. One might be tempted to wonder if Rost was the same or related to the Rozet (or Rosé) who built a French spinet in 1680, now in Besançon; the clear relationship of the Charlottenburg harpsichords to French instruments of that period might suggest that Rost, Mietke's competitor in Berlin (who also made white harpsichords, implying a possibly imitative relationship), may have been a German whose name was frenchified while he was working temporarily in France. But Rost's presumed death not long before 1747 would make an improbably long working lifetime from 1680.

54 Frederick the Great's sister Wilhelmine, as a child of nine, observed the visit to Monbijou of Peter the Great of Russia and his entourage, who were so renowned for savage living that before their visit Sophie Dorothea had the palace cleared of everything portable and breakable. See *Memoirs of Frederica Sophia Wilhelmine, Margravine of Baireuth*, trans. Princess Christian of Schleswig Holstein (New York, 1888), pp. 37–40. One wonders if her harpsichord was among the things moved out of the Czar's marauding reach.

55 Mitford 1970 p. 38; Hodgetts 1911 p. 146; and the *Memoirs* of Wilhelmine (see note 54), p. 24. Sophie Dorothea's spending power was considerable after her inheritance of three billion Thaler from her mother (Nelson 1970 pp. 110–11 and 213).

father-in-law, among other court furnishings; Frederick I, with his extravagant concert life, probably had several harpsichords in his palaces, and most or all of them would have been Mietkes. She is quoted as paying Rost for working on 'the harpsichord', which suggests that there was only one harpsichord at the location; that must have been Monbijou, for expenses for maintenance of any harpsichord at the other palaces would be paid from official funds and not from her private cashbox.

Thus it is probable that Rost came to Monbijou in February 1720, a few months after Mietke's death, to repair or refurbish a Mietke harpsichord. This possibility becomes especially interesting when we remember that the black harpsichord now in Schloss Charlottenburg was brought there in modern times from Schloss Monbijou,[56] because it so much resembled the white one that was already at Charlottenburg. Could our black harpsichord, which is almost surely by Mietke, be the same harpsichord that Rost worked on for Sophie Dorothea in 1720? One support for this possibility is Sophie Dorothea's interest in lacquer. Though Dagly had been dismissed in 1713 and his shop closed, the lacquering trade continued independent of the court and the queen bought several pieces from Andreas Völkert. She was herself a devotee of the fashionable pastime of *lacca povera*, a variant on chinoiserie.[57] The fine gold chinoiseries of the black harpsichord may have been one reason she would wish to own it.

Both the black and the white harpsichords have been enlarged in compass and altered in scale (see Appendix C). It is not impossible that the 'refurbishing' for which Sophie Dorothea paid Rost was the alteration of our black harpsichord from FF-c''' (missing FF♯ and GG♯) to its present FF-e''' (missing FF♯). But though the problem of compass and dates at this transitional time is too complicated for generalization, 1720 would seem surprisingly early for the present compass. However, Rost could still have altered it later. He died before 1747, but Sophie Dorothea may have hired him to enlarge her instrument in the 1740s, and this seems the most likely decade. By then Frederick the Great was king, and the queen mother was free to spend money on updating her instruments, and to give as many musical soirées as she liked.

C. P. E. Bach and J. J. Quantz were court musicians to Frederick the Great (from 1738 and 1730 respectively), and they both probably knew Rost. Since this harpsichord may have been owned by Frederick's concert-giving mother, whom Frederick visited at Monbijou daily when he was in Berlin,[58] it may be they who suggested the enlargement and perhaps a change of pitch. Thus the black harpsichord may be

---

56 Later than the mid eighteenth century at least, according to records and inventories. Private communication from Dr Börsch-Supan, 22 March 1980.

57 Also called *arte povera* or *lacca contrafatta*. This was a lady amateur's way of imitating lacquer with découpage, by cutting out engravings, glueing them on painted furniture, coloring them with crayons, and applying around twenty coats of varnish to disguise the bad workmanship. See Stengel 1958 p. 82. One lacquermaster complained that the queen always botched the glueing so badly that he had to keep coming to redo it for her.

58 Mitford 1970 p. 85.

a Mietke enlarged by Rost at the suggestion of Quantz (to whom pitch would be especially important if he was to play the flute with the harpsichord) or C. P. E. Bach. (If Rost did this alteration, he almost certainly altered the white harpsichord also, since the workmanship is very similar.) This is pure conjecture, of course, but it seems very probable that they would both be familiar with the black harpsichord if it belonged to the queen mother.

It might seem unlikely that the black harpsichord should remain so long in one place, at Schloss Monbijou, until modern times. But Frederick the Great was considerably distressed by his mother's death in 1757, and he had her palace kept much as she had lived in it. It was unoccupied from 1757 until his death in 1786.[59] This preservationist attitude may have protected the instrument from the usual vicissitudes of royal borrowings and gifts until it had outlived its musical usefulness, when there would be no further motive to move it.

About Michael Mietke we know only the bare facts that he had settled in Charlottenburg before 1680, and served as court instrument-builder from at least 1697 (when he was married) to 1719, when he died;[60] that he was listed as keyboard-tuner and organ-builder from 1711 until the dissolution of the orchestra (in 1713) at a salary of 70 Reichsthaler per annum;[61] and that he made 'beautiful harpsichords' and, for whatever the difference is worth, 'excellent harpsichords'.[62] About Mietke's instruments there is more information. The Mietke at Cöthen was probably the instrument J. S. Bach repaired in September 1722 and restrung and requilled in December 1722; it was still in the Kapelle in 1784, when it was listed as defective (*Dok* II pp. 73–4).

Walter Stengel lists numerous appearances of the name of Mietke through the eighteenth century taken from public announcements[63] useful for many scraps of information about Mietke harpsichords – appearance, dates, and type. Mietke

59 Edwin Redslob, *Barock und Rokoko in den Schlössern von Berlin und Potsdam* (Berlin, 1954), p. 30, and Richard Borrman (ed.), *Die Bau- und Kunstdenkmäler von Berlin* (Berlin, 1893), p. 316. Against the possibility that the black harpsichord was at Monbijou in the eighteenth century must be set the 1758 inventory of Monbijou after Sophie Dorothea's death, which mentions no harpsichord. But we know she owned at least one harpsichord, and needed it for her frequent palace concerts. It may have been away from the palace for the same reason that the white harpsichord is not mentioned in the 1705 inventory of Schloss Charlottenburg: a seasonal move, or repair, or a temporary loan. The possibility that the black harpsichord belonged to Sophie Dorothea is therefore neither strengthened nor fatally wounded by the 1758 inventory. I am grateful to Dr Helmut Börsch-Supan for this information.

60 See the wedding book of the church of Friedrichswerder, quoted Sachs 1910 p. 189; and Haase & Krickeberg 1976 p. 48; J. G. Walther, *Musicalisches Lexicon* (Leipzig, 1732), p. 405; E. L. Gerber, *Neues historisch-biographisches Lexicon der Tonkünstler . . .*, 2 vols. (1812–14), III, col. 427; Hirt 1968 p. 440; Loesser 1954 p. 15; *Dok* II p. 545; and Boalch 1974 pp. 113, 197.

61 Sachs 1910 pp. 186–7.

62 Walther: 'schöne *Clavicymbel*'; Gerber: 'vortreffliche Flügel'.

63 Stengel 1958 p. 76 notes that Curt Sachs, who completed a list of musical-instrument-makers from the entries in the *Bürgerbuch* (*Die Musikgeschichte der Stadt Berlin*, Berlin, 1908), does not know Mietke at all. Mietke might have been unlisted in the 'Citizen Book' because the records of the town of Charlottenburg were separate or because he still managed to keep his official post of court instrument-builder, functioning after 1713 as keeper and tuner of the royal harpsichords.

harpsichords are mentioned often from 1706 to 1784. It is surprising to find them valued and continuing in frequent use so late in the century, when most harpsichords so old would probably be discarded. One owner said in 1729 that the date of his Mietke was 1726, but either this is an error,[64] or the maker was a son or nephew, or Walther and Gerber were wrong in saying that Mietke died in 1719. In 1786 a Mietke harpsichord is recorded as being in the estate of another Miethke, perhaps a grandson. Another in 1781 is described with the classic disposition of three choirs, FF–e''' (the same as the present compass of both Charlottenburg harpsichords). And in 1706 the Berlin Friends of Music are reported as not liking green lacquer with gold (by Dagly?) on the Mietke harpsichord as well as the more usual black lacquer. Two announcements in 1731 and 1733 state that the Mietke harpsichords were decorated by Dagly, in one instance 'by the famous Dagly'. A spinet mentioned in 1729 is decorated all over with delicate flowers and covered with copper engravings (this may be *lacca povera*), with elaborately marquetried keywell.

But by far the most interesting announcement is that of 18 July 1778: Frau Doctorin Martini owned a Mietke, a '16' two-manual harpsichord, of which only two exist by this master'.[65] This is startling. A 16' harpsichord was a rarity anywhere in Europe, infrequent even in Germany, and almost all the surviving examples are from the Hamburg school in the middle of the eighteenth century. The earliest mention in contemporary literature of the 16' stop on a stringed keyboard instrument is Johann Christoph Fleischer's announcement in 1718 that he had invented a *Lauten-Clavesseng* (gut-strung harpsichord at 8' pitch) and a *Theorbenflügel* (gut-strung harpsichord at 16' pitch).[66] Since Mietke had already made two 16' harpsichords before his death in 1719, it seems possible that he was making 16' stops even before Fleischer's announcement. To find them made before 1719 in Berlin, by the only builder from whom Bach is known to have bought a harpsichord, is disturbing.

64 Stengel was unaware that Mietke was dead by 1726. Mietke's instruments not meant for the court would probably be signed like other North German harpsichords (including Hamburg harpsichords and the 1792 Oesterlein of Berlin, which greatly resembles the Charlottenburg harpsichords) in ink script along the front of the soundboard. Such inscriptions usually bled into the soft spruce or fir woodgrain, and often became illegible from the pen nib catching across the woodgrain grooves. '1726' may be a misreading of '1716'.

65 '16 füssiger Flügel mit 2 Clavieren dergleichen von diesem Meister nur zwei existieren.' All these quotations are from Stengel 1958 p. 76. Besides the many references to Rost and Mietke instruments, he discusses references to other Berlin harpsichord-makers too late in the century to be relevant to the Charlottenburg instruments. Most interesting, for those interested in harpsichord decoration, is the rare appearance of a named professional harpsichord-decorator: 'In Berlin, the painter and lacquerer Johann Josephy occupied himself particularly with harpsichords, and he announces at the beginning of September 1738 that he is making "precise japan/lacquerwork . . . with noble and humble figures, cupboards, night tables, jeridons [sic], coffee tables, and teaboards", and that "if anyone wants to have harpsichords [*Flügels und Claviere*] or other things properly lacquered, he can be served"'. In the *Intelligenz-Blatt* of 6 October 1760 was a notice: '"there is a demand for someone who can lacquer so well as to be able to lacquer a harpsichord, and anyone who can do that can present himself in Broad Street in the house of the clockmaker Pohlmann at any time"' (Stengel 1958 pp. 77–8).

66 Ernst 1955 p. 53.

Could Bach have had a 16′ harpsichord after all? The Cöthen harpsichord is described as large, and it was expensive at 130 Thaler, even though that included transport costs (*Dok* II pp. 73–4). The unusual cost might be because of decoration suitable for Prince Leopold (which might have been lacquer by the same Andreas Völkert from whom Sophie Dorothea bought lacquered pieces in 1720–2). But 130 Thaler is too little for chinoiserie, when Dagly charged 200 Thaler for lacquering a cabinet in white and gold in 1696.[67] Mietke's harpsichords sold for 60–80 Thaler when he was unable to pass them off as French imports.[68] It seems entirely possible that the Cöthen harpsichord was expensive and large because of a 16′ disposition, but it is distinctly stated that Mietke built only two of these instruments, and the chance that the only other one went to Cöthen is very slight. Nevertheless, it is intriguing to speculate not only on the Cöthen instrument but on the harpsichord that J. S. Bach took to Leipzig in 1733, 'a new harpsichord, the like of which no one here has ever yet heard' ('ein neuer *Clavicymbel*, dergleichen allhier noch nicht gehöret worden': *Dok* II p. 238).[69]

From having no specific type of harpsichord to associate with Bach's music on any documentary authority, we have advanced to having two superb harpsichords from a maker whose instruments can be associated not only with Bach in general, but with one of the greatest of his keyboard works, the Fifth Brandenburg Concerto. Furthermore, he may well have played on one of these surviving instruments at the very time that he was writing that concerto. We could not hope, for any composer, to find a better match between beauty of music and instrument.

Appendix A

Dagly and the Decoration

Gerard Dagly was born before 1665, brought up in the lacquering center of Spa, near Liège in Belgium, and trained by his father. He was settled in Lietzenburg (later renamed Charlottenburg) by 1686, working for the Great Elector of Brandenburg as lacquer-master. After 1687 he supervised the display of the royal collection of oriental porcelain as well as producing lacquered furniture and objects. In 1689, when the future Frederick I confirmed his appointment with a stipend of 'lodging, one pot of wine, four pots of beer, two loaves of bread daily, fodder for two horses,

---

67 Huth 1971 p. 73.
68 Loesser 1954 p. 15 (see note 51 above).
69 I am indebted to Margot Milner and Dorothea Täuberecht for procuring some important references inaccessible in Boston; to William Dowd for technical information about the two Mietke harpsichords to supplement my own less complete measurements; to Paul Guglietti for essential sources and, as always, invaluable guidance; and to my husband, whose reluctance was exceeded only by his indefatigability in propping up my German translations.

wood and coal', all the raw material he needed, and a thousand écus a year, with the title of Master of the Curio Cabinet (*Kunstkammermeister*).[70]

In 1696 he was promoted to Intendant des Ornements, in charge of interior decorations at all the court palaces, working with the architect Andreas Schlüter. He may have been lodged over the palace stables wing with the other academicians, causing it to be said that 'Frederick I keeps his asses and his horses together'.[71] He had a large shop of workmen of many nationalities. His fame increased throughout Europe, and in 1705, when the Electress of Hanover sent an English japanned watch-case to her son-in-law (the future King Frederick William I of Prussia), she apologized, saying it was only to be used as a pattern, for 'Dagly makes much better ones'.[72] However, it is unlikely that Frederick William valued the watch-case highly, since he sacked Dagly instantly on achieving the throne in 1713.

Dagly became a friend of Leibnitz, the philosopher and friend whom Sophie Charlotte had brought to her court. Dagly's scientific interests were wide-ranging, and he became famous for a variety of bizarre inventions, including a recipe for a varnish that could make silver leaf look like gold but without tarnishing (actually a shellac with gum lacci and gum sandarac stained with dragon's blood, of great use to the court librarian, who demanded the recipe before Dagly left Berlin in 1713), and an almost equally popular varnish recipe recommended for preserving the flesh of ladies' faces from 'corrupting' in the sun, but first designed for preserving leather.

He used the royal porcelain collection as inspiration and as a source for copies, and in some cases the original porcelain on which he based parts of his decorative chinoiserie can be identified. He was famous throughout Europe for his ability to imitate the texture and color of porcelain (using lacquered wood for pseudo-porcelain chimney garnishes) before it was known how to manufacture porcelain in Germany. He boasted that he could copy perfectly any oriental lacquer.

He was a cabinet-maker as well as an interior decorator and japanner, and one of his duties was to make Baroque stands on which to place the oriental cabinets (the inspiration for his imitations and copies of Eastern lacquer) imported to fill Frederick's *Kunstkammer*. Their style is similar to the white and black harpsichord stands, which are presumed to be from his shop.

None of Dagly's works is signed, but many are unique in their style, and some pieces can be identified from contemporary descriptions or engravings of the famous rooms for which he built and decorated furniture. He was particularly known for brilliant lacquered polychrome decoration on a clear white ground which did not yellow with age, and the secret of which was envied throughout Europe. We have this extraordinary polychrome on white lacquer ground on the white harpsichord at Charlottenburg, and it has still not yellowed or developed a

---

70 Interesting discussions of Dagly and Schnell can be found in the works listed below in notes 73 and 75, but reference to all facts about Dagly and Schnell cited in this appendix can be found in Huth 1971 pp. 30, 34, 66–75 (and pls. X–XI), 159–69, and 192–200, unless otherwise noted.

71 Ergang 1941 p. 15.

72 *Briefwechsel König Friedrichs I. mit seiner Familie,* ed. E. Berner (Berlin, 1901), p. 79.

craquelure, unlike most of the varnishes and lacquered whites of the eighteenth century. Though his lacquer is often so close to oriental work in design and texture that it is almost indistinguishable, he was also imaginative in his use of the technique. The brilliant coloring on white was a complete departure from oriental practice, as were the equally famous blue-on-white cabinets in which he imitated oriental porcelain instead of lacquerwork.

The white harpsichord has been frequently described in the literature on lacquering and chinoiserie as an undoubted and very important instance of Dagly's work, since this particular style is his unique specialty.[73] There is virtually no argument about the attribution despite the absence of a signature. Especially characteristic of his most unusual and personal style are the polychrome on a white ground, the idiosyncratic chrysanthemum-and-vine borders surrounding the lid and on the moldings on the apron, the use of openly spaced 'Indian' household objects (on the lid interior) and groups of two or three musicians, and a particular motif (on the right cheek of the harpsichord) of two dancers with long sleeves flowing in the air, which he used on other furniture and which are derived from a blue and white Kang-hsi vase in Schloss Charlottenburg.[74]

The white harpsichord has another of the hallmarks of his individual style, garden fences slanting diagonally through the composition with tiny landscape scenes within the fence-rails. The strong diagonals of the fences and the illogically cropped building compounds copy the accidental effect often found on real imported oriental lacquer, which was cut into expedient shapes and used as a veneer on European case furniture. Dagly has imitated the bizarre croppings that often result, producing a conscious tension between the picture and its 'frame' that is not seen again until the fashion for *Japonaiserie* at the time of Toulouse-Lautrec and Degas. Clearly this is one of the very rare instances of a surviving harpsichord unquestionably decorated by an artist of the first rank.

The decoration of the black double harpsichord in Charlottenburg is attributed by some to Dagly himself and by some, more cautiously, to his workshop.[75] The

73 See *Barock in Deutschland: Residenzen* (exhibition catalogue, Berlin, 1966), pp. 96–7 and pl. 133; H. Börsch-Supan, *Die Kunst in Brandenburg-Preussen* (Berlin, n.d.), pp. 94–5 and pl. 61; Kühn & Börsch-Supan 1980 p. 50; *China und Europa* (exhibition catalogue, Berlin, 1973), p. 228 and cover illus.; H. Hayward, *World Furniture* (New York, 1965), pp. 101–2 and pl. 341; W. Holzhausen, *Lackkunst in Europa* (Brunswick, 1958–9), p. 189 and pl. 142–3; H. Honour, *Cabinet Makers and Furniture Designers* (New York, c1969), pp. 61–3 and pl. 60; Honour, *Chinoiserie* (London, c1961), pp. 66–7; Huth 1935 pp. 16 and 18, illus.; Huth 1971 pp. 68, 71–2 and pl. X and XI; Jarry 1981 p. 152–3, 155 and pl. 168; Krickeberg 1976 p. 3 and pl. 30; Kühn 1970 I pp. 37, 61, 72, and II pl. 192 and 392; Kühn, *Schloss Charlottenburg* (Berlin, 1955), p. 34 and pl. 55; H. D. Molesworth & J. Kenworthy-Browne, *Three Centuries of Furniture in Color* (New York, c1969), p. 132; Stengel 1958 p. 75 and pl. 14; Chisaburo Yamada, *Die Chinamode des Spätbarock* (Berlin, 1935), p. 37.

74 Huth 1935 p. 16. See illustration of the Kang-hsi vase in Kühn 1970, II pl. 426. A Kang-hsi plate illustrated in *Connaissance des Arts* 218 (April 1970), p. 98, also shows a remarkable similarity to the scenes on the bentside of the white harpsichord, and to some Dagly cabinets; see Huth 1955 pl. 2–3.

75 See Kühn & Börsch-Supan 1980 p. 63; *China und Europa* p. 226; A. Conradt, 'Hamburger Musikinstrumente des 18. Jahrhunderts mit Lackmalerei', *Jahrbuch der Hamburger Kunstsammlung* 9 (1964), p. 36; Huth 1955 pp. 20–1 and pl. 5; Impey 1977 pp. 117–18, illus. 129 and plate facing 4; Jarry 1981 p. 155 and pl. 167; Kühn 1970, I p. 38, and II pl. 34.

chinoiserie is less idiosyncratic than the style of the white instrument, and more like good Eastern German lacquerwork in general, in close imitation of genuine Japanese lacquer; thus it is difficult to identify as the hand of a particular master. For this reason, and because it is less startlingly original in its conception, it has received less attention in print than the white, and some authorities seem hesitant to attribute it firmly to Dagly even though its quality is as fine as many of the works generally attributed to him.

If it is not the work of Dagly personally, it must be by his shop, for Dagly had an ironclad monopoly on the making and selling of all lacquer in Berlin after 1696 (even to the fashionable lacquered buttons) during the period when the harpsichord was probably built. The most likely hand in Dagly's shop to have risen to this level of japanning is that of Martin Schnell, who was one of his many apprentices from 1703 to 1709.[76] Schnell later became almost as famous as Dagly, working for the court of Augustus the Strong in Dresden, and his manner when working in relief gold on black was very similar to Dagly's work on black. The black harpsichord is close in style not only to Dagly's work but to Schnell's work in Dresden. There Schnell also lacquered harpsichord cases, and in 1717 he produced 'cabinets, clavicembalos and screens' worth 1,145 Thaler, including a lacquered *Clavicymbel* for the Japanese Palace in Dresden. He too never signed his work, but unlike Dagly he never produced furniture or stands.[77]

The black harpsichord is decorated in two slightly different styles, perhaps reflecting two hands in the same shop. The lid exterior and stand decoration are entirely flat, with linear, stylized flowers, and with a border treatment of red–gold speckles ('strewings', as Stalker and Parker called them in 1681) on a reddish-black ground. The case sides have landscape vignettes and figure groups in relief, in a closely observed imitation of genuine Japanese lacquer (for which Dagly and his shop were famous), worked in variations of gold, green and bronze powders on slightly raised surfaces. At first glance the black harpsichord seems different in style from the white, but in fact both styles are typical of Dagly's work,[78] and some of the motifs are especially characteristic of Dagly's shop, including the famous chrysanthemum-and-vine borders. Both instruments have fine, original stamped fire-gilt hinges, the black in a 'Chinese' style popular throughout Europe (close to but not identical with hinges used by Dagly on other furniture) and the white in a less usual design.[79]

The stands of the two harpsichords are at first glance similar, composed of a deep bombé apron with moldings above and below, seven or eight square tapered baluster legs and elaborately scrolled stretchers. But on comparison significant

76 Honour, *Chinoiserie* p. 67; and Stengel 1958 p. 74.
77 Schnell's salary as lacquermaster to the Dresden court in 1710 was 3,000 Thaler, which contrasts with Dagly's salary of 1,000 Thaler, and Bach's salary of 400 Thaler at Cöthen. See Huth 1971 pp. 66 and 74, and Stengel 1958 p. 77.
78 One of Dagly's finest cabinets has the relief gold japan on black ground on the exterior, with flat polychrome japan on white ground on the interior. See Huth 1955 p. 20 and pl. 3–4.
79 *China und Europa* (see note 75) pp. 226, 228.

differences emerge. The black stand appears to be less well proportioned and finely made. The contrast of thick and thin in the leg profile is less bold, the moldings are less complex and imaginative, the plain swollen curve of the apron lacks the splendid energy of the S-curve of the white instrument, and one misses the complexity of the tiny moldings framing each leg and making the eye dance across the surface. The expressive effect of the entire harpsichord is affected by this. It is not just that the black one is an inexpensive simplification of the lines of the white, for economy would not dictate the lessened contrast of its proportions even if it caused the unmolded and unmitered leg-framing battens. On the white, the extraordinary ins and outs of the apron and leg-top moldings, between the straight lines of case front and leg, suggests the energy of a compressed spring, while the line of the black apron is comparatively static. But the striking difference is not necessarily an indication that the black stand is not by Dagly, for it is very like his stands under other furniture.

Appendix B

Johann Rost

Though it is almost certain from circumstantial evidence that Mietke built the two harpsichords at Charlottenburg, it is not impossible that they were made by Johann Rost.[80] Several public announcements yield interesting information about Rost harpsichords.[81] A harpsichord 'made in 1706 by the famous Rost' was to be sold on 6 May 1748 in Neucölln (now part of Berlin). It was 'beautifully painted inside' and 'lacquered in white with gold bands [Leisten] outside'. It could be Dagly who did this. However, neither here nor in later announcements (16 January 1747, 'by the late Rost'; 2 June 1760) of harpsichords by Rost, which were lacquered in black, is Dagly's participation mentioned. Johann Rost appears repeatedly: for instance, on 26 February 1720, in the documents of the private cashbox of Queen Sophie Dorothea, for whom he has 'den Flügel raccomodirt'. This would mean 'repaired' or 'refurbished a harpsichord', not 'built it' as implied by Boalch.[82]

The date 1706, the location in Berlin, the fact that the Queen of Prussia was paying him for work on her harpsichord, and the fact that he is known to have built harpsichords lacquered in both white (which was never a common harpsichord-

---

80 Huth (1971 p. 68) says that 'Dagly lacquered harpsichord cases for the Berlin firm of Rost and Michael Mietke.' The same phrase was repeated in later works (presumably picked up from Huth, though without giving a reference), including Impey 1977 pp. 116–17, and Jarry 1981 p. 155. These may all derive from a hypothetical typographical error in Huth, where the passage probably was meant to read 'for the Berlin *firms* of Rost and [of] Michael Mietke', for Huth's source – Stengel 1958 pp. 75–6 – is clearly describing two separate builders, and he does not hint at any relationship between the two. Boalch (1974 p. 128) refers to two Berlin harpsichord-builders named Rost – a 'Rost' in 1760 (quoting from Gerber 1790–2 and 1812–14; this must be a later generation) and a 'Johann Rost' in 1706 (from the same passage in Stengel) – without mentioning any connection to Mietke.

81 Stengel 1958 pp. 75–7.

82 Boalch 1974 p. 128.

case color, though it was occasionally used later in the Hamburg school) and black, certainly raise the possibility that the Charlottenburg harpsichords are by Rost. However it is Michael Mietke who was specifically mentioned as the court builder to King Frederick I and Queen Sophie Charlotte, Mietke was working in Charlottenburg, not Berlin,[83] whereas Rost is mentioned only in Berlin. We have two pieces of documentary evidence that Dagly decorated Mietke harpsichords, but none that he worked on Rost's instruments. Furthermore, these harpsichords are not signed, which is normal for furniture made for a court, but not otherwise normal for harpsichords made in North Germany. One of the harpsichords was owned by Queen Sophie Charlotte (who would surely patronize her own court builder as well as court lacquerer),[84] and the white harpsichord was normally kept in Schloss Charlottenburg according to eighteenth-century records. The evidence in favor of Mietke rather than Rost is circumstantial but overwhelming.

The attribution of the white harpsichord (and, by extreme similarity, the black one also) to Michael Mietke is therefore not seriously shaken by the presence of Rost in Berlin at the same time. Unless new evidence comes to light that places Rost more strongly in contention (for instance, a signature discovered on one of these or on a very similar instrument, or proof that Mietke was away from Berlin during the few years during which the harpsichord must have been built), we may continue to attribute these harpsichords to Mietke.

Appendix C

William R. Dowd: **A Description of the Two Charlottenburg Harpsichords**

The two unsigned and undated harpsichords at Schloss Charlottenburg have long been admired by art historians but have only recently begun to attract the interest of musicologists and instrument-makers. A brief technical description of the two follows.

One is a black double harpsichord with a disposition of 8′, 4′, 8′ and a coupler. The other is a white single harpsichord with two 8′ registers. Their similarity in design, construction, and workmanship makes it almost certain that they are both from the same maker. Furthermore, the workmanship is excellent.

Each has a curved tail, continuous with the bentside. The shapes of the tails are so similar that they must have been bent on the same form. The gaps are slightly canted, the wrestplanks being 20 mm ($\frac{3}{4}''$) narrower at the treble, and the gaps them-

---

83 It is now part of Berlin, but at that time the difference was significant, for Charlottenburg was a separate town.

84 In 1696 Dagly asked for and received from the Great Elector a remarkably strict legal monopoly on all lacquering done or sold in Berlin, and King Frederick I reapproved his even more stringent demands for monopoly in 1702. In such a climate, Mietke (in a parallel though less powerful position at court) would probably make strong objections if the queen turned to an independent harpsichord-builder. See Huth 1971 pp. 68–9.

selves are tapered in width from bass to treble. The case sides of thin lime (9–11 mm, $\frac{3}{8}''$ ±) are joined at the corners with dovetails and are mounted on heavy pine bottoms. The bottoms are strengthened with two heavy interior cross-braces. Composite knees (consisting of a horizontal piece pinned to a vertical piece, both nicely shaped with chamfered edges) butt the spines, bentsides, and their liners. The liners are very heavy (28 × 28 mm, $1\frac{1}{8}''$ square for the double) and even heavier where they are sawn to fit the interior of the bentside.

The *Damms* are joined to the backs of the belly rails forming a closed barrier from soundboard to bottom. The oak wrestplanks are mounted on 25 mm (1″) pine blocks glued to the spine and cheek and filling the space from bottom to wrestplank. The front ends of these blocks have vertical pieces joined to them. These 'breadboard ends' are notched and pegged to the front ends of the wrestplanks. Above the soundboards and wrestplanks, thin linings of hardwood topped with overhanging moldings are glued to the interiors of the cases. The visual effect hints at an Italian harpsichord in its outer case.

The soundboards are undecorated, even lacking roses; the grain directions are parallel to the spines. The bridges are high and narrow, the bridge of the single and the 8′ bridge of the double having almost identical dimensions (18 × 11 mm at c′). They have equally sloping front and back sides with a molding cut into the top front edge. The pins are in the quirk of the molding. The bridges are pinned to the soundboard from the underside. These headless pins are bent at right angles and pounded into the underside of the board. The ribbing of the single is uncertain, but a normally placed cut-off bar is disclosed by a ridge in the soundboard. The double has a rather heavy cut-off bar slightly curved to follow the 4′ bridge. There is only one rib in the dead section. The normally shaped rectangular *boudin* does not join the spine liner but is cut off just after the last hitch pin. Two ribs overlap the end of the *boudin* on either side and continue to the spine liner.

The keyboards of both instruments are almost identical in style and workmanship. The very narrow octave span of 156 mm ($6\frac{5}{32}''$) is as small as many seventeenth-century French keyboards. The natural key slips of ebony have quite rounded and short heads (35 mm, $1\frac{3}{8}''$) with two pairs of cut lines. The arcades are ebony. The stained hardwood sharps are covered with thin ivory rather than bone. They are not tapered in height but are tapered in width from top to bottom by 1.5–2 mm ($\frac{1}{16}''$ ±). The key levers are lightly carved to balance. The original balance pins seem very heavy (2.9 mm, 0.115″) and the single keyboards and lower manual of the double are guided by hardwood slips in the rack.

Both instruments have full-depth box slides with the jack mortises relieved on both sides for tongue clearance. The slides of the single are tapered to increase the difference in plucking points by 10 mm ($\frac{3}{8}''$) in the bass. The taper of the double's slides is only 4 mm for all three, which is musically inconsequential. The jacks for both are neatly made and untapered. The tongues were punched for leather in modern times.

These two harpsichords, presumably made at the beginning of the eighteenth century, originally had rather limited compasses: the double, 54 notes, FF to c''', FF$\sharp$ and GG$\sharp$ missing; the single, 53 notes, GG to c''', GG$\sharp$ missing. Later in the eighteenth century, the compasses of both were extended to 59 notes, FF to e''', FF$\sharp$ missing. The cases were *not* enlarged. Extra keys were added to the original keyboards, which were then slid to the left to center them, and the additional strings were installed.

The keyboards of the double were moved two courses of strings toward the bass, thereby lengthening the scale of c'' from 295 mm ($11\frac{5}{8}''$) to 335 mm ($13\frac{3}{16}''$). The rather short original scale, like the octave span, is in the seventeenth-century French tradition, while its later scale is similar to the Hamburg school.

The single's keyboard was moved one course of strings to the bass, and its extended scale is very short: c'' is 268 mm ($10\frac{9}{16}''$), suggesting that the original scale was even shorter. Unfortunately, it is impossible to determine its exact original state, since the bridge and perhaps the soundboard date from the time of the extension. While the nut has been extended at both ends for the added strings, the bridge has neither been lengthened nor redrilled. A judicious moving of the bridge position and a realignment of the string cant could retain the original scale after the keyboard shift. The original scale was probably very close to the present scale. Two instruments extremely similar in all other respects differ significantly in their original scaling.

Dimensions of the two Charlottenburg harpsichords (in mm)

Double harpsichord (black)
total length: 2350
inside width: 860
case height: 245
soundboard down: 64 average
soundboard length: 1825
gap width: 62 to 58
wrestplank width: 207 to 187
wrestplank down: 64 average

| | *original scale* | | *scale after compass extension* | |
	8′ →	← 4′	8′ →	← 4′
e‴			133	65
c‴	153	73	174	81
c‴	295	147	335	165
c′	565	290	630	324
c	1091	552	1186	611
C	1700	927	1800	998
FF	1867	1097	1905	1195

Single harpsichord (white)
total length: 2185
inside width: 840
case height: 240
soundboard down: 62
soundboard length: 1785
gap width: 53 to 43
wrestplank width: 197 to 177
wrestplank down: 62

scale after compass extension: e‴   103
                                  c‴   135
                                  c″   268
                                  c′   520
                                  c   987
                                  C   1603
                                  FF   1840

References

Besseler, H., 'Markgraf Christian Ludwig von Brandenburg', *BJ* 43 (1956), pp. 18–35

Boalch, D. H., *Makers of the Harpsichord and Clavichord 1440–1840*, 2nd edn (Oxford, 1974)

Ergang, R., *The Potsdam Führer: Frederick William I, Father of Prussian Militarism* (New York, 1941)

Ernst, F., *Der Flügel Johann Sebastian Bachs* (Frankfurt, 1955)

Haase, G., & D. Krickeberg, *Tasteninstrumente des Museums: Kielklaviere, Clavichorde, Hammerklaviere* (Berlin, 1981)

Hirt, F. J., *Stringed Keyboard Instruments 1440–1880* (Boston, 1968), trans. from *Meisterwerke des Klavierbaus* (Olten, Switzerland, 1955)

Hodgetts, E. A. Brayleys, *The House of Hohenzollern: Two Centuries of Berlin Court Life* (New York, 1911)

Hubbard, F., *Three Centuries of Harpsichord Making* (Cambridge, Mass., 1965)

Huth, H., 'Lacquer-Work by Gerhard Dagly', *Connoisseur* 95 (1935)

——*Europäische Lackarbeit 1600–1850* (Darmstadt, [1955])

——*Lacquer of the West* (Chicago, 1971)

Impey, O., *Chinoiserie* (New York, 1977)

Jarry, W., *Chine et Europe* (Fribourg, 1981)

Kinsky, G., 'Zur Echtheitsfrage des Berliner Bach-Flügels', *BJ* 21 (1924)

Krickeberg, D., '*Meine Herren, der alte Bach ist gekommen!*' (Berlin, 1976)

Kühn, M., *Die Bauwerke und Kunstdenkmäler von Berlin*, 2 vols. (Berlin, 1970)

Kühn, M., & H. Börsch-Supan, *Schloss Charlottenburg* (Berlin, 1980)

Loesser, A., *Men, Women and Pianos* (New York, 1954)

Mitford, N., *Frederick the Great* (New York, 1970)

Nelson, W. H., *The Soldier Kings: The House of Hohenzollern* (New York, 1970)

Russell, R., *The Harpsichord and Clavichord* (London, 1959)

Sachs, C., *Musik und Oper am Kurbrandenburgischen Hofe* (Berlin, 1910)

Schweitzer, A., *J. S. Bach*, 2 vols., trans. E. Newman (London, 1911; repr. New York, 1966)

Stengel, W., *Alte Wohnkultur in Berlin* (Berlin, 1958)

Handel's 'Chandos' and Associated Anthems: An Introductory Survey

GERALD HENDRIE

(Cambridge)

The music discussed in this essay – some seventeen large-scale anthems, virtually English cantatas – was edited by me for the *Hallische Händel-Ausgabe* between 1964 and 1972.[1] The first volume is to be published in 1984.

For such an edition to remain unpublished more than a decade after editorial work is completed poses a variety of problems. Musicological fashions, like any others, are subject to change. Moreover, although up-dating of critical apparatus is both possible and to be expected, there is clearly a limit to what can be done about the musical texts. More important still, such non-publication means that much painstakingly acquired information has not been shared with others who have followed in the same field. Last, but by no means least, the would-be performer is disadvantaged.

The eleven so-called Chandos Anthems and their six Chapel Royal relations represent a significant *oeuvre* of a major composer. Moreover, despite their uneasy marriage of 'intimacy and ducal pomp',[2] any doubts about their popularity[3] would seem to be dispelled by the enormous number of surviving manuscript sources (mostly contemporary with Handel – see below) supported by the published texts of Wright & Wilkinson and of Arnold (1780s and 1790s) which, together with various nineteenth-century manuscript copies, will have kept this music in circulation until Chrysander's 1870–2 edition for the Händel-Gesellschaft. That no subsequent critical edition should have appeared in full before the tercentenary in 1985 is, to say the least, discouraging.

There is no record of Handel's appointment at Cannons, so we do not know precisely when he began, when he finished, how much he was paid, what was expected of him, whether he resided at Cannons and if so to what extent.[4] From Deutsch we

1 *HHA* III/4–6, 9, forthcoming.
2 W. Dean, 'Handel', *New Grove*.
3 H. Diack Johnstone, 'The Chandos Anthems: The Authorship of No. 12', *MT* 117 (1976), p. 601.
4 R. A. Streatfeild, *Handel* (London, 1909; 2nd, rev. edn 1910), and P. H. Lang, *George Frideric Handel* (New York, 1966). These and others suggest that Handel continued to live in London (at

note a break in newspaper references to Handel, bounded by those in the *Daily Courant* of 19 July 1717 and 16 February 1719. There is little doubt that Handel was employed by Brydges soon after the first of these dates, for Brydges's letter to Dr Arbuthnot dated 25 September 1717[5] states unequivocally that Handel had already composed four anthems expressly for Brydges and was at work on two more. It seems unlikely that Handel retained a formal connection with Cannons much beyond the following summer, for he will have wanted to be in London that autumn to engage in preliminary discussions for the establishment of the Royal Academy. Strength is lent to the case for Handel's having resided in London during his Cannons period (perhaps at Brydges's town house in Albermarle Street) by the reference to *Acis and Galatea*, that most celebrated of Cannons works, in the hand of the elder Smith: 'composed by . . . Handel . . . 1718 London'.[6] Thus although the precise nature and duration of Handel's Cannons connection remain uncertain, a reasonable assumption would be that he entered into an agreement with Brydges, perhaps quite a loose one, to be his composer more-or-less in residence (at London and Cannons) for a year or so: from August or September 1717 to about the same time the following year. This would not conflict with Mainwaring's assertion that 'two years he spent at Cannons' if we interpret 'two years' to mean parts of 1717 and 1718.

What is clear, however, is that Handel had severed his connection with Cannons by the time Brydges acquired the dukedom in April 1719, and that the term 'Chandos Anthems' has no authority other than that of custom and convenience. Moreover, the anthems cannot have been performed in the chapel at Cannons, for that was not opened until 29 August 1720.[7] They must therefore have been performed in the neighbouring church of St Lawrence, Whitchurch, which Brydges had rebuilt and modernized between 1714 and its official reopening on Easter Sunday 1716.[8]

Handel chose his anthem texts carefully, generally from the Prayer Book but occasionally from the *New Version of the Psalms* by Tate and Brady (1696). More rarely, he used a modified version of one of these sources to suit his own requirements. (Such modifications were clearly part of the overall planning and should not be confused with the occasional lapses of spelling, or other misunderstandings, found in his earlier English autographs.)

The eleven Chandos Anthems, in the order first given by Chrysander, together with their texts, are as follows. The texts are Prayer Book settings unless otherwise specified.

Brydges's Albermarle Street house) and commuted to Cannons as necessary. Dean (note 2 above) takes the contrary view. See also Beeks's account, the first essay in this volume.

5 Deutsch *Doc* p. 78.

6 T. Best, letter to *MT* 113 (1972), p. 43; P. Rogers, 'Dating "Acis & Galatea": A Newly Discovered Letter', *MT* 114 (1973), p. 792.

7 Deutsch *Doc* p. 112.

8 'Weekly Remarks' of 7 April 1716 (in *The Weekly Oracle*), quoted in D. J. Burrows, 'Handel and the English Chapel Royal during the Reigns of Queen Anne and King George I', 2 vols., Ph.D. diss., The Open University, 1981, p. 196.

PB = Prayer Book; TB = Tate and Brady

1	*O be joyful in the Lord* HWV 246	Ps. 100 [= Jubilate]
2	*In the Lord put I my trust* HWV 247	Ps. 11 v.1; Ps. 9 v.9; Ps. 11 v.2; Ps. 12 v.5; Ps. 11 vv.6–7; Ps. 13 v.6 (TB) (see pp. 154–5 below)
3	*Have mercy upon me* HWV 248	Ps. 51 vv.1–4, 8, 10–13 [= part of Miserere]
4	*O sing unto the Lord* HWV 249b	Ps. 96 vv.1 (part), 3–4; Ps. 93 v.5; Ps. 96 vv.9, 11
5A	*I will magnify Thee* HWV 250a	Ps. 145 vv.1–2, 4, 20–1 (additional non-autograph sources including one in Smith's hand – see p. 154 below – interpolate settings of Ps. 145 vv.17 and 19, and Ps. 144 v.15, before Ps. 145 v.21
6A	*As pants the hart* HWV 251b	Ps. 42 vv.1, 3 (TB modified), vv.4–5 (PB), vv.6–7 (PB modified)
7	*My song shall be alway* HWV 252	Ps. 89 vv.1, 5 (with omission), 6–9, 12 (with omission), 15, 16, 18 (first half); Alleluia (see pp. 154–5 below)
8	*O come let us sing unto the Lord* HWV 253	Ps. 95 vv.1–3, 6–7; Ps. 96 vv.6, 10 (part); Ps. 99 v.9 (first half); Ps. 103 v.11; Ps. 97 vv.11, 12 (first half) [Ps. 95 = Venite]
9	*O praise Lord with one consent* HWV 254	Ps. 135 vv.1–3, 5; Ps. 117; Ps. 148 vv.1–2 (TB); Alleluia
10	*The Lord is my light* HWV 255	Ps. 27 vv.1, 3–4, 7 (with omission); Ps. 18 vv.31, 7 (with omission), 14 (second half), 13 (second half modified); Ps. 20 v.8 (with omission); Ps. 34 v.3; Ps. 28 v.8; Ps. 29 vv.4 (first half), 9; Ps. 30 v.4; Ps. 45 v.18 (with omission); Amen
11A	*Let God arise* HWV 256a	Ps. 68 vv.1–3, 4 (first half), 19 (first four words only); Ps. 76 v.6 (with omission); Ps. 68 v.35 (last three words only); Alleluia

A twelfth anthem, *O praise the Lord ye angels of his*, published by Arnold as a 'Chandos' anthem, is stylistically quite unlike Handel; not surprisingly there is no evidence to support Arnold's claim. The matter is discussed in Johnstone, 'The Chandos Anthems' (see note 3 above).

The above order has a certain logic in that Anthems 1–6 require the same forces (STB, oboe, bassoon, two violins, continuo), whereas nos, 7–11 require the slightly larger forces of a four-part choir, or in the case of no. 10 a five-part choir; and, for Anthems 8 and 10, two recorders. Moreover, and hardly surprisingly, the Cannons 'Concert', under the direction of J. C. Pepusch, grew in number rather than diminished during the heyday of Cannons.[9]

The wording of Brydges's letter to Arbuthnot implies that Handel was composing anthems in pairs:

Mr Handle has made me two new Anthems very noble ones & most think they far exceed the two first. He is at work on 2 more & some Overtures to be plaied before the first lesson . . .

The first twelve items in the Pepusch–Noland catalogue of 1720[10] are by Handel, and

9 Implicit in C. H. Collins Baker & M. I. Baker, *The Life and Circumstances of James Brydges, First Duke of Chandos, Patron of the Liberal Arts* (Oxford, 1949); confirmed more recently and in much greater detail by G. Beeks, 'The Chandos Anthems and Te Deum of George Frideric Handel (1685–1759)', Ph. D. diss., University of California, Berkeley, 1981, chs. 1 and 3.
10 Reprinted in Baker & Baker, *op. cit.* (note 9 above), pp. 134ff.

all except the third are specifically designated as being 'in score'. (The third was most likely in score too.) These works comprise the Te Deum in B flat followed by Chandos Anthems 8, 9. 10, 2, 5, 6A, 4, 7, 11A, 3, 1 in Chrysander's (and *HHA*'s) numbering.

On 18 November 1981, items 7–12 of Pepusch's catalogue, in the form of two volumes each of three scores, were sold as Lot 122 of Christie's sale of 'Printed Books'; these were acquired by the British Library. The order of anthems in these scores is: volume I, Anthems 4, 6, 7; volume II, Anthems 11, 3, 1. That is, they follow Pepusch–Noland except for the reversed order of the anthems in the first pair. Pepusch's items 1–6, incidentally, did not appear in Christie's sale; one might reasonably assume, however, that they would have comprised two more volumes, similarly bound.[11] A further entry in Pepusch's catalogue, 19a, comprising two Chandos Anthems by Handel and two by Pepusch, did however appear in the same sale, as Lot 123, a volume similar in appearance to the previously mentioned one; this volume was likewise purchased by the British Library. The Handel anthems are nos. 2 and 5A.

Surprisingly, the compilers of Christie's catalogue for that sale missed the significance of Lot 132, a 'collection of Twelve Concerti or Sonatas, including a Te Deum, manuscript . . . 2 vols . . . parts for first violin and contrabasso only, contemporary calf panelled in gilt . . . could be by Albinoni . . . ' which are, in fact, none other than instrumental parts of Pepusch's items 1–12. (This Lot was purchased by Gerald Coke Esq. As usual, Mr Coke has generously provided written information and granted access to this material.) The order of anthems in these partbooks is: 4, 6A, 7, 11A, 3, 1, 2, 5A, Te Deum, 8, 9, 10. Table 1 sets out the contents of the three Lots. Clearly, there is a consistency about the ordering of the Chandos material in the catalogue, in the scores and in the surviving parts, and it is not unreasonable to suppose as others have done[12] that this may well reflect an order of composition, even though it conflicts with the natural supposition that as the Cannons Concert grew Handel composed accordingly: six anthems for STB and five for four or more voices – hence Chrysander's 1–6A and 7–11A.

The presence of a Te Deum among the 'anthems' is by no means surprising; for the Venite (in part) and Jubilate are present, all three being normally considered as 'canticles' for Matins. The Te Deum differs from the other two, admittedly, in not

11 Described in Christie's catalogue as 'contemporary red morocco gilt, sides gilt-panelled, elaborately tooled, with volutes and cornerpieces, enclosing centre ornament'. Catalogue title: 'Printed Books / The Property of / A Charitable Trust / The Trustees of the Stoneleigh Settlement / The Executors of the Late 4th Lord Leigh / Stoneleigh Abbey Preservation Trust Ltd / and from various sources'. The compiler of the catalogue observes that 'in 1755 James Leigh of Adlestrop, whose son later inherited Stoneleigh, married Carolina Brydges, eldest daughter of Henry Duke of Chandos, and it is likely that she owned the music and other books formerly at Cannons, which had meantime been pulled down'.

12 See the dissertations of Beeks (see note 9), ch. 3, and of Burrows (see note 8), ch. 6. Both draw support for their argument from the lost 'Cummings' MS in which ten Chandos Anthems appeared in the order 4, 6 A, 7, 11, 3, 1, 2, 5A, 8, Te Deum. This music is listed in W. H. Cummings, *Handel, the Duke of Chandos and the Harmonious Blacksmith* (London, 1915), pp. 11–12, and in Sotheby, Wilkinson & Hodge, *Catalogue of the Most Famous Library . . . of the late W. H. Cummings 17–24 May 1917* (London, 1917)

Table 1.

	Pepusch-Noland catalogue 1720	Chrysander (HG 34–6)	Christie's sale 1981		
item			Lot 122	Lot 123	Lot 132
					(contd)
1	Te Deum [in B flat]	–	–	–	Te Deum
2	*O come let us Sing unto the Lord*	8	–	–	8
3	*O praise the Lord in one Consent*	9	–	–	9
4	*The Lord is my Light*	10	–	–	10
5	*In the Lord put I my Trust*	2	–	–	
6	*I will magnify Thee O God my King*	5A	–	–	
					vol. I begins
			vol. I		with:
7	*As Pants the Heart* [sic]	6A	4	–	4
8	*O Sing unto the Lord*	4	6A	–	6A
9	*My Song shall be always* [sic]	7	7	–	7
			vol. II		
10	*Let God Arise*	11A	11A	–	11A
11	*Have mercy on me O God*	3	3	–	3
12	*[O] Be Joyful [in the Lord]* (= Jubilate)	1	1	–	1
					Vol. II
19a	*In thee O Lord I put my trust*	2		2	2
	I will magnify thee	5A		5A	5A

being a psalm. But there is no reason for an anthem to be confined to psalm texts, the splendidly open-ended wording of the 1559 'Injunctions' having paved the way for almost anything: 'for the comforting of such as delight in music . . . either at morning or evening, there may be sung a Hymn or suchlike song . . . ' Within that context, the Chandos Anthems are very conformist.

It is, of course, possible that the 'canticle' anthems were performed at the appropriate liturgical moments in the service rather than as anthems following the third Collect. Be that as it may, it should not be assumed that the Chandos setting of the opening verses of the Venite was in any way related to the Chandos Te Deum; the Venite is in A major, the Te Deum in B♭, an unlikely coupling. Indeed, if they were related Pepusch would surely have listed them in the correct liturgical order in his catalogue; as it is, they appear reversed.

The order of composition of the eleven Chandos Anthems – twelve if we include the Te Deum – remains unclear. There is little doubt that the recurring order identified above (and noted by others) warrants serious attention as does the fact, first recorded by Brydges, that Handel was composing anthems *in pairs*. All one can say with any degree of confidence, however, is that the autographs are uniform in all relevant respects. A reordering according to Pepusch's catalogue might have a certain logic and appeal. Yet Pepusch in 1720 was listing 'presentation' volumes of secondary sources whose contents therefore might equally well reflect usage or ducal preference as much as the original order of composition. Chrysander's order,

153

while unlikely to be correct in particular respects, nevertheless has a certain overall logic. I felt that the evidence for a reordering, however persuasive, was insufficiently precise to justify overthrowing Chrysander's, now hallowed by more than a century's usage. *HHA* therefore preserves the order found in *HG* 34-36. However, the Chapel Royal anthems which share Chandos material (4A, 5B, 6B, 6C, 6D, 11B) will be disentangled from their long-standing association with the Chandos Anthems and published appropriately along with other Chapel Royal compositions.

The Chandos Anthems draw upon earlier material from both Handel's Italian and first Chapel Royal periods and generate further music, most notably later Chapel Royal works. For example, Anthem 1, *O be joyful*, represents a reduction in forces for the Cannons establishment of the Utrecht Jubilate of 1713, which it follows entirely. However, the Utrecht Jubilate lacks the symphony of Anthem 1; and the Allegro of the symphony derives from the opening of the Utrecht Te Deum. However, both the Utrecht Jubilate and Anthem 1 derive from an early Italian work, *Laudate pueri Dominum*, dated by Handel 8 July 1707. The opening chorus of this motet is thirty-one bars longer than in its 'Utrecht' or 'Chandos' forms, but the musical material is the same. The opening Adagio of the symphony of Anthem 1 begins similarly to that of the 'Caroline' Te Deum in D of 1714. The entire symphony of Anthem 1 is found as the opening two movements of the Trio Sonata Op. V No. 2, published in London by Walsh in 1739.

Such a genealogy is not untypical. Moreover the anthems themselves may appear in several guises. Anthem 5B, for example, most likely dating from the 1720s, is a reconstructed version for the Chapel Royal of Anthem 5A. The magnificent opening Andante of 5A, which forms the first part of its symphony and which in 5B is woven into the solo with which the work opens, represents the archetype of the Handelian Andante, displaying that sureness of touch which removes Handel forever from the realm of lesser composers (see Ex. 1). In fact, that music, also found in the Oboe Concerto in B flat major known as no. 2, whose four movements comprise the transposed symphonies of Anthems 8 and 5A respectively, dates from as early in Handel's career as *Laudate pueri Dominum*, for it occurs in the opening Andante of the 'Sonata a 5' in B flat major of c1707.

Anthems 5A and 5B do not have much in common except their opening and closing music in A major; and as already observed, even this opening music is reworked in Anthem 5B. Anthem 5A requires the same forces as Anthems 1–4 and in its autograph version calls only for a tenor soloist. However, there are two additional movements, for soprano and for tenor, found in a number of secondary sources. Since these include one in the hand of the elder Smith[13] (one which in other respects appears to have been copied directly from Handel's autograph) these two movements, 'The Lord is righteous' (Ps. 145 vv.17 and 19) and 'Happy are the people' (Ps. 144 v.15), would seem to bear the stamp of Handel's authority. (In a further source these two movements are found interpolated in Anthems 2 and 7

13 Tenbury MS 881 (in the Bodleian Library, Oxford).

154

Ex. 1. Anthem 5A

respectively.)[14] Smith and the other score copyists who included the extra movements placed them *after* the tenor air 'The Lord preserveth'. Chrysander, however, placed them on either side of this air, presumably to permit the verses from Psalm 145 to run sequentially; that is, verse 17 ('The Lord is righteous') followed by verse 20 ('The Lord preserveth') followed by Psalm 144 verse 15 ('Happy are the people'). Not only did this disregard the evidence of the sources, but it ignored the common-sense order of text that Handel observed. For the additional movements are settings of two statements: 'The Lord preserveth all them that love him, but scattereth abroad the ungodly' and 'The Lord is righteous . . . he will fulfil the desires of them that fear him'. These are followed by the conclusion, taken from the previous psalm, 'Happy are the people who are in such a case' (in other words, happy are those who fear the Lord and whose desires are thereby fulfilled). A glance at the texts of the Chandos Anthems (see above) should serve to demonstrate Handel's care in choosing his texts and his unerring sense of liturgical and musical propriety.

14 University of Chicago Library, Dept of Special Collections MS 437: a series of twenty-six volumes of vocal and instrumental parts of the Chandos and associated anthems, together with scores of Anthems 2, 5B and 10. At the time of acquisition in 1926 or 1927, this collection was entitled only 'Music Collection, Anthems, Serenades, Violin and Organ Music', with no indication of the true content or authorship. When I was editing the anthems for *HHA* it was the article by H. Lennenberg & L. Libin, 'Unknown Handel Sources in Chicago', *JAMS* 22 (1969), pp. 85–100, that first brought this important collection to my attention.

It should be noted too that he reversed the order of verses again in Anthems 5B and 10. The additional movements to Anthem 5A are included in the *HHA* edition with their original order restored.[15]

Four versions exist of Anthem 6, *As pants the hart*, and their interrelationships are complex. No. 6A, in E minor, is scored for the same forces as Anthems 1–5A; 6B, in D minor, is for six-part choir with five named soloists, strings including violas (there are no violas in the Cannons music) and continuo; 6C, whose movements are in D minor, A minor (two), F major, G minor and B♭ major, is for six-part chorus with four named soloists and organ continuo; 6D, beginning in D minor and ending in A major, is for six-part chorus and organ continuo and, like 6C, includes 'solo' and 'chorus' directions.

Conclusions which I reached when editing this music in the mid-1960s accord with those expressed more recently by others,[16] namely that Anthem 6C was composed first during the period of Handel's first association with the Chapel Royal between 1710 and 1714; that 6A came next, with Handel rearranging the opening chorus for his Cannons forces and thereafter writing different music to the same text, his improved knowledge of the English language enabling him to correct some earlier misspellings; then 6B and 6D, for the second Chapel Royal association of the 1720s. Among the more interesting interrelationships are the four settings of 'Tears are my daily food'[17] and the obvious relationship of 6D's version to the third movement of the fourth flute sonata (Op. I No. 7) and its looser connection with the opening of the third movements of the trio sonatas Op. II No. 3 and Op. V No. 6.

Last among the dual versions are Anthems 11A and 11B. The first of these, in B♭ major, is scored for the 'usual' Cannons forces (no violas) with four-part chorus including soprano and tenor soloists; the second, a reworking in A major for the Chapel Royal, for four-part chorus and for alto and bass soloists, making six-part texture, and strings including a viola part. The autograph of 11B names 'Hughs' and 'Wheely' as soloists; both served as Gentlemen of the Chapel Royal between 1713 and 1743.

Most interestingly, there seems a distinct possibility that Anthem 11A had originally only the second Allegro movement of its symphony despite the presence of the preceding Andante in Handel's autograph score.[18] However, there is no doubt that Handel intended this Andante to be played 'before the Anthem Let God arise'; he headed it with these very words. There is no doubt either that the hand, paper, and rastrography are consistent with other works of the Cannons period,[19]

---

15 For a more detailed discussion, see G. Beeks, 'Handel's Chandos Anthems: The "Extra" Movements', *MT* 119 (1978), p. 621.

16 In the dissertations of Beeks (see note 9 above) and Burrows (note 8).

17 Summarized by B. Lam, 'The Church Music', in G. Abraham, *Handel: A Symposium* (London, 1954).

18 BL RM 20.d.6, ff. 43–76.

19 For full particulars see D. J. Burrows, 'A Handlist of the Paper Characteristics of Handel's English Autographs', typescript, The Open University, 1982.

although – importantly in view of the present discussion – this Andante is written on paper which differs slightly from that used for the rest of the anthem. (This paper reappears for the following and final anthem in the manuscript, Anthem 5A).[20] Moreover, this Andante has been wrongly bound in the manuscript, being divided between folios 43 and 50. These folios encompass the anthem's first movement (ff. 44–49') and are followed on f. 51 by the Allegro which originally served as the single-movement symphony.

What is exceedingly interesting, however, is the possible correlation between this Andante and the enigmatic reference to 'Overtures [= symphonies] to be plaid before the lessons' in Brydges's letter to Arbuthnot (a reference conveniently ignored by most commentators). Graydon Beeks asks[21] 'could our fugitive movement have been a part of one of these?' The answer could be affirmative, especially when a closer look is taken at the unusually irregular handwriting of the heading already remarked upon. The autograph handwriting is irregular because it has served more than one function. An initial reading yields:

To be played before the Symphony of the Anthem let God arise
[a] tempo ordinario, andante [erased] e staccato
No. 1 [pencil] larghetto [written between upper two staves, in pencil]

There is no doubt that the words 'Symphony of' are differently written, more faintly, more neatly, and smaller. Moreover, the second 'the' (before 'Anthem') is written over another word. The conclusion is inescapable. The original centrally placed heading was something else, short and tidy: 'Symphony of . . . '; and these first words have been encompassed later, and hastily, by Handel's present heading. The word 'the' before 'Anthem', or at least its last two letters, are boldest of all, covering, as they must, an original short word – or else one which tailed off sufficiently or similarly to be covered by the word 'Anthem' – a word whose initial letter may have been 't' or something similar. (Unfortunately, some of Handel's words, in ink and in pencil, are now very faint. Moreover this is an unusually grubby page – further evidence, perhaps, of its chequered history.)

Such a symphony could hardly have comprised only an Andante, and one cadencing on the dominant; in any case Handel's instruction 'Segue' (following his customary bar-count, in this case '26') is clear indication of a succeeding movement, no doubt an Allegro.[22] Although it might be tempting to conclude that the present Allegro was the one in question – in which case Anthem 11A would have lacked the *entire* symphony – this cannot be so, for the Allegro is headed 'Ψ 68',

20 'I will magnify thee, O God my King', ff. 77–99
21 G. Beeks, 'Handel's Chandos Anthems: More "Extra" Movements', *ML* 62 (1982), p. 155. Incidentally, Beeks states that this Andante is 'derived from a symphony in Act III sc. 7 of the 1712 *Il pastor fido*' (i.e. *HG* 59 p. 64). I cannot agree; there are syntactical similarities admittedly, but nothing in this G minor movement bears any thematic or motivic connection with the Andante in B♭.
22 The Andante ends halfway through the lower system of f. 50. To the right are the treble and bass incipits of the Allegro movement which originally began Anthem 11A; Handel may well have added these incipits later, of course, when he knew the two movements were to be united.

Handel's customary designation for psalm settings. (The first chorus lacks such a heading and so could never have begun the work.)

We do not know, of course, precisely what Brydges meant by 'Overtures to be plaid before the first lesson', but if we accept that, as seems possible, this particular Andante was the beginning of one of these overtures, then it must have been followed by a second movement *other* than the one associated with Anthem 11A. That Handel should have been able to write more than one such movement will not surprise us; indeed, we find such a movement in the same key and, as it happens, with an opening motif not very dissimilar, at the start of the masque *Acis and Galatea*, composed at Cannons about the same time (Ex. 2). Indeed, were *Acis* composed for the same forces as our Andante (*Acis* has two oboes), it would be tempting to conclude that the Andante was originally entitled 'Symphony of Acis' and that the masque thus began with a *two*-movement Sinfonia. (It is within the bounds of possibility that Handel began *Acis* with a single oboe in mind but that upon learning

Ex. 2. Anthem 11A; Acis and Galatea

that a second oboe was available he found another use for the Andante he had already composed. At this point he might have seen dramatic advantage in opening *Acis* with a fast movement – the present Presto, which, incidentally, bears no heading or title.)

Winton Dean observes[23] that

The Chandos anthems have suffered from the circumstances of their origin. They were composed for the English equivalent of a small German court and reflect at once the urbane worldliness of eighteenth-century Anglicanism and the mixture of intimacy and ducal pomp at Cannons. They are too elaborate for the cathedral repertory . . .

and H. Diack Johnstone writes[24] that

For whatever reason, chiefly perhaps their rather unusual and somewhat impractical scoring, the Chandos anthems have never been popular, and even in Handel's lifetime public performances were apparently rare.

23 'Handel', *New Grove* (see note 2 above).
24 'The Chandos Anthems' (see note 3 above).

Yet over and above the complete set of autograph scores in the British Library (Royal Music Collection and Department of Manuscripts) and in Cambridge (Fitzwilliam Museum), there are around a hundred copies, a surprising number of them in the hand of J. C. Smith the elder. Secondary sources (in reality, co-primary sources in the case of the Smith copies) are found in London (British Library; Foundling Hospital; Guildhall; Royal College of Music); Cambridge (Fitzwilliam Museum); Oxford (Christ Church; Bodleian Library, including those from St Michael's College, Tenbury); Manchester (Henry Watson Library); the cathedral libraries of Durham, Hereford and York; Dublin (Archbishop Marsh's Library; St Patrick's and Christ Church Cathedrals; Mercer's Hospital; Trinity College); two private collections in England (Gerald Coke Esq.; Lord Shaftesbury[25]) and in Denmark (Mrs Margrete Schou); Hamburg (Staats- und Universitätsbibliothek); New Brunswick (Rutgers University Library); and Chicago (University, Music Library). In addition there are printed editions of Birchall and Beardmore (Anthem 6A only), 1783; Wright and Wilkinson (Anthems 2–5A, 6A 7–10, 11B), 1784; and Arnold (Anthems 2–5A, 6A–11A, 11B), c1790. These sources are reviewed and collated in the critical commentary to the third volume of anthems for Cannons, the forthcoming *HHA* edition (III/6).

25 I am grateful to Anthony Hicks for this more recent information.

'Der Himmel weiss, wo diese Sachen hingekommen sind': Reconstructing the Lost Keyboard Notebooks of the Young Bach and Handel

ROBERT HILL

(Cologne)

Our knowledge about the influences on the early musical development of Johann Sebastian Bach and George Frideric Handel is in large part dependent on reports of keyboard notebooks that each compiled during his youth. Descriptions of the contents of these two manuscripts provide the most concrete information we have about the compositional models that influenced them during their formative years. Despite the central position of these stories for Bach and Handel biography, neither account has received critical attention. The manuscripts themselves have long since disappeared; if we wish to know more about them, we must begin by isolating those elements in the account that refer concretely to the books themselves, basing our reconstruction of their format and contents on surviving manuscripts, particularly those that indicate how keyboard repertoire in Germany was transmitted at the end of the seventeenth century.

Thanks to biographers who included it as a bit of color decorating the otherwise bare landscape of early Bach biography, the story of how the young Johann Sebastian Bach copied a manuscript by moonlight only to have it confiscated by his elder brother is one of the better-known anecdotes in musical literature. The passage in the Obituary referring to the lost manuscript reads as follows:[1]

Johann Sebastian war noch nicht zehen Jahr alt, als er sich, seiner Eltern durch den Tod beraubet sahe. Er begab sich nach Ohrdruff zu seinem ältesten Bruder Johann Christoph, Organisten daselbst, und legte unter desselben Anführung den Grund zum Clavierspielen. Die Lust unsers kleinen Johann Sebastians zur Musik, war schon in diesem zarten Alter ungemein. In kurtzer Zeit hatte er alle Stücke, die ihm sein Bruder freywillig zum Lernen aufgegeben hatte, völlig in die Faust gebracht. Ein Buch voll Clavierstücke, von den damaligen berühmtesten Meistern, Frobergern, Kerlen, Pachelbeln aber, welches sein Bruder besass, wurde ihm, alles Bittens ohngeachtet, wer weis aus was für Ursachen, versaget. Sein

1 Carl Philipp Emanuel Bach, Johann Friedrich Agricola, Lorenz Mizler & Georg Venzky, *Nekrolog auf Johann Sebastian Bach und Trauerkantate* (Leipzig, 1754) – cited hereafter as the Obituary – in *Dok* III pp. 81–2.

161

Eifer immer weiter zu kommen, gab ihm also folgenden unschuldigen Betrug ein. Das Bach lag in einem blos mit Gitterthüren verschlossenen Schrancke. Er holte es also, weil er mit seinen kleinen Händen durch das Gitter langen, und das nur in Pappier geheftete Buch im Schranke zusammen rollen konnte, auf diese Art, des Nachts, wenn iedermann zu Bette war, heraus, und schrieb es, weil er auch nicht einmal eines Lichtes mächtig, war, bey Mondenscheine, ab. Nach sechs Monaten, war diese musicalische Beute glücklich in seinen Händen. Er suchte sie sich, insgeheim mit ausnehmender Begierde, zu Nutzen zu machen, als, zu seinem grössten Herzeleide, sein Bruder dessen inne wurde, und ihm seine mit so vieler Mühe verfertigte Abschrift, ohne Barmherzigkeit, wegnahm. Ein Geiziger dem ein Schiff, auf dem Wege nach Peru, mit hundert tausend Thalern untergegangen ist, mag uns einen lebhaften Begriff, von unsers kleinen Johann Sebastians Betrübniss, über diesen seinen Verlust, geben. Er bekam das Buch nicht eher als nach seines Bruders Absterben, wieder.

Johann Sebastian was not yet ten years old when he saw himself bereft of his parents by death. He removed himself to Ohrdruf, to his eldest brother Johann Christoph, organist there, and under the direction of the same laid the groundwork for keyboard-playing. Our little Johann Sebastian's desire for music was even at this tender age unusual. Within a short time he had completely mastered all the pieces his brother had made available for him to learn. However, a book full of keyboard pieces by the most famous masters of the day, Froberger, Kerll and Pachelbel, which his brother owned was, despite all pleas, and for who knows what reasons, denied him. His zeal to progress led him to the following innocent deceit. The book lay in a bookcase locked up only behind lattice-work doors. So he withdrew it, because he could fit his small hands through the lattice openings and could roll up the book in the bookcase, since it was only bound in paper. In this manner, and by night, while everyone was in bed, he copied it, by moonlight, since he had no access to a light. After six months, the musical booty was happily his. He attempted, secretly and with uncommon eagerness, to make use of the book when, to his greatest sorrow, his brother found out, and mercilessly appropriated the copy that had cost so much effort. A miser whose ship had sunk en route to Peru carrying a hundred thousand Thaler can give us a vivid image of the sorrow of our little Johann Sebastian upon this loss. He did not retrieve the book again before his brother's death.

This anecdote is the only story concerning Bach's boyhood that Carl Philipp Emanuel Bach saw fit to include in the Obituary; indeed, outside of baptism and school records it is virtually the only authoritative biographical information that we have about Bach's life before his departure for Lüneburg. In C. P. E.'s account, Bach's keyboard background occupies the central position. Johann Christoph is mentioned specifically as Sebastian's keyboard teacher, and the book which Sebastian copied is likewise specifically described as containing keyboard repertoire, by three South German composers known primarily for their keyboard-playing and composing. This focus on keyboard-playing in Bach's early musical training is consistent with the image that C. P. E. presents throughout the Obituary of Bach as a keyboard virtuoso.

This anecdote is also practically the only point in the entire Obituary at which Philipp Emanuel attempts to sketch Bach's personality for the reader: we learn more about Bach as a person from this anecdote than from any other information supplied in the Obituary. With this in mind, we can understand C. P. E.'s emotionally loaded presentation of the events in the manuscript episode as an opportunity for him to illuminate aspects of Bach's personality, in particular his extraordinary zeal and his tendency to follow an independent course. In order to impress these traits upon the reader, C. P. E. juxtaposes with the protagonist – the young, recently orphaned Johann Sebastian – an antagonist, Johann Christoph, characterized as a provincial organist with little insight into his younger brother's gifts and equally little understanding of the tremendous efforts Sebastian expended to copy the book. C. P. E.'s attempt to illustrate early signs of Bach's musical gifts was thus accomplished at Johann Christoph's expense.

It is important to see the role that C. P. E.'s character portrait of Johann Christoph in the anecdote had in shaping the prejudice against Johann Christoph which may be seen in writings since Forkel. Johann Christoph's negative image was made even worse as a result of C. P. E.'s misconception that Johann Christoph had died around 1700 (indeed, that it was Johann Christoph's death that necessitated Sebastian's departure for Lüneburg).[2] Because C. P. E.'s date for Johann Christoph's death was inaccurate (he actually lived until 1721), Spitta concluded that the correct date could not have been of great interest to C. P. E. and thus reflected his low estimation of Johann Christoph as an influence on J. S. Bach. In turn, Spitta's rather negative opinion of Johann Christoph Bach seems to have led subsequent generations of scholars to underestimate the importance of Johann Sebastian's relationship to Johann Christoph, with the result that for years Johann Christoph was overlooked as an obvious candidate in the search for the identity of the main scribe of the Möller MS and the *Andreas Bach Buch*, the two most important sources for the keyboard music of the young Johann Sebastian Bach.[3]

Johann Christoph Bach, born in 1671, left Eisenach to study with Pachelbel in Erfurt in 1686, when he was fifteen and his youngest brother Johann Sebastian just a year old. After three years of study Johann Christoph obtained, with Pachelbel's assistance, positions as organist in Erfurt, Arnstadt and finally Ohrdruf in 1690. In considering Johann Christoph's response to Johann Sebastian's act, it is important to understand the circumstances of their relationship. We can only guess at Johann Christoph's feelings at unexpectedly becoming the guardian of two brothers he hardly knew. We know that in 1700 economic difficulties forced Johann Christoph to take on more teaching obligations than he desired. That housing and feeding his two younger brothers caused him hardship we can infer from the departure within only a year of the middle brother, Johann Jakob, who had come along with Johann Sebastian to live with Johann Christoph upon the death of their parents. Further, as soon as Johann Sebastian was fifteen – the age at which Johann Chris-

---

2 This misconception appears to have resulted from an ambiguity in the date of Johann Christoph's death as it appeared in C. P. E.'s copy of the Bach family genealogy; cf. *Dok* I pp. 259, 265. The story as it stands in the Obituary presents the facts as C. P. E. Bach understood them at a half-century's distance. It seems clear that he believed in the substance of the story, for in a reply to a request from Forkel to see any of J. S. Bach's old manuscripts of keyboard pieces by composers he had 'loved and admired', C. P. E. reported in 1775 that the manuscripts had disappeared: 'I don't have anything by Fischer, Froberger and so on. Heaven knows what's become of these things' ('von Fischern, Frobergern etc. etc. etc. habe ich nichts. Der Himmel weiss, wo diese Sachen hingekommen sind': *Dok* III pp. 292, 288).

3 H.-J. Schulze, 'Studien zur Bach-Überlieferung im 18. Jahrhundert', Diss., University of Rostock, 1977, ch. 2.

toph himself had left home – Sebastian too was sent off on his own. If we add to this Sebastian's tendency to get into mischief as a boy (a trait he did not like to be reminded of later in life),[4] then the scene is set for conflict. Finally, we should acknowledge that Johann Christoph's anger was certainly legitimate: manuscript-copying was for the most part the only way to acquire repertoire for oneself, and we may infer from Johann Christoph's response to Sebastian's unauthorized copying that he regarded this as an infringement on his rights of ownership of a body of pieces that he had gone to much trouble and possibly even expense to accumulate.

It should be pointed out that we are dealing here actually with *two* manuscripts, both now lost: Johann Christoph's manuscript and Johann Sebastian's copy. It is Johann Christoph's manuscript that we must reconstruct, since the anecdote provides some information about that manuscript but tells us virtually nothing about the copy made by Johann Sebastian. Johann Christoph is not specifically referred to as the compiler of the manuscript, but in view of his later copying activity this is a reasonable assumption. With regard to the manuscript itself, the account tells us that the book was bound in paper. This would be consistent with Johann Christoph's financial circumstances, and moreover finds corroboration in the Möller MS, which in all probability originally also had a paper binding.

Johann Christoph Bach is not known to have composed, but like his cousin Johann Gottfried Walther he was an avid copyist and collector of keyboard music. The Möller MS and the *Andreas Bach Buch* document Johann Christoph's collecting activity during roughly the first decade of the eighteenth century. These two books are what (in another context) Jakob Adlung termed 'miscellanies', that is, aggregations of various types of repertoire, without any overriding organization or order.[5] If we compare the contents of the Möller MS and the *Andreas Bach Buch* with what we know of Johann Christoph's lost manuscript, it is striking that of the three composers reported to have been represented in Johann Christoph's book only Pachelbel is represented in the two later anthologies (despite the fact that the Möller MS otherwise has a large number of pieces by composers active in the last quarter of the seventeenth century, e.g. Edelmann, Lebègue, Fabricius, Lully), and even by Pachelbel there are surprisingly few pieces for a man who was Johann Christoph's teacher and friend. The repertoire in the two later anthologies may thus be seen to complement the repertoire in the earlier manuscript, insofar as it can be reconstructed.

The Möller MS and the *Andreas Bach Buch* show Johann Christoph Bach's

---

4 C. P. E. Bach, in a letter to Forkel (Hamburg 1774?): 'many stories circulate about him; a few of them may be true and belong among his youthful pranks. The deceased wished none of them to be known, so leave out these funny things' ('Man hat viele abentheuerliche Traditionen von ihm. Wenige davon mögen wahr seyn u. gehören unter seine jugendliche Fechterstreiche. Der seelige hat nie davon etwas wissen wollen, u. also lassen Sie diese comischen Dinge weg': *Dok* III p. 286).

5 J. Adlung, in *Anleitung zu der musicalischen Gelahrtheit* (Erfurt, 1758), p. 126, describes two ways of collecting information, of which one is 'a mixed kind: *Miscellanea* in which one keeps to no order in the things but writes them down after each other as they are heard or read' ('eine gemischte Art . . . *Miscellanea* da man keine Ordnung der Sachen beobachtet, sondern solche nach einander auffschreibet, wie man sie höret oder lieset').

musical tastes to have been very sophisticated: compared to other contemporary manuscript collections of keyboard music, they contain an extraordinarily high proportion of large, elaborate pieces, which stand out from contemporary repertoire by their complexity and quality. The contrast made in the anecdote (if not merely invented for effect) between Johann Christoph's teaching repertoire for a boy of ten and the enticing repertoire in the coveted manuscript suggests that the 'moonlight' manuscript, like the later two, also contained repertoire of very high quality.

Johann Christoph would have acquired music by Pachelbel from the composer himself, most likely during his period of study with that composer in the late 1680s. And Pachelbel is also the most direct link between Johann Christoph and repertoire by Froberger, and probably Kerll as well. If we regard Johann Christoph Bach's manuscript as a student notebook compiled under Pachelbel's influence, many bits of the puzzle begin to fall into place. Just as the Möller MS and the *Andreas Bach Buch* can serve as analogous documents of Johann Christoph's collecting activity, we are fortunate to have a manuscript compiled by another pupil of Pachelbel's, Johann Valentin Eckelt. At the age of seventeen, Eckelt (1673–1728) studied with Pachelbel for three months, between Easter and the end of June 1690.[6]

Eckelt's *Tabulaturbuch*, long thought to be lost after World War II, is among the Berlin manuscripts that recently re-surfaced in Cracow.[7] The manuscript is an anthology of around ninety folios in upright quarto format, in German organ-tablature notation, containing liturgical and non-liturgical keyboard compositions by Froberger, Pachelbel and others, including many unattributed works. As with late-seventeenth-century German keyboard-tablature anthologies in general, the Eckelt *Tabulaturbuch* is a miscellany; in this case, however, the contents have a rough ordering reflecting the sources from which Eckelt obtained his repertoire.

The first two sections of the manuscript were acquired by Eckelt directly from Pachelbel.[8] These portions of the manuscript, containing predominantly a mixture of prelude and fugal forms by Pachelbel and Froberger, can give us some idea of the kind of repertoire Pachelbel made available to his pupils, though we should remember that Eckelt studied with Pachelbel for a far shorter time than Johann Christoph Bach, and that as a beginning pupil he would have been less likely to have had access to more cherished pieces.

If we use the Eckelt *Tabulaturbuch* as a model in reconstructing the format and

---

6 Some years later, in his post as organist at Sondershausen, Eckelt taught Heinrich Nicholas Gerber, who was later a pupil of J. S. Bach, and whose son was the lexicographer Ernst Ludwig Gerber.

7 DSB Mus MS 40035 (*olim* Z. 35). Although a microfilm was not available to me during the preparation of this paper, it has been possible partly to reconstruct the contents by using information furnished in R. Eitner, *Biographisch–bibliographische Quellen-Lexicon* (Leizpig, 1898–1904), articles 'Eckelt', 'Froberger', 'Pachelbel'; in M. Seiffert, *Geschichte der Klaviermusik* (Leipzig, 1899), p. 197; and *DTÖ* X/2:21 (*Johann Jakob Froberger: Orgel- und Klavierwerke*, 3, ed. G. Adler (Vienna, 1903), pp. 119–26).

8 Eckelt seems to have paid Pachelbel for some pieces: the second remark in the book is 'von ihm gecaufft zu den Cohrahlen' ('bought from him for the chorales [?]'). Seiffert, who examined the book, interpreted 'ihm' to mean Pachelbel, a conclusion I see no reason to doubt.

contents of Johann Christoph Bach's lost manuscript, the following picture emerges: Johann Christoph's book was probably an integral miscellany manuscript (as opposed to a book made up of heterogeneous gatherings bound together), notated primarily or entirely in German organ tablature rather than staff notation. The integral nature of Eckelt's book as well as the old-fashioned notation would both be consistent with other German keyboard manuscript anthologies from the mid to late seventeenth century.[9] The Eckelt *Tabulaturbuch* can also give us an idea of the Pachelbel and Froberger repertoire Johann Christoph's lost manuscript might have contained. The Eckelt book contains several large Pachelbel toccatas and chaconnes similar to but not concordant with those in the Möller MS and the *Andreas Bach Buch*, along with a number of fugues and many small pieces intended for liturgical use. Although a few Pachelbel chorales and chorale-partitas are found in a later section of the Eckelt book, it would be inappropriate to infer from this that Johann Christoph Bach's lost manuscript contained chorales, for chorale repertories tended in general to be transmitted in manuscripts devoted exclusively to that genre.[10] While it is very unlikely that a book including repertoire by Catholic composers such as Froberger and Kerll would have contained a substantial chorale repertory, the absence of such a body of chorales in the lost manuscript as well as the Möller MS and the *Andreas Bach Buch* makes it very likely that Johann Christoph Bach also compiled a collection of chorales: yet another manuscript we must count as lost.

When compared with the Froberger repertoire transmitted in collections such as the Vienna codices, and other printed or manuscript collections, the Froberger pieces in the Eckelt *Tabulaturbuch* divide neatly into three groups: three toccatas, all *unica*; three large contrapuntal pieces, all found in the well-known Froberger collections; and three 'dubious' pieces, two of which are *unica*. The third member of this last group, a small intonation prelude without parallel in the rest of Froberger's surviving works, has one concordance. It is noteworthy that the Froberger repertoire in the Eckelt book does not contain suites. It is hard to say whether or not the absence of suites reflects the availability of such material to Eckelt. In any case, the widespread dissemination of Froberger suites in other tablature manuscripts suggests that his suites would have formed a standard part of a repertory of Froberger's pieces available to Pachelbel, and thus to Johann Christoph Bach.

The Eckelt *Tabulaturbuch* contains no repertoire attributed to Kerll.[11] Kerll's keyboard output survives primarily in a few manuscripts transmitting a closed repertory;[12] so few late-seventeenth-century sources transmit Kerll's keyboard

9 E.g. the MSS SPK Am.B.340 or Mus MS 40158.

10 Examples are the J. G. Walther anthologies DSB Mus MS 22541/1–4 and the so-called *Plauener Orgelbuch* (photocopy DSB Fot Bü 129).

11 Two versets from Kerll's *Modulatio Organica* (1686) are found attributed to Vetter in the section of the manuscript containing repertoire that Eckelt apparently acquired from Andreas Nikolaus Vetter (1666–1734). Cf. M. Seiffert, *Geschichte der Klaviermusik* (note 7 above), p. 233.

12 Largely corresponding in content to the thematic catalogue of his keyboard works included by Kerll as an appendix to the *Modulatio organica*. Cf. F. W. Riedel, *Quellenkundliche Beiträge zur Geschichte der Musik für Tasteninstrumente* (Kassel, 1960), pp. 130ff.

music that it is difficult to ascertain a pattern in the nature of the Kerll repertoire that would have found its way into miscellanies. The pattern in the surviving manuscripts does suggest, however, that it was Kerll's toccatas and semi-programmatic pieces (rather than his contrapuntal pieces) that circulated in such sources and would therefore be more likely to have been available to the young J. S. Bach.

While the available information on Bach's notebook is extremely limited, we are fortunate to have slightly more information on Handel's book. The earliest report is found in William Coxe's *Anecdotes of George Frederick Handel and John Christopher Smith*, published in London in 1799. Coxe was the stepson of John Christopher Smith Junior, the son of Handel's friend. Coxe's sister Martha was the Lady Rivers, to whom Smith had willed the book, along with other manuscripts of music by Smith and Handel.[13] When the Handel biographer Victor Schoelcher purchased the bulk of Handel/Smith material from the estate of Lady Rivers in 1856, the notebook was no longer to be found.[14] The manuscript is described in a footnote on p. 6 supplementing a discussion of Handel's study with Zachow:

It has long been a matter of curious research among the admirers of Handel, to discover any traces of his early studies. Among Mr. Smith's collection of music, now in the possession of his daughter-in-law [i.e. stepdaughter], Lady Rivers, is a book of manuscript music, dated 1698, and inscribed with the initials G. F. H. It was evidently a common-place book belonging to Handel in the fourteenth year of his age. The greater part is in his own hand, and the notes are characterized by a peculiar manner of forming the crotchets.

It contains various airs, choruses, capricios, fugues, and other pieces of music, with the names of contemporary musicians, such as Zackau, Alberti, Frobergher, Krieger, Kerl, Ebner, Strunch. They were probably exercises adopted at pleasure, or dictated for him to work upon, by his master. The composition is uncommonly scientific, and contains the seeds of many of his subsequent performances.

Coxe's account conveys a remarkably concise and informative picture of Handel's notebook. He furnishes information on the book's provenance and describes its physical appearance. He identifies the main scribe, noting that the manuscript was the work of more than one scribe (perhaps teacher Zachow as well as pupil Handel?), and he even describes characteristics of the main hand. He calls the manuscript a 'common-place book', which we may understand in the sense of a miscellany, containing vocal works as well as contrapuntal pieces in genres normally played on the keyboard, composed by Middle and South German figures, most of them active at the end of the seventeenth century. Finally, he generalizes about the learned nature of the repertoire, and speculates on the pedagogical function of the collection.

13 Coxe, *Anecdotes of George Frederick Handel and John Christopher Smith* [1799], facsimile edn by Percy M. Young (New York, 1979), p. xxi.
14 V. Schoelcher, *The Life of Handel* (London, 1857), p. 9. Alfred Mann (in *Georg Friedrich Händel: Aufzeichnungen zur Kompositionslehre, HHA* Suppl. I (Kassel/Leipzig, 1978), p. 10) places the Handel notebook in connection with the manuscript collection acquired by Fitzwilliam in 1799.

It seems hardly possible that Coxe could have formulated such a methodical description without a first-hand examination of the manuscript itself. The details he provides concerning the physical appearance of the manuscript correspond closely to features frequently found in late-seventeenth-century German student or household notebooks: a date and owner's name or initials often appears on the cover or front pages of this sort of manuscript.[15] Such a personal examination seems all the more likely in view of the fact that the manuscript was owned by Coxe's sister.

Coxe's very proximity to the manuscript makes his reference to the 'peculiar shape of the crotchets' in the main hand quite problematic. If we look for evidence of such a 'peculiarity' in a score thought to be the earliest surviving Handel autograph, the *Laudate pueri dominum* dated c1702,[16] it is not the crotchet (or quarter note) that is remarkable, but rather the sixteenth note (semiquaver), which in Handel's notation of vocal lines often takes the old-fashioned South German form in which the second flag is attached to the first. While Handel retained this form throughout his life, as the opera autographs show (in particular in recitatives), there is no evidence elsewhere in Coxe's publication to suggest that he was familiar with other Handel manuscripts and hence with this notational practice. And since it is very likely that Coxe was musically literate, we can hardly blame the discrepancy between the note-values of sixteenth and quarter on mere ignorance. The possibility remains that Coxe, in putting together his book, relied on a few notes he had taken on the manuscript, and that he simply did not accurately recall which note-value looked 'peculiar'.

Coxe's characterization of the repertoire in the Handel notebook suggests that the manuscript was primarily an anthology of examples of learned counterpoint. Coxe himself hinted at this with his choice of the term 'scientific' to describe the repertoire, as well as his conjecture that the pieces were 'probably exercises selected by Handel or assigned by Zachow'. Nearly every composer included in the manuscript wrote significant contrapuntal works – works which, moreover, we can be reasonably certain were circulating in Middle Germany at the end of the 1690s.[17] A unifying thread may be traced throughout the contrapuntal repertoire that the Handel notebook will have contained: an emphasis on South German composers, with their tradition of writing pieces in strict counterpoint, often in open score, using newly composed abstract themes, with a formal emphasis on intricate contrapuntal devices introduced in a sectionalized structure, the sections often featuring contrasting meters and thematic transformation.

15 For example, the second notebook of Anna Magdalena Bach, 1725 (SPK Mus MS Bach P 225), and the Heinrich Nicholas Gerber notebook, dated 1713 and 1715 (SPK Mus MS 40268).
16 *Composers' Autographs*, ed. Walter Gerstenberg (London, 1968), vol. I, no. 35) reproduced from BL RM 20.h.7, p. 3).
17 The modifications made by scholars over the last century to the list of composers said to be represented in the manuscript reads like a comedy of errors. See G. Thomas, 'Friedrich Wilhelm Zachow', diss., University of Cologne, 1962 = Kölner Beiträge zur Musikforschung 38, ed. K. G. Fellerer (Regensburg, 1966), p. 19 note 4.

The most likely sources for such repertoire by Froberger, Kerll and Krieger will have been the prints of their music that appeared during the 1690s. The Froberger prints of 1693 and 1696[18] each contained a number of pieces written in strict style, while several *canzoni* of Kerll were available in prints from *c*1698.[19]

Of the remaining figures, the only one not working in Middle Germany in the late seventeenth century is Wolfgang Ebner (1612–65), active at the Imperial court in Vienna. Along with Froberger, he is credited with having contributed to the development of a keyboard tradition in Vienna in the mid seventeenth century. Among the handful of works attributed to Ebner is an open-score piece found in Roberday's anthology *Fugues et Caprices* (1660). As Chrysander suggested,[20] the Strungk mentioned by Coxe will have been Nicolaus Adam Strungk (1640–1700), a North German active in Leipzig at the time of his death. His capricci in strict style are transmitted in open score in the Lowell Mason Codex, a Middle German source probably from the last decade of the seventeenth century.[21] The Alberti on the list is probably Johann Friedrich Alberti (1642–1710), cathedral organist in Merseburg. His surviving chorale settings demonstrate his interest in counterpoint, and Mattheson relates that in 1968, just before Alberti suffered a paralyzing stroke, he had prepared for publication a set of twelve *ricercati* that thoroughly explored contrapuntal technique.[22] Handel owned a copy of *Anmüthige Clavier Übung* (1699) by Johann Krieger (1652–1735), whose brother Johann Philipp Krieger was Kapellmeister to the court at Weissenfels, where Handel's father had been Court Surgeon. As well as his keyboard works preserved in manuscript, Johann Krieger's prints include a number of contrapuntally intricate compositions, including a series of four fugues followed by a fifth that combines the subjects of the previous four.[23]

But it is Zachow whom we must see as the most influential figure in the manuscript: he was in a position to shape the character of the manuscript by providing appropriate pieces to stimulate and guide the young Handel's development. Mainwaring reports that Zachow had a large library from which, as Handel must have recalled to Smith, Zachow 'let him copy unusual things'. Through Zachow's library, Handel will have been able to draw on many of the prints and manuscripts he needed to compile his notebook. In the choral pieces in contrapuntal style by Zachow and others we find a repertoire which embodies both aspects of

18 J. J. Froberger, *Diverse Ingegnosissime, rarissime e . . . curiose Partite* (Mainz, 1693) and *Dive[r]se, curiose e rare Partite musicale . . . Prima Continuatione* (Mainz, 1696).

19 *Toccates & Suittes pour le Clavessin* (Amsterdam, 1698/9) and *Sonate da Organo di varii autori* (n.p, 1697/1701); cf. Riedel (note 12 above), pp. 66–7, 132ff. Handel parodied one of these *canzoni* in his oratorio *Israel in Egypt* (1739), but it seems likely that his source would have been the Walsh edition of *Toccates & Suittes* (1719, 1730) rather than the earlier Roger edition; cf. W. D. Gudger, 'A Borrowing from Kerll in "Messiah" ', *MT* 118 (1977), pp. 1039, who first proposed that Handel's source was the Walsh print.

20 F. Chrysander, *G. F. Händel* (Leipzig, 1858), p. 43.

21 New Haven, Yale University MS LM 5056.

22 J. Mattheson, *Grundlage einer Ehrenpforte* (Hamburg, 1740), p. 7.

23 Cf. *DTB* II/18, ed, M. Seiffert (Leipzig, 1917): J. Krieger's Fugues in C, pp. 46–52.

the contents of Handel's manuscript as described by Coxe. Zachow himself practiced composition in strict style. His mass for four unaccompanied voices on *Christ lag in Todesbanden*, for example, is an exercise in *prima prattica* motet style.

One of the principal differences between Handel's studies under Zachow and Bach's under his brother is that while Pachelbel and Johann Christoph Bach were primarily keyboardists, Zachow was mainly active as a vocal composer. It seems only natural that Handel's interest in vocal music should have been particularly stimulated by Zachow's activity, and perhaps it is no coincidence that the earliest surviving Handel autograph is a vocal piece, while the earliest known Bach autograph contains chorale preludes.[24] An emphasis on vocal composition is not the only important difference between Handel's and Bach's early musical studies. Probably even more significant for Handel's development was the strength of his relationship with Zachow. Zachow was an established, well-respected composer who provided a powerful model for Handel. By comparison, Johann Christoph Bach had relatively less influence on Johann Sebastian. As a teacher, he seems to have provided only an apparently rather uninspiring repertoire. And to judge from the important place of keyboard repertoire by Johann Sebastian Bach in the Möller MS and the *Andreas Bach Buch*, we could even say that within just a few years the roles of the two brothers were reversed, as Johann Sebastian began to supply Johann Christoph with pieces of his own. The fate of the manuscripts, too, reflects the sharply differing circumstances under which Handel and Bach compiled their notebooks. Handel's notebook was a precious memento he treasured throughout his life, while no trace of Bach's book is known beyond the Obituary anecdote.[25]

While the manuscripts had a practical function for their original owners, their existence was also useful to William Coxe and Carl Philipp Emanuel Bach. Coxe's description of the manuscript, the only concrete reference to documentary material in his entire collection of anecdotes on Handel, was used to substantiate an otherwise anecdotal discussion of Handel's studies with Zachow. And although the Bach manuscript story *is* anecdotal, it has an authority assured by C. P. E. Bach's privileged access to the most intimate Bach family traditions. The anecdote of the lost manuscript copied by moonlight differs strongly in character from the more common run of anecdotes such as the one (current even during Bach's lifetime) relating Bach's contest with Marchand, or that describing Bach's visit to Potsdam in 1747.[26]

In contrast to these types of anecdotes, the manuscript story is direct and personal. As C. P. E. chose to present him, Bach is portrayed not as a hero but as a boy

24 SPK Mus MS Bach P 488.

25 Johann Christoph's manuscript was perhaps lost in the catastrophic fire that swept Ohrdruf in 1753, from which the survival of the Möller MS and the *Andreas Bach Buch* remains to be explained; cf. H.-J. Schulze (note 3 above), p. 33 note 19.

26 This report of the visit has a remarkably similar antecedent in a story Mattheson relates of Kerll's appearing before the Emperor and astounding the court with his ability to improvise elaborate counterpoint (*Grundlage* (see note 22 above), p. 136).

whose craving for music compelled him to undertake a deceitful act. For both Carl Philipp Emanuel Bach and William Coxe, the manuscripts were less interesting as evidence of the early training of Bach and Handel than as tangible manifestations of an otherwise intangible genius in the two young composers.[27]

27 The materials for this discussion were assembled as part of a Harvard University dissertation, in progress, focusing on the Möller MS and the *Andreas Bach Buch*.

A biographical article by Hans-Joachim Schulze on Johann Christoph Bach, touching upon the 'moonlight' manuscript anecdote, is forthcoming in *BJ* 1985. Important new material contained in that article became available to me too late for incorporation into my discussion.

Table

MS	date	scribe	format	composers represented	nature of repertoire	source of repertoire
[GFH MS]	1698	GFH [and Zachow?]	staff notation; oblong octavo format? (80–100 ff.?)	primarily South German: Froberger, Kerll, Krieger, Ebner, Strungk, Zachow Alberti	contrapuntal repertoire?: capricci, *canzoni*? capricci, *canzoni*? fugues? capriccio? open-score capricci? keyboard fantasia? vocal repertoire *a4*? *ricercari* in strict style?	Zachow's library? prints 1693, 1695? prints 1697/8? print 1698? MS repertoire Zachow's library MS prepared for publication in 1698
['Moonlight' MS]	1695–1700	JSB	primarily German organ tablature? (50–100 ff.?)	Pachelbel, Froberger, Kerll (and others?)	large, elaborate pieces	JCB MS
[JCB MS]	before 1700	JCB?	primarily German organ tablature? (80–100 ff.?)	Pachelbel, Froberger, Kerll (and others?)	Pachelbel teaching repertoire?	Pachelbel?
JVE MS	1690–2	JVE	German organ tablature; upright quarto format (89 ff.)	(in section acquired from JP) Pachelbel, Froberger, anon.	Pachelbel teaching repertoire: small preludes & fugues, large toccatas, chaconnes (chorale partitas)	Pachelbel
Mö	1700?–1710?	JCB & others	mixed – primarily staff notation (100+ ff.); oblong format	mixed North German, French, JSB	primarily large free and fugal pieces; suites	copies from prints; MS repertoire from JSB?
ABB	1700?–1713?	JCB & others	mixed – primarily staff notation (120+ ff.); upright format	mixed North & Middle German, French, JSB	primarily large free and fugal pieces; suites	copies from prints; MS repertoire from JSB?

Did J. S. Bach Compose the F minor Prelude and Fugue BWV 534?

DAVID HUMPHREYS

(Cardiff)

Recently, in a brief contribution to *Early Music*,[1] the present writer suggested that the case for attributing the Prelude and Fugue in F minor to J. S. Bach requires closer critical examination than it has yet received. It has to be said from the outset that the ascription to Bach, which has never been seriously questioned, cannot be decisively refuted by musicological evidence. It does seem possible, however, to establish two things; first, that the ascription is impossible to confirm by external evidence and, secondly, that the flaws, weaknesses and stylistically uncharacteristic features of both movements raise grave doubts as to Bach's authorship.

The early history of the work is obscure. It is generally dated to the Weimar period (*c*1716, according to *NBA* IV/5–6 *KB*, p. 413).[2] Yet there is no trace of it in the copies transmitted by the pupils mainly associated with the organ works of the Weimar period (Walther, Kirnberger, Kellner, Krebs and others). It was also unknown to Forkel, judging by his list of incipits published in 1802.[3] Indeed, there is no record of the work until its sudden emergence in two independent, but almost certainly closely related, early-nineteenth-century sources emanating from the school of Johann Christian Kittel (1732–1809), whose status as one of J. S. Bach's last pupils constitutes the link between Bach and the sources of BWV 534. One of these is a manuscript copied by Kittel's pupil Johann Andreas Dröbs (1784–1825) as one of a collection of four Bach works in the MS Leipzig MB III.8.21. The other is an undated printed edition by another Kittel pupil, Gotthilf Wilhelm Körner, as no. 260 of the series *Der Orgel-Virtuos*.[4] Both attribute the piece to J. S. Bach. Although the textual analysis in the *NBA KB* shows that they are independent,

---

1 D. Humphreys, 'The D minor Toccata BWV 565', *EM* 10 (1982), pp. 216–17.

2 All the major commentators state or tacitly assume a Weimar dating: see H. Klotz, 'Bachs Orgeln und seine Orgelmusik', *Mf* 3 (1950), pp. 180–203; W. Emery (ed.), *The Organ Works of Bach*, Novello edn, VI (London, 1940) preface.

3 Forkel's thematic catalogue is reproduced in *BR* pp. 354–6.

4 *Der Orgel-Virtuos, oder Sammlung von Tonstücken aller Art für die Orgel* (Erfurt/Langensalza, n.d.).

there is little doubt that they both stem from a lost copy in the hand of Kittel. Körner's edition bears a footnote reading 'Nach einer Handschrift von Kittel. War bis jetzt ungedruckt' ('after a manuscript of Kittel; previously unprinted'); and Kittel was certainly the main source too for Dröbs's Bach copies. The ascription to J. S. Bach therefore hinges on Kittel's lost copy.

In 1844, BWV 534 appeared in the Peters edition, edited by Griepenkerl.[5] The fact that Körner and Griepenkerl advance conflicting claims to have published the first edition suggests that their dates of issue were very close. Whatever the truth, Griepenkerl had no access to Körner's edition and based his text entirely on Dröbs. The remarks in his preface show how little BWV 534 was known nearly a century after J. S. Bach's death; after giving Dröbs as his source and noting Forkel's ignorance of the work, he claims 'we have inquired in vain of other collectors now living for a second copy' ('auch bei anderen jetzt lebenden Sammlern haben wir vergeblich nach einer zweiten Abschrift angefragt'). Finally, the work appeared in *BG* 15 (1867), edited by Wilhelm Rust from Dröbs's copy.[6]

Many of the variants between the two primary sources are due to errors or inconsistencies of notation on the part of either Dröbs or Körner, but a second, more interesting group of variants seems to reflect the difference of approach between Dröbs, the scribe making a copy for his private use, and Körner, the editor preparing a text for publication. Körner has an occasional tendency to bowdlerize ungrammatical progressions which were almost certainly present in the original and which Dröbs leaves untouched. In bar 40 of the fugue, for example, Körner eliminates a pair of consecutive fifths by means of an unlikely-looking crotchet rest which changes the implications of the part-writing (see Ex. 1).

Ex. 1. Fugue in F minor BWV 534.ii, bars 39–40

Other variants of this type are as follows:

fugue bar 48: Körner again seems to have changed the part-writing to avoid a (quite unexceptionable) pair of doubled leading notes arising from a quaver run.

fugue bar 119: Körner reads D♮ instead of F (l.h. second crotchet), probably in order to avoid ungainly parallel sevenths with the alto.

---

5 F. C. Griepenkerl (ed.), *Johann Sebastian Bachs Kompositionen für die Orgel*, 9 vols. (Leipzig), II (1844), pp. 39–45.

6 See also *NBA* IV/5–6 *KB* pp. 413–16.

fugue bar 127: Körner reads crotchet A♭ instead of minim F in the alto (first
   beat) apparently in order to eliminate consecutive octaves.

Some at least of these solecisms are hard to explain as scribal errors, as indeed are others present in both sources (narrowly avoided consecutive octaves, fugue bar 99; doubled leading notes, fugue bar 127). Körner also modernizes the key signature from three flats to four.

The fact that BWV 534 has an obscure and unusual early history is not in itself an argument for rejecting it from the Bach canon, though it cannot fail to excite notice that nothing is known of the work until more than half a century after J. S. Bach's death. It does suggest, however, that the case for attributing BWV 534 to Bach is not proven by external evidence and requires critical examination. The teacher–pupil chain, the normal method for transmitting copies, was not always a reliable mechanism, as is well known, and many already known or suspected spuriosities in the Bach canon are there because the work of a pupil such as Krebs accidentally picked up Bach's name in the course of transmission.[7]

Initially, one notices certain mildly unusual features about BWV 534, such as the key and the use of the low pedal D♭ (prelude bar 66).[8] Far stronger suspicions arise from the character of the fugue, which is much the weaker of the two movements. Grammatical solecisms of the type quoted above could conceivably be explained as resulting from the transmission of an unpolished early draft, though it must be added that they are not common in Bach's other autograph drafts. Of much greater moment is the awkward, clogged counterpoint and part-writing, the badly thought-out tonal scheme, the profligate waste of material and the general absence of control. There is no possibility of explaining such things away by calling it an early work. From the stylistic point of view, it invites comparison with the great *allabreve* fugues of Bach's Weimar period.[9] The most obvious link is certainly with the C minor Fugue BWV 546.ii, a work whose five-part scoring (shared by BWV 534) probably suggests a connection with the French *fugue grave*; the French influence is even more apparent in the Fantasia BWV 562, which may well have originally preceded BWV 546.ii. Like BWV 534.ii, BWV 546.ii also contains much episodic material unrelated to the subject, though in the latter it is far more skilfully integrated into the overall plan. In intention, if not in realization, BWV 534 is related not to the squat, tonally restricted canzona-fugues of Bach's early years, nor directly to the *ricercar*, but to the vastly expanded scale of Bach's Weimar fugues, with their rounded tonal scheme and thematic development. Voices move

---

7 See K. Tittel, 'Welche unter J. S. Bach's Namen geführten Orgelwerke sind Johann Tobias bzw. Johann Ludwig Krebs zuzuschreiben?', *BJ* 52 (1966), pp. 102–37.

8 Leaving aside arguments about the compass of the Weimar pedalboard (before or after rebuilds), we may note that there is now no established instance of a Weimar work by J. S. Bach employing low C♯ (manual or pedal). The three works usually cited in this connection are BWV 536a (now regarded as a spurious 'simplification' of the authentic BWV 536), BWV 565 (now suspect on stylistic grounds), and BWV 534 (the subject of the present article). The Fantasia BWV 542.i, which does contain a low C♯, is almost universally dated in the Cöthen period: see Kilian's discussion in *NBA* IV/5–6 *KB* pp. 453–5. The C♯ in BWV 620 may be played in the tenor octave.

9 See P. Williams, *The Organ Music of J. S. Bach*, I (Cambridge, 1980), p. 70.

in an even-paced flow, with an aggregate crotchet rhythm maintained almost throughout. It is clear that the counterpoint is ultimately (if indirectly) derived from the so-called 'motet style'.

The fugal technique of BWV 534.ii can be compared with BWV 546.ii and 538.ii in style but not in quality. A feature of any mature Bach fugal exposition (and pre-eminently of the two fugues BWV 546 and 538) is the flow of thought straight through the purely formal articulations of entries and codettas; the conception of the music is a unity. Let us look at the opening of BWV 534: Ex. 2. The subject

Ex. 2. BWV 534.ii, bars 1–16

itself requires comment. Fugue subjects outlining the diminished seventh on the leading note are, as we know, one of the most common types of all, both with J. S. Bach and with his contemporaries and successors. But the absence from Bach's authentic works of fugue subjects featuring the diminished seventh on the raised fourth degree of the scale in a position of such prominence must raise serious doubts as to whether it was a part of his convention. Apart from this peculiarity, the subject is strikingly similar to an internal theme from the C minor Prelude BWV 546.i: Ex. 3. The correspondence (derived from a work which bears a par-

Ex. 3. Prelude in C minor BWV 546.i, bars 25–7

ticularly close stylistic relationship to BWV 534) is so exact as to suggest the possibility of deliberate modelling, the more so since the first bar of the countersubject is also concerned. Even stronger material connections between the prelude and that of the E minor Prelude and Fugue reinforce the general impression of BWV 534 as a pastiche of elements drawn from a variety of authentic works by J. S. Bach.

The exposition itself is solid artisan work, but no more. Having produced a serviceable counterpoint to his subject, the composer harmonically inverts the two motifs x and y (Ex. 2) to return to the tonic. The first and fourth entries are accompanied by amorphous non-thematic counterpoint, including unattractive clashes in bar 11 and an equally unattractive halt in the rhythmic flow in bar 12. Another short link (bars 15–16) again steers the music back to the tonic for the fifth entry. The whole exposition gives an inescapable impression of being composed piecemeal; the composer never calculates for more than the immediate needs of the situation and seems incapable of thinking over long spans. The magnificent unfolding of the expositions of the C minor and D minor fugues offers the strongest possible contrast. Even the simplest of J. S. Bach's fugal expositions (for example, that of the E major Fugue *WTC* Bk 2) give a stronger sense of overall conception than that of BWV 534.ii.

Matters do not improve later. Through the 138 bars of this prolix fugue, the feeling grows that the movement is not under control, with the composer let down at every point by an inability to conceive as a whole. In surveying the episodes, first of all, we notice that only one (bars 50–6) is based on a strong idea, and even this is not exploited or recapitulated as J. S. Bach would surely have done. Other episodes are simply stretches of padding (bars 22–6, 76–80, 105–9) or threadbare sequential ideas (bars 59–64, 113–19) which serve little purpose beyond the immediate one of keeping the movement going and steering the music towards the required tonal goal. No episode is ever recapitulated: another quite exceptional feature in a mature Bach fugue that includes episodic ideas of importance. No doubt sequential figures of equal plainness are found in authentic Bach works from time to time (in the D major Prelude BWV 532, for example), but always as part of a deliberate feature in an overall plan, not as an attempt to revive flagging momentum.

Waste of material is as widespread in the entries as in the episodes. The subject is heard with a number of counterthemes – some of them by no means unpromising – which then simply peter out (usually after one entry) in a manner wholly uncharacteristic of J. S. Bach. Examples include the flowing counterpoint to the bass entry (bars 27–30), the potentially strong countersubject which accompanies the alto entry in bars 42–5, and the figure in parallel sixths (bars 90–3). This last ushers in a wretched passage (bars 96–102) in which the movement seems to grind to a halt. The quaver figure which gradually emerges in bars 37–9 is the only recurrent thematic idea apart from the subject, and even this is buried beneath the avalanche of inchoate non-thematic material.

The lack of a coherent tonal plan is both obvious and untypical of J. S. Bach. The music seems to circle aimlessly around A♭ major (main cadences in bars 36,

47–50, 73–80), C minor (apart from the exposition, in bars 27–30, 41, 56–9, 84–95, 120–6), and the tonic F minor. J. S. Bach's method of articulating his tonal planning, with the alternation of grouped entries and developing or recapitulating episodes, seems beyond the grasp of the composer of BWV 534.

Finally, turning to the execution of the detail, there are many examples of awkward, ungrammatical or unidiomatic harmonic progressions. Examples of such moments include bars 36, 41 (crotchets 3–4), 86, 106, 109 (a highly uncharacteristic leap onto a minor ninth), 110–13 (poor shaping of the treble line) and 124, as well as the faults cited by Kilian. The counterpoint is generally more skilful in the reduced portions *a 3* and *a 4* than in the full sections, in which the constant thick doublings, awkward melodic movement and textural padding suggest that the composer had difficulty with five-part writing.

One further point concerning the fugue must follow discussion of the prelude, to which we now turn. That it can be seen to achieve both a better structure and better details than the fugue can, it seems, be ascribed to two factors: a less ambitious concept and the use of an authentic Bach model, namely the E minor Prelude BWV 548. As to the first, the composer keeps to a manageable four-part texture and a moderate length (seventy-six bars), giving the piece a clear binary shape around a central cadence (in C minor, bar 32). The tonal scheme, though narrow, is at least serviceable, avoiding many of the problems of the ramshackle fugue.

The relationship of the prelude to the prelude of BWV 548, which has been observed and discussed by Williams, sheds much light on the critical and musicological problems posed by the work. Once again, it demonstrates the impossibility of characterizing the prelude as an immature but authentic work. J. S. Bach did not evolve the mature, highly organized organ preludes which so clearly influenced the present work until well into the Weimar period. Early Weimar works such as BWV 536 or BWV 550 have preludes which are far more rooted in the Buxtehudian language and methods of J. S. Bach's earlier years, and yet seem far more expertly composed than BWV 534. Insofar as BWV 534 invites comparison with the Weimar works at all, it must be with the later stratum of works in which J. S. Bach's musical language finally seems to have reached maturity. As well as the works already discussed in connection with the fugue, they include BWV 541, 545, 537 and others. The style of the G major Prelude BWV 541.i makes an interesting comparison with the F minor prelude: the authentic Weimar work includes, and makes vastly superior use of, the same sequential patterns and characteristic melodic figures as the prelude of BWV 534. The fact that the closest relationship of all is with the Leipzig work BWV 548 reduces to vanishing point any serious prospect of regarding BWV 534 as an early and immature effort. The central argument for rejecting the Bach attribution (presumably found in Kittel's lost copy of BWV 534) is that style-critical factors pull in opposite directions: on the one hand, the work is simply not proficient enough to have been composed by the mature J. S. Bach; on the other, the idiom is too late for it to be seen convincingly as a student work.

The opening of the prelude of BWV 534 seems to be related to the opening of

BWV 548, and perhaps also to the opening of the harpsichord Toccata in E minor
BWV 914. It recalls another F minor prelude by J. L. Krebs,[10] which is a still clearer
instance of a pupil's composition based on an idea originating with the master
(Ex. 4). The main basis for Krebs's piece was Bach's B minor Prelude BWV 544.i, but

Ex. 4. J. L. Krebs, Prelude in F minor, bars 1–3

Ped.

its opening, with the patterned repetition of a motif swinging characteristically to
the subdominant (bar 2) and then returning to the tonic (bar 3), can also be related to
the opening bars of BWV 548. The essential idea is a harmonized descending scale
over a tonic pedal (handled far more mechanically by Krebs and by the composer
of BWV 534 than in authentic works of J. S. Bach). Evidently the idea held a fasci-
nation for early Bach enthusiasts. BWV 548, in fact, holds the key to many aspects
of BWV 534, with characteristic textures and figurations constantly appearing in
the preludes of both works. To a great extent, this close adherence to Bach models
would explain any superiority the prelude may be felt to have over the fugue. The
prelude, in my submission, is not a work of J. S. Bach but shows a close study of his
musical language and technique. The fact that counterpoint characteristic of J. S.
Bach exerted a strong influence on it is presumably the prime reason for the reten-
tion of BWV 534 in the Bach canon long after other works for which the authen-
tication on external evidence is equally tenuous.

Two further links with BWV 548 need to be pointed out – one musical, the other
a matter of sources. The first concerns the coda of the fugue of BWV 534 (from bar
126 to the end) which surprisingly returns to the opening figure of BWV 548, making it the basis of eight patterned repetitions which eventually dissolve into a short
measured cadenza. The motif is actually reproduced note for note in bar 133 of the
fugue. This piece of internal evidence also fits the hypothesis that the composer
already had BWV 548 in front of him. Secondly, it is interesting that in Dröbs's collection (a *Sammelhandschrift*) BWV 534 and BWV 548 occur in close proximity,
separated only by BWV 545; it would be interesting to know if the two works were
also linked in Kittel's source-copy.

From a musical point of view, the prelude of BWV 534 bears all the signs of a
competent but pale imitation of Bach's late style. The prelude can be analysed in
binary form, with the first half modulating to C minor (cadencing at bar 32) and
the second half returning to the tonic. Both halves begin with a broad pedal-point

10 Modern edition in W. Zöllner (ed.), *Johann Ludwig Krebs: Orgelwerke* (Frankfurt, 1938), pp. 16–31.

underpinning the figure derived from BWV 548. The rest of the material is formed from a characteristic broken chord (first heard in bars 8–10) and a number of sequential patterns (bars 11–13, 17–20, 43–9, 50–9) some of which can be related to similar patterns in BWV 548 and other works such as BWV 541. There is nothing intrinsically uncharacteristic in any of the main ideas, but even a cursory glance at the authentic works suffices to show the inferiority of BWV 534. The broad sweep, the inexorable movement towards tonal goals, and the far-reaching developments typical of authentic works are absent from the F minor Prelude, in which the over-all structure constantly threatens to degenerate into a patchwork of sequences. The movement to the dominant (bars 11–15) seems lacking in breadth after the long opening pedal-point, and the long preparation for the central C minor cadence is feeble and lacking in force, as indeed is the approach to bar 70.

The second half of the prelude begins with a transposition of the first ten bars into the dominant (bars 33–42) and continues with two more sequential patterns (bars 43–50, 50–9). A short development of a single four-note figure (bars 60–3) leads to a further sequence (bars 64–6) and a dominant pedal in the tonic, F minor (bars 67–9), coming to a halt with a diminished seventh chord with fermata (bar 70). The prelude closes with a measured cadenza and conventional suspension-cadence. The same observations apply here also. All the material is perfectly in accordance with authentic Bach styles; the sequence formulas match those in authentic works, and the treatment of the dominant pedal (bars 67–9) suggests a relationship with a work not before mentioned – the B minor Prelude BWV 544 (bars 16–18). What is uncharacteristic of J. S. Bach is the lack of overall cohesion and of a convincing tonal strategy. The return to the tonic is actually accomplished in one bar (bar 50); the sequential developments both before and after that point lack a genuine sense of direction and have no function beyond the maintaining of movement in tonally static conditions. The prelude as a whole sounds like an assemblage of elements drawn from Bach by a composer not gifted with his prodigious powers of organization.

For obvious reasons there are in the prelude fewer of those poorly executed details encountered frequently in the fugue; but some do occur. The passage from bars 60–3 also involves several unlikely-looking moments: the linear progression C-D-E-F-G♭ (bar 60, first crotchet), the implied consecutive octaves and doubled leading notes (bar 61), and the uncharacteristic treatment of a chromatic auxiliary note (bar 62, second crotchet). Despite its inferior quality, there is no reason to believe that the fugue had a separate origin from the prelude. The pieces were evidently preserved together in Kittel's lost copy. If any confirmation is needed that they belong together, it is provided by the already cited thematic relationships between the opening idea of the prelude and the coda of the fugue (both related to BWV 548) and by the similarity of the cadences ending the two movements. The contention here is that BWV 534 is the work of a musician with a thorough knowledge of several authentic Bach models. From the E minor prelude BWV 548.i and the Toccata BWV 914 he obtained the main thematic idea of the prelude, with

180

BWV 548.i also supplying several characteristic figures and textures in the prelude, as well as the coda to the fugue. From the C minor Fugue BWV 546.ii he took the general concept of the fugue, at the same time deriving its subject from a subsidiary idea in the prelude of the same work. Other pieces which the composer may have consulted are BWV 541 and 544, and possibly the Prelude and Fugue in F minor by J. L. Krebs.

In the search for a more convincing ascription for BWV 534 we are handicapped by the sheer lack of information about the work, but it is at least clear that its origins should be sought in the circle around Johann Christian Kittel in Erfurt and Langensalza. The most natural hypothesis to consider is that Kittel himself may have been the composer. If we posit Kittel as the composer we must assume that another hand (perhaps that of Dröbs) added the Bach ascription to Kittel's unsigned autograph. Nevertheless, the hypothesis seems at least attractive enough to be worth investigating, especially as Dröbs also paired a work by Bach with one by Kittel in another MS (Leipzig MB III.8.14). To regard BWV 534 as the work of a Bach pupil would explain its composer's evidently wide knowledge of J. S. Bach's organ works (at a time when so few of them were available in print) and the deep impression this music had so manifestly made on him. BWV 534 bears all the signs of a student work: it is not an independent artistic utterance, but a conscientious and enthusiastic imitation of J. S. Bach's language and technique. Not surprisingly, such modelled pieces are common enough among Bach's pupils, especially J. L. Krebs, among whose 'parodies' is an E major Toccata and Fugue based on Bach's BWV 540, as well as the F minor work discussed above. Most of J. S. Bach's pupils produced an uneasy mixture of their master's counterpoint with varying infusions of *galant* and Classical influence.[11] Examples of this worthy but uninspired literature continued to be produced well into the nineteenth century.

Kittel's known output consists of about three hundred pieces, most of them for organ.[12] It is unfortunate from the present point of view that there are no full-length fugues among his published works; the nearest approaches are the two unambitious fughettas published in the first part of his two-volume treatise *Der angehende praktische Organist* (1801–3), which is mainly concerned with chorale accompaniment. In fact, archaic chorale preludes, of which he produced several sets, seem to have interested him more than freely composed pieces. However, as Fellerer indicates (see note 12), counterpoint typical of J. S. Bach is much in evidence in the undated *Variationen über zwei Choräle* and the *Vierstimmige Choräle mit Vorspielen* (1803), a collection of 150 short chorale preludes paired with accompanimental harmonizations. This last collection, like the specimen chorale preludes in *Der angehende praktische Organist*, re-creates the concise convention of Bach's *Orgelbüchlein*. The description applied above to J. S. Bach's pupils in general applies well to Kittel's music, which mixes (one can hardly say 'fuses') solidly competent counterpoint with elements from later styles.

11 See R. Sietz, 'Die Orgelkompositionen des Schülerkreises um Johann Sebastian Bach', *BJ* 32 (1935), pp. 33–96; Kittel's works are discussed on pp. 74ff.
12 For a summary list see K. G. Fellerer, 'Kittel, J. C.', *New Grove*.

Although an example of direct modelling on J. S. Bach has been detected in at least one chorale prelude,[13] the work most relevant to the present discussion is Kittel's *Grosse Präludien* (undated), a set of sixteen extended preludes in a chromatically ascending series of major and minor keys from C major to G minor. The style varies a good deal, sometimes within the course of a single piece. Some, such as no. 7 in E♭ major or no. 10 in F minor,[14] are attempts to apply the idiom of the Classical orchestra to the organ, and have no stylistic link with BWV 534. Others are imitations of J. S. Bach. The opening of no. 1 (C major), quoted in Ex. 5, is

Ex. 5. J. C. Kittel, Prelude in C major (*16 Grosse Präludien* no. 1), bars 1–7

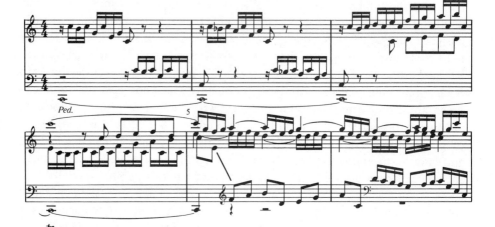

perhaps the purest Bach pastiche of all. Also belonging to the conservative group are no. 2 in C minor, no. 3 in C♯ major,[15] no. 5 in D major, no. 6 in D minor, and to some extent no. 9 in F major. The C major and C♯ major pieces both open with evocations of J. S. Bach's arpeggio or 'pattern' prelude, the latter looking back to the prelude in the same key from Book 2 of the *WTC*. The D major prelude is in the manner of the first half of a French *ouverture*, with echoes of the organ Prelude in E flat major BWV 552.i, *Goldberg Variation* 16, and perhaps the *ouverture* from Partita no. 4. Kittel's C minor and D minor preludes are the closest to BWV 534. Both are sturdy

13 See Sietz, *op. cit.*, p. 89.
14 Modern edition in W. Emery (ed.), *J. C. Kittel: Three Preludes for Organ*, Early Organ Music 6 (London, 1958).
15 See Sietz, *op. cit.*, pp. 76–7.

triple-time pieces with almost continuous semiquaver movement, built largely from the sequential formulas which dominate the prelude to BWV 534. Kittel shows a strong taste for long chains of *échappée* figures (also manifest in many of his chorale preludes) and has evidently absorbed J. S. Bach's characteristic broken-chord and auxiliary-note patterns. Ex. 6, an extract from Kittel's C minor prelude,

Ex. 6. Kittel, Prelude in C minor (*16 Grosse Präludien*, no. 2), bars 41–52

shows a strong general affinity to the closing stages of the Prelude in F minor BWV 534; the overworked sequences are especially noteworthy.

We cannot be sure that Kittel composed BWV 534. All that can be claimed is that an ascription to him would provide a convenient solution to the problems of source and style that this puzzling work creates, and that (at least as far as the prelude is concerned) it is perfectly consistent with his outlook and approach to composition. It was an outlook expressed not only through music but through the excellent verbal guidance given in *Der angehende praktische Organist* to the aspiring organist. Kittel's own advice on the subject of modelling[16] reflects a lifetime of experience as an organist and teacher:

Schaut gute Muster an. Sie sind erhabene und gefällige Führer, die die Schwierigkeiten des steilen Pfades vor unseren Augen bekämpfen und besiegen und uns getreulich die Hand reichen, wenn wir versuchen wollen ihnen nachzuklimmen.

Look at good models. They are exalted and pleasant guides which grapple with and conquer before our eyes the difficulties of the steep path, and unfailingly stretch out a hand to us if we seek to climb after them.

We may well suspect that Kittel was giving advice which he himself had followed at least once in the past. Notwithstanding the defects analysed in this essay, BWV 534 is a work which does much credit to a promising apprentice composer who was, perhaps, attempting a compositional project slightly beyond his technique. But it makes no sense in the context of the organ works of Bach.

16 *Der angehende praktische Organist*, 2 vols. (Erfurt, 1801–3), II, p. 6.

In Search of Bach the Organist

PETER LE HURAY & JOHN BUTT
(Cambridge)

Despite the close attention that has been given to performance style in recent years we are still far from any real understanding of the manner in which Bach played the organ. More than fifty eighteenth-century writers had at least something to say about Bach's playing, and all are agreed on its unique excellence.[1] The more important of these formed the basis for the fourth chapter of Forkel's biography in which the detailed discussion of Bach's keyboard technique drew mainly on C. P. E. Bach's *Versuch* (Berlin 1753, 1762) and upon information sent by C. P. E. Bach in 1774 and 1775 in response to Forkel's queries. Forkel's account seems on the surface to be comprehensive and well balanced. Certainly it avoids the anecdotal excesses of Schubart's *Bachs Bedeutung als Klavier- und Orgelspieler,*[2] which appeared some time in 1784 or 1785. Forkel's opening remarks in chapter 4, however, are sufficient to illustrate the inadequacies of all the various authorities when it comes to attempting more than a superficial understanding of Bach's keyboard technique:

Das Clavier und die Orgel sind einander nahe verwandt. Allein Styl und Behandlungsart beyder Instrumente ist so verschieden, als ihre beyderseitige Bestimmung verschieden ist. Was auf dem Clavichord klingt oder etwas sagt, sagt auf der Orgel nichts, und so umgekehrt. Der beste Clavierspieler, wenn er nicht die Unterschiede der Bestimmung und der Zwecke beyder Instrumente gehörig kennt und zu beobachten weiss, wird daher stets ein schlechter Orgelspieler seyn, wie es auch gewöhnlich der Fall ist. Bis jetzt sind mir nur zwey Ausnahmen vorgekommen. Die eine macht Joh. Sebastian selbst, und die zweyte sein ältester Sohn, Wilh. Friedemann. Beyde waren feine Clavierspieler; sobald sie aber auf die Orgel kamen, bemerkte man keinen Clavierspieler mehr. Melodie, Harmonie, Bewegung &c. alles war anders, das heisst: alles war der Natur des Instruments und seiner Bestimmung angemessen. Wenn ich Wilh. Friedemann auf dem Clavier hörte, war alles zierlich, fein und angenehm. Hörte ich ihn auf der Orgel, so überfiel mich ein heiliger Schauder. (Forkel p. 18)

---

1 See *Dok* II, *Dok* III and Forkel. For pointers towards a reassessment of Forkel's evidence, see P. Williams, *The Organ Music of J.S. Bach,* III (Cambridge, 1984), especially pp. 155, 202, 212–14.
2 *Dok* III, pp. 408–12.

The organ has much in common with the clavier,[3] but it differs in style and touch as much as it differs in the use to which it is put. What sounds well on the clavichord, or expresses something, expresses nothing on the organ, and vice versa. Even the most accomplished clavier-player may be – and usually is – a poor organist if he does not appreciate the different characteristics and functions of the two instruments. I know of only two men who can be excepted from these remarks: J. S. Bach and his eldest son, Wilhelm Friedemann. Both were accomplished clavier-players, but no trace of this was evident when they played the organ. Melody, harmony, movement and so on were all different: that is to say, everything was conditioned by the instrument and the use to which it was put. When Wilhelm Friedemann played the clavier, all was elegant, delicate and agreeable. When he played the organ I experienced feelings of reverent awe.

The problem here is a lack of focus. Is Forkel discussing performance style, is he comparing the various characteristics of the organ and the clavichord, or is he defining the kind of music that in his opinion is most suited to each instrument? As we read on, it becomes increasingly clear that Forkel is telling us not so much about the way that Bach played the organ as about the way that Bach's organ music impressed its devotees such as Forkel himself, who were living at a time when contemporary music had distanced itself by a matter of light-years from Bach's own music. Practically nothing that Forkel says about J. S. Bach can be separated from Bach the composer of organ music and from Bach the admired representative of an ideal and bygone age. The organ and Bach seem to stand in Forkel's mind for everything that is worthwhile and solid in an age of declining values. Here surely we are very close to the German Romanticism of Caspar David Friedrich, to gaunt Gothic ruins, to remoteness and to a mysticism that was far removed from the pietistic enthusiasm of the early eighteenth century.

Despite Forkel's assertion to the contrary, the basic essentials of keyboard technique will have been much the same on both organ and clavichord. Therefore, although Forkel claimed to be discussing clavichord technique in the third chapter of his book, his words are worth quoting here for they most closely describe the physical process of performance:

Nach der Seb. Bachischen Art, die Hand auf dem Clavier zu halten, werden die fünf Finger so gebogen, dass die Spitzen derselben in eine gerade Linie kommen, die sodann auf die in einer Fläche neben einander liegenden Tasten so passen, dass kein einziger Finger bey vorkommenden Fällen erst näher herbey gezogen muss, sondern dass jeder über dem Tasten, den er etwa nieder drücken soll, schon schwebt. Mit dieser Lage der Hand ist nun verbunden: 1) dass kein Finger auf seinen Tasten fallen, oder (wie es ebenfalls oft geschieht) geworfen, sondern nur mit einem gewissen Gefühl der innern Kraft und Herrschaft über die Bewegung *getragen* werden darf. 2) Die so auf den Tasten getragene Kraft, oder das Maass des Drucks muss in gleicher Stärke unterhalten werden, und zwar so, dass der Finger nicht gerade aufwärts vom Tasten gehoben wird, sondern durch ein allmähliges Zurückziehen der Fingerspitzen nach der innern Fläche der Hand, auf dem vordern Theil des Tasten abgleitet. 3) Beym Uebergange von einem Tasten zum andern wird durch dieses Abgleiten das Mass von Kraft oder Druck, womit der erste Ton unterhalten worden ist, in der grössten Geschwindigkeit auf den nächsten Finger geworfen, so dass nun die beyden Töne weder von einander

---

3 Forkel seems here to use *Clavier* as a synonym for 'clavichord' (i.e. implicitly excluding harpsichord and fortepiano).

gerissen werden, noch in einander klingen können. Der Anschlag derselben ist also, wie C. Ph. Emanuel sagt, weder zu lang noch zu kurz, sondern genau so wie er seyn muss. (Forkel p. 12)

Bach placed his hands over the keys in such a way that the five fingers were cupped, the finger ends being poised in a straight line over the keyboard. No finger was far from the key that it had to depress, and all were ready for instant action. With this hand disposition it follows that (1) the fingers cannot fall (or, as often happens, be thrown) onto the notes but are *placed* on them with a conscious awareness of the force and control that the movements require. (2) Since the weight of touch must be evenly maintained, the finger is not lifted straight from the key but is withdrawn by a gentle backward movement of the fingertip into the palm of the hand. (3) The resultant sliding action transmits to the next finger the pressure needed, as one note follows another, so that the touch is evenly regulated and distinct. Moreover, as C. P. E. Bach observed, the articulation is neither too chopped nor too sustained, but just right.

Bach played so effortlessly, apparently, that his fingers hardly seemed to move. That much at least is certain. But when all is said and done, are we any closer to an understanding of the essential point, the 'rightness' of the articulation? Just how legato was Bach's normal touch? And in any case, what precisely does 'legato' mean?

To some extent this must have depended on the fingering that Bach used. C. P. E. Bach tells us something about this in his *Versuch* (ch. 1, §7):

Mein seliger Vater hat mir erzählt, in seiner Jugend grosse Männer gehört zu haben, welche den Daumen nicht eher gebraucht als wenn es bey grossen Spannungen nöthig war. Da er nun einen Zeitpunckt erlebet hatte, in welchem nach und nach eine gantz besondere Veränderung mit dem musicalischen Geschmack vorging: so wurde er dadurch genöthiget, einen weit vollkommenern Gebrauch der Finger sich auszudencken, besonders den Daumen, welcher ausser andern guten Diensten hauptsächlich in den schweren Tonarten gantz unentbehrlich ist, so zu gebrauchen, wie ihn die Natur gleichsam gebraucht wissen will.

My dear father told me that when he was young he heard great men who used their thumbs only when they needed them for large intervals. Since he lived at a time when gradual but striking changes were taking place in musical taste he had no alternative but to develop a more comprehensive fingering system, especially in respect of the thumbs, which are particularly needed for difficult keys and which are very useful in other ways.

Sadly, though, not a note of Bach's organ music is fingered in primary sources. What is more, most keyboard scores are not even laid out in a manner that effectively and unequivocally distributes the music between the two hands. Yet C. P. E. Bach seems to suggest that his father had developed a system. Could this have been an elaborately structured method in which each piece had its carefully calculated fingerings? Or might the system have been nothing more than the use of consecutive fingers and of thumbs-under hand-position changes for scalic configurations, in place of the old paired fingerings such as those he set out for young Wilhelm Friedemann in the *Applicatio*? In his own pieces *für Kenner und Liebhaber* C. P. E. has certainly left us a highly detailed and systematic method of his own. His father, though, was by all accounts a remarkable sight-reader. Could this perhaps provide the clue to his 'method'? For sight-reading depends not on any strict adherence to a predetermined plan but on a fluently relaxed finger technique that allows the fingers to be placed *extempore* on the keys in any number of ways,

PETER LE HURAY & JOHN BUTT

many of which would probably never be used in a system that had been carefully thought out beforehand. That a totally legato organ touch could be achieved *extempore* is improbable. Bach's system, then, may have been one of general principles rather than of specific detail.

Romantic pianists and organists were brought up to believe that sustained legato was the basis of Bach playing, an idea that goes well with Forkel's solemn organ style. To achieve this they used finger-substitution extensively; we have only to turn to early-twentieth-century editions of *Das wohltemperierte Clavier* to see how persistent this tradition has been. In the few fingered eighteenth-century copies of German keyboard music by Bach and his contemporaries there are no instances of finger-substitution. For instance, whoever fingered the early version of the C major Prelude and Fugue from Book 2 of the *WTC* (J. C. Vogler's copy of BWV 870a in SPK MS P 1089) would have had to resort in places to finger-substitution if a thoroughgoing legato had been his aim. As it is, the C major fingerings let a great deal of air into the texture: ties can rarely be held for their full values, and up-beats have in many cases to be detached from their subsequent down-beats. Couperin of course did discuss finger-substitution in his *L'art de toucher le clavecin* (Paris, 1717), but in devoting so much space to it he certainly gives the impression that he considered it to be a novel aspect of finger technique. If, then, we are correct to question finger-substitution as a Baroque norm (just as we may question the extensive use of heels in pedalling) then it is equally proper to question the meaning of 'legato' in keyboard performance and to ask whether there may not be evidence in the music itself of the articulation norm that was the basis of his organ touch. Apropos touch, C. P. E. Bach writes in (ch. 3, §§5, 6):

5.§ Die Lebhaftigkeit des Allegro wird *gemeiniglich* in gestossenen Noten und das Zärtliche des Adagio in getragenen und geschleiften Noten vorgestellet . . .
6.§ Einige Personen spielen kleberich, als wenn sie Leim zwischen den Fingern hätten. Ihr Anschlag ist zu lang, indem sie die Noten über die Zeit liegen lassen. Andere haben es verbessern wollen, und spielen zu kurtz; als wenn die Tasten glühend wären. Es thut aber auch schlecht. Die Mittelstrasse ist die beste . . .

§5 *In general* the briskness of allegros is expressed by detached notes, and the tenderness of adagios by slurred notes . . .
§6 There are many who play stickily, as if they had glue between their fingers. Their touch is lethargic, and they hold the notes too long. Others, in trying to correct this, release the keys too soon as if they were burning hot. Both are wrong. Midway between these extremes is best.

The relevance of C. P. E. Bach's *Versuch* to an understanding of J. S. Bach has long been questioned. C. P. E. Bach's own music is after all worlds apart from his father's. And in disseminating J. S. Bach's music the Princess Amalie and Kirnberger seem to have been far more active than was C. P. E., who quoted not a note of his father's music in the *Versuch*. To be sure, unequivocal evidence of levels of articulation of the kind discussed by C. P. E. Bach is there to be carefully measured out in Engramelle's barrel-organ charts,[4] charts that were based on performances

4 M. D. J. Engramelle, *La tonotechnie ou l'art de noter des cylindres . . . dans les instruments de concerts méchaniques* (Paris, 1775).

188

given by the organist of Notre Dame in Paris, Claude Balbastre (1729-99). But Balbastre was the frothiest of rococo composers, and his music has absolutely nothing to do with J. S. Bach.

And yet there are hints in earlier writings – of a very general nature, certainly – that seem to suggest much the same things about articulation that C. P. E. Bach and Quantz were saying. Johann Mattheson (1681–1764) drew very clear distinctions between vocal and instrumental styles of performance:[5]

Wenn auch das gar zu sehr punctirte Wesen, absonderlich in Sing-Sachen, wenig oder nichts *fliessendes* mit sich führen kan, so . . . zu verwerffen. Im präludiren und fantasiren, wo eben keine ordentlich-fliessende Melodie erfordert wird, darff man es so genau nicht nehmen; . . . ja in Entreen und dergleichen hohen Täntzen, so wie zuweilen in Ouvertüren, wird es ausdrücklich nöthig seyn, viel punctirtes anzubringen: es klingt sehr frisch und lebhafft, druckt verschiedene, muntere, auch einige hefftige Gemüths-Bewegungen sehr wol aus . . .

Excessive articulation, especially in lyrical pieces, can have little or no *flowing* quality and is . . . to be avoided. In improvising preludes and fantasias, however, where there are no regularly flowing lines, there is no need to observe this quite so much . . . Indeed, entrées and dances of similarly elevated character, and even certain overtures, positively demand detached articulation that is fresh and vivacious and well suited to joyful and energetic pieces . . .

Mattheson devoted a substantial chapter in the third part of his book to the art of organ-playing. He was insistent (as certain Bach pupils were) that the organist should play expressively. He had actually heard both Bach and Handel. He placed both well above their contemporaries – even above Georg Böhm and J. G. Walther – and he conceded to Bach the very highest honours. Mattheson may have defined articulation in no very precise way, but his views are by no means inconsistent with those of Quantz and C. P. E. Bach.

Can it be, then, that Quantz's observations are not entirely irrelevant? And are there features of J. S. Bach's own keyboard notation that point in similar directions? There are, for instance, those puzzling slurrings and staccato markings that are scattered through the primary sources of the organ music. How much do these tell us? Though Bach was a careful copyist of pitches and rhythms he was, alas, not at all consistent when it came to the addition of articulation markings in his wind and string parts. In many cases he simply set a basic pattern in the opening bars of a movement, leaving the player to work out the rest for himself. In other cases he seems to have indicated only those slurrings that a player might not instinctively have done himself. In the keyboard music the articulation markings are so scattered and apparently inconsistent that their existence is barely noticed by either editor or player. When then did Bach add them? Could they perhaps tell us something of the normal legato touch about which Quantz writes?

A study of the slurrings in the primary sources of Bach's keyboard music shows how ready editors have been to regularize Bach's markings and brush aside the problems that the irregularities present. If the markings are properly to be evalu-

5 Mattheson, *Der vollkommene Capellmeister* (Hamburg, 1739), p. 151.

189

ated, several important questions need to be asked about the sources in which they occur. What was the function of the source? Was it a composer's draft? Was it a performer's score? Or a reference copy? Are the markings original, or were any added after the copy had been completed? Are the markings clearly drawn, or are there ambiguities that call for interpretation and comment?

The Six Sonatas BWV 525–530 for two manuals and pedals illustrate particularly well the problems that are involved. Two manuscripts are particularly relevant:[6] DSB P 271, Bach's autograph c1730;[7] and SPK P 272, largely based on P 271 (1730–3).[8] P 272 is in two sections: from bar 16 of Sonata no. 4 to the end of the cycle is the earlier portion, in the hand of Anna Magdelena Bach; this was copied directly from P 271. The remainder of the MS was added by Wilhelm Friedemann Bach, the text being derived (if not copied) from P 271. The immediate problem is the function and interrelationship of these two sources.

Both Emery and Kilian suggest that Bach used Anna's text as a teaching copy,[9] adding extra performance markings, and P 271 as a reference copy: this, they believed, contains raw text rather than material prepared for performance. There are several reasons to doubt this: P 272 was presumably taken over by Friedemann when he wrote his portion,[10] and if we believe in the conjectural date of 1730 for P 271 and assume that P 272 (with Friedemann's section) left the Bach household in 1733,[11] the period of its use as Bach's practical source would have been little longer than three years. There is no evidence that P 271 was not in Bach's possession until his death. Furthermore there are obvious errors in Anna's portion (e.g. Sonata no. 6 bar 33) which would surely have been corrected if the copy had been used for teaching purposes. Moreover, there are good reasons for thinking that P 271 was intended as a practical copy, for it is laid out in such a way that all but six of the twenty-six page-turns can be managed by the player, although five of the possible ones allow only a very short space of time: these will have been practicable if the music was well known. Anna's MS, which survives only from bar 16 of Sonata no. 4 to the end, has twenty-five page-turns: twelve are impossible, and of the rest only four are easy to manage.[12] Bach included several aids in P 271: there are far more directs than in Anna's MS; there are eight instances of words such as *volti*, six in the

---

6 Thanks are due to the curators of the Staatsbibliothek Preussischer Kulturbesitz in Berlin (West) for permission to examine SPK P 272. DSB P 271 has been examined only on microfilm, since the MS has been withdrawn from circulation; for his edition of 1957, W. Emery was similarly restricted to photographic copies only.

7 G. von Dadelsen, *Beiträge zur Chronologie der Werke Johann Sebastian Bachs*, Tübinger Bach-Studien 4/5 (Trossingen, 1958), p. 104.

8 G. von Dadelsen, *Bemerkungen zur Handschrift Johann Sebastian Bachs, seiner Familie und seines Kreises*, Tübinger Bach-Studien 1 (Trossingen, 1957), p. 18.

9 W. Emery, *Notes on Bach's Organ Works IV-V: Six Sonatas for Two Manuals and Pedal* (London, 1957), p. 80; D. Kilian, 'Über einige neue Aspekte zur Quellenüberlieferung von Klavier- und Orgel-werken J. S. Bachs', *BJ* 64 (1978), pp. 61–72.

10 He might, of course, have possessed Anna Magdalena's copy from the time of its completion.

11 When Friedemann left Leipzig; however, he might easily have collected it after this date.

12 Most movements begin in the course of a page.

190

portion relevant to Anna's copy. In her copy the word, in some form, occurs three times. Furthermore, in five places Bach actually squeezed extra music onto the bottom of a page in order to make turns possible. In Sonata no. 5, first movement, *volti* appears below the bar (72) *before* the end of the page, where only one part is playing; an easy turn is implied. In Sonata no. 5, last movement, bar 75, *volti* is added (the left hand being free) and the final system of the page is left blank. When compiling P 271, Bach possibly anticipated that the turn would be most convenient at this juncture. Thus there appear to be grounds for assuming that P 271 did indeed have a practical origin and that the performance markings it contains should not lightly be dismissed.

Much of Anna's MS does contain more slurs and ornaments than P 271; these will be considered in the light of a study of P 271. Friedemann's portion of the text contains fewer slurs than P 271, and although several are variants of his father's markings they generally occur in the same places. The exact relation of his copy to P 271 is still obscure. As his hand is not evident in Anna's portion, it can be assumed that all slurs in the latter date from before Friedemann's ownership.

A study of Bach's slurs is hampered by the fact that many of them do not seem to be carefully drawn. Some insight into Bach's writing of slurs can be gained from an examination of a graphically identical symbol, the tie. Ties would almost certainly have been written at the same time as the notes to which they are attached. In general, the ties that arch upwards are thicker at the right and tail off to the left, whilst those that arch downwards are thicker at the left. The upward-arching figures, then, may possibly have begun from the right, the downward-arching figures from the left. It would be logical then to expect the figure to be most accurately placed where the pen begins, but in every case the tie is too short: none are too long and none start too early. It may well be, then, that many of Bach's slurs are too short and that they do not necessarily begin or end over the relevant notes. Ties need not be written precisely, of course, because their function is clearcut, whereas, it could be argued, slurs must be carefully drawn if they are to have any meaning at all. It could equally be suggested, however, that Bach's slurs are no more and no less than mnemonic signs merely reminding the players of patterns of articulation that would have been common currency in contemporary performance practice. There can certainly be no question that Bach's slurs in P 271 are for the most part short, and inexactly placed. In, for instance, the second bar of the Adagio of the first sonata, the first and third slurs (rh) are drawn similarly to the accompanying ties (Plate A). Both slurs are upward-arching, seeming to span from around the second or third note to the penultimate note of each group. The equivalent slurs in bars 3–4, though, are longer; they cross the beat and are even less precise. Only one thing can be certain about these longer slurs: they imply phrasing across the beat rather than the on-beat phrasing with which the movement opens. Here, then, the slurs seem to have a mnemonic function (in the sense given above) and do not give precise instructions for articulation. The Largo of Sonata no. 2 further illustrates the poor alignment and ambiguous extent of Bach's slurs (Plate B).

Plates A and B. J. S. Bach's slurs in DSB MS P 271: from the Adagio of Sonata no. 1
BWV 525 (above) and the Largo of Sonata no. 2 BWV 526 (below).
Reproduced by kind permission of the Deutsche Staatsbibliothek (East Berlin), Musikabteilung

192

Many of the slurs starting on the first beat of each bar are little longer than the paired slurrings that follow them. The paired slurrings themselves can indicate only one form of articulation, as there are only two notes per slur. However, the placing of these slurs is so inaccurate as to warn us against literal interpretation of less obvious instances.

It appears, then, that slurs were not systematically included, nor were they written with great care. Furthermore, they are hardly comprehensive, and some show evidence of inclusion after the manuscript was completed, either by Bach or by someone else:

slurs that differ from the norm (thinner/lighter)

Sonata 1	Adagio	bar 2 rh second slur
Sonata 2	Vivace	44 rh first slur
Sonata 2	Largo	5–6 lh; 7 lh; 8 lh; 9–10 rh (after first slur); 14 rh (2nd, 3rd slurs); 18 rh; 47 rh
Sonata 4	Vivace	46 rh first slur
Sonata 6	Vivace	101–2 (ties thinner);[13] 105 rh slur thinner
Sonata 6	Lento	6 rh
Sonata 6	Allegro	41, 42 rh

slurs that are uncharacteristically drawn

Sonata 1	Adagio	4 lh
Sonata 5	Largo	3 rh
Sonata 5	Allegro (mvt 3)	93–4 rh

Despite the uncertainty that surrounds these markings, their authority may be accepted nonetheless since (as has been pointed out) P 271 probably remained with Bach until his death.

In P 272 Wilhelm Friedemann's slurs are generally consistent in appearance with the surrounding notation; only five are in any way unusual.[14] There are, however, more variations in Anna Magdalena's slurs (those marked * are not in P 271; those marked † may, from their appearance, be additions to P 271):

slurs that are thinner than the norm

Sonata 4	Vivace	26 rh (3rd* darker); rh tie of 19 is similar
Sonata 4	Allegro	50 rh*; 71 rh*; 74 rh*; 81 Ped*
Sonata 5	Allegro (mvt 3)	93 rh†; 94† two slurs (line change) 1st only
Sonata 6	Lento	2–3 rh*; 13 rh*; 17 lh* (c.f. direction marks, bar 16); 21–4* (all); 33* rh, lh
Sonata 6	Allegro	14 rh*; 23 rh*; 26–31* (bar 30 gives direct comparison with ties)

---

13 As the rhythm resembles that of the opening, without these ties, there would be good reason to assume that they are additions.

14 If he was copying from P 271, Wilhelm Friedemann evidently gave little thought to his father's slurring. If he was copying from another (lost) source, its authenticity can be only a matter for speculation.

slurs that are lighter than the norm

Sonata 4   Allegro   3 rh*; 10, 12 lh* (cf. tie in 11)
Sonata 5   Allegro   42 lh* (cf. pedal tie)
           (mvt 1)
Sonata 6   Lento   6 (1st) rh*
Sonata 6   Allegro   19 lh*; 33 lh*; 34 rh*

slurs that are uncharacteristically drawn

Sonata 5   Allegro   96 rh*
           (mvt 3)
Sonata 6   Vivace   154, 156, 158 lh* (cf. pedal ties)
Sonata 6   Lento   38–9 rh*
Sonata 6   Allegro   49–52 (all slurs*)

Although these differences could be attributed to Anna Magdalena's use of a different pen, several other features of her MS imply the involvement of two or more copyists. The clefs and key signatures are all more lightly inked than are the notes, and the handwriting of some of the tempo markings is virtually indistinguishable from that of P 271.[15] The greater incidence of slurs in the Vivace of Sonata no. 4, moreover, suggests that those not in P 272 were added after Anna Magdalena's copying, although few changes of ink are discernible here.

As Emery admits,[16] many of the additions to P 272 lack the characteristic curve of Bach's hand; he suggests that another pen could have been used during a 'hasty check' or lesson. However, most are rather systematically added (e.g. Sonata no. 6 Allegro) and are frequently placed with more accuracy than is usually attributable to Bach. It should not be forgotten that there were other members of the household who might have used this MS during the comparatively short time it is presumed to have been in Leipzig. Certainly, the detailed markings of Sonata no. 6, in particular, suggest the use of this MS for performance of some kind.

The history and function of P 271 are perhaps more easy to determine: the layout certainly suggests a performing MS, and the variants in slur style and the absence of some in the copy P 272 suggest that for certain movements (Sonata no. 4 Vivace in particular) this MS was in practical use after P 272 had been completed. Certainly it seems logical to study the markings in P 271 before any comparison is made with later and less well-authenticated copies.

As the first movement of Sonata no. 4 is the most extensively slurred fast movement in Bach's autograph, it may well contain a near-complete system of performance markings, one that was possibly developed over several years. The main figurative material of the Vivace is made up of nine elements, to be found in bars 5–13 (lh): for convenience these may be labelled as follows:

5   6   7   8   9   10 11 12 13
a   b   c   d   e   f   g   h   i

---

15 Anna Magdalena's 'd', for example, is remarkably similar to Bach's very characteristic 'd'.
16 *Notes on Bach's Organ Works* (see note 9 above), p. 54.

Subsequent appearances of the material in which the slurring differs[17] are:

bar (beat); hand	figure a–i (beat)	difference
9(2) rh	a(2)	plus slur
10(3) rh	b(3)	minus slur
14(1) lh	e(1)	plus slur
15(1,2) rh	e(1,2)	plus slurs
16(2) rh	a(2)	plus slur
16(3) lh	e(3)	plus slur
21(2) lh	b(2)	minus slur
21(3) rh	f(3)	plus slur
25(3) rh	a(3)	minus slur
26(3) lh	a(3)	minus slur
26(1,2) rh	e(1,2)	plus slurs

After this point the majority of changes are in the omission of slurs; however, the following additions are made to the basic *a–i*:

37(2,3) lh	g(2,3)
38(1,2,3,) lh	h(1,2,3)
46(1,3) rh	e(1,3)
48(1,2,3) rh	e(1,2,3)

As most of the differences take the form of omissions, the implication is that articulation patterns once established need not be repeated. Certainly figure *a*3 recurs so often that, having been established in both hands (by bar 20 it has appeared three times), no more repetitions are necessary. Similarly the slurs of *b* are well established in both hands, although the omission of *b*3 (bar 10 rh) is puzzling, especially when compared with bar 17.

The additional slurs are rather harder to explain; perhaps some of them were inserted later. The possibility of an intended difference between the two hands should not be disregarded: the additional *a*2 slur in bar 9 rh appears once more in bar 16 rh, but never in the left. It could be that an established pattern assumed in bar 5 (where the texture is thin) has to be emphasized in bar 9 because the lh is playing a group of four notes and the rh a group of two (harder to perform simultaneously?). The pitch of the respective entries might be relevant too. In bar 5 lh the pedal is very near, and in bar 9 rh both pedal and lh are more than an octave lower. Both the carrying qualities of the higher pitch and the absence of masking from other voices would mean that bar 9 rh would be heard very clearly. Thus if bar 5 lh were played too legato, the shape of line could be obscured by the pedal. However, in bar 20 the lh slur is still missing, even though it is at the top of the texture and the same figure was slurred in bar 16 rh.

The lh slur of bar 14 does not appear in bars 9 or 13, and although this slurring is what most performers would choose instinctively, it seems strange that this was not so marked in bar 9, where the rh could provide a considerable distraction. Indeed, in bars 46–8 slurs appear in the rh but not the lh, suggesting that the lh part be played more detached in order to be heard clearly.

If bars 21 lh and 36 rh are compared, the slurrings are exactly opposite: in bar 21

17 The incidence of slurs rather than their appearance is observed at this stage.

the second beat involves two leaps (while the first and third have closer intervals). Perhaps, as the rh is at the same pitch, this arpeggio figure needs to be heard more clearly, while at bar 36 rh, with the higher tessitura, the slight detachment is not required.

Visually, these slurs are as unclear as those longer marks in the Adagio of Sonata no. 1, mentioned earlier. Three points seem valid:

Bach's practice seems to be that descending adjacent semiquavers, the first being an appoggiatura, are generally slurred together (the slur covering all four notes),[18] and this is the case in bar 5(3) lh (*a*3). Bar 2(2) rh of the opening Adagio is a similar instance, although here the slur ends rather before the final note. An unequivocal example in keyboard music comes with the figuration beginning bar 34 of BWV 552.i (Prelude in E flat), a printed source.

Many other four-note patterns follow the layout of notes in which there are disjunct notes. Here the slurs cover the conjunct notes (eg. *b*(1), bar 6) with the leaps unslurred.[19] The lh figuration introduced in bar 14 seems directly akin to string techniques, with the long down-bow followed by short up-bow (when larger leaps are involved, the effect of string-crossings should be considered).[20]

The only figure that appears to be unslurred is *c* and *d* (bars 7 and 8). This could suggest that there is more separation after the tie (the appearance of the slur in BWV 527 Andante bars 5 and 7 seems to substantiate this view, as its function could be to reverse the effect of separation caused by the tie earlier in the bar). In the first movement of Brandenburg Concerto no. 1, bar 32, the fast demisemiquaver values are separate after the tie in the violin parts, so there are some grounds for believing that in movements of this tempo notes decorating short suspensions are articulated.[21]

These hypotheses can be tested immediately by comparison with an earlier version of the Vivace of Sonata no. 4: the Sinfonia to Part II of Cantata 76 (1723) in the autograph P 67. Although we must be wary of assuming the slur to have the same function in different media, some of the similarities are significant. The figures *a* and *e* are those which are most altered: the oboe slur bar 2(2) covers all four notes as suggested for P 271, as does the final slur for oboe, bar 9. Similarly the gamba bowing bar 9 shows the first three notes slurred and the fourth separated; *c* and *d* is never slurred.

The combined testimony of these two autographs would suggest that some modern editors are wrong in assuming that all these slurs simply cover all the notes of the beat. There are, however, distinct differences between P 67 and P 271, and these should not be overlooked.

---

18 For example, the Violin Sonata BWV 1001 (Fugue bar 63), and the Partita BWV 1004 (Sarabande bar 14).

19 As suggested by C. P. E. Bach, *Versuch*, ch. 3, §17.

20 Examples of this figuration in string music are found in Brandenburg Concerto no. 3, from bar 2.

21 Could this be the type of 'midway' touch in unmarked articulation mentioned by Marpurg (*Anleitung zum Clavierspielen* (Berlin 1755), I, p. 29) or C. P. E. Bach (*Versuch*, ch. 3 §6)?

differences in the initial a-i (viola da gamba, bars 5–13)

*a*2	slur added
*a*3	two slurs instead of one
*b*1,2	slurs missing
*e*1,2	slurs added
*f*3	slur added

further additions and differences[22]

9(3)	oboe (*a*3), one slur instead of the gamba's two
43(1–2)	oboe (*a*1–2), extra slur from crotchet to end of beat 2
43(3)	oboe (*a*3)
58(3)	oboe (*e*3)
58(2,3)	gamba (*e*2,3)

What is particularly interesting is the discrepancy between gamba bar 5(3) (two slurs) and oboe bar 9(3) (one slur). Possibly Bach regarded the oboe's tonguing as too incisive for more than one slur here, while the quieter tone of the gamba requires more articulation. Although the aural effect of the two is probably identical, Bach may well have intended discrepancies in articulation between parts; this is also suggested in certain features of P 271.

As it is clear that Bach did not mechanically transfer all the marks from P 67 to P 271, it is very possible that many of the markings in P 271 were added later; it is likely too that P 271 was referred to more often than the cantata, which as far as we know was performed only when it occurred in its cycle. This possibility is substantiated by the fact that there are fewer markings in P 272 copied directly from P 271, perhaps before the latter's markings were completed.

The only additional slurs in P 272 are bar 26(3) rh(*e*3) and bar 46(2) rh(*e*2). The following are omitted from P 272:

14(1)	lh(*e*1)
15(1,2)	rh(*e*1,2)
16(3)	rh(*a*3)
17(3)	rh(*b*3)
20(3)	lh(*a*3)
21(3)	lh(*b*3)
21(3)	rh(*f*3)
38(3)	lh(*h*3)

Recent scholars have chosen to consult other good secondary sources in the preparation of texts. Kilian has argued that Oley's text is an important one, deriving from Bach's instruction.[23] In Oley's text, not only is the figure *c* and *d* (bars 7 and 8) consistently slurred, but virtually every grouping in the entire movement is slurred (including the 2nd–4th quavers, pedal, bar 3). Such detailed and carefully drawn markings are rare in Bach's own hand; Oley's slurs uncharacteristically seem

---

22 Omissions are not recorded.
23 Kilian, 'Über einige neue Aspekte' (see note 9 above), pp. 69–72. Oley's text, Vienna Cod. 15528, is an exceptionally clear source, and Kilian suggests that Oley was a pupil of 'Anon 5', who was probably a Bach pupil.

to cover the entire beat, which rather deadens the effect of Bach's apparently more varied norm, found in both keyboard and instrumental scores.

Oley's further rationalization of Bach's slurrings is evident in the last bar of Sonata no. 6: here Bach used a paired slurring on the first crotchet beat and a four-note slur on the second; in performance, the paired slur creates a natural *ritenuto* for the final cadence and the four-note slur a long up-beat for the final note. Both these slurs are characteristic of those found in string music, mirroring the shape of the melodic figures. The four-note slur, in particular, follows the typical pattern of four adjacent descending notes, beginning with an appoggiatura (the first of the points noted above). Oley, on the other hand, exchanges the four-note slur for another paired pattern, thus making the effect more uniform.[24]

Am.B. 51a is another copy which Kilian suggests might have been derived from Bach's instruction (through Agricola).[25] Although this generally follows Bach's markings, twelve slurs are omitted and the only additional ones are bars 27(1) lh(*e1*), 28(1) rh(*e1*), and 37(1) lh(*g1*).

It has recently been suggested that scholars have in the past been too concerned to see consistent patterns of articulation in Baroque music,[26] a concern that may have been shared even by some of the later copyists of Bach's music, such as Oley. Clearly, if we are to reach any clearer understanding of the problem, much work has still to be done on the nature and function of Bach's keyboard slurring. If the appearance of the slur in keyboard music is not unlike that in instrumental music, did Bach assume it implied a basic legato (notes played in one bow or breath)? Or was he more concerned with the natural shaping given by a single bow-stroke or breath, of which there are no mechanical equivalents in keyboard music?

Whatever the unsolved problems may be that arise from Bach's articulation markings, there can be no doubt at all from the way in which he laid out certain textures for manuals and pedals that phrasings and detachments of various sorts must have been a feature of his playing. Whether the evidence of such textures should be used to construct consistent patterns of articulation for the related passages that are playable in a legato manner is another matter. To judge from the fingering of the early C major fugue, referred to above, the player cannot have been unduly concerned to articulate the subject in a consistent manner.

Such articulation evidence as Bach's keyboard textures yield is broadly of three kinds: articulation resulting from the juxtaposition and crossing of parts; articulation resulting from considerable changes of hand position; and articulation that is the unavoidable product of textures that do not lie easily under the hands. Some preliminary findings follow, based upon the non-chorale organ compositions.

24 Emery points out that 'certain mistakes in Oley's copies suggest that he was not fully conversant with Sebastian's habits' – W. Emery, *J. C. Oley: Four Chorale Preludes*, Early Organ Music 2 (London, 1958).

25 Kilian, *op. cit.* (see note 9 above).

26 See for instance G. Pont, 'A Revolution in the Science and Practice of Music', *Musicology* 5 (1979), pp. 1–60.

Articulation resulting from the juxtaposition and crossing of parts (Exx. 1–17). The flourish for the little E minor Prelude and Fugue BWV 533 and the well-known cadenza of the D minor Toccata BWV 565 are the fastest passages of the kind. It is, however, at the level of quaver and semiquaver movement that the problem of articulation is most pervasive, Bach's own keyboard textures suggesting a detached 'norm' of performance. Certain configurations (as for instance those of Exx. 7 and 12–14) tend to accentuate the down-beat. Others (such as those in Exx. 16–17) suggest aspirations of the kind that result from the off-beat manual changes of the *Italian Concerto* (BWV 971), the C major concerto (BWV 595; Ex. 15) and the 'Dorian' Toccata (BWV 538).

Articulation arising from abrupt hand-position changes (Exx. 18–29). While on the whole Bach does not require rapid hand-position changes in his organ music, certain passages do require speedy adjustment of the kind illustrated in Exx. 18–19. The implications again are the accentuation of a strong beat, or the phrasing of an up-beat aspiration, of the kind discussed above.

Articulation arising from awkward textures (Exx. 30–46). Exx. 30–43 are principally concerned with awkward layout, in which the division of notes between the two hands becomes a major problem. All are awkward (if not impossible) to play if a true legato touch is attempted. Exx. 44–6, moreover, remind us that Bach did not always regard written note-values as sacrosanct. Part-writing frequently necessitates the re-sounding of a sustained note two or perhaps three times, where a moving part collides with it. Many end-of-phrase notes are truncated in this way.

In conclusion, then, while the evidence of mid-eighteenth-century writers must at least be treated with caution (even if it comes from a member of the Bach family), there are grounds for believing that there may be at least a grain of truth in Quantz's hierarchy of articulations. For though so much of Bach's keyboard music is unmarked – and especially the faster music – the composer did use both slurs and staccato markings here and there as if he was seeking degrees of articulation either side of a norm. Further attention must surely be given to the defining of that 'norm'.

Ex. 1. Prelude BWV 533.i, bar 10

Ex. 2. Toccata and Fugue BWV 565, bar 133

Ex. 3. Prelude BWV 543.i, bar 36

Ex. 4. Fugue BWV 542.ii, bar 20

Ex. 5. BWV 542.ii, bar 99

Ex. 6. Prelude BWV 534.i, bar 2

Ex. 7. Fugue BWV 531.ii, bar 15

Ex. 8. BWV 542.ii, bar 43

Ex. 9. Prelude and Fugue BWV 550, bar 95

Ex. 10. BWV 565, bar 49

Ex. 11. Fugue BWV 537.ii, bar 100

Ex. 12. Fugue BWV 535.ii, bar 39

Ex. 13. Fugue BWV 564.iii, bar 37

Ex. 14. Passacaglia and Fugue BWV 582, bar 174 (cf. bars 256, 272)

Ex. 15. Concerto BWV 595, first movement, bar 3

Ex. 16. Prelude BWV 531.i, bar 23

201

Ex. 17. BWV 565, bar 54

Ex. 18. Fugue BWV 532.ii, bar 120

Ex. 19. BWV 532.ii, bar 13

Ex. 20. Fugue BWV 538.ii, bar 195

Ex. 21. Toccata BWV 540.i, bar 269

Ex. 22. Prelude BWV 547.i, bar 35

Ex. 23. BWV 547.i, bar 72

Ex. 24. Fugue BWV 545.ii, bar 38

Ex. 25. Prelude BWV 552.i, bar 94

Ex. 26. Fugue BWV 552.ii, bar 56

Ex. 27. BWV 564.iii, bar 18

Ex. 28. Corelli Fugue BWV 579, bar 52

Ex. 29. Pastorale BWV 590, third movement, bar 43

Ex. 30. BWV 532.ii, bar 64

Ex. 31. Fugue BWV 534.ii, bar 16

Ex. 32. BWV 534.ii, bar 103

Ex. 33. BWV 535.ii, bar 60

Ex. 34. Fugue BWV 541.ii, bar 27

Ex. 35. BWV 542.ii, bar 10

Ex. 36. Fugue BWV 547.ii, bar 53

Ex. 37. Prelude BWV 548.i, bar 46

Ex. 38. BWV 548.i, bar 75

Ex. 39. BWV 565, bar 100

Ex. 40. BWV 566, bar 13

Ex. 41. BWV 579, bar 47

Ex. 42. BWV 582, bar 230

Ex. 43. BWV 582, bar 197

205

Ex. 44. Fugue BWV 548.ii, bar 47

Ex. 45. Legrenzi Fugue BWV 574, bar 54

Ex. 46. BWV 582, bar 229

Keyboard Technique and Articulation:
Evidence for the Performance Practices of
Bach, Handel and Scarlatti

MARK LINDLEY

(Buckfastleigh, Devon)

Many eighteenth-century keyboard instruments had a rather facile touch[1] which helped players develop a great nimbleness in the wrist and finger joints. One might infer from Clementi's *Introduction* (Ex. 1)[2] that by 1800 the modern use of the

Ex. 1. 'Allegro by Handel' (Clementi, *Introduction to the Art of Playing the Pianoforte* (London, 1801), p. 36), bars 9–15

thumb in scale passages and extensions had quite superseded the old devices (crossing over without the thumb; extending with the middle fingers or with 2–5 rather than with the thumb). But in fact some nineteenth-century pianists had a remarkably versatile mixture of technical devices. Not only would Chopin use the thumb without hesitation on the black keys or pass it even under the little finger, but also

> With one and the same finger he took often two consecutive keys (and this not only in gliding down from a black to the next white key) without the least interruption of the sequence being noticeable. The passing over each other of the longer fingers without the aid of the thumb ... he frequently made use of, and not only in passages where the thumb stationary on a key made this unavoidably necessary.[3]

Late-Baroque players had their own compound of old and new techniques. A serious attempt to recover it might teach us a good deal about their ideas of melodic articulation and motivic organization. I imagine this attempt will be made, successfully, when the current revival of sixteenth- and seventeenth-century tech-

1 P. Williams, *A New History of the Organ* (London and Bloomington, Indiana, 1980), pp. 91–2, 105–6, 114; F. Hubbard, *Three Centuries of Harpsichord Making* (Cambridge, Mass., 1965), pp. 124–5.
2 All the extensively fingered pieces cited here will be included in the second edition of M. Lindley and M. Boxall, *Early Keyboard Fingerings, an Anthology* (London, forthcoming).
3 F. Niecks, *Frederick Chopin as a Man and Musician* (London, 1888), II, p. 186.

niques has produced a generation of players to whom some style of early fingering feels more natural than the modern fingerings which we middle-aged folk were brought up on. My own attempts, with music for which some eighteenth-century player has given us a complete or nearly complete fingering, have brought me far enough to dismiss such wilfully nescient arguments as 'Bach's technique was really the same as ours' or 'Early fingerings are merely primitive' or 'The fingering doesn't matter', and to offer, instead, a relatively disinterested account. I should say that in general:

1. The use of right-hand extensions without the thumb (Exx. 2–8) and of crossovers (Exx. 9–14) may cause the fingers to be somewhat less curved than in the 'cupped-hand' posture. How much so will vary.

Ex. 2. A. Scarlatti, *Toccata primo* (BL Add. MS 14244, ff. 52′–59′), bars 135–7

Ex. 3. F. Couperin, Passacaille (*Second livre de pièces de clavecin* (Paris, 1717), p. 35; *L'art de toucher* . . . (1717 edn), p. 68), 7th *couplet*

Ex. 4. J. S. Bach, *Applicatio* BWV 994, bar 4

Ex. 5. J. S. Bach, Fughetta BWV 870a.ii, bars 21–2

Ex. 6. J. S. Bach, Prelude BWV 870a.i, bars 13–14

Ex. 7. Zipoli/anon., minuet (Cfm Mu. MS 57, f. 23), bars 19–21

Ex. 8. Handel, Ciacona HWV 435 (BL Add. MS 31577, ff. 34′–37 = pp. 63–9), var. 7, bars 1–2

Ex. 9. J. S. Bach, Fughetta BWV 870a.ii, bars 31–2

Ex. 10. Walther, *Wir glauben all in einen Gott* (*DDT* 26, p. 243), verse 2, bars 25–6

Ex. 11. A. Scarlatti, *Toccata primo*, **bar 61**

Ex. 12. F. Couperin, 'La Triomphante' (*Second livre*, **p. 54;** *L'art de toucher*, **p. 70), second part, 3rd** *couplet*

Ex. 13. F. Couperin, 'Le Moucheron' (*Second livre*, **p. 11;** *L'art de toucher*, **p. 66), bars 22–3**

Ex. 14. Zipoli/anon., minuet, bars 9–10

Ex. 15. F. Couperin, 'Les Silvains' (*Pieces de clavecin . . . Premier livre* (1713), **p. 8;** *L'art de toucher*, **p. 47), second part, bars 1–2**

2. In lateral shifts 3 takes 'strong' or 'weak' notes as the context may render more convenient (Exx. 11–15). (This indifference can be traced back to the first half of the seventeenth century in Italy, as shown in Ex. 16, and to the late sixteenth century in Germany, as in Ex. 17.)

Ex. 16. Anonymous, from *Applicaturae* **(Breslau, 1680) (Brasov City Library, Mus. MS 808, f. 2)**

Ex. 17. Ammerbach, exercises (*Orgel- oder Instrument-Tabulaturbuch* **(Nuremberg, 1583), introduction), excerpt**

3. The wrist and thumbs are liable to move through a wide range of distances in front of the player. Often the thumb may go forward to play chromatic notes (Exx. 18–22), or (particularly in the right hand) it may often hang some distance shy of the near end of the keys, to facilitate lateral extensions among the other fingers.[4] It may move back and forth quite freely during a sequential pattern or the like (Exx. 20–22).

Ex. 18. A. Scarlatti, *Toccata primo*, bars 94–6

Ex. 19. Handel, Ciacona HWV 435, var. 13, bars 5–7

Ex. 20. A. Scarlatti, *Toccata primo*, bars 55–6 †

† For the last note of some of the right hand's eight-note groups there are variant readings of the fingering that call for 3 instead of 2. I suppose these are mistakes.

Ex. 21. J. S. Bach, Fughetta BWV 870a.ii, bars 8–9

Ex. 22. Handel, Ciacona HWV 435, var. 13, bars 1–2

4. Yet often the fingering of a sequential pattern is altered to avoid using the thumb for a chromatic note (Exx. 23–26).

5. The hand is passed over the thumb more readily than the thumb under the hand, so a modern scale fingering is more likely when moving toward the body than moving away from it (Exx. 27–33). Yet the right hand may still descend with an

---

4 C. P. E. Bach remarked that 'Wer den Daumen nicht braucht, der lässt ihn herunter hangen, damit er ihm nicht im Wege ist' ('those who do not use the thumb let it hang down so that it is not in the way': *Versuch* p. 19).

Ex. 23. F. Couperin, 'Le Moucheron', bars 14–15

Ex. 24. J. S. Bach, Praeambulum BWV 930, bars 21–4

Ex. 25. Handel, Ciacona HWV 435, var. 12, bars 1–3

Ex. 26. Zipoli/anon., minuet, bars 27–32

Ex. 27. A. Scarlatti, *Toccata primo*, bars 6–7

Ex. 28. Scarlatti, *Toccata primo*, bar 113

Ex. 29. Scarlatti, *Toccata primo*, bars 7–8

Ex. 30. J. S. Bach, Fughetta BWV 870a.ii, bar 12

Ex. 31. BWV 870a.ii, bars 13–14

Ex. 33. J. S. Bach, *Applicatio* BWV 994, bar 1

Ex. 32. BWV 870a.ii, bars 24–6

211

Ex. 34. BWV 994, bar 5

Ex. 35. A. Scarlatti, *Toccata primo,* **bars 70–1**

Ex. 36. F. Couperin, 'Les Ondes' (*Pieces de clavecin . . . Premier livre*, p. 73; *L'art de toucher*, p. 50), end of 4th *couplet*

RIGHT HAND

un-modern fingering (Exx. 34–36), and the left hand ascend 2121 (Ex. 37). I cite below some early examples of modern scale fingerings away from the body.

6. Often the same finger is used twice in succession (Exx. 38–45). Among quick notes the second one is most often metrically stronger than the first;[5] thus one tends to play the first note (at the end of a beat) with the finger alone, and then

Ex. 37. J. S. Bach, *Applicatio* **BWV 994, bars 3–4**

Ex. 38. F. Couperin, Cinquieme prelude (*L'art de toucher*, p. 57), bars 19–20

Ex. 39. Walther, *Wir glauben all,* **verse 2, bars 20–1**

Ex. 40. J. S. Bach, Fughetta BWV 870a.ii, bars 30–3

Ex. 41. J. S. Bach, Prelude BWV 870a.i, bars 14–15

Ex. 42. A. Scarlatti, *Toccata primo,* **bars 154–5**

Ex. 43. Scarlatti, *Toccata primo,* **bars 123–4**

Ex. 44. F. Couperin, 'Le Moucheron', bars 16–18

5 In this connection see F. Couperin, *L'art de toucher le clavecin* (Paris, 1717), p. 50.

212

Ex. 45. Handel, Ciacona HWV 435 (Lbm Add. MS 31577), var. 11, bars 1–4

involve the entire hand in the playing of the second note (on the beat). (This technique goes back to the sixteenth century, as in Ex. 17.)

7. Finger-substitutions are used frequently by François Couperin (Ex. 46) and occasionally by the Germans (as in Exx. 32 and, perhaps, 47), but apparently never by the Italians.

Ex. 46. F. Couperin, Premiere Prelude (*L'art de toucher*, p. 52), bars 1–6

Ex. 47. Walther, *Allein Gott in der Höh sei Ehr* (*DDT* 26, pp. 20–1), verse 2 bars 18–22

The contradictory tendencies apparent in this summary might be attributed to the 'transitional character' of early-eighteenth-century keyboard techniques. Upon using those techniques, however, one learns that often the fingerings are less systematic than modern (or for that matter Renaissance) pedagogical fingerings because they are more subtly fitted to the musical and technical peculiarities of the moment. During the first half of the century the main trend was not to simplify technique by rejecting old devices, but to expand it by adding new ones, and the choice among them all was likely to depend upon one's preferences in articulation and phrasing, or upon such a peculiar interplay among the hand, the notes and the keyboard that to derive the *ad hoc* solution from general principles would overtax the patience of even a German pedagogue. This was an age when one's technique was developed mainly by learning pieces, and not by drilling in abstract scales and arpeggios or in five-finger exercises of the kind shown in Ex. 48. The end-result was a relatively sophisticated style of playing which provided for musical and technical nuances by a variety of gestures and postures such as pianists today tend to reserve

213

Ex. 48. Friedrich Wieck, five-finger exercise (Marie Wieck, *Pianoforte Studien von Friedrich Wieck* (Leipzig, 1875), p. 1)

for more difficult music: one might have to vary with remarkable dexterity the position of the thumb (with respect to the keyboard), the angle of the hand and the curvature of the fingers.

Evidently Domenico Scarlatti was trained in this way. His father's *Toccata primo*, composed sometime around 1720[6] and typical of its genre, is of unique value, to us and no doubt to Alessandro Scarlatti's pupils at Naples and perhaps Rome, for being fingered throughout. Some of the fingerings seem pedagogically conceived: Exx. 49–51 show a progression from easier to more difficult left-hand fingerings for the same kind of passage; Ex. 20 and Ex. 52 are model demonstrations of the use of the right thumb for chromatic notes; Ex. 2 shows that diatonic

Ex. 49. A. Scarlatti, *Toccata primo*, bars 27–8   **Ex. 50. Scarlatti, *Toccata primo*, bar 102**

Ex. 51. Scarlatti, *Toccata primo*, bars 147–9

Ex. 52. Scarlatti, *Toccata primo*, bars 47–9

sixths call rather for 5–2 than for 5–1; Exx. 11 and 27 show that either 4 or 3 may have the strong notes in a scale passage away from the body; and so on. To render these examples with security one is obliged to use a marginally detached articulation and touch the keys as lightly as may guarantee the necessary choreography. I

6 In the principal manuscript (BM Add. MS 14244) the last toccata is dated 1723.

choose this term advisedly: when the technique has become familiar, it works better at full speed than in slow motion.

In Exx. 53 and 54 the left thumb and right little finger are treated analogously,

Ex. 53. Scarlatti, *Toccata*
primo, **bar 12**

Ex. 54. Scarlatti, *Toccata primo*,
bars 9–10†

† Not all the manuscripts say 'simili'.

the short finger perhaps bearing an occasional thrust of the hand into the keyboard. The same technique is evident in Exx. 55 and 56, where 2 is also used in this manner. Sometimes 4 is used thus as if it were at the edge of the hand (Ex. 57), but

Ex. 55. Scarlatti, *Toccata primo*, **bars 72–4**

Ex. 56. Scarlatti, *Toccata*
primo, **bar 28**

Ex. 57. Scarlatti, *Toccata primo*,
bar 15

Ex. 58. Scarlatti, *Toccata*
primo, **bar 99**

more often it has to maintain its independence, whereas 5 is seldom called upon to do so (Exx. 58–60 being more typical than Ex. 61). In Ex. 62, 1–4 is used only for those sixths which occupy a weak beat, and the sixth over which I have placed an asterisk is fingered 2–5 in order to bring out the second beat of a 3/2-bar hemiola – a nice example of *ad hoc* fingering for musical effect.

Ex. 59. Scarlatti, *Toccata primo*, **bars 119–20**

Ex. 60. Scarlatti, *Toccata primo*, **bars 140–2**

Ex. 61. Scarlatti, *Toccata primo*, **bars 107–8**

215

Ex. 62. Scarlatti, *Toccata primo*, bars 84–8

When we consider, apropos the right hand, those cases in which 2 serves where a modern pianist would use 1, and those in which the middle fingers without the thumb take scale figures (Exx. 11 and 27) or the *échappée*-laden figures in Exx. 49–51, we can begin to see why 1 plays altogether only about half as many notes as 2, and considerably fewer than 3 or 4 (Table 1, second row). Vis-à-vis Ruggiero Gerlin's fingering (1943)[7] for the same 1,380 notes, 1 is used some 46% less; 2 some 37% more 4 some 27% more; and 3 some 10% more (Table 1, third row).

The left hand has no quasi-thematic or decorative sixths, and the corresponding tally of its approximately 950 notes (Table 2) shows a less pronounced difference in the use of the thumb, and less use of 2 in the original than in Gerlin's fingering. Exx. 28, 49–51 and 63–65 show how 3 and, particularly, 4 are used more in the original than in the modern fingering.

As Alessandro Scarlatti is not himself our subject, one additional example of *ad hoc* fingering for musical effect will suffice:[8] the use of 3 for the A marked by an asterisk in Ex. 66. The 3 may at first seem contrived, but it imparts an extra space and articulative energy nicely calculated to compensate for the absence of semi-quavers in the bar.

Table 1. *Use of right-hand fingers in the Toccata primo*

	1	2	3	4	5
modern fingering:	24%	19%	19%	17%	20%
original fingering:	13%	26%	21%	21%	19%
comparative difference:	− 46%	+ 37%	+ 10%	+ 27%	+ 5%

Table 2. *Use of left-hand fingers in the Toccata primo*

	5	4	3	2	1
modern fingering:	13%	14%	19%	26%	28%
original fingering:	14%	18%	23%	23%	23%
comparative difference:	+ 8%	+ 29%	+ 21%	− 12%	+ 18%

7 Alessandro Scarlatti, *Primo e secondo libro di toccate*, ed. R. Gerlin, I classici musicali italiani 13 (Milan, 1943), p. 1.

8 Some additional examples are described in M. Lindley, 'An Introduction to Alessandro Scarlatti's *Toccata prima*', *EM* 10 (1982), p. 333.

Ex. 63. Scarlatti, *Toccata primo*, bar 97

Ex. 64. Scarlatti, *Toccata primo*, bar 155

Ex. 65. Scarlatti, *Toccata primo*, bars 68–9

Ex. 66. Scarlatti, *Toccata primo*, bars 29–32

With regard to scales, Ex. 67 shows that Alessandro Scarlatti would not take the hand past the thumb twice in succession. Within a few years (1724) Rameau in his 'Les Tourbillons' used an elaborate two-hand choreography for some long scale passages (Ex. 68), dividing them into three- and four-note segments rather as if only one hand were playing them in a more modern technique. (Indeed, the left hand alone could use Rameau's groupings for the same D major scale from A to a′: 4321 321 4321 4321.) Della Ciaja used a similar technique in 1727 (Ex. 69).

Ex. 67. Scarlatti, *Toccata primo*, bar 112

Ex. 68. Rameau, 'Les Tourbillons' (*Pieces de clavessin avec une methode pour la mecanique des doigts* (Paris, 1724)), bars 36–7

Ex. 69. Della Ciaja, Sonata Op. IV No. 2 (*Sonate per cembalo . . . opera quarta* (Rome, 1727), p. 15), bars 101–2

MARK LINDLEY

At other moments Della Ciaja would cross the entire hand past the thumb (Ex. 70) or else cross 4 past 1 twice in succession, or cross 1 past 4 (Ex. 71). In 1730 Peter Prelleur prescribed the latter kind of scale fingering in his *The Harpsichord*

Ex. 70. Della Ciaja, Sonata Op. IV No. 2, bar 70

Ex. 71. Della Ciaja, Sonata Op. IV No. 2, bars 29–31

Illustrated and Improv'd: Wherein is shewn the Italian Manner of Fingering; and the same fingerings were also prescribed in 1738 by Franz Anton Maichelbeck, Professor of Italian at the University of Freiburg (and an organist at the cathedral there), in his *Die auf dem Clavier lehrende Caecilia*:[9]

wann man durch eine Octave auf- oder ablauffet, so fange in der lincken mit num. 3 an, und folge mit 2, 1, 0 nach, darnach sollen die vier andere eben so also geschlagen werden. In der rechten fange mit num. 0 an, als wie zum Exempel . . .

When you run up or down through an octave, begin in the left hand with 4 and follow with 3, 2, 1; after which the other four notes should also be played thus. In the right hand begin with the thumb, as in the example [Ex. 72].

Ex. 72. Maichelbeck, scales (*Die auf dem Clavier lehrende Caecilia* (Augsburg, 1738), part 2, p. 36)

Some of Maichelbeck's other examples (Exx. 73–74) show that he was adept at returning to the thumb after 2 has been turned over it, and in two instances (where I have put asterisks in Ex. 74) his fingerings rather prompt the thumb to turn under. (He remarked that passages like the one from which Ex. 74 is taken could be found

Ex. 73. Maichelbeck, exercises (p. 36)

9 *Die auf dem Clavier lehrende Caecilia* (Augsburg, 1738), Part 2, p. 36.

218

Ex. 74. Maichelbeck, bass line after A. Scarlatti (p. 37), excerpt

'in the chamber cantatas which have been invented hundreds of times by Herr [Alessandro] Scarlatti', whom he had perhaps met as a music student at Rome in the mid-1720s.) The scales might still be performed as Tomás de Sancta María had prescribed some hundred and fifty years earlier when, recommending 1234 1234 for rapid notes in the left hand (Ex. 75), he had said that one should 'turn the hand a little in the direction of the run'.[10] Yet Ex. 76, which also dates from 1738, quite obliges the hand to face the other way.

Ex. 75. Tomás de Sancta María, scales (*Libre llamado arte de tāner fantasía* (Valladolid, 1565), f. 40)

Ex. 76. Walther, *Allein Gott in der Höh,* verse 2, bars 2–3

But another of Sancta María's injunctions – that 'the finger which has just struck should always be lifted before another is put down'[11] – was repeated in the eighteenth century. At Hamburg in 1735, Handel's longtime friend Johann Mattheson[12] said that

ein Meister seinem Untergebnen immer dazu anhalten muss, dass er eher keinen andern Finger zusetze, bis er den vorigen aufgehoben hat: ingleichen/ dass er die Tasten nur mit den Gelencken der Finger gantz säuberlich/ keinesweges aber mit der gantz steifen Hand niederdrücke.

a teacher should constantly require his pupil never to apply the next finger until he has lifted the previous one; and require him also to press down the key with merely the leverage of the finger, quite cleanly, but absolutely not with the entire hand stiff.

– thus insisting upon a marginally detached articulation while rejecting some north German counterpart of the Italian technique discussed above in connection with Exx. 53–56. (I say 'marginally detached' in deference to the lyricism of some of the fugue subjects, such as Ex. 77, in Mattheson's *Die wol-klingende Finger-Sprache,*

10 *Arte de tāner fantasia* (Valladolid, 1565), f. 38'.
11 *Ibid.* ch. 17.
12 Mattheson, *Kleine General-Bass-Schule* (Hamburg, 1735), p. 72.

Ex. 77. J. Mattheson, Fuga in C minor (*Die wol-klingende Finger-Sprache* (Hamburg, 1735), p. 11), bars 1–10

dedicated to Handel the same year, 1735.) At Berlin twenty years later Friedrich Wilhelm Marpurg[13] wrote:

Ein halber Bogen . . . bedeutet, dass diese Noten geschleiffet werden sollen. *Schleiffen* aber heisset, den Finger von der vorhergehenden Note nicht eher aufheben, als bis man die folgende berührt . . . Dem Schleiffen ist das Abstossen entgegen gesetzt, welches darinnen besteht, dass man eine Note nicht nach ihrem Wehrte, sondern sie nur etwann bis zur Hälfte aushält. Dieses wird durch Punct . . . angezeichnet. Oefters bedienet man sich dazu eines kleinen geraden Striches . . . Sowohl dem Schleifen als Abstossen ist das ordentliche Fortgehen entgegen gesetzt, welches darinnen besteht, dass man ganz hurtig kurz vorher, ehe man die folgende Note berühret, den Finger von der vorhergehenden Taste aufhebet. Dieses ordentlich Fortgehen wird, weil es allezeit voraus gesetzt wird, niemahls angezeiget.

A half arc . . . means that the notes are to be slurred. Now 'to slur' means not to lift the finger from the preceding note until one touches the next [note] . . . Detachment is the opposite of slurring; it consists of this: that one holds a note not for its [full] value, but only until about half [the value]. This is notated with [a] dot; Often one makes use of a little straight line for this . . . The ordinary procedure is opposed to legato as well as to staccato. In [this procedure], just before you touch the following note, you very quickly lift the finger from the preceding key. This ordinary procedure is never indicated [explicitly], since it is always presupposed.

A number of passages in Domenico Scarlatti's *Essercizi* (1738) want a modern scale fingering (see Exx. 78–80), yet they all seem rather moments of 'ingenious

Ex. 78. D. Scarlatti, *Essercizi* no. 10 (*Essercizi per Gravicembalo* (perhaps London, before 1740), bars 69–72

Ex. 79. Scarlatti, *Essercizi* no. 26, bars 125–30

Jesting with Art', to borrow a descriptive phrase from Scarlatti's own preface, then signs of a modern legato. Except for the music itself, and the not infrequent use of 'm' or 'd' to indicate the left or right hand, the evidence from Scarlatti himself is meagre (Exx. 83 and 85–86) and raises more questions than it answers: Which fingers should be used in Exx. 85 and 86? When the passage shown in Ex. 83 is

13 *Anleitung zum Clavierspielen* (Berlin, 1755), p. 28.

Ex. 80. Scarlatti, *Essercizi* no. 24, bars 4–6

Ex. 81. Scarlatti, *Essercizi* no. 16, bars 56–9

Ex. 82. Scarlatti, *Essercizi* no. 9, bars 24–6

Ex. 83. Scarlatti, Sonata Kk 379 (Parma, Bib. Pal. MS AG 31415, no. 22), bars 33–9

Ex. 84. Scarlatti, Sonata Kk 379 bars 77–8

Ex. 85. Scarlatti, Sonata Kk 96 (Parma, MS AG 31408, no. 29), bars 33–41

Ex. 86. Scarlatti, Sonata Kk 96, bars 140–5

Mutandi i deti

transposed up a fourth in the second half of the sonata (see Ex. 84), should a *glissando* still be used (at the expense of playing B instead of Bb)? If so, then how should one play the first bar in Ex. 82, or indeed the second bar in Ex. 81? However one may answer these questions, the effect of the rubrics is clearly to make the hand's comportment more acrobatic and less orthodox. I imagine that when a real attempt has been made by gifted players to explore the sonatas with a technique derived like Scarlatti's own (to some extent) from that of his father, we may be in a better position to speculate as to his style of playing. I think the sonatas would endure this probing even better than they did the pianistic adaptations of Czerny and von Bülow, and I dare say it would tend to show that Scarlatti's hand achieved its 'elegance and delicacy of expression'[14] by a more resourceful choreography than in Clementi's parody of 1801 (Ex. 87).

Ex. 87. 'Allegro by Scarlatti' (Clementi, *Introduction* (1801), p. 48), bar 1

The French cultivated a different style, and for a proper approach to Bach we ought to review something of their treatises.[15] Early in the century Saint Lambert said that nothing loosens the fingers better than the trill ('rien ne les denouë davantage que le tremblement')[16] and that the fingers should be curved to reach no further than the thumb ('Les doigts courbez & tous rangez au même niveau, pris par la longueur du poûce').[17] He advocated a quiet hand ('on doit toujours . . . choisir les doigts qui font faire le moins de mouvement à la main'):[18] his exact meaning can be seen by comparing Exx. 88 and 89, which are from his only known compositions

Ex. 88. M. de Saint Lambert, Minuet (*Les principes du clavecin* (Paris, 1702), p. 67), bars 11–16

14 Mainwaring p. 61.
15 For economy I have abridged this section. A more adequate account of Couperin (and Dandrieu) is in A. Dolmetsch, *The Interpretation of the Music of the XVII and XVIII Centuries* (London, 1916), pp. 392–408.
16 M. de Saint Lambert, *Les principes du clavecin* (Paris, 1702), p. 64.
17 Saint Lambert, *Nouveau traité de l'accompagnement* (Paris, 1707), p. 42.
18 Saint Lambert, *Les principes*, p. 65.

Ex. 89. Saint Lambert, Gavotte (*Les principes*, p. 67), bars 6–8

Ex. 90. Dandrieu, 'Gavotte tendre' (*Pièces de clavecin courtes et faciles (Paris, 1713)), bars 8–12

(1702), with Exx. 90 and 15, by Dandrieu (1713) and François Couperin. He decided upon reflection that for a descending right-hand *diminution* the customary use of 3232, which he himself had earlier prescribed, 'would not seem to me yet well established' ('cet usage ne me paroit pas encore bien établi'); 2121 would serve the right hand best, just as it did the left.[19] François Couperin ignored this in 1717 (see Ex. 91 – where Saint Lambert's proposal would have called for the thumb on C♯),

Ex. 91. F. Couperin, 'Allemande l'Ausoniéne' (*Second livre*, p. 90; *L'art de toucher*, p. 67), bars 30–1

but said that the successive use of $\frac{4}{2}$ for thirds had been inimical to a legato ('Cette Manière ancienne n'auoit nulle Liaison').[20] Couperin's scale fingerings (Exx. 92–93) imply a three-note anacrusis to each beat, in keeping with the other exercises in the same set (Ex. 94), but of course he sometimes phrased within the beat, as in Exx. 13 and 15.

Ex. 92. F. Couperin, 'progrès d'octaves' (*L'art de toucher*, p. 29)

Ex. 93. Couperin, 'maniere plus comode pour les tons dièsés, et bémolisés' (*L'art de toucher*, p. 29)

19 *Ibid*.
20 Couperin, *L'art de toucher le clavecin*, p. 29.

223

MARK LINDLEY

Ex. 94. Couperin, 'progrès de tierces, progrès de quartes' (*L'art de toucher*, p. 28)

Ex. 95. Rameau, five-finger exercise (*Pieces de clavecin* (1724), preface)

Rameau in the preface to his *Pieces de clavessin avec une methode pour la mecanique des doigts* (1724) prescribed that Ex. 95 be played over and over with 'equality of movement' ('Ceci se répète souvent sans discontinuer, et avec Egalité de mouvement), thus rather foreshadowing the nineteenth-century conception of the five-finger exercise as a thing of beauty *per se*. He said that in general:

le lever d'un doigt & le toucher d'un autre doivent être executés dans le même moment.

the raising of one finger and the touching of another should be executed at the same moment.

Here is a fine example of vagueness masquerading as precision, as we do not know whether 'lever' refers to the top or the bottom of the key dip. But clearly the trend was towards a legato; and this was accomodated by the left-hand scale fingerings which Rameau had given in 1722 for each of the twenty-four keys, in his *Principes d'accompagnement* (Book IV of the *Traité d'harmonie*). Wishing to be scientific, he had prescribed an ideal chord progression for each key.[21] Ex. 96 shows the progression for C major; there was a similar one (Ex. 97 shows the bass line) for D minor,

Ex. 96. Rameau, C major progression (*Pieces de clavecin* (1724), preface)

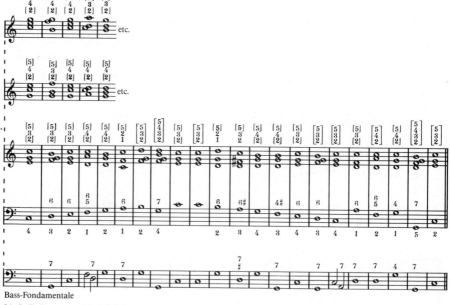

Bass-Fondamentale

21 J.-P. Rameau, *Traité de l'harmonie reduite à ses principes naturels* (Paris, 1722), pp. 381–7.

224

Ex. 97. Rameau, D minor progression (*Pieces de clavecin* (1724), preface), bass line

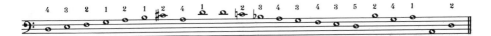

with implicitly the same right-hand chord fingerings, some of which were due to common French and Italian traditions (see Exx. 98–99), but the more difficult ones to a particular theory of Rameau's.[22] The other twenty-two keys were represented

Ex. 98. Giovanni Gentili D'Olevano, chord fingerings (mid-seventeenth-century MS treatise 'Porta musicale per laquale si entra nella scula di canto . . . contrapunto . . . cembalo' (Rome, Bib. Casanatense MS 2491), ff. 106–12) [†]

† I am most grateful to my former pupil Patrizio Barbieri for sharing with me his information about this source.

Ex. 99. Saint Lambert, chord fingerings (*Les principes*, p. 41)

by the left-hand part alone, as illustrated in Ex. 100 but with thoroughbass numbers as well. In Table 3 I have summarized the fingerings for the scalewise parts of the bass line, seven notes up and eight down. A large dot over a number means that the finger in question has a chromatic note in all the scales indicated; a small dot means it has a chromatic note in some of them. These fingerings match so often the rules published by C. P. E. Bach some thirty years later (see below) that one might wonder if the formation of his father's technique had been inspired by Rameau's

22 D. Hayes, 'Rameau's "Nouvelle methode" ', *JAMS* 27 (1974), p. 61.

Ex. 100. Rameau, bass lines for progressions in various keys (*Traité de l'harmonie* (Paris, 1722), pp. 381–7)

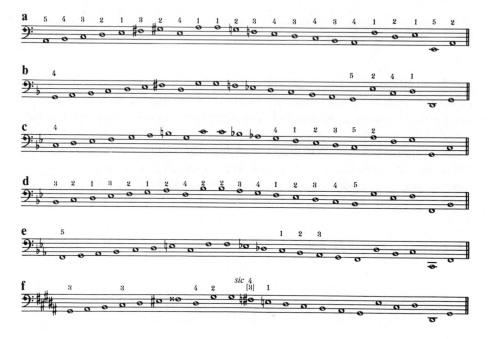

Table 3. *Rameau's bass-line fingerings.*

ascending	descending
F f 5432̇ 121	f 1231̇ 2345̇
C c G g D d 4321̇ 212̇	F C G g D d a 1234̇ 343(4)
A a E e 5432̇ 132̇	e 1234 ??35̇
Bb F# f# 4321̇ 432̇	c A E B b 1234̇ 123̇(4 or 5)
Db c# 3214̇ 321̇	f# 2343̇ 1234̇
Ab g Eb Bb 3213̇ 212̇	F# 2123̇ 1234̇
eb 2143̇ 212̇	Db c Ab Eb 2123̇ 4123̇
bb 3132̇ 121	g# 2312̇ 3434̇
	eb 2312̇ 3454̇
	Bb bb 2341̇ 2345̇

examples, had not J. S. Bach been thirty-seven years old in 1722. However, Rameau's suggestion, apropos Ex. 95, that

Pour continuer un *roulement* . . . il n'y a qu'à s'accoutoumer à passer le 1. par-dessoutel autre doigt que l'on veut, & à passer l'un de ces autres doigts par-dessus le 1. Cette manière est excellent, sur-tout quand il s'y rencontre des *Diézes* ou des *Bemols*.

To continue a *roulement* [beyond five notes] one has only to become accustomed to passing the thumb under such other finger[s] as one wishes, and to passing one of these other fingers over the thumb. This manner is excellent above all when sharps or flats are encountered.

would not have been acceptable to C. P. E. Bach, as he disapproved of crossing 5 over 1 or turning 1 under 5.

No doubt the Germans took what they wanted from these prestigious French books. At Leipzig in 1739 Lorenz Mizler, who regarded J. S. Bach as a 'good friend and patron',[23] recommended the same fingering as in Ex. 100a (towards the body) and 100e (away from the body), yet the context shows that he was perfectly content also with the fingering in Ex. 93:

Ein Anfänger wird sehr wohl tun, wenn er alle Musikleitern . . . fertig spielen lernet . . . Die Application von num. 31. und 32. [= Ex. 101b and c] kan auch wie bey [Ex. 101d] seyn, und wird die letzte allzeit bequemer gebrauchet, wenn der Daumen nach der ersten Application

Ex. 101. Mizler, scales (*Anfangs-Gründe des General-Basses* (Leipzig, 1739), Tab. IV and Tab. V

auf einen halben Ton oben kommt. Drum ist die letzte Application bey [Ex. 101e] in diesem Fall bequemer als die erste. Im Discant gibt es auf diese Art ebenfalls zweyerley Application. [Ex. 101f] ist wohl nach der ersten Application zu spielen. F dur aber [Ex. 101g] wird viel bequemer nach der andere Application gespielt. Kommt der Daumen ins auf- und nieder steigen einer Leiter auf keinem halben Ton, so gilt es in solchen Fällen gleich viel, ob man

23 G. J. Buelow, 'Mizler von Kolof', *New Grove*.

sich die erste oder die andere Application angewöhnen will. C moll kan man entweder wie
[Ex. 101h] oder [Ex. 101i] spielen. So muss man die Application durch alle Scalen nach Art.
[Ex. 101j] und [k] und zugleich den Takt den Anfängern beybringen.[24]

A beginner will do very well if he learns to play . . . all the musical scales . . . The fingering
of [Ex. 101b and c] can instead be as in [Ex. 101d], and the latter [fingering] will always be
more comfortable to use when the thumb in the first fingering comes on a chromatic note.
Therefore the latter fingering is, in the case of [Ex. 101e], more comfortable than the first. In
the soprano there are in this way also two kinds of fingering. [Ex. 101f] is well played with the
first fingering. But F major – [Ex. 101g] – will be played much more comfortably with the
other fingering. Suppose the thumb falls on no chromatic note in going up or down a scale:
in such cases it makes no difference whether one wishes to become accustomed to the first or
the second fingering. C minor can be played either as in [Ex. 101h] or as in [Ex. 101i]. So
must one teach beginners the fingering through all the scales, in the rhythmic manner of
[Ex. 101j–k], and at the same time [to keep] the beat.

J. S. Bach's little *Applicatio* of 1720 for Wilhelm Friedemann (from which
Exx. 33–34 are taken) suggests that for predominantly white-note keys he, like
Rameau in 1722, considered some of the old scale fingerings indispensable. It is
often argued that his normal fingering must have been more 'advanced', but I fail
to see how his son's innocence should induce Bach to teach him a fingering which
he himself considered awkward or outmoded. According to a later account
(1789),[25] when Friedemann grew up he reportedly

soll mit diesen beyden Fingern, wie man hier allegemein behauptet, gewisse Läufer rund und
mit einer erstaunenswürdigen Geschwindigkeit heraus gebracht haben.

would with these two fingers [3 and 4], as everyone here [in Halle] maintains, perform certain
runs straight-off and with an astonishing velocity.

This was but one aspect of a versatile technique. The same *Applicatio* has some
ornaments involving 5 in the right hand (Exx. 102–103). I suppose Friedemann

Ex. 102. J. S. Bach, *Applicatio*
BWV 994, bar 2

Ex. 103. BWV 994, bars 7–8

played it first without them, to establish the hand's choreography, and then learned
to do them 'mit einer so leichten und kleinen Bewegung der Finger . . . dass man sie
kaum bemerken konnte' ('with so easy and small a motion of the fingers that it was
hardly perceptible': Forkel ch. 3). It seems to me that some of Dandrieu's *Pièces de*

24 Mizler, *Anfangs-Gründe des General-Basses nach mathematischer Lehr-Art abgehandelt* (Leipzig,
   1739), p. 68. The *New Grove* article 'Fingering' (VI p. 571), in a passage giving an incomplete version
   of Ex. 101j and omitting the time signatures from Ex. 101b and 101d, refers to Ex. 101j and k as
   'fingered examples of music (as opposed to technical exercises)'.
25 D. G. Türk, *Klavierschule* (Leipzig and Halle, 1789), p. 148. According to 'Fingering', *New Grove*
   (VI p. 572), this passage refers to *'complex* runs' and to the *'three* middle fingers'.

Clavecin courtes et faciles (1713) want a similar approach (see Ex. 90). Of course Bach himself was a master of difficult trills, as in Ex. 104.

Elsewhere in Friedemann's notebook, a fingered *Praeambulum* shows that broken chords might often be treated as if unbroken (Ex. 105), but not always (Exx. 24 and 106).[26]

Ex. 104. J. S. Bach, Fugue in D minor BWV 851.ii (*WTC* Bk 2), bar 20

Ex. 105. J. S. Bach, Praeambulum BWV 930, bars 1–6

Ex. 106. BWV 930, bars 8–10

More telling of a fresh approach is the fingering of an early version (c1730) of the first prelude and fugue in Book 2 of the *WTC*, as written down on Bach's own paper (to judge by the watermark) by his former pupil and eventual successor at Weimar, Johann Caspar Vogler.[27] In Exx. 107–111 the use of the thumb not only recalls C. P. E. Bach's later reference to the 'other services' which it might perform (in addition to facilitating the difficult keys), but also brings out a motif of three descending quavers which is fairly vital to the composition. The motif is developed throughout the sixteen-bar prelude (see Exx. 6 and 41 above as well as Exx. 107–112), and a remarkable use of the right thumb at the end of bar 15 (Ex. 113) confirms that the three semiquavers running up or down to a beat are thematic in

26 Cf. Dolmetsch (note 15 above), p. 414, and H. Ferguson, *Keyboard Interpretation* (London, 1975), p. 78.

27 H.-J. Schulze, ' "Das Stück im Goldpapier" – Ermittlungen zu einigen Bach-Abschriften des frühen 18. Jahrhunderts', *BJ* 64 (1978), pp. 28–33.

Ex. 107 J. S. Bach, Prelude BWV 870a.i, bar 1

Ex. 108. BWV 870a.i, bar 2

Ex. 109. BWV 870a.i, bar 3

Ex. 110. BWV 870a.i, bar 4

Ex. 111. BWV 870a.i, bar 5

Ex. 112. BWV 870a.i, bars 8–10

Ex. 113. BWV 870a.i, bars 16–17

Ex. 114. J. S. Bach, Fughetta BWV 870a.ii, bar 2

Ex. 115. BWV 870a.ii, bar 3

Ex. 116. BWV 870a.ii, bars 21–2

their own right. Then in the Fughetta the same motif latent in the tail of the subject is brought out by fingerings such as illustrated (for the left hand) in Exx. 114–116. (The 2–3–4 fingerings in Exx. 115–116 are of course neutral: the 2–2–2 fingerings set the motivic pattern, which any musician will then maintain to a proper extent.)

I should like to consider some further examples in the light of Forkel's discussion of Bach's technique.[28] Forkel never heard Bach play, but made a thoughtful synthesis of information received (and plagiarized) from people who had. He said that Bach's playing differed from that of his contemporaries in that he had found a

---

28 Forkel pp. 11–18. Peter Williams points out (*The Organ Music of J. S. Bach*, III: *A Background* (Cambridge, 1984), esp. pp. 51, 66, 214) the probable importance of hindsight and of partisan motives in some of the claims made about J. S. Bach by Forkel and others.

'middle path' between too much legato and too much staccato, and thereby achieved the highest degree of clarity ('Deutlichkeit') in his touch ('Anschlag'), relying upon a 'light, unforced movement of the fingers' ('der leichten, zwanglosen Bewegung der Finger') for what I believe must have been a fairly constant, though effortless, *portato*: in general the five fingers would be bent ('gebogen') so that the fingertips 'come into a straight line', but actually in playing each note Bach would apply 'a gradual drawing back of the fingertips' ('ein allmähliges Zurückziehen der Fingerspitzen'), which would then 'glide off the near part of the key' ('dem vordern Theil des Tasten abgleitet') so that its discreet pressure ('das Mass von Kraft oder Druck') would be transferred with the 'greatest rapidity' to the next finger. (Forkel did not say at which point the finger drawing back would actually be aligned with the inactive fingers.) The object of all this was to achieve 'the highest degree of clarity in the playing [*Anschlag*] of single notes as in the pronunciation of single words'. In other words, Bach would use just enough detachment in Exx. 107–111 and 114–116 so that Exx. 112–113 and 117–119 would not sound very different (with

Ex. 117. BWV 870a.ii, bar 5

Ex. 118. BWV 870a.ii, bar 20

Ex. 119. J. S. Bach, Prelude BWV 870a.i, bars 4–5

respect to articulation), being rendered with so spare a choreography that the hand retained its rounded form ('ihre gerundete Form') and the fingers 'rose very little from the keys'. (Forkel held that the fingers never had to fall ('fallen') or be thrown upon ('geworfen') the key but needed only to be carried ('getragen') on it with a certain feeling of inner strength and command ('Herrschaft') over the motion.)

In saying that the articulation should not be very different among these examples, I mean to suggest a modicum of consistency, not uniformity. The choice of fingering does often have an effect: in Exx. 117–118 the three-note motif is transferred to the level of crotchets; the hand may dance a bit in Ex. 120; the articulation grows stronger in the middle of Exx. 112 and 121; some emphasis is added to the notes marked by an asterisk in Exx. 122–123; and so on. But these are nuances

Ex. 120. J. S. Bach, Fughetta BWV 870a.ii, bars 15–17

Ex. 121. J. S. Bach, Fughetta BWV 870a.ii, bars 15–17

Ex. 122. BWV 870a.ii, bars 32–4

Ex. 123. BWV 870a.ii, bar 10

within the grey area between notes 'blended together' (to cite Forkel again) and notes 'disjoined from each other'. This interpretation accommodates all the fingerings in Exx. 9, 21, 24, 33, 34, 40 and 41 above, and also in ex. 124, which is by C. P. E. Bach.

Ex. 124. C. P. E. Bach, *Versuch*, Tab. 3, Fig. 66

It has often been taken for granted that the technique outlined in the chapter on fingering in Emanuel's *Versuch* was simply that of his father. His own claim was more discreet; he did not say of his father's technique 'I shall expound it here',[29] but rather 'I take it here as a basis':

Vor diesem war das Clavier nicht so temperirt wie heut zu Tage, folglich brauchte man nicht alle vier und zwanzig Tonarten wie anjetzo und man hatte also auch nicht die Verschiedenheit von Passagen . . . Mein seliger Vater hat mir erzählt, in seiner Jugend grosse Männer gehört zu haben, welche den Daumen nicht eher gebrauchte als wenn es bey grossen Spannungen nöthig war. Da er nun einen Zeitpunckt erlebet hatte, in welchem nach und nach eine gantz besondere Veränderung mit dem musicalischen Geschmack vorging, so wurde er dadurch genöthiget, einen weit vollkommenern Gebrauch der Finger sich zu ausdencken, besonders den Daumen, welcher ausser andern guten Diensten hauptsächlich in den schweren Tonarten gantz unentbehrlich ist, so zu gebrauchen, wie ihn die Natur gleichsam gebraucht wissen will. Hierdurch ist er auf einmahl von seiner bisherigen Unthätigkeit zu der Stelle des Haupt-Fingers erhoben worden. Da diese neue Finger-Setzung so beschaffen ist, dass man damit alles mögliche zur bestimmten Zeit leicht herausbringen kan; so lege ich solche hier zum Grunde.[30]

Indeed, keyboard instruments were not tempered the same as nowadays, so one did not use all twenty-four keys as [we do] today, and therefore also one did not have the [same] variety of passages . . . My late father told me of having heard, in his youth, great men who did not use the thumb except when it was necessary for large stretches. Now as he lived at a time in

29 See the edition *C. P. E. Bach, Essay on the True Art of Playing Keyboard Instruments*, trans. William Mitchell (New York, 1949), p. 42.
30 *Versuch* p. 17.

which gradually a quite particular change in musical taste took place, he was obliged thereby to think out a much more complete use of the fingers, [and] especially to use the thumb – which among other good services is quite indispensable chiefly in the difficult keys – as Nature so to speak wishes to see it used. Thus was it raised at once from its former inactivity to the place of principal finger. Since this new fingering is so constituted that with it one can easily bring out every possible [thing] at the proper time, therefore I take it here as a basis.

An important difference is that Emanuel, writing at the court of Frederick the Great, gave his reader a comprehensive set of scales to practise (as Mizler had envisaged in 1739 and as Friedrich Wilhelm Marpurg had done at Berlin in 1750),[31] whereas the preliminary exercises which J. S. Bach gave to his pupils were, according to Forkel, cut from exactly the same musical cloth as the Two-part Inventions and little preludes in Friedemann's notebook:

Das erste, was er hierbey that, war, seine Schüler die ihm eigene Art des Anschlags, von welcher schon geredet worden ist, zu lehren. Zu diesem Behuf mussten sie mehrere Monathe hindurch nichts als einzelne Sätze für alle Finger beyder Hände, mit steter Rücksicht auf diesen deutlichen und saubern Anschlag, üben . . . nach einigen Monathen . . . war er so gefällig, kleine zusammenhängende Stücke vorzuschreiben, worin jene Uebungssätze in Verbindung gebracht waren. Von dieser Art sind die 6 kleinen Präluden fur Anfänger, und noch mehr die 15 zweystimmigen Inventionen . . . Mit dieser Fingerübung . . . war die Uebung aller Manieren in beyden Händen verbunden.[32]

The first thing he did in his keyboard lessons was to teach his pupils his own kind of touch, of which [we] have already spoken. To this end they had to practise for several months on end nothing but single phrases for all the fingers of both hands, with constant regard for this clear and clean touch. . . . After some months he would be so obliging as to write out little connected pieces in which these practice phrases were combined together. Of this kind are the six little preludes for beginners, and still more the fifteen two-part inventions. With this finger practice was combined that of all the ornaments in both hands.

Moreover, the *Applicatio* and Vogler's copy of the prelude and fughetta are all likely to show aspects of Bach's technique, and when we put them all together we have the image of a more eclectic approach than is outlined in the *Versuch*. Certain differences might be due to different musical intentions. J. S. Bach seems to have taken more pleasure than his son, for example, in varying sequences for the fun of it; so the odd little variations in fingering where I have placed asterisks in Exx. 125–126, which could hardly be derived from Emanuel's rules, may reflect J. S. Bach's approach and not merely Vogler's.[33] There is no evidence that Emanuel undertook to contradict his father's ideas, but as he wrote the treatise – something

---

31 Marpurg, *Die Kunst das Clavier zu spielen* (Berlin, 1750). E. L. Hays, 'F. W. Marpurg's *Anleitung zum Clavierspielen* (Berlin, 1755) and *Principes du clavecin* (Berlin, 1756): translation and commentary', Stanford University Ph. D. dissertation, 1977, suggests (p. 255) that J. S. Bach 'fashioned a scale fingering for each one of the twenty-four tonalities', and also (p. 264) 'that Marpurg recorded the scales [which he published in 1750] as he learned them from Emanuel . . . and that in the succeeding three years Emanuel had a chance to rethink and refine the scales to accord more clearly with his [own] Thumb Rule'. The author analyses the published scale fingerings in detail.

32 Forkel, p. 38.

33 In any case the fingering of the fughetta in the manuscript (SPK P 1089) is, unlike that of the prelude, in two different shades of ink.

Ex. 125. J. S. Bach, Fughetta BWV 870a.ii, bars 15–17

Ex. 126. BWV 870a.i, bars 7–8

which his father would never have done – he no doubt tried to consolidate them, and might well have lost some of their original sophistication. The amount he retained is remarkable enough.

Of the ninety-nine paragraphs in Emanuel's chapter on fingering, the first twenty-eight address matters of general approach, posture and nomenclature. The account of his father's innovations is in §7. According to §§12–14 one should play with curved fingers and relaxed nerves ('mit gebogenen Fingern und schlaffen Nerven'); and 'derjenige, welcher den Daumen nur selten braucht, mehrentheils steif spielen wird' ('he who only seldom uses the thumb will usually play stiffly'), because moderate lateral spans are more taxing without the thumb and (conversely) because the longer fingers are kept supple by frequently arching them enough to bring the thumb to the keyboard:

Dieser Haupt=Finger macht sich . . . dadurch verdient, weil er die übrigen Finger in ihrer Geschmeidigkeit erhält, indem sie sich allezeit biegen müssen, wenn der Daumen sich bald bey diesem bald jenem Finger eindringt . . . Es verstehet sich von selbst, dass bey Sprüngen und weiten Spannungen diese Schlappigkeit der Nerven und das Gebogene der Finger nicht beybehalten werden kan; . . . dieses aber die seltensten Vorfälle sind, und welche die Natur von selbst lehrt . . . Man gewöhne besonders die noch nicht ausgewachsenen Hände der Kinder, dass sie, anstatt des Hin= und Her=Springens mit der gantzen Hand, . . . die Hände im nöthigen Falle so viel möglich ausdehnen.

This [the] principal finger performs a service because it keeps the other fingers flexible in that they must bend every time[34] that the thumb presses in next to one or another finger . . . It is self-evident that the slackness of the nerves and the curving of the fingers cannot be maintained in leaps and wide stretches; . . . but these are very rare occasions, and Nature herself teaches them . . . One should habituate the hands (as yet not fully grown) of children particularly, so that instead of springing up and down with the entire hand, . . . they stretch the hands as much as possible when necessary.

The last injunction may perhaps contradict the reference in the previous sentence to the role of Nature herself, and is almost certainly at odds with Ex. 127 (where I have placed an asterisk), which is from Vogler's copy of the C major Prelude.

---

34 Mitchell's translation (note 29 above), p. 42: 'they must remain arched as it [the thumb] makes its entry'.

Ex. 127. J. S. Bach, Prelude BWV 870a.i, bars 11–12

Emanuel was not trying to make children stretch unduly, however, but only hoping to prevent them from leaping with the fingers bunched together ('auf einem Klumpen zusammen gezogen') and with the hand twisting one way and another ('bald auf diese bald auf jene Seite sich . . . verdrehen').

Paragraphs 29–65 prescribe various fingerings for the twenty-four scales, in the order

C $_a$ G $_e$ F $_d$ B♭ $_g$ D $_b$ A $_{f♯}$ E $_{c♯}$ B $_{g♯}$ F♯ $_{eb}$ C♭/D♭ $_{bb}$ A♭ $_f$ E♭ $_c$

Most of them fit the rule, given in §33, that in moving away from the body the thumb should tuck in directly after one or more chromatic notes, whereas in moving towards the body it should take a note just before one or more chromatic notes. Thus for the left hand ascending in A major 21 321 432 is 'in most cases more useful' ('bey allerley Fällen brauchbarer') than 54321 321. A few of the fingerings use 4343 in moving away from the body, and a fair number remind one of the rule for scales which Kirnberger in 1781 attributed to J. S. Bach (with whom he had studied forty years before): 'in den meisten Fällen vor und nach dem Leitton . . . der Daum eingesetzet werde' ('in most cases the thumb will be placed before or after the leading note').[35] Ex. 128 illustrates all these tendencies. In §§62 and 64 we learn

Ex. 128. C. P. E. Bach, *Versuch*, Tab. 1, Fig. 18

Ex. 129. *Versuch*, Tab. 5, Fig. 67

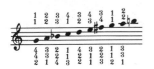 

how and why the 4343 and 2121 fingerings should be employed. They require the technique called *Überschlagen*, just as passing 3 or 4 over the thumb does, and not *Einsetzen*, which is reserved for certain ornaments as in Ex. 129. Neither technique is compatible with a modern legato:

Ueberschlagen heisst: wenn ein Finger über den andern gleichsam wegklettert, indem der andere noch über der Taste schwebet, welche er niedergedrückt hat; bey dem Einsetzen hingegen ist der andere Finger schon weg und die Hand gerückt . . . Das Untersetzen und Ueberschlagen . . . müssen so gebraucht werden, dass alle Töne dadurch gut zusammen gehänget werden können. Desswegen ist in den Ton=Arten mit keinen oder wenigen Versetzungs-Zeichen bey gewissen Fällen das Ueberschlagen des dritten Fingers über den vierten, und des zweiten über den Daumen besser und nützlicher, um alles mögliche Abset-

35 J. P. Kirnberger, *Grundsätze des Generalbasses* (Berlin, 1781), p. 3.

zen zu vermeiden, als der übrige Gebrauch des Ueberschlagens und das Untersetzen des Daumens, weil selbiger bey vorkommenden halben Tönen mehr Platz und folglich auch mehr Bequemlichkeit hat, unter die andern Finger durchzukriechen, als bey einer Folge von lauter unten liegenden Tasten.

Überschlagen means: when one finger clambers over the other at the same time that the other still hovers over the key which it had depressed;[36] whereas in an *Einsetzen* the other finger is already away and the hand has shifted . . . Turning-under and crossing-over must be so employed that all the notes thereby can be well set out together.[37] For this reason, in keys with few or no accidentals in certain cases the crossing of the third finger over the fourth, and of the second over the thumb, is better and more useful (for avoiding any possible breaking off) than any other use of crossing over or than the turning under of the thumb, since this [the thumb] has more room and hence also more ease, when *chromatic* notes precede it, to cross through under the other fingers than it does in a series of all white keys.

This distinction between *Überschlagen* and *Einsetzen* is enlightening even though it fudges borderline cases (much as the baseball umpire often does in calling a strike or ball[38]). The phrase 'der übrige Gebrauch des Ueberschlagens' ('the other use of *Überschlagen*') means other uses in general (including 3 or 4 over 1) and not one particular use.[39] Paragraph 28 rejects (as 'verwerflich') the crossing of 5 over 1 (as in Ex. 70), 2 over 3, 3 over 2, or 4 over 5, although §93 by way of exception 'excuses' (the term is 'entschuldigen') Ex. 130, which is from one of Emanuel's test pieces, because the tempo ('Zeit-Maass') is moderate. Since *Einsetzen* is reserved for ornaments, Exx. 24 and 118 elude Emanuel's system, though not Exx. 9, 34, 124, 131 *et al*. Paragraph 35 does also admit crossing 3 over 4 to pass from a natural to a single chromatic note (as in Ex. 71).

Ex. 130. *Versuch*,
Tab. 3, Fig. 54

Ex. 131, J. S. Bach, Fughetta
BWV 870a.ii, bars 26–7

As he declined to cross 3 over 2 it was only natural for Emanuel to disregard François Couperin's suggestion to sit with the right shoulder slightly closer to the keyboard than the left[40] (which would facilitate Exx. 36 and 91). Yet the discussion of intervals and chords, in §§66–86, includes a rather casual (and not very well substantiated) remark that:

36 Mitchell's translation, p. 57: 'one finger crosses another which is still depressing the key that it has struck'.
37 Mitchell's translation, p. 58: 'the tones involved in the change flow smoothly'.
38 A 'ball' is a pitch that goes by the batter below his knees or above his shoulders, or not directly over the plate, whereas a 'strike' is (among other things) a pitch which he lets go by within those boundaries.
39 That is, the definite article gives the expression 'der übrige Gebrauch' an abstract and general force, contrary to its effect in English.
40 Couperin, *L'art de toucher*, p. 4.

236

gemeiniglich der Daum und der zweyte Finger an der lincken Hand am meisten an den Oerten gebraucht wird, alwo man in der rechten Hand den Zweyten und dritten Finger einsetzt.

generally the [combination of] thumb and second finger in the left hand is used mostly in places where in the right hand one employs the second and third fingers.

Some other points from §§66–86 are that harmonic seconds are taken by adjacent fingers (as in Ex. 132); fast thirds are played mostly by one pair of fingers (Ex. 133), but not slow ones (Ex. 134); the context may call for 2 instead of 1 in an octave leap (Ex. 135), or 4 instead of 5. (But what then of Ex. 47?) The fingering of Ex. 136a is

Ex. 132. C. P. E. Bach, *Versuch*, Tab. 1, Fig. 40

Ex. 133 *Versuch*, Tab. 2, Fig. 67

Ex. 134 *Versuch*, Tab. 1–2, Fig. 42a and c

Ex. 135 *Versuch*, Tab. 2, Fig. 48

prescribed also for the analogous minor triads on C, C♯, F♯, G, G♯, B♭ and B; and that of Ex. 136b for the major triads on D♭, E♭, E, A♭, A, B♭ and B. If the C in Ex. 137 is to be sustained, the other notes are to be fingered as shown. Part-writing may call for the thumb on chromatic notes (Ex. 138). Broken chords are sometimes fingered differently from their unbroken counterparts (Ex. 139) 'because clarity is always produced primarily by an even touch' ('weil die Deutlichkeit überhaupt durch einen gleichen Druck vornehmlich mit hervorgebracht wird').

Ex. 136 *Versuch*, Tab. 2, Fig. 50a and b

Ex. 137 *Versuch*, Tab. 2, Fig. 66

Ex. 138. *Versuch*, Tab. 2, Fig. 66

Ex. 139. *Versuch*, Tab. 2, Figs. 54d and 55(1)

The rest of the chapter (§§87–99) describes some special techniques[41] ('besonderer Exempel'), among them 'omitting certain fingers because of the sequence' ('das Auslassen gewisser Finger wegen der Folge') as in Ex. 140; minimizing a shift by using the same finger after as before the thumb turns under (Ex. 141); substituting fingers (as in Ex. 142), an extraordinary ('ausserordentlich') and difficult technique which François Couperin employed 'too often and gratuitously' ('zu oft und ohne Noth'); and using one and the same finger to slur a chromatic note to an adjacent natural (Ex. 143).

Ex. 140 *Versuch*, **Tab. 3, Fig. 59**

Ex. 141 *Versuch*, **Tab. 3, Fig. 63**

Ex. 142 *Versuch*, **Tab. 3, Fig. 60***b*

Ex. 143 *Versuch*, **Tab. 3, Fig. 61**

One characteristic which I have attributed to J. S. Bach's playing seems implicit not only in Emanuel's definition of *Überschlagen* but also in a fair number of his examples shown here (and others could be cited): taken together, they are rather more compatible with Mattheson's and Marpurg's prescriptions translated on pp. 219–20 above than with a modern concept of legato. Yet nothing in the treatise quite prepares us for the remarkable integration of motivic design and fingering in Vogler's copy of the Prelude and Fughetta BWV 870a. Better players than I may better determine to what extent Bach's music could benefit from the use of a more antiquated technique than his son prescribed. It seems to me that in the English-speaking world a reasonably accurate translation of the *Versuch* would be most helpful in this regard.[42]

To judge by Burney's description, Handel's technique at the keyboard was astonishingly subtle and efficient:

His touch was so smooth, and the tone of the instrument so much cherished, that his fingers seemed to grow to the keys. They were so curved and compact, when he played, that no motion, and scarcely the fingers themselves, could be discovered.[43]

But another witness, John Mainwaring, found an 'amazing fulness, force and energy' in his playing.[44] We have no fingerings attributable with any degree of secu-

41 Mitchell's translation, p. 70: 'exceptional examples'.
42 Even Hays's dissertation (see note 31 above) has relied uncritically upon Mitchell's translation.
43 C. Burney, *An Account of the Musical Performances . . . in Commemoration of Handel* (London, 1785), p. 35.
44 Mainwaring p. 61.

rity to Handel, but contemporary fingerings are extant for parts of the G major Ciacona HWV 435 and for a smaller piece in D minor (37 bars) of which he may have composed the second half,[45] as the whole, fingered, appears next to music bearing his name in Cfm Mu. MS 57, f. 23 (inscribed '1730'). In playing this little piece I found a way to reconcile Burney's and Mainwaring's remarks. The texture is of moderately paced semiquavers in one hand (Exx. 14, 26 and 144–146) accompanied by crotchets (sometimes dotted) and quavers in the other (Exx. 7 and 147–148). For the first bar or so of each phrase the semiquavers are played with a

Ex. 144. Handelian minuet, bars 1–4

Ex. 145. Handelian minuet, bars 15–18

Ex. 146. Handelian minuet, bars 34–7

Ex. 147. Handelian minuet, bars 1–4

Ex. 148. Handelian minuet, bars 34–7

relatively quiet hand, which then moves about in the middle of the phrase, and occasionally has to make a rather pronounced *Einsetzen* (to use C. P. E. Bach's term) where a modern player would hardly think to do so (Exx. 14, 26 and 144). The only way I can negotiate these passages plausibly – but then the effect seems to me better than just plausible – is by triggering a rapid lateral shift without any reaching-out of the finger which is due to play the next note. The notes not involved in the shift have to be played energetically enough – the fingers merely supporting the action of the hand, really – not to sound weak in comparison, but only less expressive. (Perhaps one shouldn't play them all *portato*, however. Some rather pronounced phrasing will give them an Italianate plasticity; one might render Ex. 144, for instance, as Ex. 149.) I think this technique may answer both to Burney's and to Mainwaring's description of Handel's playing, *mutatis mutandis* at faster tempos.

45 The other half is by Domenico Zipoli: see his *Sonate d'Intavolatura per Organo, e Cembalo* (Rome, 1716).

Ex. 149. A rendering of Ex. 151

drive ahead

The fingerings in BL Add. MS 31577 for the G major Ciacona call for even more speculative probing at the keyboard. What might we suppose Mizler to have intended in Ex. 101 if the fifth note of each scale toward the body were not fingered (and if Mizler had not said that his alternatives were of equal value except in particular cases)? Such are the ambiguities in Ex. 150 and elsewhere in the Ciacona. They

Ex. 150. Handel, Ciacona HWV 435, var. 6, bars 2–3[†]

† The headings 'Var. 1', 'Var. 2' etc. are not in the source that has the fingerings.

can best be resolved by a consensus of historically minded players, perhaps bearing in mind that the fingering dates from some fifteen years earlier than Mizler's book;[46] my suggestions (ringed round, in Exx. 151–161) are offered as a stimulus.

In the first bar of Ex. 45, one might imagine the second C was played with the thumb to avoid taking two notes in succession with 3; but as this use of the thumb is unlikely for the B♭ a bar later, it seems unlikely here as well, in the absence of any particular indication and given the historical context represented by Exx. 42 and 43. Anyone who masters the 2343 3423 fingering may then find the use of one finger for two notes in a row more conducive to a placid hand in Exx. 151 and 152 than the alternative of shifting the thumb a seventh or (back and forth) a fifth.

Ex. 151. HWV 435, var. 7, bars 7–8   **Ex. 152. HWV 435, var. 8, bars 1–2**

Ex. 153. HWV 435, var. 8, bars 4–7

46 Terence Best in his edition of the piece (*Handel: Chaconne in G for keyboard*, London, 1979) dates this manuscript 'c1723'.

Ex. 154. HWV 435, var. 5, bars 6–8

In Ex. 153, I pair the semiquavers as in Ex. 50 rather than use the thumb for the last note of the beat, which is sometimes an F♯. In Ex. 154 I find that the use of crossovers for the scale puts the hand in a better position to take the G major triad with 235 than a modern use of the thumb would do. In the triad one must avoid 'stabbing' with 5 in order not to draw the thumb away from its A. The beats want to be emphasized (another sign of Handelian vigour?), and in that context 5432 will be more sprightly than 5321 at the beginning of the next bar – and therefore in the second bar of Ex. 151 as well. The emphasizing of the beats is evident in Ex. 155, and again in Ex. 156 where it is very nicely maintained by crossing 5 under 3 for the scale.

Ex. 155. HWV 435, var. 15, bars 1–4

Ex. 156. HWV 435, var. 11, bars 6–8

Ex. 157. HWV 435, var. 6, bars 1, 7–8

Ex. 158. HWV 435, var. 6, bar 6   **Ex. 159. HWV 435, beginning**

In Ex. 157 a modern fingering gives a motivic stamp to the scales towards the body; I think the motif is to be maintained in Ex. 158 (from the same variation) where it would be awkward for the thumb to play the F♯. A modern scale fingering is also well suited to a rhythmically undifferentiated *tirata* away from the body in Ex. 159. The left-hand fingering in Ex. 160 favours an expressive rendering of the suspensions in the middle voice, while here and in Ex. 161 the right hand evidently wants a variety of devices for a consistent phrasing and articulation, as each of the sequences is carried through different patterns of black and white keys. I imagine that if the thumb had been wanted for the last high E in Ex. 161 it would have been specified, as it was for the A a bar later,[47] where it helps 2 move into the keyboard from a white to a black key.

Ex. 160. HWV 435, var. 14, bars 1–4

Ex. 161. HWV 435, var. 5, bars 1–5

One need not agree with all my reconstructions to see that Clementi's fingering in Ex. 162 reflects a later taste. Perhaps when Clementi and Mozart encountered each other's playing on Christmas Eve 1781, and Mozart supposedly found Clementi an insipid player ('ein blosser *Mechanicus*')[48] whereas Clementi later said that 'until then I had never heard anyone perform with such spirit and grace',[49] the difference

Ex. 162. Handel, 'See the conquering hero comes' (Clementi, *Introduction* (1801), p. 24)

47 Albeit by another hand.
48 Mozart's letter to his father, 16 January 1782.
49 L. B. Plantinga, *Clementi, His Life and Music* (London, 1977), p. 65.

may have had to do with what Czerny later (in the course of praising Beethoven's legato) referred to as Mozart's 'chopped-up and clipped-off playing' ('das gehackte und kurz abgestossene Spiel').[50] Or perhaps not. In 1985 we know quite a lot about eighteenth-century keyboard instruments, but not so much about how they were played.

50 *Carl Czerny: Erinnerungen aus meinem Leben*, ed. W. Kolneder (Baden-Baden, 1968), p. 15.

Bach and Handel as Teachers of Thorough Bass

ALFRED MANN

(Rochester, New York)

More than ever before, the student of music history is aware in the celebration of the tercentenary that the question of similarity and dissimilarity of the great composers born in 1685 is a frustrating one. It seems futile to stress their dissimilarity because their very greatness rests in individuality. While this renders the issue of similarity the more vexing, the issue, decreed by the collimation of their careers in time, serves unavoidably again and again as point of departure for discussion.

What so patently links the works of Bach and Handel is their common artistic legacy, a legacy outlined by the typical attributes of the German Protestant cantor's schooling. This schooling and their similar early professional appointments as Protestant church organists – which appointments they both gave up for totally dissimilar reasons – are interestingly reflected in their teaching. Bach's approach to teaching, as his biographer writes, was

der lehrreichste, zweckmässigste und sicherste, den es je gegeben hat, und alle seine Schüler traten, wenigstens in irgend einem Zweig der Kunst in die Fusstapfen ihres grossen Meisters, ob gleich keiner ihn erreichte und noch viel weniger übertraf. (Forkel, ch. 7)

the most instructive, the most proper, and the most secure that ever was known; and all his scholars trod, at least in some branch of the art, in the footsteps of their great master, though none of them equaled, much less surpassed him. (*BR* p. 328)

We have only indirect references to Bach's typical course of teaching, though they are based on detailed accounts by his pupils.

In the case of Handel, the course of studies is directly documented in a set of autographs whose origin is suggested in a personal statement made by the composer. Asked by a visitor about his attitude towards teaching, Handel answered:

After I had left your home town anno 1706 in order to go to Italy and eventually enter service at the court of Hanover, no power on earth could have moved me to take up teaching duties again – except Anne, the flower of all princesses.[1]

1 Cf. A. Mann, *Georg Friedrich Händel: Aufzeichnungen zur Kompositionslehre*, *HHA* Suppl. I (Kassel/Leipzig, 1978), p. 11 and F. Chrysander, *G. F. Händel* (Leipzig, 1858–67), II, p. 364.

The person who recorded this remark was Jacob Wilhelm Lustig (a native of Hamburg and a pupil of Georg Philipp Telemann and Johann Mattheson), who served as music master to Princess Anne after her marriage to William of Orange, Stadholder of the Netherlands.[2] As Princess Royal, Anne, the eldest daughter of George II, had been the first of the pupils to whose instruction Handel's appointment as Royal Music Master was devoted. She was unusually gifted, and from the early lessons there developed a lifelong friendship between teacher and pupil.

As Handel's remark proves, he had done some teaching in the years of his association with the Hamburg Opera; and prior to the lessons for Princess Anne, he had concerned himself with the musical education of John Christopher Smith the younger. Smith, who later succeeded his mentor both as conductor of the oratorio seasons and as Royal Music Master, was Handel's only professional pupil, and we owe it to his care that the lessons that Handel may have designed in part for him and supplemented in teaching the princess have been preserved.[3] The list of Bach's known pupils, essentially all professionals from whom a veritable generation of later-eighteenth-century theorists emanated, numbers more than eighty. Their full listing is still a matter for research.[4]

Like all composers of their time, Bach and Handel placed the teaching of composition in the framework of vocal and instrumental performance, invariably linked, in turn, to their own creative work. The title of the Two- and Three-part Inventions is derived from Bach's preface: the purpose of instruction was

gute *inventiones* nicht alleine zu bekommen, sondern auch selbige wohl durchzuführen, am allermeisten aber eine *cantable* Art im Spielen zu erlangen, und darneben einen starcken Vorschmack von der *Composition* zu überkommen. (*Dok* I p. 221)

not alone to have good *inventiones* but to develop the same well, and above all to arrive at a singing style in playing and at the same time to acquire a strong foretaste of composition. (*BR* p. 86)

As we know, the teaching material extended from the *Orgelbüchlein* and other chorale collections to the various clavier collections, including the *Well-Tempered Clavier* and eventually the *Art of Fugue*. The resulting course of instruction was summarized by C. P. E. Bach as leading from four-part harmonization to chorales and fugues which 'commenced with two-part ones and so on'. Bach's pupil Johann Philipp Kirnberger wrote:

Seine Methode ist die beste, denn er geht durchgängig Schritt vor Schritt vom leichtesten bis zum schwersten über, eben dadurch ist der Schritt zur Fuge selbst nicht schwerer, als ein Uebergang zum andern. (*Dok* III p. 362)

His method is the best because he proceeds step by step from the simplest to the most

---

2 Lustig, *Inleidung tot de Muziekkunde* (Groningen, 1771) p. 172. Lustig gives the date of Handel's departure for Italy erroneously as 1709.

3 For a critical edition of the entire material, see note 1 above.

4 For a provisional list of pupils, see H. Löffler, 'Die Schüler Joh. Seb. Bachs', *BJ* 40 (1953), pp. 5–28.

difficult, whereby even the step to fugue itself is no more difficult than any other step.[5]

In reality, studies in the imitative style entered the picture much earlier than is suggested by either Philipp Emanuel or Kirnberger, as is evident from the very nature of the Inventions and the chorale preludes of the *Orgelbüchlein*. The same is true of Handel's lessons for Princess Anne, in which contrapuntal writing is variously introduced through compositions of the master. Together with pages from his opera and oratorio scores, there are sonatas from Op. I and keyboard pieces from various collections – as in Bach's work, the entire clavier *oeuvre* is essentially pedagogical.

The merging of the composer's own practice with teaching is typically represented by the choice of exercises in thorough bass – the kapellmeister's craft – for extensive basic studies. But are these the exercises in 'harmony' so well known to the modern student? It is important to realize that today's didactic concept of harmony did not exist when Bach and Handel began to instruct their pupils. The modern connotation of the term was created with the formulation of Jean Philippe Rameau's theory published in his *Traité de l'harmonie* (1722). Conversely, the usage of the term as understood by Bach and Handel clearly referred to a contrapuntal fabric; and this is what is borne out in their teaching of thorough bass.

Handel does not deal with, say, the six-four chord or the seventh chord as such; nor is it the chord concept itself that determines the organization of his course in thoroughbass instruction but the melodic design arising from the realization of figures – or, rather, configurations. Although the symbols are introduced one by one, they are shown at the outset with a view toward their individual flexibility and the melodic result they produce (Ex. 1). As new symbols are taken up in similar manner, they are immediately combined with the former, and the evolving contours gain in force (Ex. 2). Accordingly, the six-four chord and the chord of the

Ex. 1.

Ex. 2.

5 For the quotations from C. P. E. Bach and Kirnberger, see *J. P. Kirnberger: The Art of Strict Musical Composition*, trans. David Beach & Jurgen Thym (New Haven/London, 1982), pp. xvif.

seventh are illustrated in such passages as shown in Exx. 3 and 4. In exercises involving groups of three symbols, a melodic continuity for all four parts is, in fact, implied (Ex. 5).

Ex. 3.

Ex. 4.

Ex. 5.

The essence of this instruction is polyphonic part-writing that, despite the simplicity of the setting, maintains a melodic logic for four voices. The latter point is stressed in the documents we have of Bach's teaching. Again and again we find accounts of Bach's insistence on *Vollstimmigkeit* and good melodic realization. Bach's pupil Lorenz Mizler writes:

Wer das delicate im General-Bass und was sehr wohl accompagniren heist, recht vernehmen will, darf sich nur bemühen unsern Herrn Capellmeister Bach allhier zu hören, welcher einen ieden General-Bass zu einem Solo so accompagnirt, dass man denket, es sey ein Concert, und wäre die Melodey so er mit der rechten Hand machet, schon vorhero also gesetzet worden. (*Dok* II p. 321)

Whoever wishes truly to observe what delicacy in thorough bass and very good accompanying mean need only take the trouble to hear our Kapellmeister Bach here, who accompanies every thorough bass to a solo so that one thinks it a piece of concerted music and as if the melody he plays in the right hand were written out beforehand. (*BR* p. 231)

C. P. E. Bach is even more specific about Bach's four-part realization:

Vermöge seiner Grösse in der Harmonie, hat er mehr als einmahl *Trios accompagni*rt, und, weil er aufgeräumt war, u. wuste, dass der Componist dieser *Trios* nicht übel nehmen würde, aus dem Stegereif u. aus einer elend beziferten ihm vorgelegten Bassstimme ein vollkommenes Qvatuor daraus gemacht, worüber der Componist dieser *Trios* erstaunte. (*Dok* III p. 285)

Thanks to his greatness in harmony, he accompanied trios on more than one occasion on the spur of the moment and, being in a good humor and knowing that the composer would not take it amiss, on the basis of a sparsely figured continuo part just set before him, converted them into complete quartets, astounding the composer of the trios. (*BR* p. 277)

And a truly extraordinary report is given by Bach's pupil Johann Christian Kittel:

Wenn Seb. Bach eine Kirchenmusik aufführte, so musste allemal einer von seinen fähigsten Schülern auf dem Flügel accompagniren. Mann kann wohl vermuthen, dass man sich da mit einer magern Generalbassbegleitung ohnehin nicht vorwagen durfte. Demohnerachtet musste man sich immer darauf gefasst halten, dass sich oft plötzlich Bachs Hände und Finger unter die Hände und Finger des Spielers mischten und, ohne diesen weiter zu geniren, dass Accompagnement mit Massen von Harmonien ausstaffirten, die noch mehr imponirten, als die unvermuthete nahe Gegenwart des strengen Lehrers.[6]

When Sebastian Bach performed a church cantata, one of his most capable pupils always had to accompany on the harpsichord. It will easily be guessed that no one dared to put forward a meager thoroughbass accompaniment. Nevertheless, one always had to be prepared to have Bach's hands and fingers intervene among the hands and fingers of the player, and without getting in the way of the latter, furnish the accompaniment with masses of harmonies which made an even greater impression than the unsuspected close proximity of the strict teacher. (*BR* p. 266)

The basic difference in the documentation of Bach's and Handel's teaching is once again obvious. Whereas Handel's thoroughbass assignments are preserved entirely in his autograph but without student manuscripts in which these assignments are carried out, Bach's course of instruction has come down to us primarily in the handwriting of pupils and with a minimum of comments in the composer's hand. The brief compilation 'Some most necessary rules of thorough bass by J. S. B.' from Anna Magdalena Bach's Clavier Book of 1725 is primarily in Anna Magdelena's hand, possibly written from Bach's direct dictation. Its fifteen numbered points cover chiefly definitions and explanations, but towards the end Bach writes out a set of rules (Spitta II p. 952) which stress the aspect of four-part writing:

11) Zu $\frac{4}{2}$ greiffet man die 6. auch zuweilen statt der 6. die 5.

12) Zu $\frac{5}{4}$ wird 8. gegriffen, und die 4 *resolvieret* sich unter sich in die 3.

13) Zu $\frac{6}{5}$ greiffet man die 3; sie sey nun *major* oder *minor*.

14) Zur $\frac{7}{5}$ greiffet man die 3.

15) Zur $\frac{9}{7}$ gehöret die 3.

---

6 J. C. Kittel, *Der angehende praktische Organist*, part 3 (Erfurt, 1808), p. 33.

(11) The $\frac{4}{2}$ takes the 6 as well, and sometimes the 5 in place of the 6.

(12) With the $\frac{5}{4}$ the 8 is taken, and the 4 resolves into the 3.

(13) With the $\frac{6}{5}$ the 3 is taken, whether it be major or minor.

(14) With the $\frac{7}{5}$ the 3 is taken.

(15) With the $\frac{9}{7}$ the 3 is taken.

In their discussion of Bach's thoroughbass rules, the editors of *The Bach Reader* have singled out one point in which Bach's rules for four-part realization clearly depart from the textbooks of the time and thus 'have a peculiar significance in the history of figured-bass realization' (*BR* p. 390). This concerns sequences of sixth chords, difficult to handle in four voices and customarily treated only in three. There is an elaboration of the rules from Anna Magdalena's Clavier Book, written by another pupil and included in a manuscript once owned by Bach's friend Johann Peter Kellner, to whom we owe a number of copies made from Bach's manuscripts.[7] The manuscript shows in detail how the sixth-chord sequences are to be realized *Enquatre*.[8] Rather specific instructions are given with each of a number of examples, of which the first reads:

Man kann zur ersten 6ʹdie 6te *dupliren* zur andern aber die 8 nehmen und bis zu Ende *Con-tinu*iren. (Spitta II pp. 942–3)

For the first [group marked] 6, the sixth may be doubled, but for every alternate group the octave is to be taken, and continued to the end [see Ex. 6].

Ex. 6.

A second example deals with ascending sequences of sixth chords, and a third follows in which ascending sixths alternate with fifths, and for which the instruction reads:

Man mus mit der rechten Hand fein hoch anfangen und *per modum* [sic] *contrarium* gehen bey der 6 nehme man die 8. (*ibid*. p. 943)

---

7 The mansucript is dated 1738; see the complete reproduction in Spitta II pp. 913–50 (English Version: Philipp Spitta, *Johann Sebastian Bach*, trans. Clara Bell & J. S. Fuller-Maitland, (repr. New York, 1951), II, pp. 315ff). The compilation includes excerpts from F. E. Niedt's *Musicalische Hand-leitung* (Hamburg, 1700), the only generally available book on thorough bass at the time Bach formulated his rules. See also note 9 below.

8 I. e. in four parts – not, as the somewhat misleading translation reads, 'in groups of four notes'.

The player must begin quite high up with the right hand, and proceed *per motum contra-rium*; the octave is to be taken with the sixth [see Ex. 7].[9]

Ex. 7.

At *per motum contrarium* the original spelling is *modum*, from which Spitta concludes that the manuscript may have been taken down from Bach's dictation – an amusing hint at Bach's Thuringian pronunciation. If this is so, it would follow that Bach did not check the dictated text. The latter point is borne out more strongly by the numerous fully realized examples which are poorly done throughout and which contain mistakes that raise serious doubts about the manuscript's authenticity: the realizations can give witness only to a lesser pupil's work, not to Bach's writing.[10]

The situation is different in the case of a manuscript by another Bach pupil, Heinrich Nicolaus Gerber, the father of the well-known lexicographer. Here both the pupil's writing and Bach's corrections are fully documented. As is evident from the manuscript, Bach had assigned Gerber the bass realization of a violin sonata by Tommaso Albinoni, one of the Italian contemporaries whose works Bach had used in his own studies.[11] Here the assignment was patently done under Bach's supervision; and though Bach's corrections are small, they show the master's hand in every instance. No detail seemed too unimportant to merit his attention (Ex. 8), and each

Ex. 8.

Gerber:

Bach:

9 'Bey der 6 nehme man die 8' means that the bass note is in these instances to be doubled at the octave.
10 In his study '"Das Stück in Goldpapier" – Ermittlungen zu einigen Bach-Abschriften des frühen 18. Jahrhunderts', *BJ* 64 (1978), pp. 19–42 (especially pp. 39ff), Hans-Joachim Schulze has identified the writer of the manuscript's title-page as Carl August Thieme, alumnus of the Thomasschule and later its assistant director. Thus he may be counted among the direct pupils of Bach; yet, as is suggested in Schulze's study, the manuscript may have been prepared for his use by a less experienced pupil.
11 Cf. BWV 950 and 951; the authenticity of these works is generally accepted but not fully established. Gerber's realization, with Bach's corrections, is printed in Spitta II *Beilage*, pp. 1–11 (English edition (see note 7 above), III pp. 388ff).

minute change indicates his concern for a fuller sound in the accompaniment (Ex. 9). Even as he corrects parallel octaves he typically enriches the texture (Ex. 10), and his part-writing in the emendations is unmistakable (Ex. 11).

Ex. 9.

Ex. 10.

Ex. 11.

Gerber's lesson is all the more interesting since it has given rise to copious comment. Gerber's son, into whose possession the manuscript had passed, wrote

Dies Akkompagnement war schon an sich so schön, dass keine Hauptstimme etwas zu dem Vergnügen, welches ich dabey empfand, hätte hinzuthun können. (*Dok* III p. 476)

The accompaniment was of itself so beautiful that no solo part could have added anything to the pleasure which it gave.

On the basis of a new examination of the manuscript, Alfred Dürr has stated that the realization was indeed written as an independent setting, without recourse to the solo part – in the typical manner of a continuo-player, the elder Gerber had worked from a figured-bass part, not from a score.[12] Spitta goes to some lengths to explain that he was misled by the son's description (which he had discussed before the manuscript had become available to him) and that the realization did not represent contrapuntal part-writing.[13] His remarks, however, revert to the central issue with which we are here concerned: even in dealing with a simple harmonization, Bach thought in terms of polyphonic texture.

Dürr's essay goes to the heart of the matter since it includes a listing of the copies Gerber made from Bach's works which, for once, could be interpreted as giving us a reliable outline of the course of studies a student pursued under Bach's guidance. According to a few dates contained in the sources (which show that Gerber's tutelage commenced near the beginning of Bach's tenure in Leipzig) and Dürr's investigation of the paper and changing characteristics of handwriting, Gerber's studies moved from the Two- and Three-part Inventions to the French Suites, the suites 'avec Prelude' (English Suites), and the *Well-Tempered Clavier*. The presumable date for the realization of the Albinoni Sonata fits into the earlier part of this scheme – in any event, before that for the copy of the French Suite no. 5 BWV 816. The cantor's practice emerges with the inclusion of a setting from the 'Eighteen Chorales' among the Gerber copies, and we may assume that the study of chorales always went hand in hand with the thoroughbass studies.

A highly interesting set of illustrations which Emil Platen has given in *Bach-Jahrbuch* 1975 of chorale harmonizations by Bach and models from which Bach evidently worked in these particular instances supplements the account of 'Bach corrections' (Exs. 12 and 13) with examples for the interchange and transformation of melodic lines which – especially in the second of the excerpts quoted – give sudden overwhelming testimony to Bach's writing. Nor was the Protestant chorale absent from Handel's instructional examples. A complete keyboard setting of the

Ex. 12. *In allen meinen Taten*

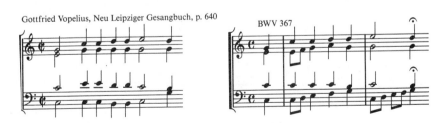

Gottfried Vopelius, Neu Leipziger Gesangbuch, p. 640

BWV 367

12 A. Dürr, 'Heinrich Nicolaus Gerber als Schüler Bachs', *BJ* 64 (1978), pp. 7–18.
13 Spitta II p. 125; the English translation (II p. 293) is inaccurate in important respects.

Ex. 13. *Wer Gott vertraut*

chorale *Jesu meine Freude* with the superscription of the German chorale title and the annotation 'Choral im Alt' (the chorale title written in German script) appears among the manuscripts for Princess Anne; and, corresponding to the beginning, a two-bar illustration for the assignment of a similar setting with the chorale tune in the soprano part is added underneath (Ex. 14).

Ex. 14. *Jesu, meine Freude*

In the continuation of the exercises compiled for Handel's pupil, however, the work on a cantus firmus gives way to that upon fugal themes. Imitative motifs are variously suggested in the advanced thoroughbass exercises. It would be difficult to realize the beginning of the example shown in Ex. 15 without recourse to the melodic phrase in bars 2 and 3 of the bass part – a typical instance to show that Spitta was, in fact, not so far off the mark in speaking about contrapuntal bass realization. Indeed, the seventh-chord sequences given in another example (Ex. 16) are embellished with a motif that in a further example is changed into a genuine

Ex. 15.

Ex. 16.

theme; its fugal elaboration is assigned with an exposition which, at the entrance of the fourth part, turns into a figured-bass exercise (Ex. 17).

The example is followed on the same page by a similar assignment, of a miniature fugue in four parts, for which Handel sketches the entrances in the letter notation of German organ tablature and once again completes the assignment in thoroughbass notation (Ex. 18).[14]

Ex. 17.

Ex. 18.

How far the thoroughbass exercises are carried in Handel's instruction is shown by the assignment for a double fugue in which, together with the figure symbols, all entrances for the theme and countersubject are marked (Ex. 19). There could be no clearer indication of the German Protestant cantor's tradition than the notation ᚐ ♮ *contrasubj. in cantu* (entrance of the countertheme after an eighth rest on the pitch H [i.e. B♮] at the octave above middle C, to be placed in the cantus [soprano]

14 Only the bass part and symbols are given in the autograph: the capital letters indicate the voices (Tenor, Alto, Cantus [= soprano]); the lines above the small letters for the fugal entries designate their respective octaves (i.e. one or two octaves above middle c′).

Ex. 19.

part). The Kellner manuscript of Bach's 'Rules and instructions for thorough bass or accompaniment in four parts', to which we have referred above, contains similar fugal examples (though without the entrance directions in tablature notation) – once again rather inadequately carried out. Spitta (I p. 715) has called attention, however, to a second similar collection ascribed to Bach, now listed as SPK P 296 and consisting only of exercises of this kind and marked with the original owner's notation 'A. W. Langloz / Anno 1763', from which we quote an example (Ex. 20).

Ex. 20.

Like the Kellner manuscript, the Langloz manuscript does not furnish convincing proof of authenticity. Wolfgang Schmieder comments on the quality of the examples:

Die Themengebilde können allenfalls aus der Zeit Bachs stammen, aber die Kompositionen Bach selbst zuzuschreiben, geht . . . schwerlich an . . . [15]

The configuration of themes conceivably suggests the time of Bach, but the manner of composition could hardly be associated with Bach himself.

In this case, too, we might be dealing with a document preserving Bach's teaching as transmitted through the work of a pupil. Nevertheless, Schmieder notes that one of the manuscript's themes is related to that of a fugue from Book 1 of the *Well-Tempered Clavier* (BWV 863), and another to that of the *Art of Fugue.*

15 W. Schmieder, *Bach-Werke-Verzeichnis* (Leipzig, 1950), p. xiii.

Tempo and Dynamic Indications in the Bach Sources: A Review of the Terminology

ROBERT L. MARSHALL

(Waltham, Massachusetts)

Unlike many of the leading musicians of his time, Johann Sebastian Bach took no active part in that most characteristic enterprise of the Age of the Enlightenment: the literally encyclopedic effort to organize the inherited corpus of musical knowledge and experience in a systematic and rational fashion. We possess no lengthy theoretical treatises, no musical dictionaries, *Versuche*, or *Anleitungen* from his pen. Perhaps Bach remained aloof from such activity because he was skeptical about such a self-conscious process of verbal conceptualization about music, with its underlying assumption that by describing, defining, classifying musical phenomena in words (or mathematical formulas) one could capture their essence. But it may be that he was simply too busy. As C. P. E. Bach related to Johann Nicolaus Forkel, 'Bey seinen vielen Beschäftigungen hatte er kaum zu der nöthigsten Correspondenz Zeit' ('With his many activities [Sebastian] hardly had time for the most necessary correspondence': *Dok* III pp. 289–90; *BR* p. 279). Indeed, the definitive edition of the surviving documents from his hand, which includes the texts not only of letters and formal reports but also of every bill and every receipt (be it ever so brief or trivial) and even the title-pages of a number of musical compositions, nonetheless contains fewer than two hundred items and would surely run to fewer than a hundred pages if one could strip away the elaborate critical apparatus.

Bach, then, was clearly not disposed to write extensively about music; but he could by no means altogether escape the necessity of using words to deal with it. First of all, part of the written form of any musical composition necessarily had to be set down in words. There was (and is) simply no other way for a composer to communicate his intentions regarding tempo, dynamics, instrumentation, and other aspects of the physical realization of his work (e.g., directions like *arco* or *pizzicato*, *con* or *senza sordino*, *tutti* or *solo*, etc). Second, Bach was not only a composer and performer but also a teacher. It was in this capacity that he prepared the explanatory material about the rudiments of musical notation and the proper rendition of ornaments that introduces the *Clavier-Büchlein vor Wilhelm Friedemann Bach*;[1] and it was surely during the course of music lessons that he dictated the elementary rules of thorough bass that survive in Anna Magdalena Bach's *Clavierbüchlein*.[2] Moreover, the title-pages and prefaces of the Two- and Three-part Inventions, the *Orgelbüchlein*, *Well-Tempered Clavier*, *Musical Offering* and *Art of Fugue* all provide explicit testimony as to the didactic function of these monumental works. In fact it would not be difficult to argue that Bach was the most self-consciously pedagogical of the great composers.

Third, owing to his reputation as an expert on organs, Bach was often called upon not only to try out newly built or renovated instruments but also to submit written evaluations of them or to draft proposals for the construction or repair of others. Finally, Johann Sebastian Bach was a civil servant whose official duties – or sense of responsibility and equity – frequently obliged him to write letters of recommendation, status reports, or even petitions and formal complaints bearing on this or that aspect of the current musical situation. The sum of these various activities and responsibilities, then, repeatedly presented Bach with opportunities to express himself in words about music or to use words simply as a necessary and unavoidable part of the process of composition. Fairly inevitably, then, he evolved a personal musical vocabulary whose range and character – as well as the manner of its expansion and revision over time – would seem destined, if seriously investigated, to provide valuable insight into his traditional and intellectual roots, his aesthetic attitudes, and his development as a teacher, performer, and composer. Such a study could even uncover welcome information of a quite practical kind.

With such reflections in mind, I have begun a compilation of the musical terms preserved in the Bach sources. So far I have managed to survey approximately six hundred sources drawn from the following 'pools':

The original documents published in the first volume of *Bach-Dokumente*, i.e. those letters, testimonials, reports, receipts, dedications, etc. written by, or at least signed and thus authenticated by, Bach himself.

The available autograph scores of the instrumental music.

The surviving autograph scores of the vocal compositions spanning the period from the earliest Mühlhausen cantatas of *c*1707–8 to the end of the first Leipzig cantata *Jahrgang* (May 1724).

A selection of autograph scores from the later Leipzig period chosen to represent the principal vocal genres: cantata, motet, oratorio, passion, mass.

The original editions of Bach's music published or prepared for publication during his lifetime.

It has not yet been possible for me to examine more than cursorily either the extensive body of original performing parts that are preserved for numerous vocal works (and for some of the instrumental ensemble compositions) or the early

---

1 See the facsimile edition, ed. R. Kirkpatrick (New York, 1959); and *NBA* V/5.

2 There are in fact two sets of thoroughbass rules in the *Clavierbüchlein*, both apparently dating from the early 1740s: the first entered in the hand of Johann Christoph Friedrich Bach, the second – and more elaborate – by Anna Magdalena. See *Dok* I pp. 252–4.

sources for those instrumental and vocal compositions which, in the absence of autographs and other original materials (e.g. copies prepared directly under the composer's supervision), may be regarded as relatively authentic.

Bach's musical vocabulary encompasses Italian, French, Latin, and German terms. The 'functional' terminology in the musical manuscripts themselves is overwhelmingly Italian, although Bach clearly prefers *Hautbois* (*Hautb.*) over *Oboe* (*Ob.*, *Oboi*, also *Obboe*) and favors French terminology in general for the dance genres. On the other hand, the musical terms found in the text documents, as well as those in the title-pages, dedications and prefaces to both manuscript and printed musical collections, are mostly German.

At this point the compilation contains over a thousand entries – an impressive figure, indeed, especially when one considers that even Johann Gottfried Walther's comprehensive *Musicalisches Lexicon* contains only about three thousand musical terms.[3] It seems prudent, incidentally, to avoid citing a more precise figure – not only because the compilation is still incomplete but also because the material inherently defies strict quantifiction, for we encounter not only equivalent terms in different languages but also numerous variant spellings and grammatical inflections (along with the uninhibited use of a variety of abbreviations) for what is presumably one and the same term in a single language. Finally, there are alternative phonetic forms (as distinct from variant spellings or grammatical forms) of the same term in the same language. (I have generally considered the latter, unlike orthographical variants and abbreviations, to be separate items.) The difficulty can best be illustrated by reproducing the five separate entries I have so far for Bach's various designations for the transverse flute. They consist of no fewer than fourteen forms: *Flaute traverso* (*Flaut: Travers:*); *Flute Traversa* (*Flute Travers.*); *Flute Traversiere*; *Traverso* (*Trav.*, *Travers.*, *Traversa*, *Traversi*); *Traversiere* (*Traversier.*, *Traversiera*, *Traversieri*) – to which could be added *Flöte(n)-Traversier*, but not *Fleute-Travers*, since for Bach the latter refers only to an organ stop.

The following discussion, owing to space constraints, will be limited in its scope to a portion of the Bach terminology dealing with performance: specifically, dynamic and tempo indications. It is intended to be regarded as a sample illustrating the potential value, and perhaps also the inherent limitations, of a systematic study of the musical terminology contained in the Bach sources.

Dynamics

The entire corpus of Bach's dynamic markings, as revealed (so far) by the sources, consists – even if one reckons single letters separately from other abbreviations and

3 See Walther 1732; also Eggebrecht 1957, especially p. 13. It is not surprising that Walther's *Lexicon* proves to be a most reliable guide to Bach's use and understanding of musical terminology. Both men, after all, shared very much the same musical tradition. Not only were they cousins who lived at the same time in the same town for close to a decade (1708–17), but they were clearly in close musical contact as well. Bach in fact later acted as the Leipzig sales representative for Walther's dictionary (*Dok* II p. 191).

fully written-out terms – of only seventeen items (see Table 1).[4] The meanings of most of these terms are neither problematic nor surprising. Walther (1732, pp. 257, 479) defines *forte* as 'starck, hefftig, jedoch auf eine natürliche Art, ohne die Stimme, oder das Instrument gar zu sehr zu zwingen' ('strong, intense, but in a natural manner, without forcing the voice or instrument too much') and *piano* as 'so viel als leise; dass man nemlich die Stärcke der Stimme oder des Instruments dermassen lieblich machen, oder mindern soll, dass es wie ein Echo lasse' ('in effect, soft; one should adjust or reduce the strength of the voice or instrument so that it may have the effect of an echo'). But one must nonetheless proceed with caution. The letters *pp*, for example, contrary to the expectations of the modern musician, are reported by Walther to stand not for *pianissimo* but for *più piano*;[5] and the sources reveal that Bach observed this usage.[6] For example, in the autograph score of the Mühlhausen cantata *Aus der Tiefe* BWV 131, dating from c1707, three of the upper instrumental parts at one point (bar 298) read *pp* while the continuo at the same time has *piu p*.[7] Similarly, we find basically the same combination in the

Table 1. *Dynamic Indications in the Bach Sources*

term	earliest observed appearance	
	year	BWV
1 *f* [*forte*]	1707	131
2 *forte* (*for:*, *fort.*)	1713	208; 596
3 *m. f.* [*mezzo forte*]	1736	244
4 *mezo forte* [sic]	1736	244
5 *p* [*piano*]	1707	131
6 *p.* [*pianissimo*]	1721	1046
7 *p: pian* [*più piano*]	1723	95
8 *pi p* [*più piano*]	1715	132
9 *pianissimo* (*pianiβimo*, *pianiss.*)	c1707	106
10 *piano* (*pi*, *pia*, *pian.*)	1707	131
11 *piano piano*	1715	165
12 *piu piano* (*piu p:*, *piu pian*)	1707	131
13 *poco forte*	1713?	63
14 (*un*) *poco piano*	1733	232
15 *pp.* [*più piano*]	1707	131
16 *p. s.* [*pianissimo sempre*]	1721	1046
17 *sempre piano* (*piano sempre*)	1713?	63

4 The table preserves Bach's usual orthography. Alternative spellings have been placed in parentheses; editorial resolutions of abbreviations in square brackets.

5 1732, p 479, which defines *piu piano* as 'wie ein zweytes *Echo*, so dass es als noch weit entlegener denn als *piano* klinge' ('like a second echo, so that it sounds as if much farther away than *piano*').

6 Walther (*ibid.*) reports further that the abbreviation for *pianissimo* was *ppp*: 'gleichsam das dritte *Echo*, welches lässt, als wenn die Stimme oder der Instrument-Klang in die Lufft zergienge' ('a third echo which lets the sound of the voice or instrument seem to fade into the air'). Bach apparently never used the abbreviation *ppp*.

7 The autograph score of BWV 131 is in private possession.

autograph score[8] of the Weimar cantata *Bereitet die Wege* BWV 132 (composed December 1715), at bar 87 of the first movement: *pp* in two upper parts (violin 2 and viola) and, simultaneously, *pi p* in another (violin 1). (This reveals, incidentally, that *pi p* is to be deciphered as *più piano*, and not, say, *piano piano*.)

Decisive confirmation of Bach's distinction between *pp* (*più piano*) and *pianissimo* is provided by a passage from the final chorus of the *St Matthew Passion* as preserved in the 1736 version of the work. In several of the performing parts (violin, viola, traverso, continuo), Bach marked the final bars of the *B* section of the movement preceding the *da capo* (bars 76–9) with the following sequence of dynamics: *piano – pp – pianissimo*.[9] At the same time this passage constitutes the earliest unambiguous indication of graduated dynamics – the succession clearly amounts to a *de facto* decrescendo – that I have encountered so far in the Bach sources. (The same sequence appears in another autograph source[10] dating from about the same time: the score of the Harpsichord Concerto in D major BWV 1054, *c*1735–45, in the viola part of the first movement, at bars 17–19 and again bars 35–7.)

The dynamic markings discussed so far – *f, p, piano, piu p, pp, pianissimo* – were all used by Bach from the beginning of his career. They all appear as early as 1707 in his first Mühlhausen cantatas: *pianissimo* in the (posthumous) manuscript of Cantata 106, *Gottes Zeit ist die allerbeste Zeit*, the others in the autograph score of Cantata 131![11] The preponderance of the softer dynamic markings here is striking; moreover, on the basis of the evidence so far assembled, it remains a hallmark of Bach's practice henceforth. More precisely, Bach not only continues to exploit the soft extreme of the dynamic range beyond *piano* to *più piano* and *pianissimo*, but will also eventually fill in the gap between *piano* and *forte* by introducing such designations as *poco piano, mezo forte* [sic], *poco forte*. But evidently he will never prescribe a dynamic level above a simple *forte*. Bach's entire dynamic spectrum, in other words, remains fundamentally 'skewed' towards the soft end; and this asymmetry would seem to reflect a basic attitude towards the performance of musical dynamics. Bach could and frequently did, of course, augment the volume level of a passage or a composition by adding more and louder instruments – a *forte* in a work scored with trumpets and drums, after all, is considerably louder than one scored for strings alone – or perhaps simply by increasing the number of polyphonic parts. (A celebrated example occurs in bars 20–2 of the B flat minor Prelude BWV 867 of *WTC* Bk 1, which one may or may not regard as ultimately rising above *forte*.)[12] But the remarkable fact remains that Bach chose, apparently,

8 SPK P 60.

9 See the movement in *NBA* II/5, as well as the facsimile reproduced in the *KB* p. 231.

10 DSB P 234.

11 The earliest source of BWV 106 is Christian Friedrich Penzel's score copy SPK P 1018, dated 1768. The earliest use of the term *pianissimo* preserved in an autograph score is found in the Cöthen cantata *Durchlauchtster Leopold* BWV 173a (DSB P 42), the precise date of which is uncertain. See *NBA* I/35 *KB* pp. 132–3.

12 Heinrich Besseler has argued that such *Ausdrucksdynamik* constituted one of Bach's major stylistic innovations: see Besseler 1955, especially pp. 25, 39.

to call for more volume (power, brilliance) only by such compositional or orchestrational means rather than by the introduction of dynamic markings (*più forte, ff, fortissimo*), something he was quite willing to do in the case of the softer dynamic levels. The practical consequences of this for anyone concerned about 'historically authentic' Bach performance seem fairly clear.

We shall shortly turn to a consideration of the later additions to Bach's palette of dynamic markings. It is first necessary, however, to make some observations about the general patterns apparently governing Bach's use or non-use of dynamic indications at all. For example, it must be mentioned that the original sources for Bach's solo keyboard and organ works – whether autographs, copies, or prints – contain (as every player familiar with *Urtext* editions has long since surmised) virtually no dynamic indications. There are of course exceptions, such as the indication of registral differentiation between leading and accompanimental parts by the simultaneous employment of *piano* and *forte* markings throughout the original 1735 edition of the *Italian Concerto* or the equally special instance of relatively rapid, echo-like *forte-piano* alternations.[13] By and large, however, it is clear that Bach considered the prescription of dynamics to be necessary only in ensemble compositions; in solo works the choice almost invariably could be left entirely to the discretion of the autonomous performer.[14]

With respect to ensemble works, Bach's normal practice – at least in the case of movements in ritornello form (arias, choruses, concerto movements) – was, as is well known, to have the tutti ensemble play *forte* during the ritornellos and *piano* during the solo sections. The principal instrumental performing parts were marked, almost always by Bach himself, according to this principle.[15] The opening ritornellos, however, typically bear no dynamic marking at all, *forte* being implied until the first (explicit) *piano* marking makes its appearance in the accompanying parts together with the (unmarked but clearly *forte*) entrance of the instrumental or vocal soloist (or chorus). It is important to recognize that the dynamic markings here are obviously fulfilling a formal rather than an expressive function: a *forte* in the accompanying parts in the later course of the movement signals the return of the ritornello or of an instrumental interlude for the ripieno ensemble, while *piano*,

13 See, for example, the echo effects in the organ Prelude in E flat BWV 552 (*Clavierübung III*), bars 34–40, as well as those in the Echo movement of the *French Overture* BWV 831 (*Clavierübung II*).

14 The argument has been put forth, quite persuasively, that there could hardly have been much if any room for discretion with regard to the choice of dynamics in the keyboard and organ works beyond the initial establishment of the registration. See Bodky 1960 p. 34, *re* the keyboard compositions, and Stauffer 1981 *re* the organ compositions. (Stauffer suggests that Bach's free organ compositions should almost invariably be performed *pro organo pleno*.) It should be observed, however, that there is also an almost complete absence of dynamic marks in the fair-copy autograph (SPK P 967) of the Sonatas and Partitas for Unaccompanied Violin – again with the exception of echo effects in the final movement of the A minor Sonata BWV 1003.iv, and the Preludio of the E major Partita BWV 1006.i. This would seem to confirm, after all, that the lack of dynamic markings in Bach's solo compositions reflects at least to some significant degree the composer's desire to grant the solo performer maximum artistic flexibility in this respect.

15 The autograph scores, especially the composing scores of the early Leipzig period, generally have few if any dynamic markings.

conversely, signals the beginning of a solo episode. The unambiguous, if tacit, assumption of a *forte* dynamic at the opening of such movements is particularly significant, for it strongly suggests that Bach regarded the simple *forte* as the normal dynamic level prevailing in a composition in the absence of any indication to the contrary.

As early as 1713 Bach began to modify this schematic loud–soft alternation. In the Weimar Christmas cantata *Christen ätzet diesen Tag* BWV 63, the duet 'Gott du hast es wohl gefüget' calls for soprano, bass, obbligato oboe, and continuo. During the course of the first vocal section (specifically, at bars 10, 15, 18), the oboe part is sporadically marked *poco forte*, in alternation with *piano*.[16] The reason for this refinement is clearly to call attention to the introduction of a thematic quotation from the ritornello in these bars and to instruct the oboist to emphasize them accordingly, despite the continued activity of the vocal soloists. The same dynamic marking, in a similar context and serving the same purpose of eliciting a 'discreet emphasis' from an instrumental accompaniment, is found throughout the aria 'Mein Erlöser und Erhalter' from the early Leipzig cantata *Lobe den Herrn, meine Seele* BWV 69a (August 1723).[17] The function of *poco forte*, then, as it is used by Bach, is still primarily formal, and this would seem to be the case as well with regard to Bach's use of *m.f.* and *mezo forte*. Both designations appear for the first (and so far only) time in the 1736 sources of the *St Matthew Passion*, where they are found in the instrumental parts of the opening chorus at most of the vocal entrances.[18] Bach's similar use of *poco forte*, on the one hand, and *mezo forte*, on the other – both as accompanimental dynamics – would seem to argue that he considered the two terms essentially synonymous. It is worth noting, however, that in the example cited above, *poco forte* follows, and thus contrasts with, a *piano*, whereas in the *St Matthew* chrous *m.f.* largely alternates with, and apparently modifies, a *forte* marking. This suggests that *poco forte* implied for Bach a more forceful rendering than *m.f.*, and that it therefore probably represented a dynamic level between *m.f.* and *f*.

The indication *un poco piano* in the string parts of the opening ritornello of the *aria a doi chori* 'So ist mein Jesus nun gefangen' (again preserved in the 1736 layer of performing parts) serves once again – like the *m.f.* markings in the opening chorus – to refine the contrast between melody and accompaniment by insuring, in this instance, that the relatively active, but secondary, strings are subordinated in volume to the thematically dominant woodwinds. That is, *poco piano* here seems actually to be quite close in meaning to the comparative *più piano* – this time 'softer' with reference to the (presumably *forte*) volume of the flute and oboes – in our terms, then, *meno forte*.[19]

16 The only original source for BWV 63 is the set of performing parts, SPK St 9. The oboe part for the duet movement is autograph. See *NBA I/2 KB* p. 11.
17 The sole source is the original set of parts, DSB St 68. The dynamics in the instrumental parts were entered by Bach.
18 The autograph score, DSB P 25, reads *m.f.*; the autograph continuo part, SPK St 110, reads *mezo forte*.
19 The dynamic markings appear only in the parts, not the autograph score. See *NBA II/5 KB* p. 164.

The introduction in the *St Matthew Passion* of such subtle, more shaded dynamics – as well as the graduated dynamics in the final chorus mentioned earlier – seems to be symptomatic of a general tendency on Bach's part during the decade of the 1730s towards greater differentiation in his performance indications. The 'Missa' of the B minor Mass, composed before July 1733, provides a different manifestation of the same tendency. The opening ritornello of the first 'Kyrie' commences in the instruments only after the dramatic four-bar choral invocation at the outset of the movement. Attached to some of the upper string parts at the change of tempo at this point (bar 5) from *Adagio* to *Largo* is once again the dynamic marking *poco piano*.[20] This time the marking serves not only the familiar formal function of clarifying the design of the movement (by introducing a dynamic contrast between vocal and instrumental sections) but also and primarily an expressive function (by contributing to the evocation of the appropriate *Affekt* of the movement – call it 'meditative' or 'somber'). That is, perhaps for the first time (at least through written prescription), Bach here is exploiting the purely expressive potential of musical dynamics.

The term *piano piano* has so far turned up only once. Like *poco piano* it is used to an expressive end – not in order to help evoke the general *Affekt*, however, but rather in the age-old service of text-illustration. The term appears in the string parts, to the accompaniment of the line 'wenn alle Kraft vergehen', in the last bar of the recitative 'Ich habe ja, mein Seelenbräutigam' from the Weimar cantata *O heil'ges Geist- und Wasserbad* BWV 165. Now although it is clear that *piano piano* is meant to be distinctly softer than simple *piano*, it is not clear whether Bach regarded it as synonymous with *piu piano*, with *pianissimo*, or perhaps with neither.[21] (It may, admittedly, be pedantic even to raise this question. Walther, at all events, was not inclined to split hairs as fine as this. Although he goes so far as to accord *piano piano* its own entry in his *Lexicon*, he is content to define it as 'wie *piu piano* oder *pianissimo*'.) At the beginning of 'Ich habe ja', incidentally, the string parts are marked *piano sempre*. This term (along with *sempre piano*) frequently appears in the string parts of accompanied recitatives, the first such use occurring in the recitative 'O sel'ger Tag' from Cantata 63 (1713). *Piano sempre* also appears on occasion in the accompanying parts of concerto slow movements: for example, in the First Brandenburg Concerto and in the D major Harpsichord Concerto BWV 1054.

As has been mentioned earlier with reference to the *Italian Concerto*, Bach at times took the trouble to prescribe different, but simultaneously executed, dynamic

20 The autograph violin 1 part reads *Largo è un poco piano*; the equally autograph violin 2 and viola parts *Largo è poco piano*. See the facsimile edition of the original parts (Schulze 1983).
21 Cantata 165 survives only in a non-autograph, but original score dating from Bach's Leipzig period. The manuscript is part of the Amalienbibliothek and is now housed in the Deutsche Staatsbibliothek under the shelf number 105. Since the source is in a copyist's hand, the question arises as to whether the *piano piano* indication is completely authentic. It is conceivable, after all, that the copyist misconstrued his source – perhaps an autograph, perhaps containing at this point an abbreviation like *pi p* or even *pp*. The *NBA* score, in any case, prints *pp*, although the critical report describes the source situation. See *NBA* I/15 p. 12, and *NBA* I/15 *KB* p. 22.

levels. Since such notation was, in effect, a way of indicating manual registration, it is encountered mostly in the sources of organ compositions. The autograph score of the D minor Concerto after Vivaldi (BWV 596), penned c1713–14,[22] provides the earliest instance. In the fourth movement, a Largo in 12/8 meter, the upper staff is marked *forte*, the lower *piano*. Similarly, in the chorale prelude *Liebster Jesu wir sind hier* BWV 634, a setting entered into the *Orgelbüchlein* c1715,[23] the canonic parts on the top staff are *forte*, the accompaniment on the bottom staff *piano*. The most striking example of simultaneous differentiated dynamics, however, occurs in an ensemble work, the opening movement of the Fifth Brandenburg Concerto. In the meticulously prepared fair-copy score Bach has carefully marked the momentarily leading parts *f* in bars 45, 51–4 and elsewhere, while the surrounding subordinate parts have *p*.[24]

Tempo and *Affekt* Indications

According to the sources consulted so far, there would seem to be forty-five discrete terms that fall into this category.[25] They are listed in alphabetical order – and according to Bach's usual orthography and capitalization – in Table 2. It is apparent at once, from Bach's use of such double (and from our point of view contradictory) formulations as *Vivace è allegro* or *Allegro e presto*, that he could not have regarded the terms belonging to this category entirely in the modern sense as objective indications of tempo (i.e. velocity) alone but must still have understood them in their earlier sense as characterizations, at least in part, of *Affekt*. Moreover, since

22 The autograph score is SPK P 330. This dating for the transcription has been suggested by Hans-Joachim Schulze; see Schulze 1978 p. 89.

23 The date is suggested in the foreword of the facsimile edition of the *Orgelbüchlein*: see Löhlein 1981 p. 18.

24 See the facsimile editions of both the autograph score (Wackernagel 1950) and the autograph parts (Schulze 1975).

25 The number could be raised to forty-seven by including *a tempo* and *a batutta* [sic]. *A tempo* is typically found in the continuo parts of recitative movements at the beginning of an arioso section – i.e. at the moment when the static recitative bass line is activated. It also occurs in accompanied recitatives in which the instrumental accompaniment develops motivic figures. The term appears for the first time during the Weimar period (in Cantatas 21 and 185) and clearly has the meaning 'in strict (that is, in measured) time'. (Walther's a definition for *a tempo* – 'nach dem Tact' ('according to the measure') – confirms this.) This of course implies conversely that the recitative was normally performed in a rather free, unmeasured rhythm in order to achieve a flexible, naturalistic declamation of the text. *A batutta*, which so far has been found only in the motivically accompanied recitative 'Ja freilich will in uns das Fleisch und Blut' from the *St Matthew Passion*, is synonymous with *a tempo*. Bach's use of the term *tempo*, incidentally, as revealed by the headings *Tempo di Borea* (BWV 1002.vii), *Tempo di Minuetta* [sic] (BWV 829.v, BWV 173a.iv), *Tempo di Gavotta* (BWV 830.vi), and *al tempo di Giga* (BWV 988.vii: an autograph addition), signified just that: tempo, speed. Walther (1732 p. 598) explains, under *Tempo di Gavotta*, 'man eine mit gedachten Worten bezeichnete Piéce, ob sie gleich keines von ihnen würcklich ist, dennoch noch dem *mouvement* derselben zu *executiren* habe' ('one executes a piece so designated, even if it is not really one of them [i.e. such a dance], nonetheless according to the *Mouvement* of the same'). And under *Mouvement* (p. 426) we read: 'die Beschaffenheit des Tacts, ob er nemlich langsam oder geschwinde sey' ('the character of the measure, i.e. whether it is slow or fast').

Table 2. *Tempo and* Affekt *Designations in the Bach Sources*

term	earliest observed appearance		number of appearances		
	year	BWV	1	2–5	25+
1 *Adagio*	1704	992			x
2 *adagio assai*	c1707	106		x	
3 *Adagio mà non tanto*	1721	1051			
4 *Adagio o vero Largo*	Cöthen?	1061	x		
5 *adagißimo*	c1704?	565		x	
6 *adagiosissimo*	1704	992		x	
7 *Affettuoso*	1708	71 (libretto)		x	
8 *Allabreve*	1733	232		x	
9 *Allegro*	1705?	535a			x
10 *Allegro assai*	1720	1005			
11 *Allegro e presto*	Weimar?	916	x		
12 *allegro ma non presto*	c1726	1039	x		
13 *Allegro ma non tanto*	c1735	1027		x	
14 *Allegro moderato*	c1735	1027		x	
15 *Allegro poco*	1704	992	x		
16 *Andante*	1707	131			x
17 *Andante un poco*	c1725	1015	x		
18 *Animose*	1708	71 (libretto)	x		
19 *cantabile*	1721	1050		x	
20 *con discretione*	c1710	912	x		
21 *dolce*	c1727–30	527		x	
22 *Fort gai*	c1725	818a	x		
23 *gay*	1714	61	x		
24 *Grave*	c1713–14	596			
25 *Larghetto*	1708	71		x	
26 *Largo*	1707	131			x
27 *Largo ma non tanto*	Cöthen?	1043	x		
28 *Lente*	1707	131		x	
29 *Lentement*	c1738	1067	x		
30 *Lento*	c1707	106	x		
31 *moderato*	1736	244	x		
32 *molt'adagio*	c1704?	565		x	
33 *molt'allegro*	1731	36	x		
34 *più presto*	1713	208	x		
35 *prestissimo*	c1704?	565		x	
36 *Presto*	c1706–10?	911			x
37 *Spirituoso*	1714	21	x		
38 *Tardò*	1707	524	x		
39 *Tempo di (Borea, Gavotta, Giga, Minuetta)*	Cöthen	173a			
40 *tres viste*	c1730	995	x		
41 *un poc'allegro*	1707	131			
42 *un poco Adagio*	Cöthen	1019a	x		
43 *vistement*	c1725	809	x		
44 *Vivace*	1707	131			x
45 *Vivace è allegro*	1723	24		x	

such 'tempo' designations had their origins in (and owed their very existence to) the breakdown of the absolute temporal values of the mensural system, they could hardly have been expected in any case to serve as precise indicators of the absolute, metronomic tempo of any compositions. Quite the contrary: the very wealth, variety, and even fussiness (or ambivalence) of a surprisingly large number of Bach's tempo markings – the *assais*, *un pocos* and *ma nons* – strongly suggest that they eluded exact quantification and were for Bach ultimately as subjective as the moods and *Affekte* from which they derived their names. Accordingly, it seems proper to group together such terms as *adagio*, *allegro*, *largo* and *presto*, which today unambiguously define tempo, along with more evocative ones such as *grave*, *affettuoso*, *gay*, *spirituoso*, and even *cantabile* and *dolce*. Bach, in fact, not only used all of these terms himself basically in the same way – almost invariably placing them at the beginning of a movement or formal section of a movement – but even had many of them serve, at least in his earliest cantatas, as in effect movement headings in the absence of form or genre designations *per se*, such as *Aria* or *Recitativo* (terms that were not to appear in his vocal compositions for another few years).[26]

The domination of Italian terminology in this category is overwhelming. Not only is the mere handful of French terms here limited to compositions in the French style – suite movements and overtures – but they are all *unica*, at least so far: *lentement* appears only in the 'Polonoise' of the orchestral Suite in B minor BWV 1067; *gay* only at the beginning of the fast section of the opening chorus of Cantata 61 *Nun komm, der Heiden Heiland*; *vistement* in the prelude of the English Suite in F major BWV 809; *tres viste* at the 3/8 section of the prelude of the Lute Suite in G minor BWV 995; and *fort gai* in the prelude of the Keyboard Suite in A minor BWV 818a.[27] This enumeration, admittedly, could be augmented by considering *grave* and *lente* to be French words. But Bach evidently did not, since *grave* and *lente*, unlike the clearly French terms, are not restricted to compositions in French style. Moreover, Walther identifies *grave* as Italian (in contrast to *gravement*) and, while omitting *lente*, offers *lento* as Italian and *lent* as French.[28] The whole thrust of Bach's usage, in any case, indicates that in general, and certainly in this connection, he viewed Italian as the standard currency of musical terminology and drew on French only when he wished to emphasize the French character of a style or genre.

It will be helpful to begin our consideration of this material with something of a

---

26 The first appearance of both *Aria* and *Recit* in the Bach sources is in the autograph score (DSB P 42) of the 'Hunting' Cantata *Was mir behagt* BWV 208, composed February 1713 – that is, if one disregards the 'Aria di Postiglione' from the 1704 *Capriccio on the Departure of His Most Beloved Brother* BWV 992.

27 The sources:

BWV	manuscript source	date	reference in *NBA KB*
1067	DSB St 154 (copy)	c1738	VII/1 p. 10
61	DSB P 45 (autograph)	December 1714	I/1 p. 9
809	SPK P 1072 (copy)	c1724/5	V/7 p. 20
995	Brussels, Bibl. Royale, Fétis MS II. 4085 (autograph)	c1727–31	V/10 p. 109
818a	SPK P 804 (copy)	c1730–40	V/8 pp. 37, 47; V/7 pp. 25–6

28 Walther 1732 pp. 290, 361.

statistical survey, noting, for example, that of the forty-five tempo markings no fewer than twenty appear quite early on in Bach's career, before *c*1710. They are (here only retaining Bach's spelling and capitalization): *Adagio, Adagio assai, adagissimo, adagiosissimo, Affettuoso, allegro, allegro poco, andante, animose, con discretione, Larghetto, Largo, Lente, lento, molto adagio, prestissimo, presto, Tardò, un poc'allegro,* and *vivace.* The earliest works, in fact – the Mühlhausen cantatas BWV 131, 106, 71; the *Quodlibet* BWV 524; the organ Prelude and Fugue in G minor BWV 535a; the Toccata and Fugue in D minor BWV 565; and the *Capriccio on the Departure of His Most Beloved Brother* BWV 992 – are particularly rich in such terms, especially the more extreme as well as some of the most uncommon indications. Twelve of these early terms, indeed, appear no more than five times in all in the Bach sources; *adagissimo, adagiosissimo, adagio assai, affettuoso, allegro poco, animose, con discretione, larghetto, lento, molto adagio, prestissimo, tardò.* But the fact is that almost three-quarters of all the tempo designations contained in the Bach sources reviewed so far (thirty-three of the forty-five, to be precise) are 'uncommon' in that they occur only five or fewer times. (In addition to the twelve just listed, the remaining twenty-one are: *adagio o vero largo, allabreve, allegro e presto, allegro ma non presto, allegro ma non tanto, allegro moderato, andante un poco, cantabile, dolce, fort gai, gay, largo ma non tanto, lentement, moderato, molt'allegro, più presto, spirituoso, tres viste, un poco adagio, vistement, vivace e allegro.*) And of these, twenty – or more than 40 percent of the total – are *unica* (*Adagio o vero largo, allegro e presto, allegro ma non presto, allegro poco, andante un poco, animose, con discretione, fort gai, gay, largo ma non tanto, lentement, lento, moderato, molt'allegro, più presto, spirituoso, tardò, tres viste, un poco adagio, vistement*).

Considered from the other end, there are only six tempo indications that occur twenty-five or more times: *adagio, allegro, andante, largo, presto, vivace.* These six would seem, then, to constitute the 'fixed points' for Bach in the scale of tempo markings, a scale which, in its essential outlines, was established early in his career and maintained thereafter. Of these six terms there is reason to believe that Bach regarded *allegro* as representing the normal tempo – the *tempo ordinario* – just as he evidently took *forte* to be the basic dynamic level. As with *forte,* there is a notable absence in the Bach sources of a simple *allegro* marking in certain strategic positions. In the cantatas, for example, *allegro* almost never appears at the beginning of a movement but only after a section in a different – typically, slow – tempo such as *adagio* or *grave.*[29] Similarly, the opening movements of the vast majority of instrumental works,[30] whether for keyboard, organ, or ensemble, carry no tempo

29 I am indebted for this observation to David M. Powers, a graduate student at the University of Chicago. The only exception so far is the aria 'Wie freudig ist mein Herz' from Cantata 199. The *allegro* marking for this aria may have been called forth by the 12/8 meter in order to insure a more vigorous tempo than would perhaps otherwise be implied by this signature.

30 The inevitable exceptions are the C major Sonata *à 2 Clav. et Pedal* BWV 529; the G major Sonata for Violin and Obbligato Harpsichord BWV 1019; the Fourth Brandenburg Concerto BWV 1049; and the B minor Praeludium (*WTC* Bk 2) BWV 893.

indication – unless it is something other than a simple *allegro*. On the other hand, the second (i.e. fast) movements of instrumental compositions in *sonata da chiesa* form (e.g. BWV 1001, 1014, 1016–1018, 1028, 1034–1035) are usually marked *allegro*, as are the final movements of three-movement concertos. In both situations, of course, *allegro* invariably follows (i.e. cancels) a different (slow) indication – that of the preceding movement – and thereby serves to restore the *tempo ordinario*. The suspicion, finally, that an *allegro* tempo constituted Bach's norm receives virtually explicit corroboration from the *Necrology*: 'und im Zeitmasse, welches er gemeiniglich sehr lebhaft nahm [war er] überaus sicher' ('of the tempo, which [Bach] generally took very lively, he was uncommonly sure': *Dok* III p. 87; *BR* p. 222).

Having ascertained the 'center', as it were, of Bach's scale of tempo designations, it is necessary to establish the extremes. The manner in which Bach linguistically manipulates the terms at the outer ends of the tempo continuum proves to be most enlightening in this connection. Whereas he exaggerates *adagio* (altering it to *adagissimo, adagiosissimo, adagio assai, molto adagio*), he moderates *largo* (changing it to *larghetto* or *largo ma non tanto*). At the other extreme Bach accelerates *presto* to *prestissimo* and avoids too rapid a tempo with the formulation *allegro ma non presto*. There are no corresponding qualifications or modifications of *vivace* – say, to *molto vivace* or *vivacissimo*. All this allows the conclusion that for Bach the slow end of the tempo continuum was generally represented by *adagio* not *largo*, and the fast end (less surprisingly) by *presto* not *vivace*.

It is now a simple matter to arrange Bach's six principal tempo designations into what was almost certainly for him their proper sequential order of increasing velocity, namely *adagio – largo – andante – allegro – vivace – presto*. This accords only in part with the ranking implied by Walther's *Lexicon* which, in its operative phrases, defines these terms as follows:[31]

Adagio: 'gemächlich, langsam' ('leisurely, slow')

Largo: 'sehr langsam, den Tact gleichsam erweiternd' ('very slow, as if expanding the measure')

Andante: 'alle Noten fein gleich . . . executirt . . . und etwas geschwinder als *adagio*' ('all the notes executed nice and evenly . . . and somewhat quicker than *adagio*')

Allegro: 'frölich, lustig, wohl belebt oder erweckt; sehr offt auch: geschwinde und flüchtig: manchmal aber auch, einen gemässigten, obschon frölichen und belebten Tact' ('happy, merry, quite lively or awake; very often also quick or fleeting; but sometimes also a moderate but happy, lively measure')

Vivace: 'lebhafft. *Vivacissimo*. sehr lebhafft' ('lively; *Vivacissimo*, very lively')

Presto: 'geschwind' ('quick': Walther does not list *Prestissimo*)

Walther, then, seems to be suggesting the order *largo – adagio – andante – allegro – presto – vivace*.

31 Walther 1732 pp. 9, 355, 35, 27, 630, 496. Walther's reference to the evenness of execution under *andante* is quite pertinent for Bach, who often prescribes the term in passages characterized by unbroken 'walking' motion in one or more parts, usually the bass (for example, the B minor Prelude BWV 869 (*WTC* Bk 1), or the Sinfonia of the C minor Partita BWV 826, at bar 8), most typically at arioso passages in recitatives where the continuo breaks into regular eighth-note motion (e.g. the fourth and sixth movements of Cantata 63).

From the instances where different tempo designations appear simultaneously (and presumably unintentionally) in different lines or parts of the same work, we can safely infer that Bach regarded the terms involved as synonymous. In the autograph score of Cantata 131, for example, the opening bars of the work are marked *Lente* over the continuo staff of the score and, simultaneously, *adagio* over the top staff (oboe); and the 'Qui tollis' movement from the Mass in B minor is marked *Adagio* in the autograph violin 1 part but *Lente* in the equally autograph alto, cello and continuo parts.[32] Similarly, in the autograph score of the early *Quodlibet* BWV 524, the continuo part at bar 15 is marked *Tardò* while the tenor has *Adagio*.[33]

A related situation is presented by the work-pair consisting of the G major Trio Sonata for Flute, Violin, and Continuo BWV 1039 and its later reworking, the Sonata for Viola da Gamba and Obbligato Harpsichord BWV 1027. The sources for both compositions date from the Leipzig period: the anonymous copyists' parts for BWV 1039 (DSB St 431) from *c*1726, the autograph score of BWV 1027 (DSB P 226) from *c*1735.[34] In the trio version the tempo for the second movement is given as *allegro ma non presto*; in the gamba version it is *allegro ma non tanto*. It seems justified to conclude from this that Bach considered the two designations to be virtually identical in meaning. On the other hand, the fourth movement of the trio is marked *presto* while that of the gamba sonata reads *allegro moderato*. Here it would surely be difficult to maintain that the two different tempo markings are to be understood as synonymous. Quite the contrary; it would seem clear in this instance that Bach intended the gamba version to be taken at a distinctly slower tempo than the trio, and changed the tempo marking accordingly.

I have already indicated that the most extreme tempo markings in the Bach repertory are concentrated in the early works. Conversely, most of the more subtle shadings do not appear before the 1720s or even the 1730s, although there are some exceptions. *Allegro poco*, *larghetto*, and *un poc'allegro* all make their first appearance in the sources of pre-Weimar compositions. To these we should perhaps add *con discretione*, a term which Bach apparently prescribes only once, in a passage from the Keyboard Toccata in D major BWV 912 (presumably composed *c*1710). The musical context in which the term appears – a passage of decorated chords marked with fermatas occurring during the course of a section marked *adagio* (bars 111–18) – strongly suggests that *con discretione* must have meant to Bach something like *ad libitum*, i.e. in free rhythm. Indeed, this impression is emphatically confirmed by Mattheson in his discussion of the fantasy style in *Der vollkommene Capellmeister* (part 1, ch. 10): 'Man pfleget sonst bey dergleichen Sachen wol die Worte zu schreiben: *ceci se joue à discretion*, oder im Italienischen: *con discrezione*, um zu bemercken, dass man sich an den Tact gar nicht binden dürffe; sondern nach Belieben bald langsam bald geschwinde spielen möge' ('One is probably also in the habit, with such pieces, of writing the words *ceci se joue à dis-*

---

32 See the facsimile editions of the autograph score (Dürr 1965) and the original parts (Schulze 1983).
33 See the facsimile edition (Neumann 1973).
34 For the datings see NBA VI/3 *KB* p. 48 (for BWV 1039) and Eppstein 1966 p. 22 (for BWV 1027).

cretion, or in Italian *con discrezione*, in order to indicate that one need not be confined to the beat at all, but according to one's pleasure might play sometimes slow, sometimes fast').[35] On the other hand, it must be reported that Walther defines *con discretione* as 'bescheidentlich, mit Masse, nemlich nicht zu geschwinde noch zu langsam' ('discreet, restrained, neither too fast nor too slow'). The expression, then, could well have signified, at least to Bach's contemporaries, a tempo much like *moderato*.[36]

As for *moderato* itself, it appears (like its counterpart among the dynamic markings, *mezzo forte*) for the first and so far only time in the *St Matthew Passion*, at the end of the accompanied recitative 'Und da sie den Lobgesang gesprochen haben' at Jesus's words 'Wenn ich aber auferstehe'. Here *moderato* follows, and in effect cancels, a *vivace* marking over a passage set to the words 'Ich werde den Hirten schlagen'.

Since in vocal music the character and meaning of the text normally suffice to define the *Affekt* and thereby suggest the appropriate tempo, it is not surprising to discover that the 'uncommon' as well as the more extreme and the more differentiated tempo markings encountered in the Bach sources are concentrated in his instrumental compositions. The extreme tempos, whether fast or slow, are largely confined to the early keyboard and organ works of the pre- and early Weimar periods: that is, to compositions for a solo instrument that were intended typically as strongly individualistic, if not unabashedly virtuoso vehicles. The more moderate, more meticulously qualified tempo markings, on the other hand, are found mainly in the later ensemble compositions: the concertos and chamber works composed during the Cöthen or even the Leipzig years. Among the latter group of designations should be included the terms *dolce* and *cantabile*. They too appear only in Bach's instrumental music: *dolce* invariably in works in 6/8 time and usually in conjunction with a *largo* or *adagio* indication (thus forming part of the movement heading),[37] *cantabile* either as a movement heading[38] or as an expression mark functioning virtually as a dynamic indication. In each of the two instances of the latter type uncovered so far, the *cantabile* indication reinforces a striking formal nuance. In the third movement of the Fifth Brandenburg Concerto at bar 148, the term calls attention to the radical transformation of the principal theme in the ripieno strings; in the final movement of the Gamba Sonata in G minor BWV 1029 at bars 19 and 24, it emphasizes the arrival and the contrasting lyric character of the secondary theme as well as the establishment of the new key of the relative major. *Affettuoso* and *grave* – like *dolce* and *cantabile* primarily character designations, although carrying obvious implications for the tempo – turn up in both vocal and instrumental works. *Affettuoso* appears for the first time

35 Mattheson 1739 p. 89 (English transl. p. 219).

36 Walther's definition of *con discretione* appears on p. 211 of the *Lexicon*. On p. 408 he describes *moderato* thus: 'mit Bescheidenheit, d.i. nicht zu geschwinde auch nicht gar zu langsam' ('with discretion, i.e. not too quick but also not at all too slow').

37 For example BWV 527.ii (*Adagio è dolce*), BWV 1030.ii and 1032.ii (*Largo e dolce*). The heading of the first movement of BWV 1015, however, reads simply *dolce*.

38 For example BWV 1015 .iii (*Cantabile ma un poco Adagio*) and BWV 769.iii (*cantabile* alone).

in the surviving printed libretto of the Mühlhausen cantata *Gott ist mein König* BWV 71 (as part of the movement heading, *Affettuoso e Larghetto*, of the chorus 'Du wollest dem Feinde')[39] and thereafter only in the headings of instrumental compositions: the third movement of the C minor Sonata for Violin and Continuo BWV 1024 (a work of doubtful authenticity)[40] and – its most familiar occurrence – the second movement of the Fifth Brandenburg Concerto.[41] The term *grave*, too, except for its isolated appearance in the Weimar cantata *Ich hatte viel Bekümmernis* BWV 21 (at the block-chord choral introduction to the final movement), is found only in instrumental compositions, in works belonging to virtually every medium: keyboard, organ, solo violin, ensemble.[42]

It is tempting to conclude this survey by presenting a grand tabulation in which all of Bach's tempo indications would be placed in their proper positions along the terminological continuum. Such a representation would of course take cognizance of the existence of synonyms: those that have been made explicit in the sources themselves through simultaneous usage, as well as those that can be plausibly inferred from linguistic equivalence (e.g. *adagio:lente, allegro:gay, presto:tres viste*, and so on). But depending on whether one adopts a 'strict' or 'free' approach to the identification of synonyms, i.e. to the separating or coupling of terms, there could be as many as twenty-two discrete points on the scale or as few as fourteen. For example: Should *largo ma non tanto* be treated as a synonym of *larghetto*, or should it be placed between *largo* and *larghetto*? Does *allegro moderato* belong between *moderato* and *un poc'allegro* or coupled with the latter? The heading *Adagio o vero Largo* (from the second movement of the C major Concerto for Two Harpsichords BWV 1061) would seem to mean something like 'between *adagio* and *largo*'. If that is so, then does it follow that the expression is synonymous with *adagio ma non tanto*, or does it mean something else? And, if it means something else, then does it signify a tempo faster or slower than *adagio ma non tanto*? In view of these and other uncertainties, it seems the better part of valor to refrain at this juncture from an all-too-ambitious peroration. We may hope and expect, though, that many of these uncertainties will be satisfactorily resolved in time as Bach's music is more closely examined and more extensively correlated with the terminological evidence than could be attempted here.

---

39 See the facsimile of the libretto in Neumann 1974, p. 385.
40 BWV 1024 is not included in *NBA* VI/1, although the reasons for its elimination are not stated in the critical report.
41 Whereas the heading of the movement in the autograph score and in the solo parts reads *Affettuoso*, the indication in the *tacet* but likewise autograph ripieno parts for this movement reads *Adagio tacet*. *Affettuoso*, then, appears in the Bach sources rather like *dolce*, i.e. in association with both *adagio* and *larghetto*.
42 See for example BWV 596.ii (*Pleno Grave*), BWV 182.i and BWV 826.i (*Grave Adagio*), and BWV 1003.i (*Grave* alone).

References

Besseler, H., 'Bach als Wegbereiter', *AfMw* 12 (1955), pp. 1–39

Bodky, E., *The Interpretation of Bach's Keyboard Works* (Cambridge, Mass., 1960)

Dürr, A. (ed.), *Johann Sebastian Bach: Messe in H-moll*, facs. edn with commentary (Kassel, 1965)

Eggebrecht, H. H., 'Walthers Musikalisches Lexikon in seinen terminologischen Partien', *AM* 29 (1957), pp. 10–27

Eppstein, H., *Studien über J. S. Bachs Sonaten für ein Melodieinstrument und obligates Cembalo* (Uppsala, 1966)

Kirkpatrick, R. (ed.), *Johann Sebastian Bach: Clavier-Büchlein vor Wilhelm Friedemann Bach*, facs. edn with preface (New Haven, 1959)

Löhlein, H.-H. (ed.), *Johann Sebastian Bach: Orgelbüchlein*, facs. edn with preface (Leipzig, 1981)

Mattheson, J., *Der vollkommene Capellmeister* (Hamburg, 1739; facs. edn Kassel, 1954); Engl. transl. by E. C. Harriss (Ann Arbor, Michigan, 1981)

Neumann, W. (ed.), *Johann Sebastian Bach: Quodlibet 1707*, facs. edn (Leipzig, 1973)

Neumann, W., *Sämtliche von Johann Sebastian Bach vertonte Texte* (Leipzig, 1974)

Schulze, H.-J. (ed.), *Johann Sebastian Bach: Brandenburgisches Konzert Nr. 5 D-Dur*, facs. edn of the parts, with preface (Leipzig, 1975)

Schluze, H.-J., 'Johann Sebastian Bachs Konzertbearbeitungen nach Vivaldi und Anderen: Studien- oder Auftragswerke?', *Deutsches Jahrbuch der Musikwissenschaft* 18 (1978), pp. 80–100

Schulze, H.-J. (ed.), *Johann Sebastian Bach: Messe in H-Moll*, facs. edn of the parts, with preface (Leipzig, 1983)

Stauffer, G. B., 'Über Bachs Orgelregistrierpraxis', *BJ* 67 (1981), pp. 91–105

Wackernagel, P. (ed.), *Johann Sebastian Bach: Brandenburgische Konzerte*, facs. edn with commentary (Leipzig, 1950)

Walther, J. G., *Musikalisches Lexikon oder musikalische Bibliothek* (Leipzig, 1732; facs. edn Kassel, 1953)

Bach, Handel, D. Scarlatti and the Toccata of the Late Baroque

GIORGIO PESTELLI

(Turin)

From the toccata of Alessandro Stradella (Rome, Biblioteca del Conservatorio S. Cecilia MS A/400)[1] to that of Ravel or of Alfredo Casella there is a strong idiomatic uniformity, a general agreement on the term 'toccata' (once something diverse and comprehensive): it is a keyboard piece, in a single fast movement, without a marked thematicism and without any interruption of the rhythm that would hinder the free flow of the *perpetuum mobile*.

The individual figures of this type of composition, considered in themselves (scales, broken chords, *passaggi* of various shapes), were already circulating in the toccatas of the sixteenth and seventeenth centuries in the fuller contexts of the multi-sectioned *versi* well known amongst organists: that is to say, short prelude-like passages of an improvisatory character, in free style though here and there fairly imitative. Very quickly this character seems to become identified with the term 'toccata', judging by a passage in Praetorius[2] which makes a derivation of the word from *Tangere, attingere* ('to touch') and mentions the Italian phrase 'toccate un poco' – in this 'un poco' there seems to be a hint of the 'diverting' prelude, without any particular structural importance. As for organ *versi*, another natural soil in which *toccatismo* ripened was that of ornamental diminutions ('toccatas are all diminutions', according to Girolamo Diruta).[3] Frescobaldi, in the first decades of the seventeenth century, offered a more original (and more often imitated) synthesis of these various threads, i.e. the measured toccata (product of ornamental diminutions in series of *partite* and variations – see for example Vars. 11 and 12 on the 'Aria della Romanesca' and Vars. 6 and 10 'Sopra la Monica') and the improvi-

---

1 Now published in E. F. McCrickard, *Alessandro Stradella: Instrumental Music*, Concentus Musicus: Veröffentlichungen der Musikgeschichtlichen Abteilung des Deutschen Historischen Instituts in Rom 5 (Cologne, 1980), pp. 255–8; see also W. Apel, *Geschichte der Orgel- und Klaviermusik bis 1700* (Kassel, 1967), p. 676, and M. Bristiger, '"Toccata" Alessandro Stradella Emendacja Tekstu', *Pagine* (Warsaw, 1972), pp. 52–7.

2 *Syntagmatis musici tomus tertius* (Wolfenbüttel, 1618).

3 'Le Toccate sono tutte Diminutioni': G. Diruta, *Il Transilvano. Dialogo sopra il vero modo di sonar organi et istromenti da penna, Prima parte* (Venice, 1593), I, p. 36.

277

satory toccata (open to all the promptings of one's own inventiveness and giving the toccata the texture of a mosaic). While in *partite* the use of *passaggi* and runs is regularized and made methodical, in toccatas it is free: the shaping of the figures almost never fits squarely, nor is the symmetry a matter of course even in short question-and-answer exchanges between hands. To the interval of a fifth a sixth will reply, to a pattern of eight notes the other voice will respond with six or four, while the fluctuating rhythm and the chromatic/diatonic alteration complicate and enrich the discourse: mature music full of allusion, token of a very ripe civilization that is distilled in an over-sensual rapture, at one with the ways of the *madrigali moderni* and the *affetti cantabili*.[4]

Of a different order, despite some parallels, is the toccata style running spasmodically through Scheidt's *Tabulatura nova*, to name the other *summa* of keyboard arts in the seventeenth century. Here ornamental diminution, the *coloratura* of the melody (as in *Versus* 12 of the chorale *Warum betrübst du dich, mein Herz?*),[5] assumes *passeggiata* figuration typical of the toccata; this becomes developed above all in the passages accompanied by the indication *imitatio violistica* (cf. *Versus* 9 of the chorale *Vater unser im Himmelreich*, or bars 190–5 of the *Fantasia super ut re mi fa sol fa*), which become very models of *perpetuum mobile*. At the end of Part I of the *Tabulatura*,[6] Scheidt explains the term *imitatio violistica* as a kind of variation that imitates the invention of 'those very skilled in this art' ('peritissimis eius artis') who 'know how to make their strings sing now more brilliantly, now more gently' ('qui modo clarius modo lenius fidibus norunt canere'); such variations, 'not unfamiliar to the skilled viol-players here in Germany' ('apud artifices Violistas etiam in ipsa Germania non infrequens'), are shown as a series of smooth semi-quavers, four at a time, with a semicircular slur above, alluding to bowed instruments. What drew Scheidt to transfer this kind of variation to the keyboard of organ or harpsichord was the 'concentus suavissimus & iucundissimus' produced by the naturalness of speech, by the fluent legato of a bowed instrument. This device also appears, not always with the heading *imitatio violistica*, in the *Toccata super 'In te, Domine, speravi'* in *Tabulatura* II, a toccata in several sections (as in Frescobaldi) in which counterpoint takes a large part and in which the toccata-like sections function as different variations and connecting episodes. With respect to Frescobaldi, however, one should note the more rational character of such *toccatismo* of Scheidt, something more regular both metrically and tonally; it lacks the rhythmic hesitancy typical of Frescobaldi,[7] and the phraseology is more primitive and predictable. Its quality can be described as *Motorik* (Apel's term),[8] a

---

4 See the preface 'To the reader' in Frescobaldi's first book of toccatas (cf. E. Darbellay, *Girolamo Frescobaldi: Il primo libro di toccate . . . 1615–37*, Monumenti Musicali Italiani 4 (Milan, 1977)), and F. Tasini, ' "Vocalità" strumentale della toccata frescobaldiana: un linguaggio tradito', *Musica/Realtà* 4/10 (1983), pp. 143–62.

5 See Apel, *Geschichte* (see note 1 above), p. 354.

6 In M. Seiffert, *Samuel Scheidts Tabulatura nova für Orgel und Clavier*, DDT 1/i (Leipzig, 1892), p. 84. See also Williams's essay in the present volume, especially Exx. 6 and 14.

7 Tasini, ' "Vocalità" strumentale' (see note 4 above), pp. 155–6.

8 Apel, *Geschichte* (see note 1 above), p. 676.

quality antithetical to the musical thought of Frescobaldi. But the 'rhythmic hesitancy' of Frescobaldi is the expression of a civilization at the peak of its maturity, something that can be perfected no further; on the other hand the *Motorik*, pure in its simplicity, will lend itself very manageably to the future developments of a new sensibility.

Connections between keyboard music and violin figures have often been drawn by scholars, for example by Apel[9] apropos Georg Muffat (the Allegro moderato of Toccata VIII in *Apparatus musico-organisticus*, 1690). But one of the most interesting cases is that of the 'Sonata' in Part II of Johann Kuhnau's *Clavier-Übung* (1692) – a piece well known amongst keyboardists because it has been mythicized in our time as a prototype of the sonata on German soil. More recently, however, it has been recognized (by Suzanne Clercx and W. S. Newman)[10] in its true context as an example of ensemble sonata transferred to keyboard. Kuhnau states clearly in his preface:[11]

Ich habe auch hinten eine Sonate aus dem B mit beygefüget, welche gleichfalls dem Lieb-haber anstehen wird. Denn warumb solte man auff dem Claviere nicht eben, wie auff andern Instrumenten, dergleichen Sachen tractiren können? da doch kein einziges Instrument dem Claviere die Präcedens an Vollkommenheit jemahls disputirlich gemachet hat.

I have also added a Sonata in B flat at the end, which should similarly please the music-lover. After all, why shouldn't one be able to compose such pieces for keyboard as well as for other instruments, the more so as no one [other] instrument has yet challenged the superiority of the keyboard?

What is particularly noteworthy in this composition is the *perpetuum mobile* of the first movement (Allegro), where there is already presented a combination of fugue and toccata (with a subject disappearing beneath passages of rhythmically uniform scales) whose technique will come to interest J. S. Bach. Kuhnau's preface conveys a feeling of novelty, the transferring to keyboard of something originating in another medium. The *perpetuum mobile* fugue can be seen exactly as a manifestation of the wish to cut a good figure on the keyboard, putting it at least on an equal footing with string music.

As regards the 'prototype' Toccata of Stradella, there are no clear indications that it derived from violin or ensemble music. Nevertheless, its figurations – arpeggios, scales, variously shaped figures – recur identically in broad sections of the works for string instruments by the same Stradella: see the conclusion of Sinfonia 11 for violin and basso continuo;[12] almost the whole of Sinfonia 12 (in the same key of A minor as the Toccata); the first movement of Sinfonia 15 for two violins and basso continuo: sections of Sinfonia 17, also for two violins; the opening of Sinfonia 22 for violin, cello and continuo. All are passages in which the

9 *Ibid.* p. 564.

10 See. S. Clercx, 'Johann Kuhnau et la Sonata', *Revue Musicale* 16 (1935), pp. 89–110, and W. S. Newman, *The Sonata in the Baroque Era* (Chapel Hill, N.C., 1966), p. 240.

11 See K. Päsler, *Johann Kuhnaus Klavierwerke*, *DDT* 1/iv (Leipzig, 1901), pp. 32–3; I give the passage as translated in Newman, *op. cit.*

12 The numbering of the sinfonias follows that of the edition cited in note 1 above.

toccatismo of the figuration has been greatly extended, and in one of them we see an example of a figure (Ex. 1) that passed into the later repertory – testimony to the persistence of common patterns.

Ex. 1.

(a) Stradella, Sinfonia 15

(b) Corelli, Op. VI No. 8, second movement

(c) Böhm, Praeludium in C

(d) A. Scarlatti, Toccata in D minor
(Naples Bib. Cons. MS 9481)

(e) Durante, Toccata (BL, Add. MS 14248)

(f) A. Scarlatti, Toccata VIII
(*Primo e secondo Libro*)

(g) D. Scarlatti, Sonata Kk 67

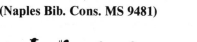
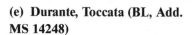

(h) J. S. Bach, Capriccio in E major BWV 993

However, more than in its motifs that recurred later and were conventionally associated with the toccata in general, Stradella's Toccata is interesting for its unifying fluency, for the drive in one direction that elements in a single tempo and developing in their own way can give it. In the complete, mixed-language toccata of Frescobaldi, the toccata-like elements of *passaggi*, diminutions and *colorature* were only one of the components. Some four decades after Frescobaldi, Stradella's Toccata and Kuhnau's Sonata testify to the encroachment and success of the *tutto passaggi* type, such as then became the best-known kind of toccata and in practice came to be identified with the term. What had been scattered moments, episodes of variable length, settled down into one single conception. In Stradella's Toccata the *perpetuum mobile* was already formed with its distinctive features; in the first years of the next century similar toccatas became common to the keyboard productions of Alessandro Scarlatti, Francesco Durante, various minor Neapolitan composers and Benedetto Marcello. During the last decades of the seventeenth century and the first of the eighteenth, between Rome, Naples and Venice, there was formed a centre for the 'crystallization' of the late-Baroque, harpsichord toccata, more and more with the intention of competing with the violinist's virtuosity even at the cost of reducing the genre to a banal and purely digital exercise. Being unable to outdo the violin in expressiveness, variety of accent and mode of attack, the harpsichord brought to the fore the advantages of its brilliant mechanism: constant rhythm, the *Motorik* character of the *perpetuum mobile*. Thus it can be argued that the *perpetuum mobile* toccata of the late Baroque is a keyboard equivalent, in the harpsichord's most flourishing period, of solo virtuosity on the violin. A new type is born: with it G. F. Handel, J. S. Bach and D. Scarlatti all come into contact in one way or another, and each of the three gives his own different response, according to the different directions given by taste, mentality and traditions.

According to the catalogue of the Biblioteca del Conservatorio of Genoa,[13] MS A 7b 63 Cass. contains five toccatas for harpsichord by Handel; however, in only one instance[14] is the attribution firm, that of the 'Toccata 3a' (ff. 97′–103′) which is ascribed to 'Hendel' by the same copyist who wrote the musical text. A later hand has then added 'Hendel' beside all the other toccatas, which on the contrary are the work of A. Scarlatti (nos. 2, 4 and 5) and Durante (no. 6). The 'Toccata 3a' of the Genoa MS has been published under the title 'Capriccio' in vol. 48 of the old Schott edition of the German Handel Society in a group of 'youthful pieces' ('aus der Jugendzeit');[15] but the piece has led to no discussion of Handel's contribution to toccata form,[16] leaving aside the negative summing-up by Valentin[17] that 'the part

13 See S. Pintacuda, *Biblioteca dell'Istituto Musicale 'Nicolò Paganini' di Genova* (Milano, 1966), pp. 421–2.

14 See G. Pestelli, 'Haendel e Alessandro Scarlatti, Problemi di attribuzione nel MS A 7b 63 Cass. della biblioteca del Conservatorio "Nicolò Paganini" di Genova', *Rivista Italiana di Musicologia* 7 (1972), pp. 103–14.

15 Information kindly given me by Mrs Kathleen Dale.

16 It was probably because of the heading *il Sassone* that the piece has been attributed to J. A. Hasse (thus A. Hughes-Hughes, *Catalogue of Manuscript Music in the British Museum*, III (London, 1909), p 114, for the MS Add. 14248). As well as the Genoa and London sources, the piece was copied in Naples Bibl. Cons. MS 71, 'Toccate per Cembalo di diversi Autori' (ff. 5′–6′), and in Cfm MS 30 H 15, 'Toccata Per Cembalo Del Sigr. Giorgio Federico Hendel' (pp. 1–7). I owe the knowledge of the latter source to information kindly given me by Prof. Keiichiro Watanabe, who also pointed out that A. H. Mann had made the following note in his catalogue (1893, p. 223): 'An unpublished Toccata, probably written during Handel's stay in Italy'. In this connection, Prof. Watanabe informs me that the paper of MS 30 H 15 carries a watermark with the name VITTORJ; the same watermark appears in Cfm MS 22 F 27, in which are copied two of Handel's trios (*Se tu non lasci amore* and *Quel fior che all'alba ride*), the first of which was completed in Naples on 12 July 1708. If not necessarily 'written during Handel's stay in Italy', the G major Toccata was certainly made widely known by Handel at Rome and Naples during his tour.

17 E. Valentin, *Die Entwicklung der Tokkata im 17. und 18. Jahrhundert (bis J. S. Bach)*, Universitas-Archiv 45 (Musikwissenschaftliche Abteilung 6) (Münster, 1930), pp. 129–30.

played by Handel in the toccata-composition of his period is suggested by some preludes in his early works (suites)' ('der Anteil Händels an der Tokkatenkomposition seiner Zeit wird durch einige Praeludien seiner Jugendkompositionen (Suiten) angegeben'). In fact, however, the confusion between the two composers in an Italian (probably Roman) source of the first decades of the eighteenth century is an interesting one in that it involves a common ground: that of the toccata–*perpetuum mobile* as practised (probably with teaching purposes in mind) by Alessandro Scarlatti. The piece unfolds over sixty-seven uninterrupted bars, prompted by a figure closely related to the opening idea of a capriccio by Zachow,[18] teacher of the young Handel in Halle (see Ex. 2). But the spirit of the 'Handelian' composition is

Ex. 2.

(a) Zachow, Capriccio

(b) Handel, 'Toccata in G major' HWV 571.ii

closer to that of A. Scarlatti's toccata than Zachow's binary capriccio, so that one can say that Handel has surpassed the Scarlatti model and left us here one of the best 'Italian' toccatas of the beginning of the eighteenth century.

That in the period of his style at Rome (1707, 1708) Handel performed in public as organist and harpsichordist is known through Mainwaring, according to whom familiarity with keyboard instruments was at that time 'his chief practice, and greatest mastery';[19] it is also from Mainwaring that we know of the celebrated trial of skill between Handel and Domenico Scarlatti at Ottoboni's court. However, it is in the repertory immediately preceding the sonatas of D. Scarlatti that one finds explicit signs of such a 'trial music': for example, Toccata VIII of A. Scarlatti in the *Primo e secondo libro di Toccate*, or the same composer's first toccata in Naples Bib. Cons. MS 9481.[20] Here are pages which have in them something of an infec-

18 See M. Seiffert, *Friedrich Wilhelm Zachow: Gesammelte Werke, DDT* 1/xxi-xxii (Leipzig, 1905), pp. 335–6. It has often been observed that this semiquaver line of Zachow's seems to paraphrase (or include within it) the same subject as that of J. S. Bach's Fugue in G minor BWV 542.ii.

19 Mainwaring p. 62.

20 See R. Gerlin and C. Sartori, *A Scarlatti: Primo e secondo Libro di Toccate*, I Classici Musicali Italiani 13 (Milan, 1943); see also G. Pestelli, 'Le toccate per strumento a tastiera di Alessandro Scarlatti nei manoscritti Napoletani', *Analecta Musicologica* 12 (1973), pp. 169–92.

tious enthusiasm and which beg, as it were, for the touch of an able performer to fill them with the warmth that, simply studied on paper, they seem not to possess. Also, without sharing Kirkpatrick's opinion[21] on the question of when 'the Scarlatti sonata' evolved, we should note the many signs that around 1710 Domenico's extraordinary creative development had not yet begun. From particular details in Mainwaring's testimony one can also have doubts about the 'trial'. Of Domenico, dead for three years, he writes that he is 'now living in Spain'; for him the most famous Scarlatti is Domenico; speaking of Handel's stay in Venice he speaks of 'Scarlatti' clearly meaning Domenico, while the first time he mentions Alessandro he takes the opportunity of giving in a note some details of information on 'the elder Scarlatti'. Is it possible that Mainwaring's memory, writing half a century later about these encounters in Rome, could have succumbed to a desire to measure his Handel by the Scarlatti who by 1760 (in England especially[22]) was the better known? It is only conjecture, but quite apart from there being no other evidence about the Handel/D. Scarlatti trial, it seems much more probable – on the grounds of the music's idiom and technique – that the meeting had been with Alessandro and had involved the toccata–*perpetuum mobile* species of virtuoso inspiration.

A further text deserves attention: a spacious toccata preserved in Naples Bib. Cons. MS 71 ff. 19'–23', a piece with no other title than 'Arpeggio' attributed to 'Federico Hendel Il Sassone'. After the 'Arpeggio' section (8 bars) there follow 50 bars of an [Allegro], 32 bars of a further [Allegro] in 12/8 time and lastly a [Fuga] of 88 bars. No other source is known for the piece, which cannot confidently be ascribed to Handel; and at various points (e.g. in the fugue bars 34–6, 80) the text gives both doubtful and evidently corrupt readings. But the general tone is more Handelian than not, and it is difficult otherwise to explain the imposing dimensions, the fullness of phrase and the very rich eloquence. The opening 'Arpeggio' can be compared with the 'Arpeggio' preceding the Suite in F sharp minor (BL autograph);[23] more relevant to our present discussion is the following [Allegro], a riotous filigree of virtuoso scales and of jagged dialogue between the two hands, in the style of an improvisation. But the fugue also – too long (88 bars) to be the work of an Italian composer? – includes frequent episodes in which fugue and toccata converge. Virtuosity enters the fugue, an area in which the contrapuntal potential of the keyboard gives it an advantage over the violin. Two passages from this toccata (still unpublished, as far as I know) may prompt the reader's recognition: Ex. 3. In the piece, firmly welded into one whole, it is generally easy to catch the 'public' flavour of trial music, an echo of the *accademia* around Cardinal Ottoboni that found in Handel an active participant, according to his first biographer. The Toccatas in G minor HWV 586 and A minor (doubtful) are the vestiges of Handel's contribution to the toccata, a contribution fuller than the extant material suggests.

---

21 *Domenico Scarlatti* (Princeton, N. J., 1953).
22 See R. Newton, 'The English Cult of Domenico Scarlatti', *ML* 20 (1939), pp. 138–56.
23 R. Steglich, 'Ein Arpeggio für Klavier von Haendel ("Handeliana")', *Musica* 10 (1956), pp. 613–14.

Ex. 3. Handel?, Toccata in A minor (Naples Bib. Cons. MS 71)

(a) [Allegro]

(b) [Fuga]

On the question of the combined forms – of fugue dissolved in toccata – J. S. Bach certainly had more to say. The crucial piece for the link with Italian toccatas is the Toccata in E minor BWV 914, or more correctly the fugue that is its last section. This piece, as I have shown in a previous essay,[24] is the elaborated version of a fugue probably by Benedetto Marcello contained in Naples Bib. Cons. MS 5327 (ff. 46′–49′) and is thus to be added to the list of pieces developing thematic material taken from Italian composers (the fugues on themes of Legrenzi BWV 574, of Corelli BWV 579, and of Albinoni BWV 950 and 951). Even if it is not possible to establish today from what source Bach got to know the Fugue in E minor preserved in the Naples MS, it is probable (given the similarity in date between BWV 914 and the MS concerned) that the channel was that through which the young Prince Johann Ernst fed his Italian interests in the first Weimar period (1708–13).

The authenticity of this fugue has not gone unquestioned: doubts were expressed (on the basis of the MS tradition) by Karl Grunski,[25] who observed how the composition appears to have been conceived as a toccata in its own right, one moreover transmitted in different readings, with variants and corrections.[26] The fugue in the Naples MS contains sixty-six bars, that in BWV 914 seventy-two; the subject is somewhat modified in the first half of the first bar (Ex. 4). The two fugues

Ex. 4.

(a) B. Marcello? Fuga in E minor (Naples Bib. Cons. MS 5327)

(b) BWV 914

24 'Un'altra rielaborazione bachiana: la Fuga della Toccata BWV 914', *Rivista Italiana di Musicologia* 16 (1981), pp. 40–4.

25 K. Grunski, 'Bachs Bearbeitungen und Umarbeitungen eigener und fremder Werke', *BJ* 9 (1912), pp. 79–80.

26 Grunski (*ibid.* p. 80) notes 'an old copy' of the fugue of BWV 914 with two closes, of which the shorter (by six bars) makes the fugue the same length as that in the Naples MS.

correspond as far as the first half of bar 8, then diverge as Bach adds a bar (bar 9) before the third entry of the subject. But certain parallels remain: groups of beats appear related between the two texts (compare, for example, bar 19 of the Naples fugue with BWV 914 bars 37 and 50), and minor events are treated in a similar way. The Naples fugue closes with five bars of 'arpeggio' (in the Handelian sense noted above) which lead the piece into E major; BWV 914 also closes in this key, though without 'arpeggio'. As for this last point, it looks as if Bach kept the original in mind but did not lay too much stress on original solutions or elaborate counterpoint, limiting himself to giving the piece greater thematic coherence, without the diversions given by the Naples fugue, whose one originality is its subject.

From a consideration of this fugue subject (Ex. 4) various points arise. It belongs to that type of idiomatic string music in which various intervals alternate around a note that remains as a pivot. The most famous example of this type is without doubt the fugue subject of the Toccata BWV 565, recently discussed by Peter Williams[27] in the light of its violinistic character and its 'oddities' as a piece of organ music. What Williams writes apropos BWV 565 – 'this is a fugue subject so unlike the normal thing that the composer could find nothing better to do for a countersubject than run around the subject in 6ths and 3rds' – could well be repeated to the letter for the Toccata BWV 914. Many scholars have noted with a certain amazement the naive simplicity of the fugue of BWV 914, from Spitta, who spoke of it as 'so leicht und schlank, wie eine holde Gestalt' ('so light and slender, like a lovely form'),[28] to Alberto Basso, who pointed out the anomaly of 'vistosi scorci a due voci' ('showy simplicities in two voices').[29] Naples MS 5327 confirms that the suspicions of its being too naive for Bach's normal practice were legitimate, insofar as BWV 914 is none other than a fugue in Italian style on an Italian subject.

The Naples piece's attribution to Benedetto Marcello is likely if not certain. In Marcello's keyboard sonatas examples of string idiom are not rare: the Presto of the first movement of Sonata 12[30] is difficult to consider as anything other than an imitation or transcription of string music; and it is interesting to note that the piece has been published separately in recent times under the title 'Toccata'.[31] The term 'toccata' reappears in Paris BN MS Vm[7] 5289 for the first movement of Sonata no. 4, a page on which there are many violin figures around a pivot: Ex. 5. We are thus

Ex. 5. B. Marcello, Sonata No. 4

27 'BWV 565: A Toccata in D minor for Organ by J. S. Bach?', *EM* 9 (1981), pp. 330–7.
28 Spitta I p. 437.
29 A. Basso, *Frau Musika. La vita e le opere di J. S. Bach, I (1685–1723)* (Turin, 1979), p. 506.
30 The numbering of Marcello's sonatas follows that in L. Sgrizzi and L. Bianconi, *B. Marcello: Sonates pour clavecin*, Le Pupitre 28 (Paris, 1971).
31 See W. S. Newman, 'The Keyboard Sonatas of Benedetto Marcello', *AM* 29 (1957), pp. 28–41.

still in the realm of that music in Italy around the turn of the century when violinistic gesture was transferred to the keyboard and given the kind of virtuosity associated with it: these are figures which in themselves produce 'an effect rather empty on the organ' (Williams)[32] but which are compensated for on the harpsichord by the effectiveness of *Motorik* treatment. The virtuoso character was to remain basic to this kind of figure even when it came to be transferred to the piano. To it Clementi gave over the whole of Study no. 36 and passages of no. 76 in *Gradus ad Parnassum*; and did not Beethoven make broad use of it in the first movement of the 'Kreutzer' Sonata, a work far from the spirit of the Viennese classics and turned in quite other directions (as frankly suggested by the unusual original title, 'Sonata scritta in uno stile [crossed out: brillante] molto concertante quasi come d'un concerto)'?

That Bach was not the originator of the fugue subject of BWV 914 can therefore lead to new discussions and researches of similarly toccata-like fugue subjects, whether in 'doubtful' works (Fugue in C minor BWV 909) and those seldom attributed to him (BWV 948), or in totally authentic works like the E minor Fugue BWV 855.ii (*WTC* Bk 1) and the A minor BWV 944. This last piece is preceded, in the principal sources, by ten bars of 'Arpeggio', like the Handel (?) in Naples MS 71, and the first bar of the subject (six bars long) transforms and amplifies a typical toccata incipit: Ex. 6. An extraordinary piece, BWV 944 unfolds without a break

Ex. 6.

(a) A. Scarlatti, Toccata VIII (*Primo e secondo Libro*)

(b) BWV 944

over 198 bars; the polyphony (within the limits of three voices) is rigorous; and the *violinismo* is totally transformed into idiomatic harpsichord writing. Perhaps it was the last word, in the Cöthen years, in a series of youthful experiments and essays in fusing the static quality of this fugue subject with the driving flow of a *perpetuum mobile*.

As in all aspects of Domenico Scarlatti's artistic personality, so with his involvement with the toccata: the received documents are scarce, contradictory and ambiguous. It does not follow that Domenico never used the term 'toccata' to indicate anything precise or different from his sonatas; certainly the toccatas of Alessandro were known to him, but with only a few exceptions[33] Domenico was content to use the term 'Sonata' for all that he wrote. Some Scarlatti sources, however, can lead

32 Williams, 'BWV 565' (see note 27 above), p. 335.
33 Kirkpatrick, *Domenico Scarlatti* (see note 21 above), p. 141.

one to make other suppositions: four sonatas in the copy Coimbra Bib. Univ. MS 58 are grouped under the title 'Toccata 10' (the Sonatas Kk 85, Kk 82 a fugue, Kk 78 a *Giga*, and Kk 94 a *Minuetto*). Thus at first sight the Coimbra Toccata looks more like an odd suite or *sonata da camera*; but it is possible to see that (leaving on one side the gigue and minuet) the first two pieces comprise the usual pairing of the Italian toccata and that of Alessandro Scarlatti in particular: Allegro–Fuga. In general terms one can say that the *perpetuum mobile* idea was not something that would meet the taste of Domenico Scarlatti. The various characteristics associated with him – the repeat of a particular (even slight) idea, the alliteration (beginning successive motifs on the same note), the ritornello elements, the use of whole empty bars separating passages in distant keys – are all features at the antipodes of the *perpetuum mobile*. We might say too that even the general tendency towards a piece full of effect (trial music) is removed from the spirit of intellectual sobriety that distinguishes the *arte scarlattiana*. However, there is a vast difference between the two Domenicos: the more famous Scarlatti (a model unto himself, from the *Trenta Esercizi* of 1738 onwards) and the young Scarlatti, mysterious composer of 'Italian' sonatas and uncertain (even not so well versed) follower of Corelli, Alessandro Scarlatti, Marcello and Vivaldi. To this nebulous composer belongs the Sonata Kk 85, which indeed is one of the very few that depart from the binary shape with central cadence to the dominant. It is thus a question here of the *perpetuum mobile*, if only of forty-nine bars, and one that can be easily exchanged for one of Alessandro's toccatas (e.g. the first of the collection *Primo e secondo Libro di Toccate*).

Thematic figures around a pivot note (see Ex. 5 above) also characterize the whole of the subject of Kk 82 which, like BWV 944, dilutes the fugue in a *perpetuum mobile* of 196 bars. It is not only a question of a single violinistic figure, however, but of the general climate. Kirkpatrick observed:

as in similar works of Benedetto Marcello and J. S. Bach, this brilliant harpsichord approximation of the string orchestra has much in common with the international style of the early eighteenth century which stems from Vivaldi's concertos.[34]

There remains the oddity of including a gigue (Kk 78) and a minuet (Kk 94) under the title 'Toccata'; but at least for the coupling of the first two sonatas the Coimbra manuscript's compiler could draw on some part of the manuscript tradition coming from Roman circles in the first decades of the eighteenth century. Other sonatas too that can be assigned to this phase of archaic composition make it possible to trace Domenico Scarlatti's involvement with the Italian toccata of the period: Kk 61 (a theme with thirteen variations, unique in the Scarlatti *oeuvre* and notable for the violinistic nature of various figurations), Kk 31, Kk 35 – all compositions that could be attributed to father Alessandro without difficulty. For all these sonatas one could repeat what Kirkpatrick said about Kk 85: they 'might easily represent the kind of music Scarlatti was playing when he competed with Handel at Cardinal Ottoboni's in Rome'.[35] But since the reservations voiced above about

34 *Ibid*. p. 151.   35 *Ibid*.

Mainwaring's account still seem valid, we prefer to leave Handel competing at the harpsichord with both the Scarlattis.

If at this point one leaves Domenico's early productions, joined directly as they are to Italian repertories, and plunges into the sea of hundreds of sonatas, for which no chronology over any length of time can yet be established from documents, the questions concerning toccatas become more difficult and subtle. It looks as if Domenico sometimes made references to the toccata as a historical idea or tradition, alluding to it in the course of his sonatas, rather in the manner of quotations. In a secondary source at Münster,[36] three further sonatas are called 'Toccata': Kk 104, 141 and 211. The Sonata Kk 141 has become *the* Toccata of Domenico Scarlatti since Longo called it so in his old edition, and occasionally one still sees it so called in concert programmes today. The chief element in the piece is the repeated note, transformed from an exercise into a sonorous invention which, somewhat more pungent, one finds again only in Ravel or Falla. The violinistic origins are now discarded and replaced by suggestions of another instrument (the guitar), and yet the writing is essentially that of harpsichord idiom; the *perpetuum mobile* is as it were mocked in its course by the unexpected halts at seven perfect cadences, two of which are emphasized by empty bars (bars 32, 123) followed by distant keys, themselves then discarded. The *Motorik* character is looked at from on high with an ironic distance, refined into total originality. The other two 'toccatas' in the Münster MS, Kk 104 and 211, have in common with Kk 141 only some more or less long passages of repeated notes; but it is the only link that can have led the copyist to use the term 'toccata', from which kind of music Kk 211 especially is distant, being an Andantino.

Allusions to the toccata are also traceable in what can be considered the turning-point in Domenico Scarlatti's artistic development: the volume of *Trenta Esercizi* (London, 1738) and those other sonatas which can be considered, through particular similarity of style, close to this collection. The Scarlatti of the *Esercizi* is an artist absolutely through and through, with a maximum economy of means, the very antithesis of the young 'Italian' Scarlatti. Already in the opening 'exercise' (Kk 1) the first bar fuses together into one figure the loose or free opening arpeggiations of Alessandro Scarlatti's toccatas. And this feeling of 'geometric synthesis' exercised on a protoplasm is given above all by the Sonata Kk 67; the point of departure here is the same as in Alessandro's Toccata VIII (the two incipits are in Ex. 1 above). Alessandro's toccata, once under way, forgets the point of departure and grows in passing across page after page until it encounters the final chord; in twenty-two bars, Domenico's sonata proceeds with a cartesian rigour so that all can be deduced from the first proposition, with no single note superfluous or replaceable – it is a toccata too, but it seems to have been designed in deliberate contrast to the *perpetuum mobile* type without head or tail. It is as if Domenico was saying, 'this is how to do it, with four notes and no more'. In the *Trenta Esercizi* there sur-

36 Münster, Bischöfliche Santini-Bibliothek MS 3964–3968; see Kirkpatrick, *Domenico Scarlatti*, p 399 and 141 (footnote).

face many details of this kind – types of openings that are like toccatas dried out and placed under glass, such as Kk 12, 24, 25 and 29. This last sonata gives more extended passages of this sort, all disguised in the costume of Harlequin in which only the cadence to the dominant (in the centre of the piece) gives any order; the *perpetuum mobile* is (as it were) refused as being too riotous, the *Motorik* is exhausted with a calculated strategy; and as for material taken from the virtuoso *violinismo*, it is interesting to note in bars 10–13 the same motif that many years later Brahms was to use in no. 3 of the set of *Paganini Variations*.

If the *Esercizi* already can be viewed from a broad perspective as an affirmation of rigorous high craftsmanship, how much more this impression is given spontaneously by the sonatas that followed, those works probably originating from the period around 1750 when the *style galant* was dominant! A work like the Sonata Kk 517 can be understood as refuting the *style galant*: in the face of the simplicity associated with this style it marks a return to a more austere and straightforward tradition, looking as if it is once again exploiting the spaciousness and feathery style of Alessandro Scarlatti's toccatas. There is no theme, no *galanteria* in the sense suggested by Mattheson,[37] only the central cadence of the sonata damming the flow of *perpetuum mobile* but without lessening the 'aggressive' feel typical of trial music. Even the pattern later called the 'Alberti bass' (though not here used as a bass) is drawn into the *Motorik* and ceases to be a mere support of the melody. And is not the Sonata Kk 427 (one of Domenico's most personal and idiomatic works) a bringing together of the essence of toccatas? Does not the indication *presto quanto sia possibbile* release the dynamic unity of *perpetuum mobile* on a more spectacular level, the anapaestic chords underlining it all like the click of castanets? Certainly the striking of an attitude of 'return to the toccata', as in Kk 517, is exceptional in the way it is sustained throughout the sonata (though something similar occurs in Kk 445). Often it is a case rather of referring to toccata-like elements in the opening bars of the sonata, as a form of beginning; one can see the Sonatas Kk 382, 418, 469, 486 and 545 in this sense, all probably composed in the late years of the composer's life. The phenomenon is rarer in the course of a sonata, but here too there are examples of toccata allusions in an episode that surfaces and disappears in the fluid stream. Limiting examples to those using one of the toccata-like ideas already mentioned (Ex. 1 above): the motif appears in Kk 414 as a coda figure (see Ex. 7), while bars 12–13 of Kk 427 can be considered a new way of employing the figure, varied and now modernized from its usual form (Ex. 8). In the Sonata Kk 551, a piece far from toccata-like in character, the motif is treated as a theme, again in the nature of a resolute coda (Ex. 9). These are all ways of applying a language that belongs to a musical culture by now fading into the middle of the eighteenth century, applied with an archness which goes from sophisticated quotation (the last examples above) to a more controversial standing out against the sheer simplicities of *style galant*.

As far as Domenico Scarlatti's rapport with the new currents of taste is con-

37 J. Mattheson, *Das neu-eröffnete Orchestre* (Hamburg, 1713), III, p. 137.

Ex. 7. Kk 414

Ex. 8. Kk 427

Ex. 9. Kk 551

cerned, extent documentation – usually so meagre for our Neapolitan – gives a hint worth keeping in mind: Dr Burney[38] recorded that M. L'Augier (a *connoisseur* who kept frequent salon in Vienna) had heard Scarlatti himself remark

that the music of Alberti, and of several other modern composers, did not in the execution, want a harpsichord, as it might be equally well, or perhaps, better expressed by any other instrument; but, as nature had given him ten fingers, and as his instrument had employment for them all, he saw no reason why he should not use them.

On D. Scarlatti's scanty sympathy toward the modern composers there is evidence too in his only letter to come down to us, that written in spring 1752 to the Duke of Huescar,[39] where we read incidental but convincing praise 'for the true law of writing in counterpoint' ('della vera legge di scrivere in contrappunto'), something for which Scarlatti feels that few of those 'moderni teatristi compositori' whom he observes around him can be praised. Now as far as it concerns the harpsichord, the 'moderni teatristi compositori' were those masters of the *style galant*. The virtuoso idea of the toccata may well have been for Scarlatti something like counterpoint for

38 See P. A. Scholes (ed.), *Dr Burney's Musical Tours in Europe* (London, 1959), II, p. 87.
39 See the reproduction in Kirkpatrick, *Domenico Scarlatti* (see note 21 above), fig. 39 and pp. 120–1.

Bach, in connection with which he was accused of lacking naturalness. One does not know if Domenico found himself engaged in an argument of the Birnbaum–Scheibe kind, but in a similar way the sonatas of Scarlatti do sometimes involve an advanced mastery of the keyboard such as to make them unique and removed from the contemporary scene. *Style galant* cannot have been unknown to him, even in his Spanish isolation, and elements in the Sonatas Kk 300, 192 and 251 speak for this; but the occasional surfacing of *toccatismo* may indicate a denial of, or at best only a minimal interest in, those gaudier aspects of the simple style advocated by the new taste.

It seems likely that in their work all three of the composers born in 1685 came across the genus *perpetuum mobile*, species *Motorik*, a late fruit of the toccata tradition, produced by the stimulus to imitate brilliant Italian violin virtuosity of the seventeenth and eighteenth centuries. Handel takes it up as only he can, striving to achieve in his characteristic way the highest possible degree of efficiency; J. S. Bach joins it to the principle of fugue, achieving in such works as BWV 944 an unrepeatable amalgam of the materials employed; Domenico Scarlatti, for whom it is more a matter of 'quotation', revives it in a fragmentary way as one of the kinds of vocabulary for his kaleidoscopic sonata. All three aim for sounds more or less removed from their period but all three transformed them by enriching the expressive means, according to the craftsmanship and artistry of each of them.

Translated by editor

Does 'Well-Tempered' Mean 'Equal-Tempered'?

RUDOLF RASCH

(Utrecht)

Introduction

One of the unique aspects of Bach's *Wohltemperirtes Clavier* (*WTC*) is the reference to tuning contained in the term *wohltemperirt*. From the second half of the eighteenth century well into the middle years of the twentieth century, it was generally agreed that *wohltemperirt* meant 'equal-tempered'. The *WTC* was considered to be one of the first examples of what could be done with the tonal system when all twelve semitones were of equal size, so that all keys sounded the same. Only Barbour (1947 p. 69, and 1951 p. 195) was a little less sure about the unquestioning identification of 'well-tempered' with 'equal-tempered'. He remarked that since Neidhardt (1706) the Germans had used the term *gleichschwebend* ('equal-beating') to mean 'equal-tempered', and that *Das Wohltemperirte Clavier* might possibly been better translated as 'The Well-Tuned Piano'. He explained 'well-tempered' as a term implying that all keys can be played, with the common ones (the 'central' or 'diatonic' keys, with only a few or no sharps or flats) sounding better than the uncommon ones (the 'chromatic' or 'peripheral' keys, with many sharps or flats). All this was prompted by a quotation from the *Hodegus curiosus* of Werckmeister (1687).

The last two decades have seen in the practice of early music the rise of unequal temperaments and also of several 'Bach tunings'. Since the *WTC* is the work of Bach's in which the tuning question is most pressing, it is no wonder that many recent authors have focused their attention on this work. Three authors will be singled out for special consideration: Kelletat (1960, 1967), Kellner (1976–1980), Barnes (1979), and Billeter (1979). Their unequal Bach temperaments have been constructed on rather diverse arguments, but agree with each other surprisingly well. They follow the leads of Barbour. The central, diatonic fifths (between naturals) are a little too small; the peripheral, chromatic fifths (between raised keys) are pure. Because of this, the central keys sound better than the peripheral ones, although all of them are tolerable. In fact, the peripheral keys sound Pythagorean.

293

This article largely falls into two halves. In the first half, an investigation is made of whether German music theory of the beginning of the eighteenth century might give us the meaning of the term *wohltemperirt* or might say something about playing in all keys. The second half of this article will then be devoted to an analysis of the modern unequal Bach tunings, particularly to finding out in which aspects they could be thought to go wrong. Views from the second half of the eighteenth century on Bach's own tuning procedure are also reviewed.

Werckmeister

Andreas Werckmeister is the author of a rather extensive list of texts concerned with music theory; in nine of his works (1681, 1687, 1691, 1697, two works of 1698, 1702, 1705, 1707) tuning problems are discussed, and in five of these works (1681, 1687, 1691, *Anmerckungen* 1698, 1707) the term *wohltemperirt* can be found. The first encounter with the concept of *wohl temperiren* is on the title-page of his first printed work, the *Orgel-Probe* of 1681. The subtitle contains the following clause:

Unterricht wie durch Anweiss und Hülffe des Monochordi ein Clavier wohl zu temperiren und zu stimmen sey, damit man nach heutiger Manier alle modos fictos in einer erträglichen und angenehmen harmoni vernehme.

Instruction how, with the help of the monochord, to tune and temper a keyboard well so that in accordance with contemporary practice all *modi ficti* can be heard in a tolerable and agreeable way.

Indeed, on pp. 26–40 there is a chapter 'Von der Temperatur und Stimmung' ('On temperament and tuning'). Werckmeister rejects the then current meantone tuning, and also the use of split upper keys or *subsemitonia*. His rejection of meantone tuning is based on the uselessness of the wolf intervals (fifths and thirds), and that of the *subsemitonia* on the confusions arising in keyboard-playing technique. He provides two alternative tunings that make use of twelve tones per octave (without *subsemitonia*) and do not possess wolf intervals. That means that all tonalities can be performed on a keyboard tuned this way. These two tunings return ten years later in his *Musicalische Temperatur* (1691), as numbers III and IV. The first of these (III) is recommended for a *Clavier fictè* (peripheral keys), the second one (IV) for the *regular-Modi* (central keys). It is important to note that a single tuning allowing all keys to be playable without retuning is not being sought. 'Werckmeister III' is now considered to be Werckmeister's most important and most useful contribution to the repertoire of tunings. It is seen as a tuning which makes all keys possible but favours the central keys. Today, a so-called 'Werckmeister tuning' is to be equated with Werckmeister III, and already in the eighteenth century this tuning was quoted as *Werckmeisterische Temperatur* (Sorge 1748, Marpurg 1776, Türk 1808). This is not quite in accordance with Werckmeister's own views on his tunings, however, for he assigned his no. III to the *peripheral* keys. For the common keys no. IV was to be preferred, a tuning that is much less satisfactory in modern perspective. However, it is this tuning that is accompanied by a tuning instruction in both the 1681 and 1691 books, and it is the one applied to the newly built organ of the court church of Quedlinburg by Zacharias Thayssner in 1677 (Werckmeister 1681 p. 36). In the text of the *Orgel-Probe* the term *wohltemperirt* does not occur.

Werckmeister's second book is entitled *Musicae mathematicae hodegus curiosus* (1687) and deals with 'mathematical music' or 'musical mathematics'; chapter 40 (pp. 116–20) concerns the monochord and temperament. The term *wohltemperirt* is used twice, to designate a tuning in which all tonalities can be performed: firstly,

Derhalben sind diese Transpositiones fictae nicht schlechter Dings zu verwerffen, bevorab, wenn unser Clavier wol temperiret ist, wenn wir nur eine gewisse Ordnung dabey halten . . .

Therefore these transpositions to the peripheral keys need not simply be disregarded beforehand if our keyboard is well tempered, i.e. if only we keep to one particular arrangement . . .

and secondly,

Wenn wir hingegen ein wohl temperirtes Clavier haben, können wir aus jeglichen Clave alle Modos haben . . .

When however we have a well-tempered keyboard, we can have all tonalities [starting out] from each finger-key [as the tonic].

The *Hodegus* does not describe the tuning further.

Werckmeister's *Musicalische Temperatur* of 1691 is his only work devoted entirely to problems of tuning and temperament. In fact, it is a large-scale elaboration of the chapter on tuning in the *Orgel-Probe* of 1681. Werckmeister repeats to a large extent his views and positions of 1681, including the tunings described there. The term *wohltemperirt* can be found twice. First, in the title, in which much of the subtitle of 1681 has been included:

Musicalische Temperatur, Oder deutlicher und warer Mathematischer Unterricht, Wie man durch Anweisung des Monochordi Ein Clavier, sonderlich die Orgel-Wercke, Positive, Regale, Spinetten, und dergleichen wol temperirt stimmen könne, damit man nach heutiger manier alle Modi ficti in einer angenehm- und erträglichen Harmonia mögen vernommen werden.

Musical temperament, or clear and true mathematical instruction how (with the help of the monochord) to tune a keyboard well-tempered, especially organs, positives, regals, spinets, etc., so that, in accordance with present practice, all *modi ficti* can be heard in an agreeable and tolerable harmony.

Secondly, *wohltemperirt* appears on p. 61, when the possibility of enharmonic use of tones is being discussed. This possibility, he says, also holds for the augmented fourth:

Vom h. bisz ins f. war vorhin eine quarta, kan aber in scalâ ficta eine quinta werden, als h a gis fis f, wenn nun ein Clavier wohl temperirt ist . . .

From B to F the interval used to be seen as a fourth; but in a *scala ficta* it can also be a fifth (such as B A G♯ F♯ E♯) if the keyboard is well tempered.

The term *wohltemperirt* occurs here in a rather loose way, not as a technical term with strict meaning. The idea of well-temperedness is also expressed by Werck-meister in a number of alternative wordings like *gute Temperatur* (good tempera-ment) and *richtige Temperatur* (right temperament). It denotes a tuning without any of the disturbing wolf intervals and without any *subsemitonia*: one in which all tonalities can be performed. There is also a not very explicit reference to equal tem-perament in the *Musicalische Temperatur* (p. 75):

denn wenn man sich an keinen Modum in Stimmen will binden lassen, so kan man nur alle Tertias majores in die Höhe schweben lassen, als: Wann C–G. G–d. D–A. A–e. so weit und nicht weiter herunter gelassen, dass C und e eine in die Höhe schwebende Tertiam geben, so viel das Gehör vertragen kan, so ists schon gut. Weiter wird die quinta E–H. wieder so hoch gebracht, dass G und H eine in die höhe schwebende Tertiam geben, so viel das Gehör ertra-gen kan, von H ins fis, wird es wieder also gemachet, dass fis vom d scharff in die Höhe schwebet, und also durchs gantze clavier.

When in tuning one wants not to be bound to one single key, all one can do is allow all the major thirds to beat sharp: i.e., when C–G, G–D, D–A, and A–E have been flattened so far (but no further) that C–E gives as sharp a third as our hearing can tolerate, then it has been well done. Further, the fifth E–B is set up in such a way that G–B gives as sharp a third as our ears can tolerate, and the fifth B–F♯ is done the same way so that F♯ beats sharp to the D; and so on through the whole keyboard.

If the last phrase is meant literally, there is no other explanation of this description than equal temperament. It is interesting to note that this procedure is especially recommended when no particular key is to be favoured in the tuning.

Tuning is discussed again in chapters 9–11 (pp. 26–39) of the *Hypomnemata musica* of 1697. Equal temperament is mentioned explicitly, but rejected at the same time:

Wer aber eine Temperatur verlanget da alle consonantien in einer Gleichheit stehen der lasse alle quinten $\frac{1}{12}$ eines commatis herunter schweben, so werden die tertiae majores $\frac{2}{3}$ die Minores $\frac{3}{4}$ commatis schweben . . . Bissher habe ich dieser Meinung nicht können Beyfall geben, weil ich lieber die Diatonischen claves reiner halten wollen, damit dasselbe genus, welches am meisten gebrauchet wird, desto reiner behalten würde.

However, anyone who seeks a temperament in which all consonant intervals are equal must take care that all fifths beat $\frac{1}{12}$ of a comma flat, so that all major thirds beat $\frac{2}{3}$ of a comma and the minor third $\frac{3}{4}$ of a comma . . . So far I have not been able to agree with this view, because I prefer to keep the diatonic notes purer so that the diatonic keys which are used the most would be kept that much purer.

In this instance the requirement of a tuning that favours the central tonalities has been stated explicitly. In the *Hypomnemata* the term *wohltemperirt* does not occur. No specific tunings other than equal temperament are described or men-tioned in this work. Werckmeister did not have a single term for equal tempera-ment. Instead he used terms referring to the commata, an indirect description that returns in later publications (*Anmerckungen* 1698, 1702, 1707).

Of prime importance for the present discussion is Werckmeister's basso-continuo instruction book *Die nothwendigsten Anmerckungen* (1698). This work includes a short appendix (pp. 61–70) entitled 'Kurtzer Unterricht und Zugabe, wie man ein Clavier stimmen und wohl temperiren könne' 'Short instruction and appendix how to tune and well-temper a keyboard'. Two tunings are mentioned. One is equal temperament; the other is an unequal temperament. Equal temperament is asked for when all the twelve major and minor keys play their parts. With unequal temperament it is possible to favour the central keys, and this is the procedure asked for when these keys occur most often:

Wir wollen aber . . . das Werck also beschreiben, dass das Genus Diatonico-Chromaticum, welches heutiges Tages am meisten gebrauchet am reinesten bleiben.

We will, however, describe the procedure in such a way that the keys most commonly used today (the diatonic-chromatic genre) are the purest ones.

By 'diatonic' and 'chromatic' keys he means the keys up to and including (let us say) four sharps or flats in the key signature. The unequal temperament is described by way of a tuning instruction rather than an exact theoretical description. The tuning instruction is as follows (pp. 64–6; see Ex. 1):

3	C–G beating a little downward
4	G–D beating a little downward
6	D–A beating a little downward
8–9	C–E test: tolerable, not too sharp
11	E–B beating a little downward
12	G–B test: beating a little upward, as much as is tolerable
13	G–B–D test: tolerable
14	B–F♯ beating a little downward
16–17	D–F♯ test: beating upward
18	F♯–C♯ beating a little upward
19	A–C♯ test: beating upward
21	C♯–G♯ test: almost pure
22	E–G♯ test: a little sharp
23	G♯–D♯ is allowed to beat a little upward
24	B–D♯ test: tolerable
25	D♯–G test: tolerable
27	D♯–B♭ can also beat a little upward
28	B♭–D test: tolerable
29	B♭–F again beating a little upward, or pure

In this tuning, eight fifths in a row (C – G♯) must be tuned a little flat. Two fifths (G♯–D♯ = E♭–B♭) are a little sharp. The fifth B♭–F may be a little sharp, or pure. The closing fifth, F–C, has not been specified, nor is the extent of the tempering indicated. A range of temperings, from $\frac{1}{8}$ to $\frac{1}{12}$ part of a (diatonic) comma, is mentioned in a later paragraph (p. 69).

The information given is hard to fit into a theoretically compatible tuning scheme. If all flat fifths from F–C to C♯–G♯ are tempered by $\frac{1}{8}$ comma, the sum of these temperings is $-\frac{9}{8}$ ditonic comma. From this, $-\frac{1}{8}$ comma must be compensated for by a positive tempering of one or more fifths, i.e. fifths that are a little too large. This can be done either by tuning G♯–D♯–B♭–F $\frac{1}{24}$ comma too large, or by tuning G♯–D♯–B♭ $\frac{1}{16}$ comma too large and B♭–F pure. In any case, the result is a

Ex. 1. The order in which the intervals are tuned, according to Werckmeister's *Anmerckungen* 1698 (P = *Probe*, i.e. the interval or chord one should test at that point)

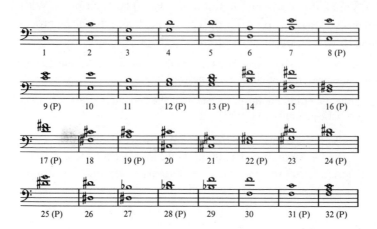

tuning that is only slightly unequal, differing much less from equal temperament than any of Werckmeister's temperaments of 1681 and 1691.

In 1698, an enlarged and corrected reprint of the *Orgel-Probe* of 1681 was also issued, as *Erweiterte und verbesserte Orgel-Probe*. In the final chapter (32), organ tuning is discussed. The explicit descriptions of tuning in the 1681 editions are not repeated, and instead only general remarks are made. The term *wohltemperirt* does not occur.

The tuning question is treated again in the *Harmonologia musica* of 1702, mostly in section 27 (pp. 15–18). This section is a direct argument for equal temperament, based on the possibilities of unlimited transposition and enharmonic changes. It is emphasized that the tempering of consonant intervals in equal temperament just follows the order of sensitivity to tempering of the intervals, but in the opposite direction. The fifth is the most vulnerable interval; it is tempered only a little. The major and minor thirds are less sensitive to tempering and are accordingly tempered more strongly. The word *wohltemperirt* does not enter into the discussion.

In *Organum Gruningense* (1705), Werckmeister describes in detail the repairs and alterations carried out on the organ of the Schloss-Kirche of Gröningen, near Halberstadt. One of the alterations concerned the tuning of the instrument (sections 50–64). Meantone tuning is declared inappropriate for the demands of recent music, and although its alternative is not clearly stated, it must be equal temperament. This is clear from the following analogy, in which a full glass of pure wine must be understood as a pure fifth and the water added to it as the tempering (sections 63–4):

Ich habe 12. Maass Wein, und 12. Löffel Wasser, wenn ich denn in ein jedes Maass Wein, einen Löffel voll Wasser giesse, so werde ich das Wasser wenig, oder gar nicht schmecken,

wolte ich aber alle zwölff Löffel voll Wasser in ein Maass Wein giessen, so würde das Wasser
mercklich geschmecket werden, und keine gute Temperatur seyn: Dieser Krug würde gegen
die andern nicht accordiren.

Nichts anders ist es mit den Quinten . . .

I have twelve glasses of wine, and twelve spoonfuls of water. If I pour one spoonful of water
into each glass of wine, I shall not taste the water, or only a little. If, however, I should pour
all twelve spoonfuls of water into one glass of wine, then the water would be tasted clearly
and would be no good temperament: this draught would not agree with the others.

It is the same with the fifths.

The comparison between tuning and blending is interesting, since the term *Temperatur* is derived from the Italian verb *temperare*, which can mean to mix paints.

Werckmeister's last opus is entitled *Musicalische Paradoxal-Discourse* and was
published after his death, in 1707. It is a rather unsystematical volume in which alle-
gorical interpretations of musical concepts play central parts. The subject of tuning
is treated, together with transposition, mostly in chapters 10–14 (pp. 48–80) and
23–4 (pp. 104–14). Werckmeister's position is the same as in the *Harmonologia* of
1702: because transposition without limits as well as enharmonic changes must be
possible, equal temperament is generally required. This requirement is reinforced
by comparing equal temperament with true Christianity (p. 110):

Wir schreiten weiter, und wissen, wenn die Temperatur also eingerichtet wird, das alle
Quinten $\frac{1}{12}$ Commat: . . . schweben, und ein accurates Ohr dieselbe auch zum Stande zubrin-
gen, und zustimmen weiss, so dann gewiss ein wohl temperirte Harmonia, durch den gantzen
Circul und durch alle Claves sich finden wird. Welches dann ein Vorbild seyn kan, wie alle
fromme, und wohl temperirte Menschen, mit Gott in stets währender gleicher, und ewiger
Harmonia leben, und jubiliren werden.

We go further, and know that if the temperament is settled in such a way that all fifths are
tempered . . . by $\frac{1}{12}$ of a comma, and carried out and tuned by an accurate ear, then there will
surely be a well-tempered harmony through the entire circle of fifths and throughout the keyboard. Which can be an example of how all pious and well-tempered people will live and
rejoice in a consistent, equal and eternal harmony with God.

The *unrichtige Temperatur* is compared to false Christianity. On pp. 111–14 Werckmeister apologizes for his earlier propaganda for unequal temperaments. He states
that he has already mentioned the shortcomings of the old meantone tuning and
that his unequal tunings have paved the way for equal temperament. Equal temperament had been on his mind from about thirty years earlier – so from about
1675 – ever since he had read Harsdörffer's *Philosophische Erquickstunden* (1651,
1653). His monochord in the *Musicalische Temperatur* could have been extended to
equal temperament by dividing the comma distances in twelve parts. He refers to
Neidhardt, who (1706) indeed carried out such a monochord with equal temperament.

Three stages of development in Werckmeister's views can be discerned:

In his early writings (1681–1691) Werckmeister discussed explicitly only unequal
temperaments. He described two of them (1691 nos. III and IV) in detail, of which

one (no. III) is for the peripheral keys (many sharps or flats), the other one (no. IV) for the central keys (few sharps or flats).

In his middle writings (1697–1698) both equal and unequal temperaments are discussed. Equal temperament is judged best for that exceptional circumstance in which all keys are of equal importance. Unequal temperament is judged preferable for the common condition in which the central keys are the prevailing ones.

In his later writings (1702–1707) equal temperament is brought to the fore as the only reasonable thing, because of the unrestricted possibilities for transposition and enharmonic changes. The term *wohltemperirt* is nowhere defined as a technical term; more important still, it occurs never as a single word, but always as a verb with qualification. If it is given a specific meaning, it must be something like 'appropriate tuning'. But what is appropriate in tuning is something that depends on the music in hand.

Neidhardt, Mattheson, Sorge

The preference for equal temperament evident in Werckmeister's later work is also to be found in the writings of the most influential German music theorists of the eighteenth century: Neidhardt, Mattheson, Sorge and Marpurg. Werckmeister's position in his middle writings – that one needs equal temperament if all keys are needed, unequal temperament if the common keys are predominant – is treated as a reasonable alternative in the writings of all but the last of these authors.

In his *Beste und leichteste Temperatur* (1706) Johann Georg Neidhardt describes only equal temperament, while in the *Sectio canonis harmonici* (1724) some nuances are added. He describes four numbered tunings, of which the first one is plainly unequal, the second one less outspokenly so, the third one only slightly; his fourth system is equal temperament. The application of these tunings is explained with a metaphor (p. 20):

Meines Erachten schickt sich die Erste, mehrentheils, am besten vor ein Dorff, die Andre vor eine kleine Stadt, die Dritte vor eine grosse, und die Vierdte vor den Hof.

In my opinion, the first tuning is mostly fit for a village, the second for a town, the third for a city, and the fourth for the court.

This must be read as a metaphor for the musical continuum from traditional or archaic (village) to progressive or avant-garde music (court). In the *Gäntzlich erschöpfte mathemathische Abtheilungen* (1732) Neidhardt repeats his views with some changes in detail.

In his writings on music theory Johann Mattheson was a tireless propagandist for equal temperament and contributed to its application a set of figured-bass examples in all twenty-four keys (1719, 1731). He credited equal temperament equally to Werckmeister and Neidhardt (1725 p. 162). In his *Critica musica, Tomus secundus* (1725), he discussed the tunings that were applied by the organ-builders Silbermann and Wender (p. 235):

Diese Meister . . . haben sich doch zu dergleichen Neidhardtischen exacten Temperatur nicht verstehen wollen; sondern weil sie wissen, dass bey Kirchen-Musiquen die diatonische Modi, und nächst diesen die transponirten, welche nicht gar zu tieff in das Chroma fallen, die vexatissimi Martyres sein . . . so haben sie noch immer auf das diatonicum Genus meistens regardiret.

These masters have not been converted yet to Neidhardt's exact [= equal] temperament, since they know that in church music the diatonic keys first, and then the transposed keys with not too many sharps or flats, are those most severely made to suffer [i.e. most often used]. They have therefore mostly kept diatonic keys in mind.

Georg Andreas Sorge discussed equal temperament in many of his writings. He also composed a set of pieces in all keys, the *Clavier-Übung* (1739–42), prior to his theoretical writings, which began to appear in the 1740s. The relation between the use of all twenty-four keys and the application of equal temperament is most overtly stated in the following sentence from his *Vorgemach der musicalischen Composition, Ander Theil* (1746 p. 131):

Bey heutiger musicalischer Praxi, da man aus allen Ton-arten setzet und spielet, ist ohnstreitig die gleichschwebende Temperatur die beste, denn sie stellet alle 24. Ton-Arten gut und brauchbar dar.

In present musical practice, in which all keys are used in composition and performance, equal temperament is without question the best, for it makes all twenty-four keys good and useful.

Sorge deserves our attention for a second reason as well, namely because he uses the term *wohltemperirt* in one of his writings. It is in his *Zuverlässige Anweisung Claviere und Orgel zu temperiren und zu stimmen* (1758), which includes a section entitled 'Methode die Orgeln wohl temperirt zu stimmen' (p. 17: 'Method of tuning organs well-tempered'). This section is not essentially different from Werckmeister's instructions for well-tempered tuning in his *Anmerckungen* (1698). Two possibilities are given: first, the *rational-gleiche Temperatur* ('the rational-equal temperament', Sorge's name for equal temperament); secondly, a good unequal temperament, of which one example is described by Sorge on p. 20 of his book. It is a tuning that strongly recalls Neidhardt's unequal temperaments, especially in its use of $\frac{1}{6}$ and $\frac{1}{12}$ parts of a comma as tempering units. Like Werckmeister, Sorge writes *wohltemperirt* never as a single word but rather as a compound, and without a technical definition.

Bach

What is the meaning of the term *wohltemperirt* in the title of Bach's collection? If the use of the word in the theoretical works of Werckmeister and Sorge is followed, it must mean 'appropriately tuned'. The appropriate tuning for a work which progresses through all twenty-four keys can be derived from the given statements by Werckmeister, Neidhardt, Mattheson, and Sorge: equal temperament. It is interesting to note that these authors disagree vehemently on numerous topics but are surprisingly unanimous as to the application of equal temperament. However, one may not say that *wohltemperirt* equals 'equal-tempered' but rather that *wohltemperirt*, in the context of music requiring all keys to be playable, is the equivalent of 'equal-tempered'.

In the second half of the eighteenth century a number of statements were made about Bach's tuning procedures. First, the Obituary (*Dok* III p. 88):

Die Clavicymbale wusste er, in der Stimmung, so rein und richtig zu temperiren, dass alle Tonarten schön und gefällig klangen. Er wusste, von keinen Tonarten, die man, wegen unreiner Stimmung, hatte vermeiden müssen.

He knew how to tune and temper harpsichords so pure and right that all keys sounded beautiful and fine. He did not know of any key that had to be avoided because of impure tuning.

Secondly, Friedrich Wilhelm Marpurg says in his *Versuch über die musikalische Temperatur* (1776 p. 213) that he had learnt about Bach's tuning from Bach's pupil Kirnberger, but that this was quite different from what Kirnberger had described in his *Kunst des reinen Satzes* of 1771 (*Dok* III p. 304):

Der Hr. Kirnberger selbst hat mir und andern mehrmahl erzählet, wie der berühmte Joh. Seb. Bach ihm, währender Zeit seines von demselben genossnen musikalischen Unterrichts, die Stimmung seines Claviers übertragen, und wie diese Meister ausdrücklich von ihm verlanget, alle grosse Terzen scharf zu machen. In einer Temperatur, wo alle grosse Terzen etwas scharf, d.i. wo sie alle über sich schweben sollen, kan unmöglich eine reine grosse Terz statt finden, und sobald keine reine Terz statt findet, so ist auch keine um 81:80 erhöhte grosse Terz möglich. Der Hr. Capellmeister Joh. Seb. Bach, welcher nicht ein durch einen bösen Calcul verdorbnes Ohr hatte, musste also emfinden haben, dass eine um 81:80 erhöhte grosse Terz ein abscheuliches Intervall ist. Warum hatte derselbe wohl seine aus allen 24 Tönen gesetzte Präludien und Fugen die Kunst der Temperatur betitelt?

Several times Kirnberger himself told me and others how the famous J. S. Bach (during the time of the former's musical instruction under the latter) made over to him the tuning of his keyboard, and how that master expressly desired him to make all major thirds sharp. In a tuning with all major thirds sharp, no pure major third can occur, but as soon as no pure major thirds are found, so too no major third can be found [which is] a comma ($\frac{81}{80}$) sharp. J. S. Bach, whose hearing was not impaired by bad arithmetic, must have heard that a major third a comma sharp is a disgusting interval. Why else did he entitle his collection of preludes and fugues in all twenty-four keys the Art of Temperament?

Pure and comma-raised major thirds occur in Kirnberger's own tunings, described in 1771.

Thirdly, Carl Philipp Emanuel Bach informed Johann Nikolaus Forkel for the latter's book about Bach, in an undated letter (1774? see *Dok* III p. 285), about Bach's tuning procedures:

Das reine Stimmen seiner Instrumente so wohl, als des ganzen Orchestres war sein vornehmstes Augenmerck. Niemand konnte ihm seine Instrumente zu Dancke stimmen und bekielen. Er that alles selbst.

The pure tuning of his instruments as well as of the whole orchestra was his most important aim. Nobody could have any thanks for tuning and quilling his instruments for him. He did everything himself.

302

Fourthly, Forkel used this and other information in his Bach biography of 1802 (p. 17) in the following way:

Seinen Flügel konnte ihm Niemand zu Danck bekielen; er that es stets selbst. Auch stimmte er so wohl den Flügel als sein Clavichord selbst, und war so geübt in dieser Arbeit, dass sie ihm nie mehr als eine Viertelstunde kostete. Denn waren aber auch, wenn er fantasierte, alle 24 Tonarten sein; er machte mit ihnen was er wollte. Er verband die entferntesten so leicht und so natürlich mit einander, wie die nächsten; man glaubte, er habe nur im innern Kreise einer einzigen Tonart moduliert.

Nobody could have any thanks for quilling his harpsichord for him; he always did it himself. Also the tuning of his harpsichord and clavichord was his own affair, and he was so practised in this work that it did not take him more than a quarter of an hour. But then, when he improvised, all twenty-four keys were his; he could do with them what he wanted. He connected the most remote keys together as easily and naturally as the nearest; one could believe he was modulating only in the inner circle of a single key.

From these passages the following conclusions can be drawn:

Bach took special care to ensure that the tuning of his instruments was as perfect as possible (C. P. E. Bach, Forkel).

Bach had great skill in setting a tuning on an instrument (Forkel).

Nothing is being said explicitly about the tuning(s) practised.

All keys could be played beautifully and equally well (Obituary, Forkel).

There were no discernible differences between near and remote keys (Forkel).

All major thirds were (equally) sharp (Marpurg).

The conclusion must be that the quotations refer to the use of equal temperament, or something not perceptibly different.

None of the authors cited considered Bach to adhere to any clear system of unequal temperament, although knowledge of unequal systems was widespread and easily available through the works of Sorge, Kirnberger, Marpurg, and others. Equal temperament was becoming the norm for tuning during the second half of the eighteenth century. If works of Bach like the *WTC* asked for a tuning substantially different from equal temperament, it is at least surprising that no eighteenth-century author had said so.

The statement that the *WTC* expects an equal-tempered keyboard must not be understood as meaning that equal temperament is a *conditio sine qua non* for all keyboard works by Bach. Bach's keyboard *oeuvre* covers a wide range of Neidhardt's spectrum from village to court. Many organ works, the keyboard suites, the Two- and Three-part Inventions, etc. are clearly orientated to the traditional, central, tonalities. An unequal temperament of the Werckmeister–Neidhardt–Sorge types serves them very well. On the other hand there are the 'experimental works': the *WTC*, the Four Duets, a number of fantasias, etc. For these pieces equal temperament is appropriate.

Kelletat, Kellner, Barnes, Billeter

Each of these recent authors has contributed a 'Bach tuning' to the repertoire of available unequal tunings. In all four cases the *WTC* is one of the principal applications. Before discussing these temperaments in detail separately, it must be said that they share the following shortcomings:

They use elements of Werckmeister's theories as building-blocks, but restricted mostly to the early writings of Werckmeister, notably the *Musicalische Temperatur* of 1691. His middle writings, which give equal temperament a place beside unequal temperament, have been overlooked, as have his later writings that put equal temperament in the foreground.

The rejection of equal temperament is not free from fashionable elements. Equal temperament is seen as an essential element of nineteenth-century and early-twentieth-century music and of 'non-authentic' interpretation of earlier music during these periods. This does not do justice to the role of equal temperament in eighteenth-century music. Equal temperament has been described and discussed so often in eighteenth-century writings as a practical system that it must have played an important part in musical performance.

Kelletat (1960) linked Bach with his pupil Johann Philipp Kirnberger, who described several unequal temperaments, now known as Kirnberger I, II (both described first in the preface of the fourth volume of his *Clavierübungen* of 1766) and III (described only in a letter to Forkel of 1779: see Bellermann 1871). These tunings have one, two, and four tempered fifths respectively. In his exclusive description of unequal temperaments and rejection of equal temperament, Kirnberger (1771 p. 11) stands quite alone. Although in many respects Kirnberger showed himself to have been a good pupil of Bach's, this does not imply that every sentence of the *Kunst des reinen Satzes* of 1771 reflects Bach's views. The *Kunst* was written more than twenty-five years after he had studied with Bach. In the meantime he published, among other things, a graphic construction of an equal-tempered monochord (about 1760) and composed for keyboard a *Musicalischer Circul* that passed through all the keys. Kelletat's 'Bach temperament' of 1967 (p. 26) is similar to but not identical with Kirnberger III. He calls this tuning

... eine empirische Wohltemperierung auf der diatonischen und chromatischen Basis der klassischen Mitteltönigkeit. Sie folgt den tonsystematischen Grundsätzen des Bach-Schülers Johann Philipp Kirnberger (1721–1783) und wird u.a. bestätigt durch die Analyse des Intervallbestandes im *Wohltemperierten Clavier* von Johann Sebastian Bach.

... an empirical well-tempering on the diatonic and chromatic basis of classical meantone temperament. It follows the foundations of the tonal system laid by Bach's pupil Kirnberger and is confirmed amongst other things by the interval analysis of Bach's *WTC*.

However, what is presented as evidence is no more than a series of opinions stated in undefined terms. For example, what exactly is meant by 'empirical well-tempering'? What is the 'diatonic and chromatic basis' of 'classical' meantone temperament? Kelletat's tuning proposal cannot claim any authenticity because both its construction and its background lack any firm foundation in documented history.

Kellner's (1976, 1977) procedure is not very different from Kelletat's. Kellner too conceives of undocumented ideas which are implanted in Bach's mind; this time it is numerological evidence. Kellner assumes that the fifth and the major third in the major and minor triads should be equal-beating, that is, beating equally fast. To achieve this, he postulates a well-tempered fifth, which is tempered flat by $\frac{1}{5}$ of a ditonic comma. If we use four such fifths to construct a well-tempered major third, this major third is tempered by a syntonic comma minus $\frac{4}{5}$ of a ditonic comma (about 2.5 cents). It can be shown that in a well-tempered major triad of this kind the fifth and the major third have beat frequencies in the ratio 35:36 (which is nearly 1:1); in the well-tempered minor triad, 6:7 (which differs a little more from 1:1). If a well-tempered fifth is tempered $\frac{1}{5}$ of a comma, there must be five well-tempered fifths in the circle of fifths. Kellner places them in a manner that strongly reminds one of Werckmeister III. Now, what is wrong with this Bach tuning? First, there is no reason to believe that Bach ever thought of well-tempered fifths or thirds or triads. Secondly, the laws governing beat frequencies were still unknown in the first half of the eighteenth century. Of course, the equal-beating fifth and major third could have been found by trial and error, but this is a tough and tedious procedure. Thirdly, no single concept or step in Kellner's reasoning has any documentary foundation.

The tuning has found some remarkable applications on Bösendorfer grand pianos for a post-Baroque repertory (see Tanner 1979, Kellner 1979). It is mentioned as Bach's tuning in the preface to Walter Dehnhard's edition of Book 1 of the *WTC* in the Wiener Urtext Edition (1977).

Thirdly, there is the Bach tuning of Barnes (1979). Barnes proceeds quite differently from the German authors by taking into account internal evidence, that is, the notes or text of the *WTC*. Having investigated all the major thirds in the twenty-four major-key preludes, he puts them in five categories of 'prominence', i.e. vulnerability for tempering. The categories are defined as follows: *A*, tuning error very obvious; *B*, fairly obvious; *C*, easily perceptible; *D*, barely perceptible; *E*, imperceptible. Then the mean prominence is calculated for each of the twelve major thirds of the chromatic scale, and a tuning is constructed in such a way that the most prominent major thirds are the least tempered ones. The result is a Werckmeister–Kellner-like tuning, but now with six tempered fifths, the tempering being $\frac{1}{6}$ of a diatonic comma. Although this procedure looks elegant and promising in the beginning, it contains a remarkably large number of weaknesses. What is missing is a perceptual definition of 'very obvious', 'fairly obvious', 'easily perceptible', etc., and a strict procedure for categorizing major thirds in the music itself. Without these definitions the method is open to any kind of bias. Then: Why only the major-key preludes? Why not also the fugues (50% of the music) and the minor-key preludes (another 25%)? Moreover, are the two books of the *WTC* alike in this respect?

If we look at the numbers given by Barnes, some of them are very striking. Eight out of nine *A*-prominent major thirds C–E come from a single prelude (*WTC* Bk 1 no. 1), which gives a very strong weight, not to say bias. (The numerous F♯–A♯

major thirds in the D sharp minor Prelude of *WTC* Bk 1 have not been counted.) Also, the categories are rather unequal as to magnitude. Only 14 major thirds have prominence *A*; 33 have *B*. But there are 155 in category *C*; 303 major thirds are used in such a way that a tuning error is stated (by Barnes) to be barely perceptible; and of 307 major thirds the tuning errors should be imperceptible. There is fewer than one *A*-prominent major third per prelude on the average, and fewer than two *B*-prominent ones. Such a numerical base is not very fit for statistical treatment. Moreover, Barnes constructed his tuning from the numerical base by trial and error, bypassing the mathematical procedures developed by Hall (1973, 1974) for a similar undertaking.

The use of internal evidence always implies an interpretation model. Unless such a model is given by external evidence, it must be constructed anew by the twentieth-century investigator and is bound to be arbitrary. Barnes's interpretation model includes (e.g.) the supposition that tuning errors (deviations, temperings) should be heard as little as possible. Now, most adherents of unequal temperaments for the *WTC*, including Barnes himself, mention the differential effects on the tonal colours as one of their inspirations. In Barnes's case, however, this leads to a contradiction, because by minimizing the perception of the temperings, the tuning differences between tonalities are also minimized instead of emphasized. Another assumption is that the pattern of use of the major thirds should faithfully reflect the pattern of temperings. The latter assumption means that a musical work can be considered to be meant for playing in equal temperament only if all major thirds occur equally often.

Billeter (1979 pp. 30–1) proposed still another Bach tuning. Two fifths are narrowed by $\frac{7}{24}$ of a diatonic comma (D–A–E), and five fifths with $\frac{1}{12}$ of a diatonic comma (F–C–G–D and E–B–F♯), so that this tuning is not essentially different from the other Bach tunings. Since Billeter himself has already called the tuning 'hypothetical', we need not discuss it further here.

It is not my intention to say that the proposed unequal Bach tunings are bad tunings. They are variants of tunings well documented in history, and they can be included in the repertoire of good unequal tunings which can be used for a large stock of late-seventeenth- and early-eighteenth-century keyboard music. However, they are unable to meet the special demands of music that proceeds through all twenty-four keys, major and minor. Personally, I dislike the many Pythagorean major thirds that arise with these tunings when playing preludes and fugues with five to seven sharps or flats.

The class of tunings to which the 'Bach tunings' belong is categorized by tempered fifths in the central part of the circle of fifths (the 'diatonic' fifths C–G, G–D, etc., or the lower-key fifths), and pure fifths in the peripheral part (the 'chromatic' fifths F♯–C♯, C♯–G♯, etc., or raised-key fifths). Because of this situation the central major thirds (C–E, F–A, etc.) are the best ones (i.e. tempered least), the peripheral major thirds (F♯–A♯, etc.) the worst ones (i.e. tempered most: viz. a syntonic comma, 21.5 cents). Since the tempering of the major thirds (varying from zero to

21.5 cents) seems to be more decisive than that of fifths (which ranges only from zero to about 5 cents), the central tonalities (C, F and G major, A minor and D minor, etc.) sound better than the peripheral tonalities (B, F♯, D♭ major, etc.).

Jorgensen, Di Véroli

Barbour (1951) indicated for the first time the possibility of unequal temperament for Bach's *WTC*, without going into detail. The same position was also held in two recent general texts about historical tunings, those by Jorgensen (1977) and Di Véroli (1978). These authors also consider unequal temperament as an essential element in the performance of the *WTC*, without mentioning one specific system. In a response to Barnes's article, Di Véroli (*EM* 9 (1981), p. 129) proposes the Vallotti or Young tuning as optimal for the *WTC*. This tuning contains six successive tempered fifths, and so differs only slightly from Barnes's temperament.

Jorgensen gives the terms 'well-tempered' and 'well temperament' a very specific and interesting meaning. In his view, a tuning is well-tempered if none of the fifths is larger than pure, if none of the major thirds is smaller than pure, if none of the minor thirds is larger than pure (this requirement follows from the first two points), and if the temperings of the major thirds increase gradually from central to peripheral, or, going from C–E over G–B, D–F♯, etc. and over F–A, B♭–D, etc. to F♯–A♯ (= G♭–B♭). These conditions are met by many of the good unequal temperaments of the seventeenth and eighteenth centuries, and also by the modern unequal 'Bach tunings'. The first three conditions result in a situation in which the mean tempering of all consonant intervals in the tuning is minimal, and equal to 10.428 cents. Marpurg (1776) and Türk (1808) called such a tuning a *Mittel-Temperatur* ('middle temperament'). The fourth condition is no different from the tuning quality that I call 'concentric'.

Tuning by retuning?

So far, it has been supposed that only one tuning should serve the whole *WTC*. Is there a possibility that not all pieces ask for the same tuning? The question of adapting tuning to key deserves a study to itself. Werckmeister (1681, 1691) assigned his tuning no. III to the peripheral keys, no. IV to the central keys. The literature of the seventeenth and eighteenth centuries is conspicuously silent about tuning-adapted-to-key, with Cima (1606: see Rayner 1969) as a notable exception. Barbour (1951 p. 192) supposes 'adaptive' tuning for the late-seventeenth-century keyboard repertoire; but although small tuning adaptations are not uncommon for concert performances and recordings, in the case of Bach's *WTC* they are an unlikely solution to the tuning problem. The order of pieces is chromatic, not following the circle of fifths (like that of a comparable set such as Sorge's *Clavierübung*), which means that, unless the order is completely changed, tuning time is longer than performing time.

An extreme view on tuning by retuning has been put forward by Hafner (1974). His proposal is to use meantone temperament adapted per key, using the row of fifths from B♭ to D♯ for C major, from D♭ to F♯ for C minor, and so on. Hafner tried this all out for Book 1 of the *WTC* on a Scalatron, an electronic keyboard with variable intonation. A 31-tone equal-tempered keyboard would do the same job without retuning. Hafner is the first to bring meantone tuning into the discussion about the tuning of the *WTC*. This reminds one of Friedrich Suppig who, in Dresden, wrote a multi-section keyboard fantasia going through all twenty-four keys, entitled *Labyrinthus musicus*, in the same year that Bach dated the title-page of Book 1 of the *WTC*. From Suppig's comments it appears that meantone tuning (without retuning, merely accepting the wolf intervals) or 31-tone equal temperament was what he had in mind for tuning.

Conclusion

During the nineteenth century and the first half of the twentieth, virtually nobody ever doubted the view that Bach's *WTC* was intended to be played on an equal-tempered keyboard, and that *wohltemperirt* or 'well-tempered' meant 'equal-tempered'. This view was adopted as self-evident and not based on any particular research. During the last three decades doubts have been cast upon this opinion, and several musicologists have proposed unequal Bach temperaments, designed especially to serve the *WTC*. While they have looked for a variety of arguments as foundations for their Bach tunings, the resulting tunings are rather similar 'concentric' tunings, not unlike Werckmeister III, Kirnberger III, Vallotti's tuning, etc. Other authors have not gone further than stating that *wohltemperirt* should mean unequally tempered with possibilities for all twenty-four keys. The latter opinion has been shared by many musicians.

In this article, I have presented evidence from late-seventeenth- and early-eighteenth-century German music theory that points to equal temperament as a particularly appropriate tuning for a musical work of the kind of Bach's *WTC*, with its emphasis on the equal importance of all twelve major and minor keys. It has been shown as well that the arguments put forward in favour of an unequal temperament for Bach's *WTC* are at best undocumented modern views. The conclusion must be that the traditional view, that Bach's *WTC* expects an equal-tempered keyboard, is correct.

I wish to express my hope here that, just as the unequal temperaments have their right places in the performance of early music, equal temperament will not be denied its right to be one of the tuning variants available for the performance of early music, whenever it is appropriate.

References

Barbour, J. M., 'Bach and the Art of Temperament', *MQ* 43 (1947), pp. 64–89

Barbour, J. M., *Tuning and Temperament* (East Lansing, Michigan, 1951)

Barnes, J., 'Bach's Keyboard Temperament', *EM* 7 (1979), pp. 236–49; see also responses to this article by C. Di Véroli (*EM* 8 (1980) p. 129), P. P. Jones (*ibid.* pp. 511–13), H. A. Kellner (*EM* 9 (1981) p. 141), and again C. Di Véroli (*ibid.* pp. 219-21)

Bellermann, H., 'Briefe von Kirnberger and Forkel', *AMZ* 6 (1871), pp. 565-72

Billeter, B., *Anweisung zum Stimmen von Tasteninstrumenten in verschiedenen Temperaturen* (Kassel, 1979)

Di Véroli, C., *Unequal Temperaments* (Buenos Aires, 1978)

Forkel, J. N., *Über Johann Sebastian Bachs Leben, Kunst und Kunstwerke* (Leipzig, 1802)

Hafner, E., 'The Forty-Eight Revisited in Thirty-One', *Well Tempered Notes* (November 1974), pp. 2–3 (also included in *Xenharmonikôn* 3 (Spring))

Hall, D. E., 'The Objective Measurement of Goodness-of-fit for Tunings and Temperaments', *Journal of Music Theory* 17 (1973), pp. 274–90

Hall, D. E., 'Quantitative Evaluation of Musical Scale Tunings', *American Journal of Physics* 42 (1974), pp. 543–52

Harsdörffer, G. P., *Delitiae mathematicae et physicae. Der mathematischen und philosophischen Erquickstunden Zweyter Theil* (Nuremberg, 1651); *Dritter Theil* (Nuremberg, 1653)

Jorgensen, O., *Tuning the Historical Temperaments by Ear* (Marquette, Michigan, 1977)

Kelletat, H., *Zur musikalischen Temperatur* (Kassel, 1960; 2nd edn 1980)

Kelletat, H., *Ein Beitrag zur musikalischen Temperatur der Musikinstrumente vom Mittelalter zur Gegenwart* (Reutlingen, 1967)

Kellner, H. A., *Wie stimme ich selbst mein Cembalo?* (Frankfurt am Main, 1976; 2nd edn 1979)

Kellner, H. A., 'Eine Rekonstruktion der wohltemperierten Stimmung von Johann Sebastian Bach', *Das Musikinstrument* 26 (1977), pp. 34–5

Kellner, H. A., 'Was Bach a Mathematician?', *English Harpsichord Magazine* 2 (1978), pp. 32–6

Kellner, H. A., 'Die ungleichstufige Wohltemperierung Bachs auf Bösendorfer-Konzertflügeln', *Das Musikinstrument* 28 (1979), pp. 1179–80

Kellner, H. A., *The Tuning of My Harpsichord* (Frankfurt am Main, 1980)

Kirnberger, J. P., *Construction der gleichschwebenden Temperatur* (Berlin, [c1760])

Kirnberger, J. P., *Die Kunst des reinen Satzes in der Musik. Erster Theyl* (Berlin/Königsberg, 1771)

Marpurg, F. W., *Versuch über die musikalische Temperatur* (Breslau, 1776)

Mattheson, J., *Exemplarische Organisten-Probe* (Hamburg, 1719)

Mattheson, J., *Critica musica. Tomus primus* (Hamburg, 1722); . . . *Tomus secundus* (Hamburg, 1725)

Mattheson, J., *Grosse General-Bass-Schule* (Hamburg, 1731)

Neidhardt, J. G., *Beste und leichteste Temperatur* (Jena, 1706)

Neidhardt, J. G., *Sectio canonis harmonici* (Königsberg, 1724)

Neidhardt, J. G., *Gäntzlich erschöpfte mathematische Abtheilungen des diatonisch-chromatischen, temperirten Canonis Monochordi* (Königsberg, 1732)

Rasch, R. A., 'Wohltemperirt en gelijkzwevend', *Mens & Melodie* 36 (1981), pp. 264–73

Rayner, C. G., 'The Enigmatic Cima: Meantone Tuning and Transposition', *Galpin Society Journal* 22 (1969), pp. 23–34

Sorge, G. A., *Vorgemach der musicalischen Composition. Ander Theil* (Lobenstein, 1746)

Sorge, G. A., *Gespräch zwischen einem Musico-theorico und einem Studio Musices* (Lobenstein, 1748)

Sorge, G. A., *Zuverlässige Anweisung Claviere und Orgeln zu temperiren und zu stimmen* (Lobenstein, 1758)

Tanner, R., 'L'Accord inégal bien tempéré appliqué à un Bösendorfer', *Das Musikinstrument* 28 (1979), pp. 770-2

Türk, D. G., *Anleitung zu Temperaturberechnungen* (Halle, 1808)

Werckmeister, A., *Orgel-Probe* (Quedlinburg, 1681)

Werckmeister, A., *Musicae mathematicae hodegus curiosus* (Quedlinburg, 1687)

Werckmeister, A., *Musicalische Temperatur* (Quedlinburg, 1691)

Werckmeister, A., *Hypomnemata musica* (Quedlinburg, 1697)

Werckmeister, A., *Die nothwendigste Anmerckungen und Regeln, wie der Bassus continuus oder General-Bass wol könne tractiret werden* (Aschersleben, 1698; 2nd edn 1715)

Werckmeister, A., *Erweiterte und verbesserte Orgel-Probe* (Quedlinburg, 1698)

Werckmeister, A., *Harmonologia musica* (Quedlinburg, 1702)

Werckmeister, A., *Organum Gruningense redivivum* (Aschersleben, 1705)

Werckmeister, A., *Musicalische Paradoxal-Discourse* (Quedlinburg, 1707)

The B minor Mass – Perpetual Touchstone for Bach Research

HANS-JOACHIM SCHULZE

(Leipzig)

The composition that the Zurich publisher Hans Georg Nägeli called in 1818 'the greatest musical artwork of all time and of all nations' ('das grösste musikalische Kunstwerk aller Zeiten und Völker') is not only the latest but still the most puzzling and controversial amongst the oratorio-like works of the Leipzig *Thomaskantor*.

The significance of this *opus summum* seems only gradually to have struck the generation of Bach sons and Bach pupils. The Obituary, written in 1750–1 and published in 1754, makes no special mention of the work; and only some two decades later, starting in Berlin, does it begin to be dispersed in copies, made in the circle of pupils and admirers of the composer. About the same time documents show an increase in the number of those recognizing that Bach's masses were works 'of sublime splendour and passion' ('mit erhabener Pracht und Feuer'). At one point in 1775 there is mention 'of a great mass of the late J. S. Bach' ('einer grossen Messe des seligen J. S. Bach'), the original score of which appeared eventually in the literary estate of the second-eldest son, C. P. E. Bach, under the heading 'the great Catholic mass' ('die grosse catholische Messe'). Whether this term 'great Catholic mass' was transmitting a reliable tradition or merely betraying the inadequate knowledge of later generations is still a matter of disagreement – in favour of the reliable tradition argues the fact that in the family circle the *St Matthew Passion* was given a similar epithet by 1750 at the latest and was known as the 'great Passion' ('grosse Passion').[1]

A milestone in the history of the impact made by the B minor Mass was reached when, at a benefit concert given in Hamburg in the early part of 1786, Philipp Emanuel performed the whole nine-movement Credo (along with works by Handel and himself) and thereby prompted a press report that praised it as 'one of the finest musical pieces ever heard' ('eins der vortrefflichsten musikalischen Stücke, die je

---

1 Many an argument today proceeds from the assumption that the Lutheran Bach could in no circumstances have composed a Catholic mass, whether the B minor Mass or any other. No convincing explanation of the matter from any line of approach, however, has yet been prepared.

gehört worden'). It seems also to imply a gradual recognition of the Mass at the turn of the century that copies of it not only got as far as England but found themselves in the possession of Joseph Haydn and others, and that some time later Beethoven too tried to obtain a copy – alas without success, so that the *Missa solemnis* came about without any knowledge of Bach's B minor Mass.

That this was the first and for a long time the only one amongst the great choral works of Bach to arouse the interest of a publisher[2] is itself token of imminent recognition. It seems a quirk of history that in the same year that this occurred (1805) a mass for two choirs falsely attributed to Bach was actually published in Leipzig and performed in the Gewandhaus. To the listeners, this work – not composed by Bach, only copied by him – appeared 'like an obelisk excavated from the ruins of the grey past', awakening in those present a 'thrilling awe for the power and might of our ancestors and for the greatness and holiness of their art' ('wie ein aus der Ruinen der grauen Vorzeit herausgegrabener Obelisk . . . Schauer der Ehrfurcht gegen die Kraft und Gewalt der Vorfahren und gegen das Grosse und Heilige ihrer Kunst'). Against Nägeli's intention to publish a genuine work of Bach's new obstacles were constantly arising, so that only in 1833 could a beginning be made of printing the score (the year in which the Berlin Singakademie had ventured on the first steps towards a performance, and exactly a century after the Kyrie and Gloria originated), and the whole Mass was not ready until 1845, nine years after Nägeli's death.

In 1818 Nägeli had expressed the hope that the planned edition of the Mass should not be missing from any collection of church music, from any singing academy or from any library of musical scores – because the edition, undertaken 'through the participation of great and wealthy promoters, would be brought into the hands of worthy professionals and students', an edition of music 'equally important for the organist as for the player of fugues, and for the scholar as for the composer' ('durch die Theilnahme grosser und reicher Kunstbeförderer . . . in die Hände würdiger Künstler und Kunstjünger gebracht werde . . . dem Organisten wie dem Fugenspieler, dem Kunstgelehrten wie dem Componisten gleich wichtig'). But by 1832 he was convinced otherwise. Resignedly he remarked 'that for such things we have a really small public', since even the public performances in Berlin and Frankfurt 'had come about [only] because of enthusiasts for Bach's music' ('dass wir für solche Sachen ein gar kleines Publikum haben . . . [Aufführungen nur] durch Enthusiasten für die Bachische Musik erzwungen worden'). Normally the choral unions were not inclined 'to take on vocal music so immensely difficult and inimical to the voice' ('sich mit so ungeheuer schwieriger und organwidriger Singmusik zu befassen').

Nevertheless, despite all difficulties and setbacks, the public became more and more aware of the 'powerful five-part mass comparable to no other piece of music' ('gewaltige und mit keinem andern Musikwerke vergleichbare fünfstimmige Messe', in the words of the Berlin scholar Adolph Bernhard Marx, 1825), even if it

2 In 1805 Hans Georg Nägeli acquired the original score with the intention of publishing it.

was not as exposed as the *St Matthew Passion*, revived by Mendelssohn in 1829. After a partial performance in 1841 in the Leipzig Gewandhaus, Robert Schumann wrote:

Den tiefsten Eindruck machte vielleicht das Crucifixus, aber auch ein Stück, das nur mit andern Bachschen zu vergleichen ist, eines, vor dem sich alle Meister aller Zeiten in Ehrfurcht verneigen müssen.

The deepest impression, perhaps, was made by the 'Crucifixus' – a piece which is to be compared only with other Bach works, a piece before which all composers of all time must bow in awe.

Though the B minor Mass occupies an especially favoured position in the modern repertory (and has the advantage over the Passions of being free of translation difficulties in non-German-speaking countries), it is the legitimate subject not only of praise but of relatively sharp criticism, even today. The critique, drawing on historical, theological and even philological arguments, is directed most particularly to the work's considerable dimensions which leave it apparently unsuited for liturgical use both in the present and obviously at the time of its composition.[3] To this end certain arbitrary details in the text are invoked to show that the Mass supposedly corresponds neither to Protestant nor to Catholic use.[4] Furthermore, comment is made on a 'tonal imbalance' (the preponderance of D major) and a 'disturbing lack of uniformity' in the scoring for instruments and particularly voices (changes between four, five, six and eight parts in the choir). In particular, however, a 'heterogeneous quality in the compiling of the work' is claimed, too great a proportion of parodied movements, resulting from a decline either of the composer's creative power or of his interest. Accordingly, it would follow that the score left by the composer has been taken only through a historical error as the document of a work intended as a unity, and that what we are really dealing with is several compositions independent of each other.

This line of argument, much discussed in the mid-1950s and finding an echo in the edition of the Mass for the *NBA*,[5] is not so misleading as it first appears. It follows from the complicated history of the work's origin, a solution to which could not be achieved by the traditional methods of research at that time. Only later investigations could bring more light into the darkness that surrounded the work.[6] Present knowledge suggests the oldest part of the Mass – if one ignores a cantata movement of 1714 that served as model for the 'Crucifixus' – to be the six-part Sanctus that Bach produced for the First Day of Christmas 1724 and will have performed in the main church of Leipzig, the Nikolaikirche. To all appearances this composition left behind it an unusually strong impression, for one of the most

---

3 Or is here the wish – that it cannot be a Catholic mass – father of the thought?

4 In particular, this is a reference to the added 'altissime' in 'Domine deus'; but this corresponds to the old Leipzig tradition and can be traced from the late-medieval *Thomasgraduale* right down to the Leipzig hymnbooks of the Bach period.

5 Cf. F. Smend, *NBA* II/1 *KB* (Leipzig/Kassel, 1956).

6 G. von Dadelsen, 'Friedrich Smends Ausgabe der h-moll-Messe', *Mf* 12 (1959), pp. 315–34.

engaging musical Maecenases of the time, Count Franz Anton von Sporck (1662–1738) – resident in Bohemia but often in Dresden and occasionally visiting Leipzig – asked the composer for a set of parts. When Bach came to prepare a repeat of the Sanctus in 1727 he had to have new parts written out, since Count Sporck had not given back the borrowed copies.

If it is difficult to explain how it came about that the D major Sanctus so suddenly and markedly surpassed other mass movements of Bach, it is more immediately clear why that is also the case with the next sections to be composed, the Kyrie and Gloria of 1733. In that year there was an exceptional event comparable to that in autumn 1727 when Bach composed his *Trauer-Ode* after the death of the Electoral Princess of Saxony. On 1 February 1733 the Elector of Saxony, Friedrich August I ('August the Strong'), had died in Warsaw, and as in 1727 there was an extended period of national mourning. For Bach, national mourning meant a period in which no music was allowed, and thus a marked drop in supplementary income. As for the effect of this on his musical activities: above all, evidence suggests that the main event of the year, the Passion performance on Good Friday, had to be given up. But the composer used this interim in his own way.

After ten years in the office of *Thomaskantor* he was familiar with all the potential and all the limitations in his field of activity. The promises which had drawn him to Leipzig, and his own high-flying plans, had been only painfully reconcilable with reality. The striving towards a new definition of the *Thomaskantorat* – less in the sense of a traditional school post, more in the direction of a municipal music-directorate – had been only partially successful. By 1733 Bach's wide-ranging memorandum on the need to improve fundamentally the financial and artistic possibilities of the church's music already lay some years in the past. Much the same could be said for the significant letter Bach wrote to his old friend Georg Erdmann in Danzig, in which he quite openly solicited a new position because in Leipzig 'the authorities are strange and little interested in music' ('eine wunderliche und der Music wenig ergebene Obrigkeit'). If Bach was not able to resign his Leipzig position, he must have tried to build it up as far as his powers allowed him. In this respect Dresden, the brilliant electoral capital, with its lavishly equipped, courtly music-making, served as a guiding light very different from that given by the mean city fathers of the middle-class commercial capital, Leipzig. So on 27 July 1733 Bach turned with a written appeal to the successor to the throne, asking for a court title to be bestowed on him and committing himself to produce church and orchestral music. Bluntly he let the country's ruler know that he was not merely pursuing a title for its own sake, but that this would provide a means with which he could deal with 'injuries' ('Bekränkungen') of the kind he had already had to suffer and with the 'reduction in extra fees' ('Verminderung derer Accidentien') that had lowered his income. The 'slight token of that knowledge which I have achieved in music' (geringe Arbeit von derjenigen Wissenschafft, welche ich in der Musique erlanget'), referred to in this letter to the Elector Friedrich August II, consisted of the performing parts for the Kyrie and Gloria of the later B minor Mass.

Evidently Bach chose the moment for this dedication with careful thought. Only a few weeks had elapsed since his eldest son, Wilhelm Friedemann, had successfully competed for the organist's post in the Dresden Sophienkirche, and was now installed at the newest and finest organ in the Residence, an instrument of Gottfried Silbermann. Meanwhile the countrywide ban on music had been lifted, so that in the middle of June 1733 Bach's Collegium Musicum at Leipzig could pick up again, while 2 July was planned as the beginning of church music. Since on this day (2 July) one of the three Marian feast-days fell, it is not out of the question that for this purpose Bach rearranged his Christmas Magnificat of 1723 (the most brilliant and festive creation of his first year in office at Leipzig) and performed it in the new D major version.[7] On 19 July, a Sunday, there was a family event at court (the baptism of a prince) that gave the opportunity at many places in Saxony, including Leipzig, for the performance of a Te Deum with trumpets and timpani. In the following week Bach must have travelled to Dresden, though whether it was only on his own account or in connection with the appointment of his eldest son it is not possible to say. The petition to the elector is dated 27 July. On the title-page of the presentation parts of the *Missa* is written: 'To His Royal Highness and Electoral Majesty of Saxony has been shown in the accompanying *Missa* . . . the obedient devotion of the author J. S. Bach' ('Gegen Sr. Königlichen Hoheit und ChurFürstlichen Durchlaucht zu Sachssen bezeigte mit inliegender Missa . . . seine unterthänigste Devotion der Autor J. S. Bach'). Since both letter and dedication were written in Dresden, it can be accepted that Bach formulated them only after he had found an opportunity to produce the work. For this one can think above all of the Sophienkirche. Its organ was pitched not in the so-called *Chorton* (the pitch of most of the Leipzig organs, a whole tone above *Kammerton*) but in *Kammerton* itself; the figured-bass part of Bach's *Missa* too is in *Kammerton* and was not transposed, unlike those for the Leipzig cantatas. In Leipzig, on the contrary, no performance with the sources as we have them can have taken place (such as on the occasion of the Oath of Fealty for the new elector on 21 April 1733), although a 'Lutheran *Missa*' could have found a place in the liturgical order of the main churches in Leipzig as well as the Sanctus alone had done.[8]

7 For this purpose a new, distinctly calligraphic copy of the score was made, causing one to think of Dresden and presentation copies.

8 The idea that with the B minor Mass it is a question of a 'Lutheran *Missa*' composed for the Leipzig service, and only later (as suitable opportunity arose) dedicated to the Catholic king, belongs to the favoured hypotheses of Bach research. Because of the connection with the Oath of Fealty at Leipzig there has even been a thought that it is literally political music, according to which the Kyrie and Gloria signify in turn a musical equivalent of the old motto *le roi est mort – vive le roi*. Careful investigation of the Dresden parts, however, largely removes the foundation for such speculations. Everything suggests that this set of parts was the first and probably only set, copied from the composer's score; that it was thought of primarily for Dresden and not for a previous performance in Leipzig; that it consisted of exactly notated and complete, practical material, except that Bach took out the duplicate parts (other than violin 1 ripieno); and that it served in fact as performing material. The peculiar dedication formula 'bezeigte mit inliegender Missa' anticipates through the use of the past tense the fact of a performance, as was then usual; because as already noted this text had been written in Dresden – thus at its intended destination – a mistake cannot easily be imputed. See also H.-J. Schulze, *J. S. Bach: Missa h-Moll BWV 232¹*, facs. edn of Dresden parts, with commentary (Leipzig/Neuhausen–Stuttgart, 1983).

One must rest content with surmises and the adding of two and two together in this way: there is neither documentary evidence about any supposed performance, nor any hint about the reception that this unusual work might have had amongst the friends and patrons of music in Dresden. From the direction of the court there was evidently no reaction. Bach's note was passed on only on 19 August and then remained unanswered; similarly without success was his attempt to attract attention to himself outside Leipzig by musical activities, particularly through music written in homage on the occasion of birthdays and name-days in the royal family. More than three years passed before Bach – in the meantime involved in risky questions of jurisdiction apropos the Thomasschule – decided to renew his petition and so at last reached his goal. As 'Royal Polish and Electoral Saxon Court Composer' he was henceforth as well protected from fundamental criticism of his professional conduct as he was against financial loss resulting from the restrictive measures of the Leipzig council.

When it was that Bach took the decision to enlarge his two-part *Missa* into a complete five-part Catholic mass (*Missa tota*) one cannot say. It is certain that at the end of the 1730s or a little later he wrote other 'Lutheran masses' (though whether exclusively for Leipzig is unknown); he also copied out similar works by other composers, as he had done since the Weimar period, and had them performed. After 1745 the Sanctus from 1724 had another performance, and the *Missa* from 1733 was also brought out again: by rearranging three of its most important movements Bach produced a Latin Christmas piece, though for what occasion is still not known.[9] It is worth noting that it was also to the years after 1740 that Bach's copy of a complete Palestrina mass belongs – a token of his involvement with the contrapuntal style of the sixteenth century – and particularly suggestive of the requirements at Leipzig is the fact that he prepared for performance only the Kyrie and Gloria of this mass.

It looks very much as if one must seek some external reason for the impetus to compile the B minor Mass. Above all Dresden itself is in question, even though no relevant circumstance is to be found: a commission could have been given by those noble patrons of music who came from countries partly or largely Catholic, such as Bohemia, Moravia, Austria, Poland or Silesia. Some of the people known to have had contact with Bach in his late years suggest an answer in this direction. It is not to be supposed that any sort of commission was sufficient to induce Bach in his last years to start on such an extensive task; important, perhaps even decisive, must have been the readiness of his state of mind. Indicative of the situation in which the composer found himself – ageing, perhaps plagued by lingering illness, hindered by increasing eye trouble – is the way in which he prepared the full score of nearly 190 pages (the whole scarcely earlier than 1748) and came through that critical meeting-point between slackening powers and increasing demands.

For the Kyrie and Gloria Bach used his score of 1733, needing to make only

---

9 Perhaps it was intended for Wilhelm Friedemann, who had been working in Halle since 1746 and into whose possession the score came.

minor improvements. The *Missa* was given a new title-cover and the number 1. For the Credo – the Nicene Creed, rich in verbal imagery, and headed *Symbolum Nicenum* by the composer – no older draft existed and he had to make a new complete score from scratch. To this section numbered 2 the Sanctus was added as no. 3. For the Sanctus Bach could have made use of his composing copy from 1724 but decided to write out the ten pages of score again and to make a series of alterations. For the remaining parts from the 'Osanna' to the 'Dona nobis pacem' there was again no previous draft, so these had to be newly copied out and were then collected together as no. 4. In this way there came about a score that can be regarded on the whole as a fair copy, even if it does not achieve the calligraphic level of the famous score of the *St Matthew Passion*. The striking arrangement in four sections leaves it perfectly clear – from the composer's point of view as from ours – how the single parts had different origins, and so there was no attempt to dress it up as a unity. The groupings also underline, no doubt with an eye to the circumstances of performance, the changing distribution of parts in the four sections.

Whether during Bach's lifetime a set of parts was prepared from this score is something we do not know; it would have made sense only for someone on the outside (so to speak) commissioning them, for one cannot think of a performance of such a *Missa tota* in any Protestant church in Leipzig or elsewhere. Nevertheless Bach worked yet further on the score after it was ready. Only subsequently did he compose the 'Et incarnatus est' as a choral movement, which caused some alteration to the duet 'Et in unum', to which that text had originally belonged; similarly the transition to the 'Crucifixus' was altered, and that chorus now has a short introduction for instruments. Details of this kind show how much care Bach gave to the new *magnum opus* and what store he set by perfecting it.

Any such conclusion seems to collide strikingly with the fact that the twenty-six movements of the Mass include numerous known or supposed arrangements of older compositions, so that against these parodies the original movements total less than one-third.[10] 'Domine deus', 'Et resurrexit' and 'Osanna' go back to homage cantatas for the electors of 1727 and 1732; the sources for the 'Gratias' (and 'Dona nobis pacem') and the 'Et expecto' are to be found in church cantatas for the Leipzig election of 1731 and for a marriage service (1729 at the latest); cantata movements from 1723 and 1714 supply the models for 'Qui tollis' and 'Crucifixus', while the ancestor of the 'Agnus dei' can be found in a secular wedding cantata of 1725. So far the original versions of the 'Christe', 'Gloria', 'Laudamus te', 'Qui sedes', 'Quoniam', 'Et in spiritum sanctum' and 'Benedictus' have not been discovered. Some cases are complicated by the fact that known alternative versions are not to be related to each other directly but possess a common ancestor that has now disappeared: this is the case with the 'Osanna' and the movement 'Preise dein Glücke, gesegnetes Sachsen', with the 'Agnus dei' and an aria from the *Easter*

10 Cf. K. Häfner, 'Über die Herkunft von zwei Sätzen der h-moll-Messe', *BJ* 63 (1977), pp. 55–74.

Oratorio, and also with the 'Patrem omnipotentem' and the opening chorus of Cantata 171, 'Gott, wie dein Name, so ist auch dein Ruhm'.

The attempts to account for the fact that so celebrated a work as the B minor Mass, the four smaller masses, or the *Christmas, Easter* and *Ascension Oratorios* consist mainly of older movements with new words, reflect an ambivalent attitude of Bach research to the technique of parody. While it was boldly maintained in the nineteenth century that secular originals were to be understood only as first steps and sketches *en route* to the real fulfilment of this or that movement through its association with a sacred text, so the tendency in later times was to excuse what seemed to be necessary measures taken by the composer as being forced on him by shortage of time or by economy of effort. For late works of Bach there would also be the question of failing creative powers. Against this, however, newer interpretations suggest that Bach's compact musical diction generates a surplus of quality in respect to each and every text, a surplus that allows a justifiable association between many movements and various, even contradictory, texts.[11]

As far as the B minor Mass is concerned, it is also to be noticed that throughout his life – already during his musical education, sources suggest – Bach showed a great talent for selectivity. It has long been observed that in the choice of cantata movements taken over into the Mass Bach sought out those best suited at each moment, often movements that in *Affekt* or theological content already bear some relationship to the corresponding section of the mass text. He took great care to underlay the Latin text as well as possible to the movement in hand and to apply as became necessary changes to rhythm, metre, instrumentation or number of parts – as well as reducing some movements to their fugal skeleton whilst making others more compact by leaving out the instrumental introductions.

To generalize, it can be claimed that for the *Missa tota* Bach did not take merely any of his 'Lutheran masses' or any agreeable Sanctus but the *Missa* and the Sanctus that he regarded as his most successful. This must already have been his procedure in 1733 when it occurred to him to create the *Missa* – perhaps his first composition of this kind – for dedication to the new ruler of Saxony. Around 1748 he applied himself further to the choosing of fine-sounding choruses and highly expressive arias, and the procedure is bound to have had consequences for the sublime work of the aged Bach in the newly composed movements 'Credo', 'Et incarnatus est' and 'Confiteor'.

Such a way of going about things, that sets out to bring together the best and the most important, pressing ahead with the creation of a new and higher unity out of heterogeneous elements, is not directly comparable to the contemporary *florilegia* in poetry or *pasticcii* in opera. A closer comparison would be with the heterogeneous text – one that reaches such a striking quality – in the first Leipzig Passion music, the *St John Passion*. Nor in the case of the B minor Mass is it quite enough to invoke the hypothesis of a 'commission from the outside'. Without doubt there

11 Cf. L. Finscher, 'Zum Parodieproblem bei Bach', *Bach-Interpretationen*, ed. M. Geck (Göttingen, 1969), pp. 94–105.

is also involved the matter of 'inner development', the desire of a mature artist on the threshold of old age to bring something permanent to the present and future world: a work that, in the realm of vocal music, would no more go out of date than would the *Art of Fugue* in the realm of instrumental music.[12] The timeless Latin text was in any case free of the danger of ageing, unlike the madrigalesque cantata and Passion poetry whose ephemeral nature Bach must have been aware of in his last years.

Thus the B minor Mass stands before posterity, grown beyond the requirements of ecclesiastical duty or external commission, a *summa* of artistic development and religious experience, a product of the struggle over decades for the greatest possible perfection-in-composition,[13] from the early period of mastery at Weimar through the maturity of the first decade at Leipzig to the spiritualized late style of the last years. Despite the difficulty with which the origins and history of the Mass are clarified, it cannot be denied that the composer's intention had been to create a unified work. How far he succeeded in doing so could lead to differing opinions. One will not easily be able to disregard the concentrated power of organization that gives order to the most varied types of movement and that can bring together opposite and seemingly incompatible elements.

How deeply the composition plumbs the venerable mass texts from the theological point of view certainly varies from movement to movement and must depend on the nature of the originals gathered here and there; but it must also be influenced by the intention behind the choice of movements. Thus it should not be forgotten that the *Symbolum Nicenum* is symmetrical in shape, and that through the subsequent composition of the 'Et incarnatus est' as a choral movement the 'Crucifixus' is moved into the central position. Many symbols used in the shaping and working out of themes, in rhetoric and the use of *figurae*, in large- and small-scale structuring, can be unlocked after some trouble, while others remain uncertain. Certainly Bach saw more deeply here than any of his contemporaries or most of his predecessors. On the other hand, in the case of the 'Dona nobis pacem', based on a previous movement, or the contrapuntal setting of the plainsong 'Credo' intonation, he seems to have leant towards models of South German/Austrian/Italian provenance of the kind he will have got to know in Dresden. Even the overall structure as a 'cantata mass' – assembled from closed choral movements and arias (though free of *da capo* forms) – follows previous examples circulating as far as Vienna, Venice and Rome. Nevertheless, for the shape and contents of the B minor Mass as a whole and of its single movements no prototype is either to be found or expected.

A quarter of a millennium after the origin of the *Missa* as the basic germ-cell form of the later *Missa tota*, scholarship and practice still confront many unresolved problems. As already said, the last and most controversial of the

---

12 Neither the *Art of Fugue* nor the B minor Mass has an authorized title for the work as a whole.
13 Cf. C. Wolff, 'Die sonderbaren Vollkommenheiten des Herrn Hofcompositeurs: Versuch über die Eigenart der Bachschen Musik', *Bachiana et alia musicologica: Festschrift Alfred Dürr zum 65. Geburtstag*, ed. W. Rehm (Kassel, 1983), pp. 356–62.

oratorio-like works of the *Thomaskantor* reflects in its later history much of the state of Bach scholarship at various times. A final note here concerns Bach's use – still not fully elucidated – of the invocatory formula *JJ* (*Jesu juva*) and closing colophon *SDGl* (*Soli deo gloria*) in the score of the B minor Mass. The *Missa* of 1733 (no. 1) contains both, being at that moment a complete work in its own right; in 1748 the *JJ* could remain since it still served the planned completion, but although the *SDGl* had no function any longer it would have been blasphemous to eliminate it. The Credo (no. 2) was newly composed, so the composer wrote *JJ* over the first brace of staves; he avoided any final note since the work was certainly not ending with the Credo. The Sanctus (no. 3) remained without a mark, being a mere copy (though improved in detail) of a composition already to hand. The final section of the Mass from 'Osanna' onwards (no. 4) was newly composed like the Credo[14] and received, logically, a *JJ* at the beginning. Then after the 'Dona nobis pacem' is written *Fine SDGl*, the final colophon for the *Missa tota*, 'the great Catholic mass', the *opus summum*, puzzling now as before.

Translated by editor

14 In section 4 as in section 2, 'new' includes the parodying of older movements.

Remarks on the Compositions for Organ of Domenico Scarlatti

LUIGI FERDINANDO TAGLIAVINI
(Bologna)

It is not very original to claim that in Domenico Scarlatti's output of keyboard music the harpsichord occupies a predominant position. The great Neapolitan's sympathy for this instrument rather than for the organ has, moreover, received 'official' sanction ever since the moment of his famous musical contest with Handel in 1709.[1] Nevertheless, we are not without pieces by Scarlatti in which performance on the organ appears quite legitimate: works whose writing is not idiomatic to the harpsichord, particularly those compositions in contrapuntal style that return to the traditional ambivalent phrase 'for harpsichord or organ' (*per cembalo od organo*). Then there are the pieces certainly and explicitly intended for organ. In his still basic monograph on Scarlatti, Kirkpatrick identifies five sonatas as expressly conceived for organ,[2] to which he gives the numbers Kk 254, 255, 287, 288 and 328, that is to say two pairs and a single sonata.[3] Kirkpatrick's hypothesis has been generally accepted, and the five sonatas have been published as works for organ in editions by Douglass Greene[4] and Loek Hautus[5], the latter complete with the fugues Kk 41, 58 and 93.[6]

There is no doubt that the pair of Sonatas in D major Kk 287 and 288 was intended for organ: indeed, the first of them is headed 'Per Org⁰' and 'Per Organo da Camera con due Tastature [*sic*] Flautato e Trombone' in the Venice and Parma sources respectively,[7] and in addition both sonatas carry (in both manuscripts)

---

1 The 'trial of skill' between Domenico Scarlatti and Handel, promoted by Cardinal Pietro Ottoboni, is an anecdote told by Mainwaring, pp. 59–62. The passage is quoted by, amongst others, R. Kirkpatrick, *Domenico Scarlatti* (Princeton, N.J., 1953), pp. 32ff. Did the story come from Handel himself, as the one about the abortive Marchand–J. S. Bach contest probably came from Bach himself?
2 Kirkpatrick, *Domenico Scarlatti*, pp. 185ff.
3 In Longo's edition (Milan, 1906–8) the five sonatas received the numbers 219, 439, Suppl.9, 57, and Suppl.27 respectively.
4 *D. Scarlatti: Five Organ Sonatas* (New York: Schirmer, 1962).
5 *D. Scarlatti: Sonaten und Fugen für Orgel –Sonatas and Fugues for Organ* (Kassel, 1968).
6 The fugue Kk 41 is missing from the Longo edition; the other two appear as nos. 158 and 336.
7 Venice, Bib. Marc. MSS 9770–9784; Parma, Bib. Pal. MS AG 31406–31420.

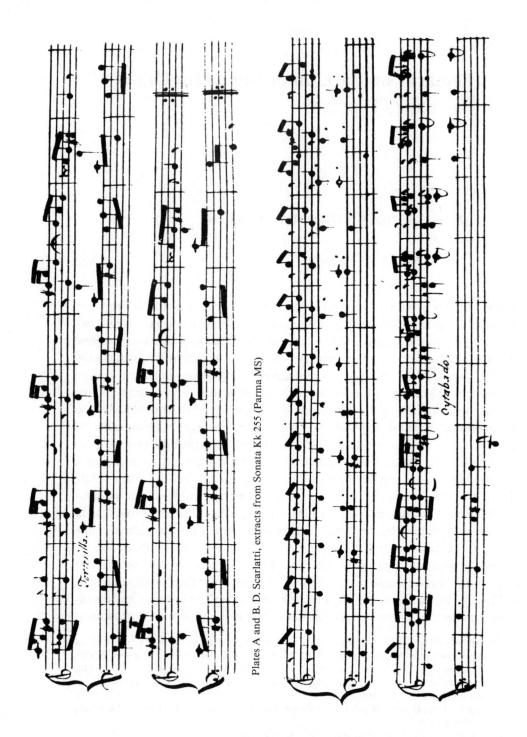

Plates A and B. D. Scarlatti, extracts from Sonata Kk 255 (Parma MS)

precise indications for the changing of manuals.[8] Nor does it seem open to doubt that the Sonata in G major Kk 328 is intended for organ, since in both of the sources cited there are directions, constantly alternating, for 'Org̥' and 'Fl̥'.

The case of the pair of Sonatas Kk 254 (C minor) and Kk 255 (C major) is on the contrary very different. As I have already shown elsewhere,[9] the idea that they were intended for organ rests on a misunderstanding: it is based on the indications 'Oytabado' and 'Tortorilla' placed (identically in the Venice or Parma manuscripts) at bars 37 and 64 respectively of the Sonata Kk 255 – indications taken by Kirkpatrick, Greene and Hautus as registration signs. Greene interprets the first term to mean 'octaved' (past participle) and supposes that it can refer to a registration of $8' + 4'$, while Hautus hazards the guess, difficult to accept, that the term derives from *octava tapada* ('stopped octave') and hence refers to the 4' *bordone* (stopped Diapason). As for 'Tortorilla', both editors attempt to interpret the term (signifying 'turtle-dove') as alluding to a clear combination of stops: 'stops of a clear flute quality' (Greene) or 'bright registration, e.g. $8' + 2'$, or $8' + 1''$ (Hautus). Any such interpretation of the term carries little conviction: one really cannot see why 'Tortorilla' should indicate a particular combination of stops. The only plausible explanation in organ terminology would rather be some reference to the effect of twittering birds often found in Baroque organs. But it is enough to consider the passage given this indication (see Plate A) to realize that the term can be interpreted in a quite different sense. 'Tortorilla' is certainly not an indication of stops or in any way of performance but is a clear allusion to the onomatopoea contained in the passage: the characteristically incisive melodic–rhythmic element repeated no fewer than five times towards the end of the first part (f♯-g-d) of the sonata, as too in the second part (b-c-g), is evidently an imitation or stylization of the turtle-dove's call.

In a similar direction can be found an explanation of the term 'Oytabado', a word whose form can be reduced to Portuguese or Galician. It concerns a passage, beginning at bar 37 of the same sonata, that is based on a characteristic rhythmic motif (Plate B). In fact, the term seems to be an allusion to a specific dance rhythm: the *oitavado* was a popular Portuguese dance.[10]

With the certainty that the two terms in question are not stop-indications, the reason for considering the pair of Sonatas Kk 254 and 255 as organ pieces collapses. Besides, in neither of these two sonatas can anything be recognized as an idiomatic expression of the nature of organs, unlike the sonatas certainly conceived for organ (Kk 287, 288, 328), where various details in style and writing – contrasts between two levels of sound, contrapuntal passages, sustained notes such as the

8 The indication takes the form of a little hand with forefinger pointing up or down, corresponding to each passage on upper or lower manual. See facsimile (based on the Parma MS) in R. Kirkpatrick, *D. Scarlatti: Complete Keyboard Works in Facsimile from the Manuscript and Printed Sources* (New York/London, 1972), p.x.

9 Review of the edition by L. Hautus (see note 5 above), in *L'Organo* 8 (1970), pp. 111–14.

10 Cf. C. de Figueiredo, *Novo dicionário da língua portuguesa*, 5th edn (Lisbon, 1937), II, p. 471; also *Grande enciclopédia portuguesa e brasileira* (Lisbon, 1945), XIX, p. 158.

pedal-point towards the end of the Sonata Kk 288 – show themselves clearly inspired by the sonority and resources of the organ. On the contrary, certain passages in the Sonata Kk 255, in particular the sections based on the *oitavado* rhythm, have a catchy quality that seems decisively harpsichord-like. Besides, the Sonata Kk 254 requires a keyboard with a completely chromatic first octave or at least one lacking only the C♯ – in fact the E♭, F♯ and A♭ are used – while the three sonatas of Scarlatti certainly intended for organ can be played on instruments with short bottom octave, as was usual in Italy and the Iberian peninsula at the time.

Of the three organ sonatas one deserves special mention: that in G major Kk 328, composed in the form of a dialogue on two levels of sound carefully distinguished (as noted) by 'Org̣' and 'Fḷ' Hautus thinks that it was composed for a typical Italian organ with single manual and considers that the dialogue can be realized as an alternation between a *plenum* (*ripieno*, with which the term *organo* is to be considered synonymous) and a *flauto in ottava* (a 4′ flute) played an octave below – something possible, given the high compass of the passages marked by the rubric 'Fḷ' The changing of stops would be made possible by using the *tiratutti* lever. This hypothesis, though interesting in itself, is not easy to accept since there is no evidence that the term *organo* was equivalent to *plenum* (at least, not in the context of Italian–Iberian organs). The former term is on the contrary to be understood as *primo organo* or *organo principale* (therefore the main keyboard), in the same way that in German-speaking countries the term *Werk* can be understood to mean *Hauptwerk*. As for the rubric 'Fḷ', it is probably an abbreviation for the term 'Flautato' that figures in the text of the Sonata Kk 287. The dialogue in Kk 328 is then to be realized, in my opinion, by means of a change of manual. It seems likely, in short, that this sonata too was composed for that *organo da camera con due tastature* intended for the pair of Sonatas Kk 287 and 288, or at least for an instrument of very similar type.

An examination of the three compositions reveals that the passages given to the upper manual in Kk 287 and 288 – like those headed 'Fḷ' in Kk 328 – do not go lower than tenor a. The organ for which they were written was thus provided with one complete manual and a second manual restricted to treble only, probably beginning at a; on such a kind of *récit* would be placed the open flue 8′ stop (Flautato) – appropriate to an *organo da camera* precisely because of its missing bass pipes – while on the main manual would be found (probably along with other stops) the Trombone. In all probability this last is to be understood as a regal,[11] a stop which unlike the Flautato can run down into the bass as far as C because of its short resonators. From the text of the three sonatas one can be largely certain of the compass of the instrument concerned: the top of both manuals was surely d‴ (a note played frequently, whereas it looks as if e‴ was impossible.[12] In addition, the

---

11 The term *trombone* referring to a regal is found in Italian sources from the end of the sixteenth century onwards; in the form *tromboncini* it became standard in the Venetian organ of the eighteenth century.

12 Hautus draws attention to bar 27 of the Sonata Kk 288, where it seems clear enough that expedients had to be devised to avoid the e‴.

bass octave of the main manual was very probably short, given that in none of the three sonatas do the lowest four chromatic notes appear. Although the term *trombone* (with reference to a regal) occurs often in Italian organ terminology, *flautato* seems definitely to refer to the Iberian organ; also, a little chamber organ with two manuals would be, in the field of Italian organs at this period, a quite unique example.

From the considerations aired here it appears that the registration of the Sonata Kk 287 should be realized in a manner exactly opposite to that suggested by Hautus[13] and generally adopted by performers: it seems the passages marked 'Flautato' ought to be played on the short upper manual and those marked 'Trombone' on the lower, and not vice versa.[14]

Translated by editor

13 The registration that seems to me correct is indicated in Greene's edition (note 4 above).
14 The two changes of manual suggested by Hautus (note 5 above) in bars 21 and 25 of the Sonata Kk 287 are therefore to be rejected. The whole passage from the last crotchet of bar 19 to the third of bar 26 is in fact characterized by the high tessitura which distinguishes the upper manual of the *organo da camera*. The changes of manual indicated by Kirkpatrick (*Domenico Scarlatti*, p. 363) are also inexactly placed.

Figurae in the Keyboard Works of Scarlatti, Handel and Bach: An Introduction

PETER WILLIAMS

(Edinburgh)

Like other intimate details in the arts of composition and performance, *figurae* (motifs, figures, *Figuren*) are studied today far less often than topics concerned with context or sources. Yet when one looks at the actual notes composed and the way they behave, it is possible to understand directly what priorities were engaging the original composer and thus what it is the performer is actually playing, whether or not he knows or communicates it.

It is not yet possible to give either a full theoretical backing to some of the ideas expressed in this essay or indeed a full survey of the issues involved. In many areas in the performance of old music, one could well doubt if we are yet able to see what the questions are, much less answer them. One such basic question would be: Are performers to express in the way they play the nature of the motifs as worked out (with much trouble and care) by the composer, or is that merely to expose the bones of the structure and make explicit what was left implicit? In at least one case, the answer must be that the performer does make it explicit: J. S. Bach generally, and Handel often, slurred the note-pairs of the so-called 'sighing motif' shown in Ex. 1. Now, whatever this *figura* is supposed to 'mean' or 'express' or 'symbolize', whatever its instrumentation, its position in the composer's chronology, its thoroughness of application in a particular piece etc., it seems clear enough that the player is to mark it by playing each pair of notes as if it had a nature distinct from other motifs – as of course it does. But is he always to mark *figurae* in some such way, give to each its own kind of articulation, and so draw attention to their nature, variety and inventiveness? Is he to mark the 'sighing motifs' of Ex. 1 in the same way in the works of Scarlatti, who never slurs them? How is one to know? Have we yet grasped the scope of *figurae*?

When the idea of *Figurenlehre* was formulated – one might say 'invented' – in German musicology of the earlier twentieth century, it was not for the sake of deducing articulation or other basic details of performance but as a means of showing that

Ex. 1.

(a) J. S. Bach, *O Lamm Gottes, unschuldig* BWV 618

(b) G. F. Handel, Gavotte Double (bar 28) from G major Suite, *Second Set* (1733)

composers were illustrating the 'rules' drawn by certain old theorists. The theorists used for these purposes were usually German, and it was not always made clear – nor is it yet – that what these theorists said was the result of what they could observe of Italian madrigals and other vocal music (or German imitations thereof). Today's treatment of German theorists often disguises the fact that they were well to the rear of the advances made during the seventeenth century: the theorists of less backward and provincial countries (Italy, England, France) had a less developed interest in listing and naming *figurae*, for they had already moved on. In any case, the remarks of (e.g.) J. G. Walther are now examined by musicologists not to suggest that during their early years together in Weimar both Walther and J. S. Bach were involved in *figurae* as compositional elements *per se*, but to demonstrate that what older theorists had said was still alive and that their motif-lists (insofar as there was such a thing) implied one or other *Affekt* in the rhetorical palette of music. From the reading of such theorists as Walther or Mattheson grew another twentieth-century invention, *Affektenlehre*, which led to such astonishing assertions as that a piece of 'Baroque music', as it is called, has only one *Affekt* throughout its course. No thinking performer ever gave such an idea more than a passing smile, however seductive the theory and however useful it might be in 'proving' some other theory (such as that organists should not change manuals in long ritornello fugues). But the significance of *figurae* lies not in such areas at all – at least, not in the case of the top-rank composers of whom we are thinking – but in the more down-to-earth details of composing and playing.

Of course, some *figurae* are bound to be associative. It is difficult to see how the chromatic fourth in Ex. 2 could ever be anything than grave or melancholy. Yet the

Ex. 2.

madrigal composers would not use it to suggest melancholy – to pluck melancholy out of the air, so to speak – but simply because the association was natural[1] and because the motif ('which our organists use', as Morley noted in 1597) is useful in counterpoint of a serious cast. At least up to the time of Mozart, this *figura* (part of the species called by Bernhard *passus duriusculus*, a term apparently borrowed from earlier non-musical rhetoricians)[2] usually had a melancholy, or ecclesiastical, or old-fashioned, or serious-minded feel to it. The chromatic fourth is after all the fugue subject *par excellence*, and it is likely that without it the whole history of fugue might well have been different; it is certainly extremely useful as a counter-subject or as one of the subjects in a permutation fugue. Its sudden colouring of a passage in a madrigal could obviously produce a sudden melancholy *affetto* too, of course, and this dual nature – its usefulness to both counterpoint and *affetto* – remained with it. Mozart's use of it in D minor in the early Quartet K 173 (with a fugal answer precisely of the kind Fux had said was incorrect – see Fux 1725 p. 235) reflected its contrapuntal potential, as do the G minor and A minor versions of it in the Quartet K 387; but the same chromatic fourth in the cello part of the Minuet in the later D minor Quartet K 421 certainly contributes to the melancholy feel in the quartet as a whole. In short, this particular *figura* traditionally appeared both for subjective and objective purposes over the whole period from Lassus to Mozart and indeed beyond.

Although other motifs too may have been related by Walther to the Italian vocal arts of embellishment and good word-setting, they can have had nothing like the same strength of allusion. For example, the *figura suspirans* might well occur in Monteverdi for a sighing *affetto*, as in Ex. 3, but such motifs are in themselves free

Ex. 3. C. Monteverdi, *Il Ritorno d'Ulisse*, Act I Sc. 8

---

1 Even then, the chromatic fourth in D minor does not inevitably bring with it gravity, as any admirer of the Habañera in Bizet's *Carmen* will know.

2 Is it possible that Bernhard or others recognized a pun and saw that *duriusculus* ('somewhat hard') could also mean 'somewhat major' – i.e., that some of the notes in such progressions are those of the major scale, some of the minor, and that only one pair (C♯-C♮) is strictly chromatic? Morley pointed out something similar when he remarked that the motif 'is not right *Chromatica*, but a bastard point patched up, of halfe *chromaticke*, and halfe *diatonick*' (1597, 'Annotations' to p. 2, 'vers 26'). Two centuries later, Manfredini was still calling such motifs those 'of the *genere misto*' (1775 p. 25).

of allusion or *affetto*. They might be used for sighing or they might not, while for the keyboardist they produce lines or patterns very comfortable for the fingers. Thus, on the one hand, for the keyboardist they are useful in their own right; on the other hand, for very highly expressive purposes in vocal music, a composer would soon learn to use other, more marked ideas. Neither Monteverdi nor Handel use the *figura suspirans* frequently for 'sighing' purposes, the younger composer preferring a more striking gesture (as in Ex. 4a); the old *suspirans* may have been more versatile, but this also meant that it was more 'neutral' and thus useful especially in keyboard works (see Exx. 4b and 4c). Other versions of the *suspirans* would be

Ex. 4.

(a) G. F. Handel, Cantata *Mi palpita il cor*

o-gnor ge- mi e so - spi-ri?

(b) G. F. Handel, Allemande from D minor Suite, *Second Set* no. 4

(c) D. Scarlatti, Kk 258, bar 32 (passage repeated)

etc.

more positive, even jubilant, serving such themes as the Resurrection (Ex. 5),[3] though early works of Bach in particular (and probably also Handel and Scarlatti) are full of lines and textures built up from the *suspirans* motifs so well suited to fingers on a keyboard. At the same time, obviously the way the motif is scored, the tempo in which it is played or the direction in which it goes (ascending/descending)

3 BWV 66 is the Leipzig version, for the 2nd Sunday after Easter, of a birthday cantata for Leopold of Anhalt-Cöthen (BWV 66a, 1718), of which the relevant text was 'Der Himmel dacht' auf Anhalts Ruhm und Glück'.

Ex. 5.

(a) J. S. Bach, *Erstanden ist der heil'ge* **Christ BWV 628**

(b) *Heut' triumphiret Gottes Sohn* **BWV 630**

(c) BWV 66.i, bar 13

can all produce variable *Affekte*. Here, therefore, is a good example of a motif originally related (at least by Printz and Walther) to a vocal text or applied as a kind of vocal ornament becoming for a good keyboard composer a versatile means of writing idiomatic music.

But a key question is: Did such a motif *ever* have much to do with 'sighing' except in the fancy of theorists or those seventeenth-century German composers anxious to catch up with the musical nations of Europe, in particular with Italy? Were not such *figurae* already part of the keyboard composer's repertory before, or in any case irrespective of, the madrigalists of either *prima* or *seconda prattica*? Certain things are natural to fingers on a keyboard, however long the keys and whatever the fingering conventions, and one can imagine that even when a composer is supposed to be (for example) 'imitating the viols' with his *figurae* (as is the case with Scheidt's *imitatio violistica* – Ex. 6), the bowing or slurring marks produce nothing that is

Ex. 6. S. Scheidt, *Wir glauben all'*, **Verse 3 (bar 36) from** *Tabulatura nova*, **I**

331

unnatural for keyboard-players' fingers. A similar point can be made about those lines of semiquavers in the English virginalist school which, however plain they may look, are made up of *figurae* whose subtle cross-rhythms are brought about by certain natural fingerings and articulations. When we can find a composer of the first rank playing with conventional *figurae*, it becomes important to ask several questions. Is he doing so with an *affetto* in mind, one that would otherwise not be apparent? Is he doing so under the assumption that the *figurae* suggest particular articulations and are to be played in a certain way and thus distinguished from each other? Is he doing so because he knows what a contemporary theorist says or because he knows other music using them? Of these basic questions not a single one can be answered with certainty for any of our three composers; but much can be learnt from addressing them.

At least the first question can be answered 'No' with reasonable confidence, not least because, as Bernhard himself implied, *Affekte* also involve (and influence) the manner of performance (1963 edn p. 37) – something we should need no theorist to tell us. Even the chromatic fourth is allusive only when associated with certain texts – that is, either set to words in a vocal piece (descending in 'They loathed to drink of the river' in *Israel in Egypt*, ascending at 'And Israel by Philistine arms shall fall' in *Saul*) or related to a 'situation' in an instrumental piece (the lament in J. S. Bach's Capriccio in B flat BWV 992). In, say, a harpsichord sonata or an organ concerto, it must be more neutral if still 'serious', especially when it appears in D minor, like a passage near the end of the Spiritoso of the Organ Concerto Op. VII No. 3 – see Ex. 7a. If 'They loathed to drink of the river' originated as a keyboard fugue (no. 5 in A minor from the *Six Fugues* of 1735), and one composed some twenty years before publication, one could imagine the composer searching amongst his keyboard works for what might be called a potentially allusive fugue, just as when he came to teach fugal techniques he would naturally turn to a subject type that was apt and useful (see Ex. 7b). It seems that for J. S. Bach in particular the chromatic fourth is virtually *de rigueur* in D minor counterpoint (*tonus primus*): the final statement of the D minor Three-part Invention, the fugue subject of the D minor Fugue *WTC* Bk 2, occasional moments in works composed in other keys,[4] a countersubject for one of the fugues in the *Art of Fugue*,[5] and so on. In fact, consider-

4 It is clear from BL Add. MS 35021, f. 1' that the D minor chromatic fourth in the middle of the opening prelude of Book 2 of the *WTC* (Prelude in C major BWV 870.i, bars 18–20) is the result of revision: it was not there at first, at least not in this copy.

5 It is surely significant how seldom the chromatic fourth appears in the *Art of Fugue*, considering the work's key and the wide-ranging survey it gives of fugal counterpoint. Did the composer regard the chromatic fourth as having outlived its usefulness? Was it so much a mere formula for him in his earlier work? Is the absence of the chromatic fourth from the D minor Toccata BWV 565 (especially when compared with the D minor Canzona BWV 588, the D minor Concerto BWV 596, etc.) another reason to doubt the authenticity of BWV 565? Is the presence of the chromatic fourth in another key in an early work (e.g. the Albinoni Fugue in B minor BWV 951) 'proof' that it did not originate as a keyboard fugue or as one composed by J. S. Bach? Obviously the F minor chromatics in the Capriccio in B flat BWV 992 are a particularly strong gesture.

Ex. 7.

(a) G. F. Handel, Concerto in B flat for Organ, Op. VII No. 3, third movement, bar 127

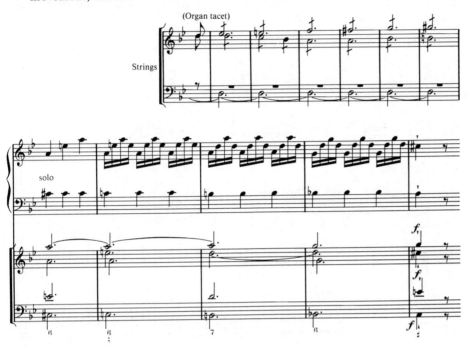

(b) G. F. Handel, *Kompositionslehre* (ed. A. Mann, 1978), p. 87 (and cf. p. 100)

ing its formula-like nature in the chorale *Das alte Jahr* BWV 614 (including the curious fact that it could have been worked into the counterpoint of the piece as it now exists more often than it actually is), can one claim that BWV 614 is not as melancholy as it usually thought, since in the end 'conventionality' can be seen as a 'neutral' quality?[6]

In the case of the second question posed above – are *figurae* to be played in certain ways specific to each? – the answer may well veer more towards 'Yes'. Although in his harpsichord sonatas Scarlatti may appear to have had no particular awareness

---

6 Note too that since BWV 614 carries no *largo* or *adagio* marking (as found in some other chorales in the *Orgelbüchlein*) and that since the hymn itself is a text not for 31 December but for New Year's Day, 'melancholy' may well be inappropriate on several grounds.

of – or habit of using – the D minor chromatic fourth (such sonatas in D minor as Kk 89 and Kk 90 present many opportunities for it which are not exploited), some sonatas, including Kk 89, do make a suggestion about other close-interval motifs that raises an important question for the player (see Ex. 8). It is this: Are chro-

Ex. 8.

(a) D. Scarlatti, Sonata Kk 89, bar 15 (original slurs)

(b) Kk 474, bar 4

(c) Kk 16, bar 18 (the print of 1739)

matic or close-interval motifs in keyboard music associated with and/or slurred legato touch? Even perhaps a super-legato or sostenuto, as too when Scarlatti slurs the notes of a broken chord? In any set of variations (e.g. Handel's C major Suite HWV 443.v or Bach's chorale-partita BWV 767), the chromatic passages are obviously given a marked character when played in this way. But how could one begin to answer such a question when so few slurs are written into keyboard music, and when those that are are usually for other motifs only (see Ex. 1)?[7] The grounds for

7 Why the motif shown in Ex. 1 is slurred, so consistently, when it could hardly be played any other way, is itself a large question. It looks as if it was a 'necessary' part of J. S. Bach's notation, automatic, whether or not the first note is an appoggiatura, and whether or not later copyists or transcribers understood it (for example, the violin's autograph slurs in the fugue of the G minor Sonata BWV 1001 are omitted in the non-autograph sources for the organ transcription BWV 539.ii bars 13–14). Of course, such slurs must often function as a warning against taking too lively a tempo: the detail they introduce into the articulation (also in string music, such as the finale of the C minor Concerto for Two Harpsichords BWV 1060) compels a steadier tempo than might otherwise be taken.

　　Of the various decorative *figurae* still listed by Bach's pupil Kirnberger (1776 p. 86), only this motif receives a slur. In the second of A. della Ciaja's *Sonate per cembalo* (Rome, n.d.) a similar motif is slurred and figured (r.h.) 3232; is the slurring in Ex. 8c a warning not to pair off the semitones?

thinking that chromatic *figurae* might of themselves suggest legato touch – though they are rarely slurred – would have to be derived from analogy, practicability and supposition. *Analogy*: smooth chromatic motifs or lines are suggested by analogy with other instruments, such lines having the nature of phrases played under one bow by violin[8] or in one breath by flute. *Practicability*: a smooth chromatic phrase is usually easy for the fingers (and, in organ music, for the alternate-foot technique of pedalling). *Supposition*: one may suppose that it is natural to desire contrast, and a legato chromatic line contrasts with the prevailing *détaché* touch. Of these three arguments, the first is no proof, since obviously strings, voices and woodwind can all be expected to perform some chromatic phrases smoothly, others not.[9] The second and third are better reasons, though by nature inconclusive. In Ex. 9, a

Ex. 9. G. F. Handel (?), 'Sonatina' (*HHA* IV/21), bar 5 (with added signs)

primitive and archetypal example, the independence of contrapuntal lines – a 'counterpoint by articulation' – seems to suggest *détaché* for one theme, legato for the other. In the chorale BWV 614, already referred to, the organist could create a more sophisticated contrast by playing the chromatic phrases legato, the bass cadences (clearly marking the end of each line) *détaché*. In the Italian counterpoint

8 Kk 89, having a figured left-hand staff, may well have originated as a sonata for violin. The characteristically slurred chromatic motifs that are frequently found in Italian string music – particularly towards the end of a movement or cadenza or section – can also be found in Bach transcriptions (e.g. BWV 596.iii bar 15; BWV 1064.iii bars 169–74). Such 'preparatory chromaticism' on what is usually a simple harmonic idea (e.g. dominant pedal-point; or the drone of a pastorale such as BWV 590 bars 28ff; or that in Zipoli's *Sonate d'intavolatura* (Rome, c1716), closing bars) is certainly emphasized by slurring.

9 For example, at moments in the D minor Chaconne the violin has the chromatic fourth (D minor, G minor) in anything but legato contrast; on the contrary, it is *marqué*. The same could be said about its appearance as the countersubject to the fugue in the C major Sonata BWV 1005. In both violin works, the chromatic fourth contributes a vivid, 'somewhat hard passage' to the movements as a whole – indeed, two of the very few examples that justify or illustrate Bernhard's term *passus duriusculus* in music composed during the period after the central Italian madrigalists. For most so-called Baroque composers, the chromatic fourth was 'very melancholy', not 'somewhat hard' – *maestissimus*, not *duriusculus*.

335

of the D minor Canzona BWV 588, it clearly makes good sense to have a sliding or legato chromatic line surrounded by a *détaché* leaping counterpoint in the other parts – until, that is, the chromatic fourth is actually marked to be played *détaché* (as in bars 116ff). A chromatic countersubject being so often one of the lines of a fugue with more than one subject, it would always make sense to mark it with its own articulation or touch. This is true too of chromatic lines in other contexts – such as the 'hidden' line dispersed within the broad lines of a fluent movement (Ex. 10a), or the sudden and unexpected gesture in the course of a jolly, extrovert movement (Ex. 10b), or the coda-like air of finality that chromatics can supply at the close of an otherwise very diatonic movement (Ex. 10c). In general, one could

Ex. 10.

(a) G. F. Handel, Courante from C minor Suite (*HHA* IV/17a), bar 40

(b) D. Scarlatti, Sonata Kk 441, bar 77 (with added signs)

(c) J. S. Bach, *Allabreve* in D major BWV 589, bar 180 (with added signs)

claim it to be at least useful for the keyboard-player to begin with the assumption that a chromatic line is best marked by being played legato or even super-legato.

Other *figurae* too may well have their own natural articulations as a matter of course, i.e. because of the kind of motif that they are. A good example is the triplet of fast notes, whether slurred (in Scarlatti's *Essercizi per gravicembalo*, London 1738, Kk 6, Kk 7 and Kk 17) or instead marked '3' (L. Giustini's *Sonate da cimbalo di piano e forte*, Florence 1732; *In dulci jubilo* BWV 608, autograph copy in DSB MS P 283, where the triplets, like many of Scarlatti's, are notated twice too fast). Whether to set them off from each other as groups of three, or run them together in longer lines, must depend on how they are used by the composer; either way, they are not *détaché* like those in *Vater unser* BWV 682, which must be a sign of newer styles in musical performance. In view of its other *galant* elements, it is likely that BWV 682 was consciously reflecting the refinements of newer playing style in this very detail: i.e., staccato flute-like triplets.

Another example of the *figura* bringing with it an associated articulation is the off-the-beat motif in Exx. 3, 4 and 5. Whether or not we are justified in calling it the *figura suspirans*, its chief characteristic is that it begins after one beat and moves towards another, even when it appears several times in the course of one phrase (as in Ex. 11 and Ex. 4b, 4c). Elsewhere, both the Passacaglia BWV 582 and the Sonata Kk 258 exploit motifs that undoubtedly begin *on* the beat, as in Ex. 12. Therefore,

Ex. 11.

(a) J. S. Bach, Passacaglia BWV 582, bar 48

(b) cf. Partita BWV 767. iii

Ex. 12.

(a) BWV 582, bars 104, 120 (slurs original – copy of autograph?)

(b) Kk 258, bar 19

it could be argued, one could convey the composer's exploitation of different ideas (motifs, *figurae*) by articulating them differently: some lead towards a main beat, others away from it.

Indeed, even when a line looks unbroken and continuous, it will generally be found to be made up of such *figurae*, and it may well have been understood to be broken and *dis*continous. A particularly good example is the scale, for a scale is no more than a pattern of adjacent notes, rising or falling, less or more extensive. Before it became customary for all performers to practise the gamut of scales – a topic itself worth a major study – any line of adjacent notes was likely to have a much more carefully thought-out function and character. Scarlatti or his copyists often – even generally (except Roseingrave in the additional pieces in his edition of *XLII Suites*, London 1739) – slurred fast scales, sometimes to indicate *glissando* (as too in the third of della Ciaja's *Sonate per cembalo*), but sometimes not. Whether *glissando* or not, in most of these cases the scale was longer than an octave or so – longer than, say, the scale-like colorations running up and down in at least one movement of a set of variations by Handel or Bach. This kind of slur is indeed the most common in the Scarlatti sources, drawing attention to the fact that scales of this kind are embellishments, decorative fill-ins (whether *glissando* or not) between the important beats, corresponding to what the German theorists (picking up what they could of older Italian singing habits) called *tirata*. But decorative scales are a different species from the kind of line built up in the Passacaglia out of what are essentially off-the-beat *figurae*: the two types of scale are shown in Ex. 13. Similarly, the *perpetuum mobile* character of such lines as the paraphrased right hand in *Nun freut euch* BWV 734 is also built up of *figurae*: see Ex. 14. Here the motif is not off the beat but on it, looking very like Scheidt's *imitatio violistica* (cf. Ex. 6), which of course may well have been still very familiar indeed both to the young Bach and to Scheidt's fellow Hallensian Handel. One can guess that, in comparison, the easy fluency of many of Handel's *perpetuum mobile* lines (B flat Suite of the *Second Set*, etc.) suggests they are to be played without subtle articulations. But the degree of articulation in Exx. 13 and 14 is also conjectural because an abso-

Ex. 13.

(a) BWV 582, bar 80

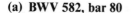

(b) Kk 454, bar 18

Ex. 14. J. S. Bach, *Nun freut euch* **BWV 734**

(chorale: G   G A   B   A G A   A   B)

lute seems to be operating: one simply cannot separate off *figurae* beyond a certain degree.

That is a particularly difficult problem for the player eager to convey the thoroughness with which *figurae* are often exploited by J. S. Bach and Handel: How far can be afford to mark off the *figurae*? For example, given that the Magnificat Fugue BWV 733 has some form of the *figura* shown in Ex. 15a in virtually every bar, he simply cannot mark it off conspicuously bar after bar. Yet an unbroken continuity is unsatisfactory to those aware of the composer's skill in handling the motif throughout a substantial fugue. In the case of the Prelude from Handel's E major Suite, the *figura* (Ex. 15b) takes more varied forms, so that even

Ex. 15.

(a) J. S. Bach, Magnificat Fugue BWV 733

bar 2   or bar 10   cf. BWV 546.ii, bar 60

(b) Handel, Prelude from E major Suite

or bar 3   or bar 12

though the piece is shorter, the composer has still made things easier for the player by producing (on a small scale) a varied phraseology. Similarly, elsewhere in the music of Bach (C minor Fugue BWV 546.ii; *Italian Concerto*) the motif, or one very like it, can afford to be more conspicuously marked simply because it occurs less often. In the music of Scarlatti, if often looks as if the composer left open how far the player was to break continuity and where he was to break it. Several solutions could be found for articulating the scales in Ex. 16. When in chapter 10 of his book on continuo-playing Gasparini suggests a short run before and into the $\frac{4}{2}$ chord, one can assume it to be a smooth *tirata*, a mere filling-in; but the excerpts in Ex. 16 suggest anything but a mere filling-in. On the right instrument, marking the groups as in Ex. 17 draws attention to how the music is constructed and plays with the motifs as if each has its own identity. Perhaps such composers left it to the player, assuming that anything but an overall legato would be natural. It should not be forgotten that the end-result of all articulation signs in all written music, including those rare examples of extensive slurring in Scarlatti sources (e.g. Kk 440), is to

339

Ex. 16.

(a) D. Scarlatti, Sonata Kk 216, bar 129

(b) J. S. Bach, Partita in G BWV 829

Ex. 17.

limit choice. The more effete a musical language and the more petite its effects, as for example in the hands of French composers *c*1750, the more it matters what precisely the articulation is.

The third question posed above concerns the degree to which composers are influenced by theorists and/or other composers, and it is safe to assume that every composer has his own pattern of events in this respect. A particularly clear connection was that between J. S. Bach and J. G. Walther: that Walther's ability with motifs as domonstrated in *Ach Gott und Herr* BWV 693 (once attributed to J. S. Bach) is inferior to Bach's as shown in the *Orgelbüchlein* might even suggest that the latter felt a particular reason for developing the techniques further.[10] One could make a similar point about the German keyboard music known to the young Handel, for naturally enough Zachow's preludes too use many of the same *Figuren*, as also do those of his successor Kirchhoff, and it cannot have been of prime importance to such men what it was that W. C. Printz happened to write in a book published in the 1690s. Evidently the Thuringian composers of *c*1700 thought very much in terms of basic motifs, like the *passus* or *saltus duriusculus*, the *figura suspirans*, the *figura corta* (dactyl and anapaest patterns) and so on, and

10 Of course, it is through his own chorales, rather than through his uncompleted book on music theory, that Walther is relevant to our understanding of the *Orgelbüchlein* and other chorales of J. S. Bach. That the melody of the chorale *Ach Gott und Herr* was treated in the Bach circle to figural and canonic workings is suggested by several kinds of example: Walther's BWV 693 (with its four-note motif that rises and falls, in augmented, diminished and regular forms); BWV 714 (by J. S. Bach or J. L. Krebs? similar motifs in canon etc.); and also the music example in Kirnberger's *Kunst des reinen Satzes* (1771, ch. 11) that shows how to set a chorale and give it different treatments (like BWV 693 but also exploiting the chromatic fourth).

340

it is tempting to assume that the more conventional a work's *figurae*, the earlier it is in the composer's worklist – although as is well known both Bach and Handel looked back late in life to specific old styles, if for different reasons.

When it comes to assessing how inventive a composer was in the way he exploited conventional *figurae*, it is clear that Bach is usually 'superior' to Handel and to their elders like Böhm; the *figurae* in Ex. 5 are developed in a way neither Handel nor Böhm would have considered useful,[11] and it is possible to think that the motif of Ex. 15 is itself a developed form of the same *figura* – a kind of extension or 'logical furthering' of a kind peculiar to J. S. Bach. Although the sets of variations and the ostinatos of Handel that are undoubtedly authentic do not 'further the motif' in the same way, they do suggest him to have been responsive to the local tastes of his adopted homeland, tastes far removed from the old Thuringian organists he left behind. One can accept that at times any chromatic fugue is going to involve the chromatic fourth, but Handel's sets of variations show more individuality of motif. Perhaps the English tradition of division-playing was in some way an influence. For example, the ostinato movement opening the B flat Organ Concerto Op. VII No. 1 suggests this in several of its details. The bass theme itself is not far removed from the *passamezzo moderno* of an earlier period,[12] while other traditional elements include the figural variation of the bass theme (Simpson's 'breaking the Ground' – 1665 pp. 28ff), the changes of mood 'to express Humour and draw on Attention' (*ibid*. p. 56), the nature of some of the patterns, the chordal variations (unusual outside the divisions tradition), perhaps the succinct close. Several of these details are absent from an early (?) set of variations more in the Pachelbel mould, the D minor *Aria* (HWV 450.v), where the *figurae* are totally standard and open to simple 'figural articulation' of the kind suggested in Ex. 18.

Ex. 18. G. F. Handel, *Aria* (Var. 1), *HHA* IV/12, bar 17 (with added signs)

Scarlatti's Variations in A minor (Sonata Kk 61) show, if it needed to be shown, that keyboardists find it natural to do certain things with the fingers. Not only did he not need to pick up such patterns from theorists, he would not have needed to pick them up from other composers. Clearly he aimed to create motifs encouraging

11 This remark is less a biographical speculation than a way of explaining in what way Bach was 'superior'. It is always difficult to imagine the flair of Handel being conducive to the mastering and careful calculation of figural *minutiae*.

12 A simple form of this bass, archetypal in its tonic–subdominant–dominant progressions, would naturally crop up throughout the diatonic period (e.g. Biber's Violin Sonata in A major (1681), the second subject of Schubert's A flat minor Impromptu (1827), etc.).

finger dexterity *per se* and composed music inventively from whatever motifs he had in hand. There was no developed Italian doctrine of *figurae*, and if there was ever a German one it had been assembled from vocal arts that were simply no longer to the fore in Italy itself. Presumably many of the typical Scarlatti motifs originated not as textbook *variationes* or *colorature* (as Bernhard claimed the Italians called them – 1963 edn, p. 73) but as finger-motifs: Ex. 19. Kirnberger, who cites Ex. 19c, thought this particular form of the motif (which indeed is curi-

Ex. 19.

(a) D. Scarlatti, Sonata Kk 345, bar 6

(b) C. Bernhard, 'Exempel der Variationen zur Secunda hinaufwärts'
('Example of variations on rising seconds', 1963 edn, p. 73)

(c) D. Scarlatti (cf. Kk 326), quoted by Kirnberger 1771 p. 89

ously rare in Scarlatti's repertory) unpleasing and uncomfortable to sing. But a sonata like the A major Kk 101 seems a mass of differentiated motifs, calculated to exercise the fingers: legato scales, legato broken chords, *détaché* broken chords, rising and falling sigh motifs, angular motifs in octaves and so on. Because they are all elemental ideas in keyboard-playing, some will resemble *figurae* used in (e.g.) Book 1 of the *WTC*.

In the case of Scarlatti's use of the chromatic fourth, various points can be made:
Any minor fugue would very likely have some reference to it, though (as is also the case with Corelli and other composers of violin sonatas) it had no particular associations with modes 1, 2 or 3.
Example: Kk 58, a C minor Fugue including diminutions, probably early, and perhaps originally in three parts (two violins and continuo?).
The progression could be used for simple rhythmic impetus, not contrapuntal but essentially decorative or contrasting.
Examples: Kk 260, where one of its appearances seems deliberately to surprise the ear about the eventual key; Kk 3, four, five or six bars of super-legato?

Chromatic lines are still derived from the chromatic fourth even (*a*) when in
mature pieces they may not look like it, or (*b*) where the sequence produces a
longer chromatic line as it proceeds.

Examples: (*a*) Kk 58, 373 and 55; (*b*) Kk 84, 115 and 126.

Each of these points may well seem common to a good deal of Italian keyboard
music composed in the period after the toccatas of Michelangelo Rossi, though
contemporary composers such as Marcello and Vivaldi (final bars of Concerto in
D minor Op. III No. 11, transcribed as BWV 596) kept more to the old key associations. Many elements common to Italian styles were rare outside Italy itself – for
example, the harpsichord *acciaccatura*, which has a right to be considered a kind of
figura (see Williams 1968). The slipping in of non-harmonic notes can be found in
what looks Scarlatti's early work without his ever having needed to be bewitched by
the flamenco guitar styles to which such dissonances are often attributed today. As
Ex. 20 shows, the D minor Sonata Kk 64 adds such notes to progressions otherwise

Ex. 20. D. Scarlatti, Sonata Kk 64, bar 8

very conventional as does the *arpeggiato nell'acciaccature* movement in Giustini's
Sonata no. 5 (1732). One can imagine that even those Thuringian or Saxon com-
posers/writers who eventually became aware of Italian idioms (as Heinichen did
after reading Gasparini) would not have thought to compose or play such things.

Since the *figurae* listed by the German theorists were vocally inspired, it is not
surprising that they would be so little prominent in Scarlatti, not because the
Italians misunderstood the vocal arts but because for them all music idiomatically
conceived (including vocal) was constantly changing. Their notions of vocal, string
or harpsichord idioms left no room for harking back (which is what *Figurenlehre*
did), although some Italian theory books continued to illustrate the *figurae* or (as
Penna called them – 1696 pp. 47–9) *movimenti sopra le note grosse*. Decorating
vocal lines, as illustrated by Zacconi in 1596 and still complained of by Fux in 1725,
was an art described throughout the period, and at least the better theorists were
able to see that one could not be pedantic about the 'meanings' of these or any
figurae. Even minor keys were not necessarily to be associated with *mestizia* or *lan-
guidezza*, as Sabbatini noted, illustrating his point by showing a rising chromatic
fourth set to the words 'et vitam venturi saeculi' (1802, I p. 94).

The origin of one particular device characteristic of Scarlatti – the opening solo
melody in the right (and less often the left) hand – is a further example of his
branching out from common traditions. G. B. Martini, whose detailed understand-

ing of old music makes his words relevant to many generations of composers, devoted several paragraphs in his widely circulated treatise to the various kinds of fugue subject: the distinctions he draws between *soggetto*, *attacco* and *andamento* themes are borne out in many a sonata of Domenico Scarlatti whether or not his versions of such themes are treated fugally in the sonata as a whole (see Ex. 21). Of

Ex. 21.

Martini's three types, the long 'walking' theme is perhaps the most familiar; but Scarlatti's sonatas contain many brief appearances of themes of the *attacco* kind (note that Martini's example is actually in the form of a *figura suspirans*), and it could well be that the middle-sized *soggetto* is a type of theme characteristic of his earlier works. When such solo lines appear in the bass (e.g. Kk 388), they seem to recall the opening basso-continuo statement of a vocal aria; when they appear in the treble, they suggest a kind of updated canzona-fugue (Kk 82) or even an Italian two-part invention (Kk 67). But the Sonata Kk 79 suggests how Scarlatti learnt to develop the formal function of such themes, in addition to giving them his own melodic flavour.[13] Individual motifs are not striking in themselves, nor are they

13 Martini's three types of fugue subject are those of a late theorist categorizing musical practices. But that Scarlatti grew up in a musical context in which such distinctions were made is suggested by the clear examples of them in the works of Corelli: in the Op. V Violin Sonatas, for example, a *soggetto* can be heard in no. 7 (third movement), an *andamento* in no. 7 (opening movement), and an *attacco*

developed and 'logically furthered' in the way mentioned above in connection with
J. S. Bach. But in Kk 79 it is impossible to guess what is to come next, for originality is geared towards producing the unpredictable and to harnessing caprice
without destroying a sense of paragraph.[14] Awareness of Scarlatti's way with
figurae would suggest that Kk 79 is an early piece moving towards the unique
caprice of the maturer sonatas. Or, to put it another way, any hypothetical chronology of Scarlatti's sonatas would have to offer some such analysis of his use of
figurae. Similar points could be made about Handel's keyboard music, for though
in general his early indebtedness to older German composers is gradually becoming
clearer, his type of *Figurenkontrapunkt* and the degree to which he uses old *figurae*
will surely be found to deserve close stylistic analysis.

References

Bernhard, C., *Die Kompositionslehre Heinrich Schützens in der Fassung seines Schülers
    Christoph Bernhard*, ed. J. Müller-Blattau, 2nd edn (Kassel, 1963)

Buelow, G. J., 'Rhetoric and Music', *New Grove* (London, 1980)

Deggeller, K., 'Materialien zu den Musiktraktaten Christoph Bernhards', *Forum
    musicologicum* 2 (1980), pp. 141–68

Eggebrecht, H. H., 'Zur Figur-Begriff der musica poetica', *AfMw* 16 (1959), pp. 57–69

Fux, J. J., *Gradus ad Parnassum* (Vienna, 1725)

Gasparini, F., *L'armonico practico al cimbalo* (Venice, 1708)

Handel, G. F., *Georg Friedrich Händel: Aufzeichnungen zur Kompositionslehre,* ed.
    A. Mann, *HHA* Suppl. I (Kassel/Leipzig, 1978)

Heinichen, J. D., *Der Generalbass in der Komposition* (Dresden, 1728)

Kirnberger, J. P. *Die Kunst des reinen Satzes in der Musik*, I–II (Berlin, 1771, 1776)

Kretzschmar, H., 'Allgemeines und Besonderes zur Affektenlehre', *JbP* 18 (1911), pp. 63–77,
    and 19 (1912), pp. 65–78

Manfredini, V., *Regole armoniche o sieno precetti* (Venice, 1775)

Martini, G. B., *Esemplare o sia saggio fondamentale pratico di contrappunto fugato*, 2 vols.
    (Bologna, 1774–5)

Morley, T., *A Plaine and Easie Introduction to Practical Musicke* (London, 1597)

Penna, L., *Li primi albori musicali* (Bologna, 1696)

Printz, W. C., *Phrynis Mitilenaeus oder Satyrischer Componist,* 2nd, rev. edn (Dresden/
    Leipzig, 1696)

Sabbatini, L. A., *Trattato sopra le fughe musicali* (Venice, 1802)

Scheidt, S., *Tabulatura nova*, I (Hamburg, 1624)

in no. 8 (finale). J. S. Bach's borrowings from Italian sources also observed the distinctions between
themes in this respect, though no doubt he remained unaware of the terms; the borrowings include
examples of *andamento* (Albinoni Fugue BWV 951), *soggetto* (Legrenzi Fugue BWV 574), double
subject (Corelli Fugue BWV 579), and *attacco* (in the form of a stretto-motif opening the finale of
Vivaldi's Concerto in D minor, transcribed as BWV 596.iv).

14 It seems to have become a particular aim of Italian composers, as the eighteenth century progressed,
to work the old conventions as capriciously as possible. For example, in his Op. II Violin Sonatas
(London/Florence 1744) Veracini gives the violin several themes recognizably of the *attacco* or
andamento kind but developed in less recognizable ways: they are even longer, or they vary in length
on each appearance, or they leave the listener uncertain what is to happen next, etc.

PETER WILLIAMS

Schering, A., 'Die Lehre von den musikalischen Figuren', *KmJb* 21 (1908), pp. 106ff

Schmitz, A., 'Figuren, musikalisch-rhetorische', *MGG*, IV (Kassel, 1955)

Schmitz, A., 'Die Figurenlehre in den theoretischen Werken Johann Gottfried Walthers', *AfMw* 9 (1952), pp. 79–100

Simpson, C., *The Division Viol*, 2nd edn (London, 1665)

Walther, J. G., *Praecepta der musicalischen Composition [1708]*, ed. P. Benary (Leipzig, 1955)

Walther, J. G., *Musicalisches Lexicon* (Leipzig, 1732)

Williams, P., 'The Harpsichord Acciaccatura: Theory and Practice in Harmony, 1650–1750', *MQ* 54 (1968), pp. 503–23

Zacconi, L., *Prattica di musica* (Venice, 1596)

Ziebler, K., 'Zur Aesthetik der Lehre von den musicalischen Figuren im 18. Jahrhundert', *ZfMw* 15 (1932–33), pp. 289ff

Index of Bach's Works cited

BWV: W. Schmieder, *Thematisch-systematisches Verzeichnis der musikalischen Werke von Johann Sebastian Bach* (Leipzig, 1950)

Index of Bach's Works cited (BWV)

Index of Bach's Works cited (BWV)

Index of Handel's Works cited

HWV: B. Baselt, 'Verzeichnis der Werke Georg Friedrich Händels (HWV)', *Händel-Jahrbuch* 25 (1979), pp. 9–139 (no reference is made in the following index to revised HWV numberings as yet (1984) unpublished)

Index of Scarlatti's Works cited

Kk: R. Kirkpatrick, *Domenico Scarlatti* (Princeton, 1953), catalogue pp. 442–56

Index of Names

This index does not include J. S. Bach, G. F. Handel and D. Scarlatti